Bankers, Builders, Knaves, and Thieves

Bankers, Builders, Knaves, and Thieves

The $300 Million Scam at ESM

DONALD L. MAGGIN

CONTEMPORARY
BOOKS

CHICAGO · NEW YORK

Library of Congress Cataloging in Publication Data

Maggin, Donald L.
    Bankers, builders, knaves, and thieves : the $300 million scam at
ESM / Donald L. Maggin.
      p.   cm.
    Includes bibliographical references.
    ISBN 0-8092-4547-7 : $19.95
    1. ESM Government Securities, Inc.   2. Savings and loan
associations—Ohio—Corrupt practices.   I. Title.
HG2153.O3M34   1989
364.1′68′09771—dc20

          89-37336
          CIP

Published by Contemporary Books, Inc.
180 North Michigan Avenue, Chicago, Illinois 60601
Manufactured in the United States of America
International Standard Book Number: 0-8092-4547-7

Published simultaneously in Canada by Beaverbooks, Ltd.
195 Allstate Parkway, Valleywood Business Park
Markham, Ontario L3R 4T8 Canada

I dedicate this book to
the memory of a surpassing and inspiring artist—
Bird, Charlie Parker.

Contents

Acknowledgments ix

Prologue 1

1   $300 Million Is Missing   3

2   The Patriarch   18

3   He Wanted Everything   36

4   The World of the Bond Daddies   59

5   Anatomy of a Scam   74

6   The Stags Lock Horns   106

7   Masterful Maneuvers   121

8   The First Domino Falls   134

9   Devastation in Ohio   146

10   Reconstruction in Ohio   179

11   The Demons of Stephen Arky   194

12   Tom Tew—Ace Receiver   203

13   Criminal Justice   218

14   In the Web of the Law   244

Epilogue: Where Are They Now?   257

Notes   264

Sources   291

Index   295

Acknowledgments

I became interested in the ESM case while writing an article, "The Repo Men," which appeared in the magazine *Management Review* in early 1986. So the first person I want to thank is Tony Rutigliano, my editor at *Management Review*, who encouraged and guided me in preparing the article. I had excellent research help from Daphne Weaver, Julie Edelstein, and Jill McManus.

Jill—jazz pianist, teacher, writer, *Time* magazine veteran—stayed with my project through all its phases and provided stalwart assistance in digging out data on subjects ranging from the mores of the Memphis "bond daddies" to the structure of the U.S. debt to the care and feeding of show dogs.

The godfather of *Bankers, Builders, Knaves, and Thieves* is Donald Gropman. If not for him, my efforts would have stopped with my article. He read it and saw in it the possibilities of a book and introduced me to Helen Rees, who became my agent. She definitely saw a book lurking there, and under her vigorous tutelage, I developed a proposal which helped her sell our concept to Contemporary Books, Inc.

Donald Gropman provided vital help in shaping and researching the proposal and in researching the book. He is probably the most effective interviewer in the United States, with an uncanny ability to extract information from the most recalcitrant of subjects. He is also a deep repository of both city and country wisdom, a fine writer, and a jazz lover who is hip to everyone from Jelly Roll Morton to Cecil Taylor.

Sharon Chase, my personal assistant, ably organized our research files, set up our computer operation, and conducted many important interviews.

She and I were both unhappy in July 1988 when she had to leave my employ for personal reasons, and I was fortunate in finding Tom Bruce to step into her shoes. He has done a prodigious job in seeing the text through its various transformations, providing editorial assistance, and keeping the masses of data organized.

Several journalists have helped us with their insights and information. First among them are Mary Yost of the *Columbus Dispatch* and Sharon Maloney of the *Cincinnati Post*. I want also to thank Sharon Sharkey and Tom Suddes of the *Cleveland Plain Dealer*, Claudia Winkler of the *Cincinnati Post* (now with its parent company Scripps Howard), Michael Curtin of the *Columbus Dispatch*, Jim Otte of Columbus, Ohio, radio station WOSU, Bill Cunningham of Cincinnati radio station WLW, Martha Brannigan of the *Wall Street Journal*, Larry Birger of the *Miami Herald*, Brian Dickerson of the *Miami Herald* (now of the *Detroit Free Press*), Dale Keiger, a freelance magazine writer, and Lane Kelley of the *Fort Lauderdale News/Sun-Sentinel*.

Fran Bermanzohn of the Public Securities Association, and Jon Corzine, Paul Jacobson, and Tom Pura of Goldman, Sachs & Co. helped me greatly to understand the complex workings of the government securities market.

Mark Raymond, an outstanding young lawyer with the Tew Jorden firm, sharpened my insights into the legal issues of the myriad ESM cases, considerably shortened my path through the masses of trial data, and provided valuable background concerning key players in the drama.

Special thanks go to JoAnn Touri and Lisa Winbourne of the federal trustee's ESM depository. They performed daily miracles in locating obscure documents from among the one-and-a-half million they had under their wings. Ruth Oregar of the *Miami Herald*, Jennifer Belton of the *Washington Post*, and Tom Hart of Ohio State Senator Dick Finan's staff also provided important archival help.

Many people have contributed to our efforts by consenting to be interviewed. Their names are listed in the Sources section at the end of this volume.

Finally, I want to thank Bernard Shir-Cliff, my editor at Contemporary Books, Inc., for his wisdom, skill, and patience in shepherding me through the task of writing this book.

Prologue

This is a story of prodigious crimes and the hurt, tragedy, and triumph that followed in their wake. It reaches into every corner of the United States, but its center is a modest office building in Fort Lauderdale, Florida. All the major actors in the drama were knit together by what happened there on a hectic March weekend in 1985.

Marvin Warner and Shepard Broad, the business tycoons; Tom Tew and Steve Arky, the fiercely competitive corporate lawyers; Ronnie Ewton, George Mead, and Nick Wallace, major players at ESM, the obscure government securities dealer in the middle of it all; Laurie Holtz and his team of investigators; Jose Gomez, the CPA from the big auditing firm; Ohio Governor Richard Celeste—their lives and the lives of millions of others were forever changed by the events of Saturday and Sunday, March 2 and 3, 1985.

1

$300 Million Is Missing

Laurie Holtz managed his accounting firm so that he didn't have to work on Friday afternoons. He usually played tennis. But on March 1, 1985, he was doing a public service chore for his hometown, Miami Beach. He was on the board of its convention center, and he was attending a boring meeting there concerning its expansion; they were arguing endlessly about the architectural plans. He doodled as he thought about the hitch in his forehand stroke. He couldn't stop fidgeting. He had to get out of there, so he walked into the corridor and phoned his office for messages. One was important. It said: "Call Tom Tew—urgent."

Tom Tew was a Miami attorney with whom Laurie had worked closely on several projects and whom he respected greatly. Tew asked Laurie to come to his office. He was meeting with some people from a Cincinnati bank, and they had a problem and Tom thought Laurie could help.

Laurie got there at 3:00 P.M., and Tom introduced him to David Schiebel, president of the Home State Savings Bank of Cincinnati, and Don Collins, a lawyer for Home State. The three men seemed somber, troubled. Particularly Schiebel. Laurie recalls, "He was white as a ghost, and I just remember saying to myself, I feel very sad. Something very bad is happening to this man."

Tom explained that Home State was the largest customer of ESM Government Securities, Inc. (ESM), a Fort Lauderdale brokerage firm that specialized in securities issued by the U.S. government. Just the night before, George Mead and Nick Wallace, ESM's principal officers, had hired Tom as a special legal adviser. Bill Cagney, a neighbor of Tom's and a former colleague, had introduced him to Mead, the "M" in the company name. Cagney, a criminal and civil litigator, had been asked to represent ESM and quickly realized that ESM's legal problems were primarily financial and that he did not have the financial savvy to serve his client properly. He asked Tew to help him because Tom had specialized for years in securities law, financial

3

litigation, and bankruptcy. Tom was a partner in Finley Kumble Wagner Heine Underberg Manley Myerson & Casey (Finley Kumble), at that time America's fourth-largest law firm.

Tom told Laurie that what concerned him, Schiebel, and Collins was the 1984 audited financial report for ESM. That morning, just after Tew's firm had agreed to work for ESM for a $500,000 retainer, Alexander Grant & Company, a giant accounting partnership ranked eleventh in the United States, had withdrawn the audit, saying "it could not be relied upon." There was no other explanation. The report had been issued only the day before.

Such a withdrawal is almost unheard of. Audits take months to prepare, and the big firms double- and triple-check every number before they issue a report.

Tom had kept a copy of the withdrawn report and gave it to Laurie to read. He remembers:

> They handed me this thing and said, "What do you make of it?" And I'm reading it and I'm saying to myself, "They want a magic answer in one second."
>
> I felt pretty much on the spot because I was looking at this financial statement that had $3 billion on it, and I don't see any of those with my clients. I thought, "This is the biggest thing I've seen."
>
> They started asking questions, and I told them there was something bothering me. It was in a footnote describing $1.6 billion in transactions with an affiliate. $1.6 billion! The footnote raised lots of questions, answered none. It read:

> > The company entered into repurchase and resale agreements with customers whereby specific securities are sold or purchased for short durations of time. These agreements cover securities, the rights to which are usually acquired through similar purchase/resale agreements. The company has agreements with an affiliated company for securities purchased under agreements to resell amounting to approximately $1,621,481,000 and securities sold under agreements to repurchase amounting to approximately $1,324,472,000 at December 31, 1984. Accrued interest receivable from and payable to the affiliated company at year end were $11,174,000 and $64,410,000 respectively.

> The amazing thing was they didn't describe the affiliate. I said to myself, "Who is this affiliated company? What is it? What kind of company could have $1.6 billion in transactions with it?"

Tom broke in to say that Mead, who was a sales executive with virtually no background in accounting, was disturbed by the withdrawal of the audit. He had given Tew a green light to dig out the facts surrounding it, and Tom had decided to spend the weekend making his own investigation at ESM in Fort Lauderdale. He asked Laurie to join him. He needed top-flight accounting talent to get to the bottom of the Grant audit mystery. Schiebel and Collins strongly supported the idea.

Laurie had serious problems with the weekend. He and his wife were bringing his whole family together to celebrate his mother's eightieth birthday on Saturday night—brothers, sisters, in-laws, nieces, nephews. They were flying some of them down from Washington and New York; it was no ordinary party.

Besides, he felt sure they would be spinning their wheels at ESM. You couldn't call people on the weekend and expect to find them at their offices, ready to answer your questions. It was going to be hell, but he couldn't say no. He'd never seen anything this large, this intriguing, in his thirty-two years as an accountant.

Laurie said yes and called his six partners and told them to meet him at ESM at 9 o'clock the following morning. He wanted only experienced people—just partners, no staff. He didn't tell them what they would be doing. Why should they have a lousy Friday night too?

Schiebel left to catch a plane to Cincinnati. Before departing he gave Laurie some computer runs that tracked Home State's transactions with ESM. The computer runs indicated that Home State had a lot to lose if anything was wrong at ESM. That's why Schiebel was so shaken by the withdrawn audit. It was his bedrock, and now it had turned to dust.

Laurie lugged the computer runs and the ESM audit home with him. He couldn't stay away from them, and he couldn't sleep. He got up at 3:30 A.M. and spread the papers out on his kitchen table. He spent four hours studying, staring, punching his calculator, cross-referencing. He never noticed the rising sun chasing the shadows away in the kitchen. He wanted to have all the key numbers memorized by the time he got to Fort Lauderdale. He was panicked by the responsibility. Forget about whether Tom would ever call him again. The responsibility was enormous.

At 8:45 A.M., Laurie got within a block of ESM, and he couldn't believe what he was seeing. There were barricades blocking the street. And police cars with those crazy revolving lights on their roofs. What the hell was going on? Then he saw some sweaty runners struggling by. A policeman explained that they had closed off the street for a Heart Fund charity marathon race. Laurie made a U-turn and got out of there. He drove along side streets and hit dead ends. He thought he'd never find his way around the race.

He finally got to ESM an hour later. The setting was lovely, very un-Fort Lauderdale. Nearly everything in the city looks new—glass and metal towers glinting in the sun, terraced condos rising out of raw earth, streets torn up for sewer pipe and fresh bundles of electric cable. You can go for miles and find nothing built before 1970.

ESM was housed on the ground floor of a forty-year-old structure, a solid, three-story, stucco building which surrounds a quiet courtyard filled with trees and flowering bushes. The wooden beams supporting its metal roof were weathered by sun and salt air, the roof itself had the green patina of old copper, and the palm trees, whose foliage shades most of the second and third stories, were as old as the building.

Everyone else had problems with the marathon. Laurie's partners checked in one by one, then Collins drove in, and finally Tew arrived with Cagney. They were met by two young women and a young man—puzzled and apprehensive ESM employees who George Mead had asked to help in the investigation. Mead and Nick Wallace were also there. After George and Nick introduced everyone, they left. They said they would be back early in the afternoon.

Tom huddled with the lawyers, and Holtz headed for the accounting department. Work began immediately. Laurie set up three teams. One was to look into the profit and loss records, another was to check out the assets and liabilities, and the third team, headed by Laurie himself, was to analyze the intercompany records. That footnote about intercompany transactions had bothered him all night, and he suspected that it was the key to the audit withdrawal. But he didn't really expect to find the essential records that weekend. If something were wrong, the evidence was probably buried somewhere far out of reach.

Laurie tried anyway. He asked one of the young women whether she could show him where the intercompany financial statements were. Laurie remembers, "She looked at me and waited a second, and she said, 'Sure.' To her it was just an answer. It was one of the happiest moments of my life. I mean, after all this buildup of nervousness, and fear of the responsibility, she showed up and she knew where every-thing was. And it was all there."

While the accountants plowed through the numbers, Tew—with the help of a young woman who had been an ESM secretary—examined the premises. The executive offices were on the perimeter, surrounding the trading room and the accounting department. They bypassed the accounting offices where Laurie's staff was ensconced, and entered the windowless trading room. Twelve desks were crowded there in a horseshoe shape. Tew's guide told him that the action in this area was noisy and hectic; they often bought and sold more than $100 million worth of securities in a single day. Not corporate stocks and bonds like regular brokerage houses, she said, but securities of the U.S. government—Treasury bills, Treasury notes. The traders sat on the periphery of the horseshoe and barked their orders to the clerks who sat in the center and recorded the transactions. The desks were a mess; they were covered with note pads and computer printouts, Rolodexes, potted plants, computer screens, calculators, ashtrays, and telephones.

Tom and the young woman stepped out to the executive offices, which all had the same look: beamed ceilings, expensive brass light-ing fixtures, textured beige Chinese wallpaper, and traditional Brit-ish furniture. The largest office was actually a suite which opened onto a garden patio. On one side of the working area was a meeting room with a mahogany table which sat eight, and on the other side was a full bathroom with shower. Both the office and the meeting room sported large, glitzy bars. Tom was puzzled because the bars were not stocked, and the suite seemed unused.

His guide told him that it was, in fact, unused. She said that it had belonged to Ronnie Ewton, the "E" in ESM and a founder of the company, and that Ronnie had resigned five weeks earlier. No one else had moved into the suite yet. She added that it always looked unused, even when Ewton was still with ESM, since he was the "outside" man constantly on the go seeking new clients.

The last office on Tew's tour looked like its occupant might return at any moment, but it had the smell of a place that hadn't been used for a long time. Tew stepped inside, but his guide hung back in the doorway as if she were afraid to enter. She told him that this had been the office of Alan Novick, ESM's "Mr. Inside," the man who ran the shop and bought and sold all the securities. Novick, an intense, hard-driving gentleman, only worked about half the time in his office, because he spent hours every day in the trading room directing the action there. She pointed to a tattered old couch to the left of the door; Novick had died there from a heart attack three months before. His office had remained empty since then. He was only forty-four when he died.

At 11:30 A.M., Tew took a phone call from a lawyer for the Grant accounting firm. The previous day, Grant had promised to send people to ESM to help with the weekend investigation. The lawyer now told Tew that Grant had changed its position and would send no one. "My new client's got serious trouble," Tom thought. "I don't know its shape or form, but it's trouble."

While Tom had been touring the premises, Laurie and his men were weaving together the books of ESM and its affiliate, ESM Financial Group, Inc., and, when they treated them as one entity, they found that there was a $300 million loss. If you looked at the ESM audit by itself, you couldn't find the loss. The footnote was the culprit. The jargon-filled, $1.6 billion footnote shuffled the loss over to the affiliate. Laurie had been on the right track from the beginning.

The outside world never saw an audit of the affiliate. What it saw was the ESM audit which showed the company to be highly prosperous instead of hopelessly insolvent.

A massive fraud had been committed. The ESM statements certified by Grant were phony. They were a deception whose intent was to hide the $300 million loss from the world. And the 1984 audit, withdrawn the previous day, was just the last in a string of seven. The fraud went back to at least 1978.

Two analyses prepared by Laurie's partners confirmed his discoveries. One showed that ESM had borrowed more than $1.9 billion and in turn had loaned out more than $1.6 billion, indicating that losses approximated $300 million. It appeared that ESM was being forced to pay back some of its borrowings, and that was the cause of its current crisis. In addition, Laurie's partners had examined the tax returns, and they showed that the affiliate had been losing huge amounts of money for eight years. The ESM guys had told the IRS the truth, because they didn't want to pay taxes on fictitious profits. And Grant knew it, because they had prepared the tax returns. Laurie was amazed; he had never seen an accounting firm, major or minor, involved in anything like this.

He was also relieved. It was noon, they were two hours into the assignment, and they had found what they were supposed to find. Laurie's frame is small and never seems capable of containing the energy that is always bursting out of him. He almost charged into Ewton's office where Tom was working. Two of Laurie's partners followed him carrying the crucial paperwork. He said, "I'm glad you're sitting down for this one. I think we've got the answers. They're $300 million in the hole, and somebody's committed fraud."

Tom couldn't believe it. He was stunned. He kept repeating, "You must be joking; you must be joking."

They quickly convinced him that they were serious. When they finished telling him about their findings, he asked, "Who was responsible for the audits? Who at Grant was on this?" The answer: Jose Gomez, managing general partner of Grant's South Florida office. He had been supervising the ESM account for the previous nine years.

Laurie Holtz had never heard of Gomez, but Tew knew about him. Tom was aware of Jose as one of the rising stars of Miami's Cuban-American community and a man deeply involved in civic affairs, so he was shocked to discover his involvement in the fraud. And, like Holtz, Tew was amazed that seven years of fraudulent audits had slipped by undetected from a major firm like Alexander Grant.

Most accounting partnerships have a rigorous internal review process to detect the kind of scam which had been pulled off at ESM. Besides, audit fraud almost never happened. Audit integrity is too important to our financial system; it is the foundation for almost all of the important investment decisions made by American businessmen.

Tew and his team had found the fraud. Now it was time to do something about it. Their overriding concern was recovery—helping their clients track down the $300 million and getting back as much as they possibly could. But first, they had to think about security. There were more than one million pieces of paper in the ESM files, and if anything happened to them, the true story of ESM would probably be lost in the mists. Besides, they had nagging worries about the legitimacy of their own situation. Tom remembers, "One of the things that scared the devil out of us—Laurie and I—was that we might be in a Mafia bust-out. We may have had one ESM officer give us the authority to do this, but some other guy could come home from out of town and say, 'What are you guys doing in this office?' We were vulnerable. We had auditors running all over the place tearing books off the shelf."

They called in Cagney and told him about their stunning discoveries. Then Tew had all on-premise ESM books and records secured in the interior offices. Holtz directed his most meticulous partner to make a map and carefully chart the contents of every drawer in every file cabinet and desk. Then they had all the locks changed at ESM and at warehouses where other ESM records were stored. They also brought in armed security guards to stand watch round the clock. Finally, they ordered lunch.

Over sandwiches, Holtz and Tew started asking the key questions: Why is there a loss? Who got the money? Where is it? How do we get it back? There were many, many things to be learned, and they had to be learned very quickly.

The two men had been in situations like this before, and they knew that a crucial source of help in the intense inquiry that lay ahead would be ESM's own employees. The office workers always knew where everything was. They had all kinds of answers, and they probably had never done anything wrong. So Tom and Laurie decided to hire them all at the earliest opportunity. Then they returned to their staff and the massive job of research.

A half hour later, Laurie was back in Ewton's office. He was excited. He said to Tew, "This is unbelievable. It looks like the main victims were the customers. ESM conned them into leaving large bundles of securities down here and then ESM borrowed against the customers' securities to cover its losses. The big losers are American Savings & Loan here in Miami with a $60 million hit, and Home State with at least $140 million. No wonder Schiebel and Collins were worried."

At this point, Mead and Wallace returned with a workman. Mead explained that the workman was going to help him take home one of his trophies, a stuffed sailfish which hung from a wall in his office. Tom told George not to worry about the sailfish for now. There were important matters that Tom and Cagney had to discuss with him and Wallace immediately.

Tom described the morning's discoveries and then said:

> You were smart to bring us in here so soon after Grant withdrew the audit. It's allowed us to get a handle on this thing quickly.
>
> Bill Cagney and I are not accusing you of the fraud we've uncovered. But we urge you as our clients, first of all, to disclose the situation to the authorities, and secondly, to close down operations.

The shares of American Savings & Loan, one of the big losers, are traded on the New York Stock Exchange, and by law they will have to issue a press release before the stock market opens on Monday. You guys have roughly $2 billion in open transactions on your books and if you try to do business on Monday, after the disclosure by American, there will be absolute havoc in the markets. Besides, you're hopelessly broke; you can't survive anyhow.

Cagney backed Tew up and advised Mead and Wallace that it was clearly in their self-interest to close up shop and make a clean breast of things. The Securities and Exchange Commission, the market watchdog of the federal government, would be very distressed if ESM caused chaos in the markets on Monday. They and the state authorities would be far happier if the company cooperated in an investigation and liquidation. All the facts had to come out, and the sooner they were revealed, the less damage there would be for everyone.

The two men weren't ready to face the magnitude of what was happening. They told Tew and Cagney that they would get back to them the next day, and they hurried to leave the building. Mead and the workman removed the sailfish from the wall and got out of there, and Wallace ran off to do some serious shopping.

Tew then met privately with Don Collins, Home State's lawyer, to tell him the startling news. Collins immediately called Schiebel and a group of top Home State people who had assembled for an emergency meeting in Cincinnati, and told them of ESM's massive insolvency. Tom felt badly that Don was spending his weekend this way. He liked and respected Collins and felt he was a real professional, an excellent and practical securities lawyer.

One of Holtz's partners, who had been nursing a bad hangover all day, left at 5:00 P.M., but everyone else worked past the dinner hour. Laurie left the premises at 8:00 P.M. and headed directly to the restaurant where he and his family were celebrating his mother's birthday.

The Tew/Holtz team was back into it early on Sunday: reading through the ledgers, the correspondence, the tax records, the transaction sheets—anything and everything that would tell them where the $300 million went. Laurie remembers, "I was going to put every hour in I could, because I knew every moment I was working I was finding something. It was like when they had the first oil well in Texas.

Wherever you put your finger in, oil came out. Whatever I touched was valuable. The ESM guys probably should have burned the records or dumped them in the Gulf Stream but they didn't."

Mead and Wallace arrived at midmorning. They told Tew and Cagney that they would follow their advice; they would close shop and go public with the news of ESM's staggering loss. They seemed relieved that the drama was coming to an end. Mead, a big bluff man, had held his large body at rigid attention while listening to the lawyers the previous day. Now he was relaxed, and lounged comfortably in his chair. Wallace, whose face was a mask on Saturday, smiled easily now and said, "OK. Do what you have to do."

Tew and Cagney were elated that their clients were allowing them to get the facts out fast. It seemed likely that hundreds of thousands of people were going to be hurt by the ESM debacle; Home State alone had ninety-two thousand depositors. Letting the situation fester would compound the damage. Prompt disclosure would limit it.

An important part of the accountants' task was to compile a list of ESM's customers and calculate exactly where each of them stood with ESM. As they worked through the list, Holtz's people came across a curious item which they brought to Tew's attention. More than 99 percent of ESM's past and present customers were institutions—cities, towns, savings and loans, other brokerage houses, pension funds. But, tucked into a separate category were three recently closed personal accounts in the names of Burton Bongard, Marvin Warner, and Stephen Arky.

Bongard, who turned out to be a predecessor of David Schiebel as president of Home State, was unknown to Tew. Tew had never met Marvin Warner, but he had heard of him. Warner was well-known for his aggressive investments in Florida banks, and he was the owner of Home State. But Tew's eyes stopped at Arky's name. Stephen Arky, a prominent Miami lawyer, he knew.

There was a long-standing, vaguely defined animosity between Arky and Tew. They were both in their early forties, both energetic, ambitious men. Miami in the seventies and eighties has been a boomtown, growing explosively in banking, business, and construction. Their law firms of Finley Kumble and Arky, Freed were among the city's top five, and they had clashed frequently in the courtroom and in the pursuit of big clients and big fees.

In 1981, for instance, the firm which Tew later merged into Finley Kumble had put together a complex and lucrative airplane leasing deal, which was brought to clients of Steve's firm (whose full name was Arky, Freed, Stearns, Watson, Greer and Weaver). The Arky, Freed clients told Tew that they didn't like the deal, but, in fact, pulled an end run and completed it without Tew's firm. To make matters worse, they used much of the legal documentation which Tew had created. Tom sued Steve Arky's clients and won a cash settlement.

But there was more than professional competition behind the animosity between Arky and Tew. There were deeper reasons that had to do with lifestyle, personality, background, and even physical appearance. Tew was a tall, handsome man, so good-looking that he had worked his way through Dartmouth as a TV model. His movements were easy and graceful, he dressed Florida casual whenever possible, and he was usually even-tempered. Arky was the opposite. Described by a friend as "a short guy with a big head," Arky was five feet, five inches tall, relatively stiff in most situations, and almost all of his suits were of somber hues.

Tew preferred to negotiate and work things out, but Arky was a born litigator with a reputation for belligerence. A Miami financial writer has said, "Steve Arky couldn't help it, couldn't contain himself; he loved it when his law firm kicked the other guys' asses. . . . Arky, Freed's lawyers had to make it clear that they weren't going to be pushed around, that they would punish anybody who tried to take advantage of their clients."

As Tew studied the three personal accounts, it appeared that each had been profitable. Bongard's account had been dormant for almost a year. But Arky's was closed on January 17, a scant six weeks earlier. Warner's account was closed even later, on January 28.

Like everyone else in Miami's business and law community, Tew was aware that Warner, a man of great self-made wealth, was Arky's father-in-law. Everyone knew that Warner's patronage had helped Arky, Freed become one of the most successful law firms in Miami, and that Arky, who was frequently the middle man in Warner's Florida business transactions, had made a name for himself as someone who could skillfully and swiftly put together a profitable deal. Tom remembered clearly the *Wall Street Journal* profile on Arky that appeared on Arky's fortieth birthday. They called him one of the hottest lawyers in the country.

Tew cut short his musings about Arky and Warner, because he had to approve the text of a telegram which would go out to each of ESM's customers. It read, "E.S.M. has terminated its business and will not open on Monday, March 4, 1985. The Company has retained special counsel, and all inquiries may be directed to them: Thomas Tew, Esq., or William P. Cagney, Esq."

Tom and Laurie wanted to be sure that they informed Shepard Broad, who controlled American Savings & Loan, and Marvin Warner, because of the magnitude of their potential losses. Tew knew that the two men had been partners only seven weeks earlier, when— in a widely publicized deal—Broad had bought out Warner's interest in American Savings & Loan at a profit to Warner of $12 million.

On Sunday it is difficult to find people at home in sunny Miami, and Tew searched all day for Shepard or a surrogate from American. He finally reached Shepard's son, Morris, and at 7:00 P.M. Morris was led, ashen and shaken, into ESM offices to see the terrible numbers for himself.

Tew felt comfortable about Marvin Warner because he had, throughout the investigation, been briefing Don Collins, Warner's legal representative, and Clark Hodgson, a partner of Collins, who had arrived in Fort Lauderdale on Sunday. Tom knew that Collins and Hodgson had been in touch with Warner and Warner's people during the entire weekend.

Tew's people completed the customer list at ten o'clock Sunday night, and Tom sent telegrams to all of them. Then they went home.

Tom's first job on Monday was to inform the government authorities and the media about the disaster at ESM. He got to his office early and, at 8:00 A.M., issued a press release. It ended with the words, "ESM is unable to meet its financial obligations to its customers as they mature. ESM has terminated operations on the advice of its special counsel and will not open for business on Monday, March 4, 1985."

At 8:30 A.M., Tom tried to get through to the Securities and Exchange Commission (SEC) and the Florida Division of Securities to report the fraud. Charlie Harper, the number-one man in the Miami SEC office, called back at 9:15 A.M. Charlie knew both Tew and Holtz from their work on the Greenman case, a $90 million 1982 fraud, so he and Tom were able rapidly to get down to the basics of the ESM situation. In fact, Charlie and two of his investigators were in Tew's office by 10:00 A.M. At 10:15, a Florida official called. As soon as he had the facts, he indicated that Florida would revoke ESM's state licenses and would let the SEC take the lead in prosecuting the ESM case.

Charlie Harper is just the opposite of the stereotypical federal bureaucrat. His manner is "down home," informal; he never waffles, and he likes to get things done rapidly. His speech is unlike that of the South Florida natives, which tends to be bland and uninflected. He speaks in the relaxed rhythms of the hill country of eastern Tennessee where he was raised.

He recollects that Monday morning:

> I was going to Federal court as soon as possible and get the judge to appoint a receiver for the company, a receiver to protect the interest of those who had been hurt.
>
> What happens in these situations is the creditors all start scrambling like crazy to lock up the assets, and it becomes a race of the swift, and fairness goes out the window.
>
> But when I met with Tom Tew, I wanted to be sure of my ground. So I sent two guys over to Holtz's office to make sure they hadn't made an error. Because if I go charging into court and say ESM is $300 million under water, and somebody's made an error, I'd look pretty darn stupid.

Charlie gathered up the key documents from Tew, hurried back to his office, and called his boss in Atlanta. He told him that he planned to sue ESM for fraud that day and that he wanted to get a judge to close the company down and name a receiver. And he asked his boss to deal with the five SEC commissioners up in Washington, who are appointed by the president of the United States himself. Charlie couldn't bring a lawsuit without their approval.

Then he started drafting the reams of papers he would need for his rendezvous with the judge—a complaint, a temporary restraining order, a motion, an affidavit, a certification, and a memorandum of law. Charlie remembers:

> So I start getting all these papers done lickety-split and parcel them out to the secretaries—"You type this, you type that."
>
> As I'm getting these papers together, I'm asking: Who the hell should I get as receiver? I usually don't put somebody in that's had any relationship with the company. I put somebody in fresh. But I've been with the SEC in Miami for fourteen years, and I know about the big law firms. I know Arky's firm is out. And I know two other firms have conflicts of interest, and a couple are just too busy.
>
> So I'm thinking maybe Tew's the man. I know he had a receivership for the Atlanta office, and I called them back, and they're tickled to

death with him. At about noon, I called Tom and asked if he would
switch sides and be the receiver.

Harper had put Tew on the spot. Tom already had the $500,000
from ESM in his firm's bank account. If he became the receiver, he
would have to return the $500,000, and his compensation would
depend on recovering substantial monies from the ashes of ESM.
Based on the sketchy information he had that Monday afternoon, this
looked like a bad bet.

Weighing on the other side was the professional prestige and honor
of being chosen by the judge to take up the cause of those who had
been defrauded. Tew decided to throw in his lot with the ESM creditors and give back the retainer—if he could surmount an important
obstacle. He had to get Mead and Wallace to release him as attorney.

So he had Bill Cagney bring them over to his office. Mead and
Wallace decided that their best option was to cooperate with Harper
and the federal authorities, and they let Tew go. Cagney agreed to
continue as their lawyer, and he hurriedly drafted a release document,
which they signed.

At 5:00 P.M., Harper had his approval from Washington. He called
the federal courthouse and said he was coming over with a big case
and needed to see the duty judge immediately. He jumped in a car,
picked up Tew, and went over to the courthouse. There they met
Laurie Holtz, Don Collins, and Clark Hodgson.

The judge, William Hoeveler, was hearing a jury trial, and Charlie
sent a note up to him, and he immediately adjourned it. They went
into the judge's chambers, and Hoeveler remembered Harper, Tew,
and Holtz from the Greenman case. He said with a laugh, "You three
again? This must be trouble."

Charlie answered, "It is, judge. We've got a $300 million fraud."

And Hoeveler replied, "Did you say $3 million?"

Charlie said very slowly, "No, your honor, $300 million."

Hoeveler replied, "You had better give me those papers right now."

He ran through them quickly, and he said to Charlie, "It looks like
a lot of people, a lot of poor people, are going to be hurt by this. We've
got to act. Who's your receiver?"

Charlie told him that he wanted Tom Tew. He explained that he
didn't ordinarily recommend someone who had been representing the
culprit for three days. But with so much at stake and with tremendous
time pressure, it was the right thing to do.

Hodgson and Collins backed Charlie up. They told Hoeveler that as representatives of Home State, potentially the biggest loser, they strongly supported Tew's appointment.

When Judge Hoeveler signed the papers at 6:30 P.M., he brought down the curtain on act 1 of the ESM drama by doing two things: he put the company out of business, and he made Tew the protector of the interests of all those harmed in the debacle.

2

The Patriarch

S hepard Broad looked at what he humorously called "the ego wall" in his office, and his eyes moved slowly over the plaques, the framed newspaper clippings, and the letters from governors and U.S. senators. He was tired, he was seventy-six, and he had just signed the papers that spelled retirement.

His eyes stopped at the oldest clipping, the one from the *Montreal Daily Star* of July 30, 1920, which told of his arrival in Canada: "Boy of 13 Came From Poland" the headline read. And then the subhead: "Traveling Alone to New York After Narrowly Escaping Starvation." He remembered the pains of hunger in Pinsk, where he was born on July 8, 1906, and where his journey to North America had started. Bloody Pinsk on the Eastern Front, fought over by the armies of the czar, imperial Germany, the Bolsheviks, and newly born Poland.

Szmuel Bobrowicz (Shepard's given name) lost his mother when he was three and was orphaned at ten when his father died in 1916. After that, he and his younger brother were cared for by his paternal grandparents. World War I shredded their lives. As Shepard tells it:

> Those were terrible dark years, the German occupation. After Father died, there was nobody in our family that the Germans could use in the labor force. If you didn't contribute anything to the war effort, you didn't eat. So, first of all, the net worth disappeared, next everything that was saleable or hockable. After that, we were really with our backs against the wall.
>
> One way or another, we would scrape together something to get a loaf of bread. Grandfather would dole out four slices—one for me, one for my grandmother, one for my brother, and one for himself. Fearful that maybe I might find out where he hid the loaf of bread, he would make marks so there would be no way that I could slice off a piece.
>
> By four o'clock, mine was gone, my brother's was gone, my grandmother's maybe. He had two-thirds left of his, and he'd subdivide it and give it to us.

That was months, that was weeks and weeks and months. It was terrible—those were rough, rough times.

After Shepard's father died, his grandparents had two surviving sons: Usher in Kiev and Daniel in New York. Shepard's grandfather believed that America was the land of the heathen, its people corrupted by materialism; he would have none of them. So, when things grew unbearable in Pinsk, he looked for refuge in Kiev with Usher.

In late 1918, while the Bolsheviks occupied Pinsk, Shepard got passes for his grandparents and his brother to migrate east to Kiev. To Shepard, at age twelve, Kiev was nowhere, a stifling backwater. He had picked up every scrap of information he could about New York, and it filled his head with images of color and energy—big muscular bridges spanning the rivers, brightly lit theaters on Times Square, streets filled with people amusing themselves, shopping, dodging motorcars. And in this city of his imagination, everyone dressed elegantly, ate well, and lived in beautiful homes. Above all, for Shepard, New York was "a place where I could be somebody, where I could show people I too had a belly button."

He would do anything to get there, and he knew that his uncle Daniel was working to bring him to New York. So, when his grandparents and his brother went to Kiev, they left Shepard with other relatives in Pinsk.

Finally, after more than a year of effort, Daniel arranged for Shepard's passage from Warsaw to New York. The catch was that Shepard had to get to Warsaw, three hundred miles west of Pinsk, on his own. The boy had very little money for the trip overland, and he couldn't get out of Pinsk while the Bolsheviks were in control. In the spring of 1920, the Bolsheviks were forced out by the new Polish government, and Shepard saw his chance.

Wearing an ill-fitting suit he made for himself in a tailoring class at school, and carrying a small valise with all his belongings, he hopped a freight train which had been crudely converted to transport refugees. He had no ticket and eluded the conductor the first night by hiding behind the skirts of a large and cooperative peasant woman. But in the morning he was discovered and thrown off the train. He walked for two hours to get to the nearest town, Kobrin.

There was, in Kobrin, the first evidence of an informal, Jewish "underground railway" which was to help Shepard on all stages of his journey to New York. On arriving in the town, he headed straight for the synagogue. His aim was to get to a place called Brest-Litovsk, which had a direct rail link to Warsaw.

At the synagogue, he was introduced to one of the worshippers who was a drayman, a horse-and-wagon man. The drayman was touched by the young refugee in the funny suit, and, after the services ended, pulled Shepard up onto his wagon and drove him on rough cobblestone roads to Brest-Litovsk. Shepard bought his ticket and caught his train to Warsaw, and there, following his uncle's instructions, sought out a Mr. Davitch, an official of the Pinsk Relief Society, a Jewish organization. Shepard remembers that "no plenipotentiary put forth more eclat, more class, more importance than he attached to his mission." Davitch skillfully worked the bureaucracy to get him the credentials to pick up the tickets that Daniel had provided.

The next stage of the journey, a train trip to Antwerp, went without a hitch. But in Antwerp, as Shepard recalls, there was trouble:

> I went to the docks to board this ship, *The Lapland*, of the Red Star Line. But there was no room, and no way they would let me on. When that damned boat sailed away, I was sick. It would be two weeks before I could book another boat on the Red Star Line.

> I was broke. Empty pockets and no place to stay. So I started walking away from that damn pier towards the town. About a hundred yards away there was a row of houses, and there was a great big woman—her rear end looked like a Belgian horse really—sweeping a stoop.

> So I tried to speak in sign language. Somehow she understood that I was up a tree. I offered like I wanted to help her sweep. She was laughing, she enjoyed that episode. So she walks me up to the third floor landing and there's a big trunk. She points to it. Okay, so I slept on it. It was a boarding house, and the next morning I was helpful there in the dining room, bringing out platters, etc.

> I finished with that, and as I was walking towards the center of town, I came across a photographer's showcase. And for the first time in my life, I saw a picture of a black man. Being steeped in the Talmud, I figure I've found one of the Ten Lost Tribes. I couldn't get over his looks and appearance, and I'm totally engrossed in the thing. While I'm standing there, this rather nice-looking gentleman—who he is, to this day I don't know—opens up in Yiddish to me: Who am I? Where am I from?

> I told him what happened to me the day before. He said right around the corner he's got a friend in the travel business, and he thinks he can

work it out for me. It's interesting when you have nothing to lose you listen to anything anybody might tell you.

The travel agent made a deal with Shepard. He exchanged his Red Star Line ticket to New York for one to Quebec City, on *The Gramphian*, a Canadian ship, plus a railway ticket from Quebec to New York. *The Gramphian* was a tiny one-lunger that would take more than three weeks to get to Canada. But it was leaving the next day and that was all the penniless boy cared about. He had met his immediate needs for food and shelter.

The Gramphian was carrying mostly British sailors and Canadian soldiers, with a few civilians in the hold. Shepard was so small, he had trouble grabbing enough food in the hurly-burly of the mess. Then, while walking on the deck, he struck up a conversation in Yiddish with a Jewish businessman from Warsaw who, it turned out, was friendly with the first mate. Shepard's new friend told the officer of his plight, and the first mate took the skinny kid under his wing as something of a mascot. He gave him a cot in his cabin and allowed him to eat the copious rations of the officers' mess.

Shepard's idyll ended when he stepped off *The Gramphian* in Quebec City. Canadian immigration hauled him away to a detention barracks as "an alien with no visible means of support." On his fifth day of detention, Shepard was interviewed by Adolf Stark, a wealthy Montreal insurance executive and the president of the Canadian Jewish Immigration Society. Two days later, a young man, a representative of Stark, arrived and convinced the immigration officials to release Shepard in his custody. Shepard recalled:

This fellow fed me a great dinner, and took me to his home in Montreal. I had a bath in the first porcelain tub I ever saw. At breakfast there was another first, with a miracle flavor—orange juice! Then this guy takes me to a photographer, which I hated, gets me a haircut, outfits me from head to toe (I finally got rid of my homemade suit) and brings me to the *Montreal Star* for my interview. I was so excited, I blabbed too much.

Finally, we went to Stark's beautiful house where Stark took me in. We called my uncle long-distance in Brooklyn and that was a happy moment. I stayed with Stark for a few days before heading for New York. We became lifelong friends. He urged me to become a lawyer, and he was proud years later when I told him I had passed the bar.

Shepard moved in with his uncle Daniel and Daniel's wife on August 4, 1920. They had exchanged the name Bobrowicz for Broad. Shepard did likewise and also transformed Szmuel to Shepard. Daniel, who never had a child of his own, became a true father to him, his beloved "Pop."

Shepard swiftly put the educational system to work for himself and, at eighteen, entered New York Law School, one of three in New York State which did not require a college degree for entrance. He graduated in June 1927 and was in a hurry to start practicing. He wanted to take the bar exam in October and not wait for the next round in February. But there was a hitch: he had to become a U.S. citizen first.

New York State had a law in those days aimed at preventing the stuffing of ballot boxes with the votes of newly created citizens. The law stated that no one could become a citizen in the thirty days before the November elections.

Shepard did not become eligible for citizenship until Saturday, October 8, 1927. He had to be sworn in on that day because Monday, October 10, fell within the thirty-day preelection period. The next opportunity for citizenship would therefore be after the elections, and he would miss the October bar exams. So Shepard found an old federal judge, who had the unlikely name of Grover Moscowitz, and pleaded with him to make him a citizen that Saturday morning.

When the day came, Shepard was cursing. He was standing outside the federal courthouse, and he was soaking wet. It was raining buckets, and it seemed like the old judge would never arrive. But finally, Moscowitz, clad in rubbers, a raincoat, and a rain hat, and holding his umbrella aloft, came into sight. When they got inside, the judge reminded Shepard that the law required that the oath of citizenship be taken in a public place. Moscowitz was a stickler for form and opened a large, ornately decorated courtroom for the ceremony. The lone witness was a court clerk.

Shepard passed his bar exam later that month and went to work for a lawyer in Manhattan. He went out on his own in 1932, the year that he married Ruth Kugel.

Shepard met Ruth in the summer of 1929 in her hometown of Warrensburg, New York, in the Adirondacks just below the Canadian border. He and his "Pop" were driving to Montreal to visit the Starks, and Pop suggested that they drop in on his widowed friend Mrs. Kugel for an hour or so en route. Shepard was so taken by Mrs. Kugel's daughter Ruth that their visit extended to the next day. Ruth had just finished her sophomore year at Syracuse University. A year after she graduated, they were wed. They had two children: a daughter, Ann, born in 1933, and a son, Morris, born in 1935.

Shepard prospered in law and in politics during the mid-1930s. In fact, in 1936, he was scheduled to become a candidate for a safe, Democratic seat representing Brooklyn's Canarsie and Flatbush neighborhoods in the New York legislature. But, at the last minute, as a crowd waited in the clubhouse to hear the New York fire commissioner nominate Shepard, the local boss, Joe Whitty, called Shepard in and said that he would have to replace him on the ticket because the name Broad didn't sound Jewish enough.

The district was heavily populated with Irish and Jews, and the boss wanted to score heavily with both groups. The other candidates on the ticket were Whitty himself and a woman named Murphy. So Shepard's name was pulled and replaced by that of Leo Rafiel, son of Hymie Rafiel, a well-known magistrate. Shepard was disappointed but he went along. He made the nominating speech for Leo.

The Brooklyn machine took care of its own. Whitty found Shepard a client whose legal fees made up for the $3,000 per-year-salary of a legislator. The client was John J. Flannery, who worked part-time as U.S. commissioner of jurors, and who owned a lucrative bus line with a monopoly on transporting handicapped children to public schools all over New York City.

On Christmas morning 1938, Flannery called Shepard and said, "My son and I are leaving for Key West at noon, in our single engine-plane, the Stinson. We're going deep-sea fishing. You've worked hard for me all year. Come on and join us."

Shepard went, and it changed his life. In Florida, he felt a stirring, a release. In Brooklyn, you were hemmed in by the el lines, the dark buildings with their grim fire escapes, the endless gray streets. Brooklyn had lots of limitations; Florida seemingly had none. Florida was open, it was beautiful. There were miles and miles of gorgeous beaches, thousands of acres of tropical forest, and water everywhere—ocean, lakes, canals, streams, bays. You had to like this. Millions of people would like it if they could only afford to come down and see it.

And there was something else that was important, very important. Things were on a different scale here, a much larger scale. You weren't making deals for brownstones eighteen feet wide. You were buying 200-acre, ocean-front tracts and building beautiful homes on them. Shepard felt he could do big things in Florida.

Shepard returned from his vacation to his usual round of activities, but there was a difference. He would be working on something—arguing before a judge in court, negotiating a deal—and he would find himself thinking of Florida. He could never dismiss it totally from his mind. It was always there—a magnet with a strong force field.

In the summer of 1939, Shepard was worried about "Pop." Daniel Broad was part of a team liquidating a large mortgage company, a depression casualty, and the assignment was about to end. Pop was fifty-three, and there were no prospects for a new job. So when a fellow Shepard had met in Key West called him about an attractive business proposition there, he saw an opportunity for Pop and sent him down to check it out. The deal was a good one, but Pop's wife didn't like Key West. It's a sleepy town now; in 1939, it was positively somnolent. She preferred Miami. So Shepard and Pop found a lot on Miami Beach and built the Balfour Apartments, a modest structure with six hotel rooms and twelve "efficiencies." Pop managed the building. He became a permanent resident of Miami Beach and an advance scout for Shepard.

Pop became friendly with Roy Calamia, a real estate broker, and when Shepard came down to Miami during the 1939 Christmas holidays, the three spent a lot of time together.

Roy kept hammering at Shepard that his talents were needed in South Florida. He said, "There are many real estate deals down here with big fees attached, and you've got the talent and drive to handle them. Besides, there are lots of Jewish buyers. The local real estate people and lawyers don't know what makes them tick. You understand them, and they understand you. You will be able to pull off deals that nobody else can."

In the spring of 1940, Calamia introduced Shepard to Ed Fleming, a prominent Miami lawyer, and Fleming asked Shepard to come down and be his partner.

Ruth Broad resisted initially. They had recently traded Brooklyn for the ultimate early 1940s Jewish suburb—Great Neck, Long Island—and Shepard's law practice was thriving. Why change? But she knew that the Florida virus in her husband's system was too tough for her to fight, and she turned him loose. In June 1940, Shepard went down to Tallahassee to take the Florida bar exam. He remembers, "The headline on the newspaper was that Paris fell and France surrendered. The world was in flames, and I said to myself, 'What am I doing trying to pick up stakes and move here?' But I was in Tallahassee already, so I took the bar."

He passed the exam and proceeded to form Fleming and Broad. Their two practices didn't mesh well—Fleming was a litigator and Shepard a real estate man. After a year, Shepard went out on his own. He did well from the start; so well, in fact, that he was able to put aside some money to invest for himself. Mostly he invested in the field that he knew best—real estate. His biggest holding was a half-interest in a good-sized office structure in downtown Miami, the Biscayne Building.

While he prospered during World War II, Shepard agonized as millions of Jews were being slaughtered in Europe. He was convinced that, if the Jews were to have any future at all, they must have a homeland. He felt that, "homelessness, in and of itself, was a badge of shame." His response was to organize a Miami Beach chapter of the Zionist Organization of America. It became one of the strongest chapters in the United States and raised large sums of money for the Zionist cause. His resolve had been strengthened by the rumors, later confirmed, which he had heard about the fate of the Jews of Pinsk. There were forty thousand when the Germans arrived in 1941, and fewer than one hundred survived the Nazi death squads.

In late June 1945, Henry Montor, director of the United Jewish Appeal, invited Shepard to a meeting on Sunday morning July 1 in New York City. Shepard was to tell no one about it. The subject of the meeting: Palestine. The guest of honor: David Ben-Gurion, at that time a little-known general in the Jewish underground army, Haganah.

In the summer of 1945, Hitler had been defeated. But Ben-Gurion took no solace from that. The British ruled Palestine, and he believed that they were convinced that their self-interest required a Holy Land dominated by Arabs. Ben-Gurion predicted that the British would leave and would do everything they could to ensure Arab hegemony after their exit.

Ben-Gurion saw only one survival option open to the Jews: arm yourselves and fight. He wanted to arm and train Jewish fighters under the noses of the British. And he wanted to swell their numbers by bringing to Palestine the Holocaust survivors and every other Jew who wanted to come. Both tasks would be very difficult, particularly since the British had imposed a strict naval blockade against immigrants and arms.

Ben-Gurion came to America in June 1945 to plead his case privately and informally to the U.S. Jewish community. The American Jewish establishment reacted with distrust and distaste. They felt that they had earned their place in the American sun by being good Americans, and most of Ben-Gurion's agenda violated an important American law which prohibited American citizens from aiding clandestine, foreign armies. Besides, England was America's staunchest ally. American Jews were still fighting side by side with the British in the war against Japan and expected to do so for some time to come. The atomic bomb had not, as yet, been unleashed, and the end game in the Japanese war was expected to be long and bloody. Some of those guns that Ben-Gurion wanted might be used to kill British troops.

To the American Jewish establishment, providing food, medicine, and doctors for Holocaust survivors was okay. But creating a secret army and running refugees and arms through blockades was out of the question.

After three weeks in America, Ben-Gurion was weary and frustrated. He felt like a pariah. He turned to his friend Henry Montor and asked him if he could round up any American Jewish leaders who would, at least, give him and his militant cause an open hearing. Montor went to his card file and started calling those Jewish leaders whom he felt possessed a Zionist fervor. He invited Shepard and sixteen others to meet with Ben-Gurion.

July 1, 1945, in New York was as hot as anything Shepard had experienced in Florida. More than fifty thousand people had slept on the city's beaches the night before. In those days, air conditioning was something you found in movie houses, not in private homes. Not even in the palatial duplex penthouse in which the group gathered. It was located on Sutton Place, a bastion of the city's old wealth, and it was built on a grand scale. The men met in a beautifully appointed living room fifty feet long and two stories high. An antique Oriental rug covered its floor, and two massive chandeliers provided its lighting.

The apartment belonged to Rudolf G. Sonneborn, and the men at the meeting later dubbed themselves collectively "The Sonneborn Institute." Sonneborn's profile fit that of the Jewish establishment which had found Ben-Gurion's program so distasteful. He was a member of a wealthy German-Jewish family from Baltimore, who had transformed a small business in New York into a major force in the petrochemical field. He had played football for Johns Hopkins, and had flown for the U.S. Navy in World War I. But he had worked directly with the Holocaust survivors, and their suffering had shaken loose his old establishment convictions. He had swung over to Ben-Gurion's camp because he feared another Holocaust if the Jews didn't make a stand in Palestine.

Shepard remembers the give-and-take with Ben-Gurion:

> We were skeptical at first. These things Ben-Gurion was predicting, they were not widely held notions in that day.
>
> But after a while, it began to ring true to me. What Ben-Gurion was saying was that no people ever had freedom handed to them. You had to be prepared to spill your blood for freedom. And that made sense to me. From what history I knew, it seemed to me he was right.
>
> Yet there was one question that I had to have answered before any of what he was suggesting to us could make any sense. I had to know what the Jews in Palestine were like. Were they prepared to spill their blood? Were they willing to fight for the freedom we were talking about?
>
> So towards the end of the meeting, I turned to Ben-Gurion and I asked him, what kind of people are the Jews in Palestine? Will they fight?
>
> And he said to me, "Look, what is an Iowa farmer like? If you were to walk up to the front door of an Iowa farmer's home and ring the bell and he comes to the door and you say to him, this is my land now. You must take your things and get off it immediately. You know what he'll do? He'll say excuse me and he'll go back inside and when he returns he'll have a shotgun in his hands. He'll aim it at your head and then he'll say, now what was that you just told me?"
>
> So I said all right. If that's what the Jews in Palestine are like, then I'm willing to do all that I can to help.

The seventeen men were given no specific assignments that day. They were told to go home and keep absolutely quiet about their meeting. They would be contacted later when their help was needed. Their activities were compartmentalized. Each project would be undertaken separately, and each participant would be given knowledge only of his own project.

Jacob Dostrovsky, who arrived in the United States in January 1946, was the only man who knew the details of every undertaking. He was the coordinator, the master tactician. He had fought alongside the British in Hitler's war and had risen to a high rank in the Haganah.

Later, he would become its chief of staff and, after the creation of the Jewish state, he would take the name of Jacob Dory and become the first chief of staff of the Israeli Armed Forces.

Shepard's assignment was straightforward and of questionable legality. He was asked to buy a couple of old freighters and bring them into a shipyard on the Miami River where they were to be outfitted to carry refugees. Shepard reflects:

> It gives me a good feeling today to think about it. Dostrovsky gave me the money to buy the ships and have them outfitted. I hired very few Jews to work on the project because I wanted in no way to draw any attention to what we were doing.
>
> What I did was tell everyone the ships were going to be used to haul bananas from Honduras. That way I was able to get the proper documentation, and the fact that we were building all those racks down below aroused no suspicion. Even the workmen thought bananas would be laid on those racks.

Shepard was never told exactly what happened to his ships:

> I know that once out beyond the twelve-mile limit, they changed course from Honduras to Marseilles. And I know that the French were very helpful to our cause, that the job of loading the refugees in Marseilles was one of the easier tasks involved. But what happened after that I really don't know. I suspect that only one of the boats got through the blockade.

Shepard's current contributions to Jewish causes are much less warlike. He has given many times to hospitals, schools, and universities. He has built a theological seminary in Jerusalem, and in 1986 he completed the construction of two small synagogues in a suburb of that city.

The urge to build has been with Shepard a long time. In fact, during the summer of the Ben-Gurion meeting, he was itching to make a career change in that direction. He didn't mind being a landlord—particularly of a profitable office building—but he preferred the role of developer. He saw his opportunity when World War II ended. Wartime regulations, which directed all building materials to the defense effort, had stopped development in its tracks. So, almost five years of pent-up housing demand was about to burst forth, and

Shepard wanted to be one of the people who would meet it.

He was constantly looking for appealing sites to develop. What he considered appealing often took lots of imagination to visualize. For instance, he was attracted by a mosquito-infested mangrove swamp which at high tide was under water. It was situated strategically in Biscayne Bay between North Miami on the mainland to the west and Bal Harbour on the slender Miami Beach peninsula on the eastern or ocean side.

The swamp was owned by Pierre Bailey, the son of a wealthy Frenchman. His father was killed when the Nazis captured Paris in 1940, and Pierre came to the United States soon after. He was eager to fight the Germans and tried to join the U.S. Navy, but he was stymied because the FBI thought they had evidence linking him with the French government in Vichy which was collaborating with the Nazis. The evidence proved spurious, and Pierre was eventually cleared to join the Navy. But the whole experience had rankled him. He was particularly angry with the FBI, whom he felt had unfairly harassed him during its investigation.

The swamp was one of several pieces of South Florida real estate which Pierre had bought at bargain prices. In October 1945, Roy Calamia told Shepard that Pierre wanted to sell it for $600,000. Shepard remembers how the transaction proceeded:

I told Roy, "It's not a bad price. It's reasonable. I don't know of anybody that would be especially interested, but if he wants to trade me for my equity in the Biscayne Building, I would do it." He asked me who the biggest single tenant was there, and I said it was the FBI. He said, "How much space do they have?" They had two-and-a-half floors. He said, "Do they have a lease?" And I said, "No." He said, "Pierre would love it; he'd love to get even with the FBI and throw them out."

He calls Pierre in upstate New York, and Pierre is excited. He takes the coach—in those days it wasn't possible to get Pullman—and travels almost two days by coach. We meet him on Sunday in the railway station at the back of the courthouse where Roy says to him, "The FBI doesn't have a lease." And Pierre says, "Shep, do you really want to make this swap?" And I said, "Yeah." So we made the swap.

We closed the deal in November 1945. My wife was very concerned that I had traded good security for a swamp. So to accommodate her, I took in a partner, the chairman of the Mercantile National Bank, Ben Kane.

Shepard and Ben called the development Bay Harbor Islands. Shepard was the active, managing partner; Ben was in the background looking after the finances. They envisioned two islands, separated by a waterway. The eastern island would be for multifamily dwellings and commercial buildings, and the western one was reserved for single-family homes. They were aiming for wealthy buyers and, therefore, did not apply for any of the postwar federal housing subsidies, whose purpose was to stimulate home construction for working- and middle-class families.

Once they had detailed maps drawn up, they were ready to sell. The first dredge arrived on March 8, 1946, and the sales office opened on April 1. By June 1, from the drawings alone, they had sold $3 million worth of lots. They collected $1 million in deposits and used it to finance the construction. They did not have to borrow from banks, because a strong flow of sales deposits continued as building progressed.

During the rest of 1946 and most of 1947, Shepard was constantly at the site—swatting away the bugs and directing the dredges, the barges dumping bay-bottom sludge and rocks for fill, the piledrivers, the drainage rigs.

The town was incorporated in April 1947, and Shepard and Ben had their first building open for occupancy by Christmas of that year; it was a fifty-room hotel. Soon after, they opened an eight-unit apartment house.

All the heavy construction was done by the end of 1948. By the time they were finished, they had created three hundred acres, fifty of which were used for streets and waterways. In 1951, the town completed a causeway with bridges linking the two islands to both the mainland and the beach peninsula. Its name: Broad Causeway. Shepard looks back on those times happily: "If you pick up Genesis, you can see the joy the Creator gets out of creation. After He created everything, He looked at it, and He said, 'This is good.' That's what we felt in terms of taking a swamp and turning it into a pretty livable place."

Bay Harbor Islands is more than "pretty livable." It is a community where sleek yachts bob in berths next to $750,000 homes, where sprinklers click endlessly over soft, deep-green lawns, and where residents visit the supermarkets in Mercedes and Cadillacs.

Today, 5,000 people live there, and 600 work in its hotels, office buildings, shops, banks, and restaurants. The current value of its real estate is $500 million, a far cry from the $600,000 Shepard paid Pierre Bailey for the swamp.

Shepard has a photo of himself at the controls of one of the swamp dredges and, excepting that his hair has turned from black to white, his appearance is not very different from today. A caricaturist would emphasize the intense, determined eyes looking out from under bushy eyebrows, the strong line of his mouth, the bow tie, the small, trim body.

Shepard is as determined about giving his money away as he is about making it. In addition to his philanthropies in Israel, he has given generously to a Catholic hospital and to a Catholic college (where he was chairman of the board of trustees), the prestigious Mt. Sinai Medical Center in Miami Beach, the University of Florida, and his alma mater, New York Law School, where he has established several scholarships.

When he committed himself to Bay Harbor Islands, Shepard realized that he would have far less time to give to his law practice. So on January 1, 1946, he brought in a partner, Alvin Cassel, and changed the name of the firm to Broad and Cassel. Today, the firm is thriving with more than 150 employees in seven cities.

To service his growing real estate empire, Shepard needed a savings bank. As he put it, "The city, the banks were clients of the law firm. The banks made loans for the houses. This was in the day when you didn't worry so much about conflicts of interest."

In 1948, he attempted to get a federal savings bank charter but was stymied when people already in the business convinced the federal authorities that there was already too much competition in the Miami area. They thought they had their man beaten, but they didn't know Shepard. He went to the state legislature and, in 1950, got the first state charter ever issued in Florida. He called his bank American Savings & Loan.

Before 1980, the savings and loan industry was closely regulated by the federal government to achieve its stated social purpose: to encourage home ownership by making mortgage money readily available. The government accomplished this by subsidizing and regulating interest rates to give the savings banks a comfortable operating margin. The federal authorities practically guaranteed a profitable enterprise for the reasonably intelligent entrepreneur. It was, as Shepard has said, "a no-brainer industry."

There were two main ingredients for success. First, you wanted to locate your branches in areas of population growth, because such areas would provide both a good supply of deposits and a heavy demand for mortgages for new homes. Secondly, you had to exercise prudence; for example, you didn't want to give a $100,000 mortgage to a fellow who was only making $100 a week.

The second ingredient was built into Shepard; he was a naturally prudent man. And South Florida certainly provided the first ingredient; the 1950–1980 era was a golden period of growth for the area. Shepard had started with one small branch in 1950, and, by 1980, he had forty-five of them with more than $2 billion in deposits. That made American the third largest savings and loan in Florida and the twenty-sixth in the nation. The company went public in 1976, and its shares were listed on the New York Stock Exchange in 1979.

If the rules of the game had not been changed, the 1980s most likely would have seen a continuation of American's robust expansion. South Florida did not run out of steam in the 1980s; its growth accelerated, and American had a seasoned management team to take advantage of it.

The troubles began in the late 1970s with Jimmy Carter's double-digit inflation and double-digit interest rates. Money market funds sprang up everywhere in response to these phenomena. The funds paid the highest interest rates available in the open markets, and thus drew deposits away from the banks and savings and loans, which were restricted to paying the lower regulated rates. The banks and savings and loans were hurt but managed to hold on to the great majority of their customers, mainly because their deposits were federally insured, while cash invested in the money market funds was not.

Powerful depositor groups wanted both high rates and federal insurance, and their pressures coincided with that of another highly vocal political constituency of the late 1970s—those who were pushing for deregulation. Congress had already freed the airlines and the trucking industry from government control, and banking was next on the deregulators' agenda.

Congress responded to the pressures by passing a new law which changed the rules of the savings and loan game and which dealt an almost-lethal blow to the industry.

The new law was called the Depository Institutions and Monetary Control Act of 1980 and is better known as the Banking Deregulation Act of 1980. It affected both savings and loans (S&Ls), whose purpose was to provide mortgage loans, and commercial banks, which made all the other kinds of loans.

Both kinds of banks survive on the "spread" between what they pay out in interest to depositors and what they earn in interest from borrowers. Prior to 1980 when the government controlled the interest rate paid to depositors, it pegged it low enough to provide a spread big enough to give the lender a reasonable chance to make a profit. The 1980 bill took the government out of this business. It no longer kept a lid on deposit interest rates, letting them find their own levels. The rates shot up immediately in all-out competition for the depositor's dollar.

A typical S&L would face numbers like these: pre-1980, it might have had a comfortable three-point spread (paying depositors 5 percent and lending on mortgages at 8 percent). Its expenses (rent, salaries and wages, advertising, etc.) would probably eat up 2 percent of the 3 percent spread, leaving a reasonable profit from the remaining 1 percent. After the bill's passage, the S&L would see the rate paid to depositors leap from 5 percent to 7 percent, reducing the spread to 1 percent. With expenses at 2 percent, it had fallen into the red.

The big problem was on the income side, that is, on the money earned by lending to borrowers. And the income problem was far worse for S&Ls than for commercial banks. The reason: S&Ls were stuck with long-term, fixed-rate loan commitments to their borrowers—20- and 30-year mortgages—and couldn't raise their interest income quickly to keep pace with the rise in interest rates they were paying for deposits.

In contrast, the term of commercial bank loans averaged less than two years; the banks knew that they could replace low-income, low-interest-rate loans with more profitable ones in twenty-four months or sooner. The S&Ls, on the other hand, faced many difficult years as old mortgages were slowly paid off and were replaced by more profitable ones. The replacements were "variable rate" mortgages, a new breed which allowed the S&Ls to change their rates in line with money market conditions and thus maintain a profitable spread.

What seemed like a bright spot for S&Ls in the 1980 act was a provision which allowed them to diversify into all kinds of financial services: discount brokerage of stocks and bonds, insurance, investment banking, even commercial banking. However, success in these new fields would not come easily or rapidly. They required considerable experience and skill. The $100 billion lost in the S&L bankruptcies of the late 1980s have confirmed this.

American Savings & Loan, no exception to industry norms, was bleeding red ink in the early 1980s, and Shepard knew he needed an infusion of new capital to survive. He shopped widely for affluent merger candidates or venture capitalists but came up empty. No one he talked to had sufficient faith that American could pull out of the tailspin caused by deregulation.

Shepard was surprised, therefore, when, in March 1982, Steve Arky called to say that he had a potential investor. Shepard knew Arky as one of the most aggressive and successful of Miami's young business lawyers, and he had run into him from time to time at social functions, but they really didn't know each other. When Arky asked for a meeting, Broad agreed, and they met for lunch that same day.

The potential investor turned out to be Arky's father-in-law, Marvin Warner. Broad knew who Warner was, his name was in the newspapers often enough; and he had built quite a reputation among Shepard's peers in the Miami banking community. He knew that Warner had been U.S. ambassador to Switzerland, that his lifestyle ran to Sabre jets, thoroughbred horses, and beautiful women, that he had amassed a fortune in real estate, and that he owned a major S&L in Cincinnati. Most importantly, Shepard knew that Warner had taken two moribund Florida commercial bank chains, American Bancshares and ComBanks, and, with hands-on, hard-driving management, had rapidly turned them into highly profitable institutions.

So it appeared to Shepard that Marvin Warner offered, in addition to essential hard cash, proven management skills. When he met Marvin, he encountered a man full of energy and ideas. Marvin couldn't wait to take over the reins at American if a deal could be worked out. He made it clear to Shepard that he was eager to pick up American's $2 billion bundle of assets and run with it.

Shepard, at age seventy-six, was finally looking to reduce his workload, and he knew that his son Morris, now forty-seven, did not have the drive and desire to succeed his father as CEO. Besides, Warner had a program to turn American around. He wanted to take it into new areas. He told the press he favored taking more risks with American and said, "S&Ls traditionally have made loans on real estate, but we must expand into sophisticated commercial banking services, international banking, and consumer lending."

The Broads negotiated with Arky and Warner for several months, and the deal they worked out was fairly complex.

First of all, American would issue 124,000 new shares to Warner in exchange for 124,000 Warner shares in another savings and loan,

Freedom. American would then turn the Freedom shares into fresh liquid capital by selling them for $1.3 million.

Warner would pour in $10.2 million more in fresh capital in exchange for seven hundred thousand newly issued shares in American. With the shares he already owned, this gave him 28 percent of American as against the 16 percent owned by Shepard and Morris.

All shares owned by Warner and the Broads would be pooled in a voting trust and voted as a unit for ten years by Marvin and Shepard. The Broads and Warner would each name six directors to American's twelve-member Board.

Marvin would become chief executive, and the executive committee of the board of directors would be comprised of Shepard and Morris Broad, Warner, and someone to be named by Warner. His choice was his friend Ronnie Ewton.

As the final element in the deal, Warner and Broad executed a "buy-sell" provision concerning their American shares. It could be triggered by either man as initiator. The initiator would set the price but the other party got to choose whether to be the buyer or the seller. The initiator had some leverage, however, because if he set the price high enough, he could almost force the other party to be the seller. The other party had sixty days to declare which side of the buy-sell option he would choose.

The contracts were signed on December 8, 1982. It was a taxing and highly emotional day for Shepard. It wasn't easy handing over an enterprise which he had coddled, nurtured, and sweated over for thirty-two years.

After the deal was closed, Shepard's people, Warner's people, and the lawyers left Shepard alone with the "ego wall" and his musings about arriving in Canada. It had all started in Quebec, and, if Shepard had assessed Warner properly, the end had begun when Shepard signed the papers.

What if he was wrong about Warner? Shepard had covered that contingency—that's why he had the voting trust, that's why he had the buy-sell agreement.

3

He Wanted Everything

Marvin Leon Warner was born June 8, 1919, in the Jewish neighborhood of Fountain Heights on the north side of Birmingham, Alabama. Some people say it was blue collar, others that it was lower middle class. All agree it wasn't affluent. There wasn't much money, but there was work. The jobs were there because Birmingham, alone among Southern cities, had an industrial base. It sat on millions of tons of iron ore and coal, and its steel industry undergirded its economy.

Fountain Heights was populated mostly by East European immigrants and their children. People from Poland, Russia, Latvia, Rumania, Hungary. As in many American cities, the German-Jewish population, which had arrived a generation or two before the East Europeans, lived in a separate community. They were on the south side of Birmingham. They had blended into the mainstream; spoke, dressed, and acted like Americans; and did not look too kindly on the rough *shtetl* ways and heavy accents of their East European brothers.

The residents of Fountain Heights, who represented 4,000 of Birmingham's 250,000 souls, possessed a real feeling of community when Marvin was growing up in the 1930s. You knew just about everybody, and people helped out if you were sick or had lost your job. Those were Depression times; things were tough. But you scrimped and hustled, and one way or the other you got by, sometimes with help from your friends. You didn't feel that you were alone.

The principal focus of the neighborhood—especially for the kids— was the Jewish Community Center, which housed the YMHA. It was an imposing three-story, yellow-brick structure with a Moorish look. The women's clubs met there, scholars gave lectures on Jewish history, and the kids played basketball or just hung out. And that's where many important functions took place—parties, dances, banquets.

In the spring of 1936, they held a special celebration at the center. Three local Jewish boys had swept the Alabama state oratorical contests, and the community decided to honor them. The college winner was Mel Israel, later to become the Mel Allen who chronicled the exploits of Joe DiMaggio, Yogi Berra, and Mickey Mantle as the radio and TV voice of the New York Yankees. The high school victor was Marvin Warner, and the grade school champ was a boy named Joe Kanter. Each winner was given a gold watch and a gold medal. The event got some press coverage, because several local politicos came by to sing the praises of these "future leaders of America."

Marvin's family operated a local institution, which in some ways was as important as the Jewish Community Center. It was called the Bohemian Bakery and Restaurant, and it was owned by his mother's brother, Philip Randman. Philip was a tall, slender fellow who acquired the nickname "Tom Mix" because he resembled that old cowboy star. Randman was an astute businessman, and he was something of a hero in Fountain Heights, because, in a small way, he was a philanthropist. He frequently gave or lent money to those in need. Marvin's mother and father, who later ran their own restaurants, worked at the Bohemian when Marvin was growing up.

The Bohemian offered home-cooking from the old country in a homey atmosphere. It was a place where you could sit and talk for hours over coffee and cheese blintzes. Or you could order a main course like brisket of beef. The bakery was known for its strudels and its breads, the pumpernickel and the challah Sabbath bread, which was a rich lacquered brown on the outside and yellow and soft on the inside. In later years, Marvin could remember the abrupt change from the sweet smells of the bakery to the pungent aromas of the restaurant: stuffed cabbage, mushroom barley soup, potato pancakes laced with garlic.

Presiding over the clatter of dishes and conversation was Marvin's mother Rose, an imposing woman, tall and handsome. She was the cashier, and she worked long hours. She kept track of everything for Philip, joked with the customers, had a smile for everyone. One of her contemporaries remembers Rose: "She wasn't here long from Latvia, but she spoke English with hardly the trace of an accent. She Americanized very well. She was an aristocratic lady for her generation." Rose was active outside the business and was an energetic presence in several Jewish social and religious groups.

When Rose married Marvin's father Samuel in 1916, she was a twenty-eight-year-old widow with a four-year-old daughter. Sam, a strong, healthy chap, was working in the warehouse of a produce company. He became a baker at the Bohemian after the marriage, and eventually helped to manage it and other restaurants he and Rose were involved with. Sam was a rough, rude, plain sort. He never fully adopted American ways, and his Polish-Jewish accent stayed with him all his life. Unlike his wife, he did not achieve standing in the community beyond his job, and he didn't push hard for financial success. He seemed satisfied to do his work and collect his paycheck.

Rose wasn't satisfied with the status quo. Her immigrant generation had found roots in this new country and had fought through the depression and other hardships. For the new generation, it would be better. Rose had big plans for her only son. She was determined to prepare Marvin for success. She was always there—supportive, understanding, loving—letting him know that with his energy and talent, he could have whatever he wanted. Young Marvin must have listened eagerly to her words of encouragement because, as it turned out, he wanted everything—fame, fortune, applause, influence.

Marvin has been conspicuously silent about his father. He seldom talked about him to his friends, and Sam is scarcely mentioned in the numerous biographical articles written during Marvin's career. Marvin may not be ashamed of his father, but it does not appear that he has a whole lot of pride in him either.

Marvin revered Rose and at every opportunity would tell people how much she meant to him. She died in 1979, and in 1982, Marvin built a handsome Jewish student center at the University of Cincinnati in her honor. The dedicatory booklet for the center spoke glowingly of her, mentioned her brother Philip twice, and listed her children and grandchildren. There was not a word about Sam Warner.

Marvin was a wiry, blue-eyed, sandy-haired kid. He was a force, an engine as he was growing up, rocketing through grade school and high school. He hated to lose. If he wanted something, he went after it with a thoroughness and zeal that amazed his contemporaries. He earned good grades, helped run the student government, and traveled all over the South winning oratorical medals.

The beat went on after high school. Always working, always hustling, always looking for the right contacts, he drove himself through college, law school, and a postgraduate law degree. His college roommate, Dave Sokol, remembers:

> He would thrust himself into situations. I would notice that when he was introduced to people, he'd pronounce his name very distinctly, so

whoever heard it would remember it very well. At a party or a meeting or something, he'd be talking to you but looking around to see who else was there; if he saw somebody he thought was more influential, the first thing you knew he'd be over talking to that other guy.

Sokol told him, "Marvin, you're going to be a wealthy man one of these days. You're going to be a real big success in life. But you're going to be as big a son of a bitch as you are now."

Marvin, Sokol, and their buddies who went to the University of Alabama in the thirties look back at it now in a haze of adoration. Those were happy years for them, a time of growth and friendship. Although they couldn't join the Christian fraternities, there was little anti-Semitic feeling, and there were no barriers to achievement in any campus organization. Marvin, for instance, was treasurer and secretary of the student body, wrote for the newspaper, and led the debating team. Students who came from the East said that anti-Semitism seemed considerably more severe at the Ivy League colleges. Fifty years later, Marvin and his friends make heavy financial contributions to the university, go to reunions, and are avid followers of the football team, the Crimson Tide. Marvin majored in commerce, made important gifts to the School of Commerce, and was awarded an honorary degree in 1980.

He entered the Army in 1941 as a lieutenant in the Judge Advocate's Corps and married his high school sweetheart Jane Blach in 1942. Jane was a member of one of the leading southside German-Jewish families. Their business, a department store, had been started in the 1850s. Some of the Blachs had fought for the Confederacy; others had helped organize Temple Emanuel, the oldest and most socially prominent synagogue in Birmingham.

Blach's department store, which closed down in 1988, catered to the carriage trade. It was quiet, upscale, and carried only the highest quality goods. Jane's father, Mervin, owned a significant piece of the business but was not a leader in its management. He spent much of his time working for charitable causes and sold his interest to one of his brothers in the 1960s. Jane's mother died in 1941.

The Blach family was not happy about Jane marrying the son of Fountain Heights immigrants. Of all the Blachs, Mervin was the least disturbed by the idea of the marriage, and by Jane's wedding day, he had won grudging acceptance from his relatives. Jane was spectacularly beautiful that day, her delicate features framed by lustrous black hair. One wedding guest said that Marvin and Jane were the handsomest couple in all of the South.

Marvin spent most of the war with an engineering unit fighting the Japanese and was mustered out as a major in early 1946. When he returned home, he found that the outlook for young lawyers in Birmingham was bleak. He would say later, "They offered me $150 a month; I couldn't live on that. Now I pay them $150 an hour." Marvin's father had died in 1944; and he, Jane, and their daughter Marlin (who was born in 1943) were living with his mother when he decided to take a shot at working for his uncle, George Warner, in the insurance and real estate business.

George has been described as "a real, good, warm, Yiddish fellow," a crusty bachelor who could hardly say two sentences without throwing in a few "Yiddish words." He had built up a solid business serving his Fountain Heights neighbors. He would occasionally rebate commissions to his cronies, the accounting system was antiquated, the pace was slow. Marvin wanted to change all this, bring the business into the modern world, and sparks soon flew between him and George. Marvin started searching for a way out and found it when he studied the Veterans' Emergency Housing Act of 1946. He thought he saw a way to be his own boss, to make money, and to meet his own housing needs in the bargain.

Housing demand in 1946 was enormous, and it was unprecedented. America had never seen anything like it before. There were four main reasons for this.

First, there were virtually no homes built during World War II. Every scrap of copper, steel, glass, wood, aluminum was commandeered for the war effort. There were a few isolated exceptions, such as the new town the government built for the workers at the atomic energy facility in Oak Ridge, Tennessee. But that was about it. The government controlled the raw materials, and it wouldn't let you have any to build a house.

Second, there were more people. In 1940, there were 132 million Americans, and in 1946, there were 142 million—a gain of 8 percent. The third factor was increased prosperity. Income per person in real terms made a dramatic 29 percent rise to $1,475 from 1940 to 1946.

And the fourth factor was the condition of the existing housing. President Roosevelt in 1937 said that he saw "one-third of our population ill-nourished, ill-clad, and ill-housed." That bad housing was nine years older in 1946, and much of it had not been well maintained during the war. When your plumbing sprang a leak or your wiring fizzled out, you didn't replace it, you patched it, because the essential materials were needed for the war effort.

Filling the housing gap became a major political issue in 1946, and the sharpest spotlight fell on veterans' housing. There were twelve million people in the armed services on V-J Day in August 1945, and in the rush to demobilize, ten million had become civilians by the end of 1946. To complicate matters, most of the veterans were creating or expanding families. Many of them had postponed having children for four or five years and were making up for lost time.

The national magazines like *Life* and *Newsweek* and the newspapers kept running photographs of veterans living in shacks or of veterans and their wives and kids doubling up with in-laws. Pundits such as Gabriel Heatter and Walter Lippman talked about young lives being stunted by over-crowding. And radio talk shows featured irate citizens calling for emergency solutions to the housing crisis. They were saying that we could beat the Nazis and the Japanese in the biggest war in world history, that we could put twelve million people under arms, and that we could develop the atomic bomb and manufacture fifty thousand planes a year, but we couldn't build a two-bedroom house for a brave veteran.

The main political response to the housing crisis was the Veterans' Emergency Housing Act, passed on May 22, 1946. It built on a New Deal base of federal activity in housing, but its scope was unprecedented, both in terms of the money involved and of program design. The act attacked the housing problem from both the supply side and the demand side. It encouraged supply by providing generous loans to private-sector builders. And it supported demand by having the federal government guarantee payments on all veterans' mortgages. As a last resort, in communities where these measures failed, it provided for the government itself to be the builder and landlord.

There were abuses and there were important policy mistakes, but, over all, the 1946 act was one of the most successful pieces of social legislation in American history. It met the demand, and by the early 1950s, the crisis had passed, and America was housed far better than it had ever been before.

The act was a very American response to the challenge. The European democracies such as England and France met their demand by having the government build millions of units. The private sector had no significant role. But here, the Housing Act worked to encourage entrepreneurs to provide the homes. The government subsidized and aided and abetted, but basically stayed on the sidelines.

The main beneficiaries of the act were working class and middle-class Americans. The typical person the government was trying to help was a twenty-five-year-old veteran with a couple of kids who hadn't saved any money yet and was just starting his career. The people who voted for the act were saying they had faith in him. The critics, mostly Midwest conservatives such as Senators Mundt, Bricker, and Capehart, said the government would surely take a big bath in red ink, that you shouldn't guarantee a loan to a penniless veteran with a family and uncertain prospects. But the optimists turned out to be correct. The veterans were able to pay for their housing, and the percentage of foreclosures was minuscule. The twenty-five-year-old veteran with the wife and two kids had the energy and the brains to hold a job which would allow him to pay his rent or meet his mortgage obligations.

Marvin Warner, age twenty-seven, living in cramped quarters with Rose, Jane, and Marlin, and chafing at the old country ways of Uncle George, was attracted by Section 608 of the act. He decided to become a 608 builder.

Section 608 was designed to encourage multifamily rental housing by providing government loan guarantees for 90 percent of the builder's estimated costs. In other words, if a bank lent Marvin $100,000 on a project and the project failed, the federal government would stand behind Marvin, would guarantee to the bank the repayment of 90 percent of the loss, or $90,000. The bank also had the building itself as collateral, so it was virtually a no-lose proposition. In addition, the interest rate was set at an attractive level for that time—4 percent. If a project made any sense at all, it was like Christmas Day to the bank every time they made a 608 loan.

The way it worked was this. The prospective builder would buy a plot of land and would go to the Federal Housing Authority (FHA) with his plans to develop it. He would have to show that there were sewers and other utilities available and that the site had good access to shopping centers, schools, and transportation. Most importantly, he had to produce architectural plans that showed that the building could be constructed at a reasonable cost and that it would meet FHA quality standards. The FHA would check out every detail of the project—engineering drawings, building schedules, insurance, legal fees, architectural fees, the availability of labor, the availability of materials. In addition, the builder had to show that he had a good record for paying his bills. Abner Johnson, who handled most of the 608 projects for the FHA in Birmingham, remembers, "The need for the housing was so great in this country that our underwriting requirements were relaxed a great deal. . . . The program was designed so that a man did not have to have a lot of cash money. What he needed was a good reputation. . . . They just had to show us that they had the ability to go out there and build that project in accordance with the plans and specifications completely."

Finally, the FHA would require that the builder give veterans preference over nonveterans when he went to rent his apartments.

Once the builder had his FHA approval and 90 percent loan guarantee commitment, he would go to his banker and arrange the construction financing. This was a two-step process. The FHA would not give its guarantee until the building was up, and it had assured itself that all specifications and standards had been met. So the builder would first get a construction loan from the bank. Then, when he had the building completed and the FHA had accepted it, the bank would convert the construction loan to a 33-year guaranteed mortgage loan.

Marvin Warner borrowed $4,200 from Rose and bought a vacant lot in a residential section on the south side of Birmingham. He worked with a designer to develop plans for a modest, ten-unit complex on the site. It comprised two one-story buildings, one with six apartments, the other with four. He went to the FHA, and Abner Johnson approved the project. Marvin called it Saipan Gardens for a Pacific island that he had helped wrest from the Japanese. He completed it in 1947 and moved into the tenth apartment with Jane and Marlin.

Joe Kanter, one of the winners with Marvin of the oratorical contests in 1936, was twenty-three in 1946. He had landed at Omaha Beach on D day with the 102nd Infantry and had fought all the way across France and into Germany. He was discharged as a staff sergeant and returned to Tarrant, his hometown, a blue collar suburb of Birmingham about twenty miles from where Marvin was living.

His father had died, and there wasn't any real family business to go into. Joe had read a newspaper story about a hundred people answering an ad for an apartment for rent, and some of his best friends were living in houses that were falling down around them. It seemed like everybody in Birmingham needed a new place to live. He reasoned that he couldn't lose if he got into the construction business.

Joe found a plot of land, got some backing from a local lumber company, and bought a set of plans from the same designer that Marvin was using. The project had eight apartments. Joe was his own general contractor and, when needed, would do some of the carpentry and plastering work himself.

When Joe finished his project, he made a bracing discovery. He had come in well under his estimated costs, so when he got his FHA guaranteed mortgage, he had about $4,000 in his bank account. He hurried over to his lawyer and asked him if he had done something illegal; and the lawyer assured him that everything was aboveboard. Joe could use the $4,000 to repay part of the mortgage, or he could keep the money as an attractive loan from Uncle Sam.

Joe had discovered that the FHA cost standards were calculated for the average builder nationwide. If you happened to be efficient the way Joe was, and you were in a relatively cheap labor market such as Birmingham, you could beat those standards. If you came in at 90 percent of your estimate, you didn't have to invest any of your own money at all. You owned a building, and all you had needed to put into it was your intelligence, your sweat, and your energy. And if you came in at 80 percent, you pocketed the difference between 80 percent and 90 percent as a highly favorable government loan. In other words, if you had done your job really well, Uncle Sam gave you money.

Of course, all the builders were not as efficient as Joe Kanter. Abner Johnson remembers several projects which were financial failures because actual costs were well above the estimates.

Marvin Warner was also efficient and had beaten the estimates on Saipan Gardens. He met Joe through a mutual friend, Joe's lawyer, and they started comparing notes. They soon decided that each could do better if they pooled their resources, and in 1948 they formed a corporation, a fifty-fifty joint venture called Warner-Kanter Company.

Joe and Marvin would be together for ten years, and they would always work through corporations in which each owned 50 percent. They were true partnerships in that the men shared responsibility, authority, and ownership equally. Both men were involved in all the business aspects of their ventures—land purchases, financing, construction, sales.

If there was one area where the responsibilities were somewhat unequal, it was politics. Joe, a more private person, did not especially enjoy the hurly-burly of the public arena, but Marvin loved it. He courted major politicians and, in particular, John Sparkman, the Alabama senator, who was to become Adlai Stevenson's vice presidential running mate in 1952. Sparkman had made himself an expert on housing and was a powerful advocate of the industry in the Senate. Marvin became a familiar figure in his Washington offices, lavishing flowers and boxes of candy on his secretaries and aides. He was also an important contributor and fundraiser at campaign time. Dave Sokol recalls, "He was a master politician. He knew how to do for those fellows to get them obligated to him. When Marvin would go to Washington, he'd just go into Sparkman's office and take over. Anything Marvin wanted, he got."

Marvin threw himself into American Legion activities in Birmingham and became the first World War II veteran to head the organization. He was an active leader and, of course, fired up the membership to lobby for more dollars for veterans' housing in the area. He also got them to take a stand against Ku Klux Klan anti-Semitism.

There were always two sides to Marvin the businessman. The outside world saw the politician, the smooth-as-silk persuader. But on the job, he was not an easy person to deal with. He hounded his suppliers, hassled his contractors, and drove his employees. One of his executives remembers: "He motivated through fear . . . he was driven and expected the people around him to be driven. The day started at 6:00 or 6:30 in the morning, and he didn't think twice about having you there at 8:00 or 9:00 at night. He was seldom satisfied with what was being accomplished; he constantly expected more."

He seldom negotiated a contract that he didn't want to change. One of his old competitors says, "He just keeps at it. With some people you might think you're done, that you've made your negotiations, and it's over. With Marvin, it's always up in the air until it's put to bed. He probably could have won more friends and made just as much money if he hadn't been quite as tough." Back in the late forties, Marvin told one of his father's friends that you had to step over people to get ahead in the world. The older man answered, "That may be your way, Marvin. It's not mine."

If you're looking at them head-on, Joe and Marvin are quite different because their faces are so dissimilar. The bone structure of Marvin's face is rugged and angular. You immediately take note of his jutting jaw and his long aquiline nose. Joe's face is rounder and flatter, and his features are much softer. If you spin them around, however, and look at them from the rear, the two men are remarkably similar. Both are about five feet, eight inches, slim-waisted, lean, athletic. Their bodies testify to lots of hours toning muscles at gyms, swimming pools, and jogging tracks, and they both move with bouncy, energetic strides. They were a formidable pair when they were in their twenties building up a storm in and around Birmingham.

They started with two small projects and then went for a major one, a twelve-story structure they would call The Essex House. The price of the land was $175,000, a very fancy number for those days, and it was totally beyond the boys' means. But that didn't stop them. They knew that the local contractors badly needed work at that time. The builders had almost starved to death during the war when there was virtually nothing for them to do, and now their tongues were hanging out for big projects.

Marvin and Joe went to the largest contractor in the city and said, "We'll give you the project to build—and it's a major one at around $2.5 million—if you'll lend us the $175,000 for the land. We'll pledge our total ownership in the project as collateral until we repay the loan." The contractor, who stood to make a profit of perhaps $300,000 on the construction, accepted the deal.

Now Marvin and Joe, with the land and a good set of building plans in hand, got a $3 million plus commitment from the FHA to cover 90 percent of all costs. Because they were efficient, when they had the building completed and had gotten their mortgage money, there was more than enough cash available to pay off their loan from the contractor.

Abner Johnson, over at the FHA, was monitoring the Birmingham situation very carefully, because he did not want to see the city overbuilt with rental units. He approved only four major projects, The Essex House and three others. He says, "We had fulfilled the need here. If I had approved everything that everybody wanted, instead of four buildings . . . we would have had thirty. You know how builders are. If anybody will finance them, they'll keep on building. Don't make a damn if there's a need or not."

Home construction, particularly when done on a small scale, has always been one of the least efficient sectors of the American economy. Warner and Kanter were appalled by the wasteful practices of the contractors on their first two projects, and they were sure they could do better. They had read about prefabrication techniques and decided to start a prefab facility near Birmingham in Fort Payne, Alabama.

By the time they were building The Essex House, they had a professional operation underway at Fort Payne. They were able to cut costs significantly by delivering important construction elements— wall sections, full bathroom units, floor s¹abs—to the site in finished condition. They married a pool of cheap, nonunion labor with the best technology available and ended up with perhaps the lowest cost operation in the United States.

Their technological know-how became a major plus when they were forced to look elsewhere because Abner Johnson had closed down the Birmingham market on them. In 1949, they traveled all over the Midwest looking for new opportunities. They found that developers in the major cities were very wary of the 608 program because they were afraid they were on the high side of the FHA cost standards. For instance, they did not believe that they could build a four-and-one-half-room apartment for less than $9,000, and the FHA standard was $8,100. Their labor was expensive and frequently unionized, and they had little know-how or investment in the new prefab technology.

Marvin and Joe were confident that by using the Fort Payne facility, volume purchases, and other cost-cutting techniques they could build profitably in the Midwest. They went for big projects because high volume was so crucial to keeping down costs. They found their first ones in Cincinnati and St. Louis, and they outfitted specially designed flatbed trucks which would move prefab sections overnight from Fort Payne to the building sites in these two cities.

Constantly expanding, they were perpetually short of cash. Often they relied on contractors to help with their finances. In addition, at times they found lenders who were so enamored of the 4 percent loans with the big federal guarantees, that they paid Warner-Kanter an extra fee for the privilege of lending them money. Marvin and Joe used these fees to cover land purchases and other preliminary costs.

There was terrific political pressure on the FHA to get 608 housing built in the Midwest. The congressmen, the senators, and the state and local politicians were screaming for 608 money to flow to their states and communities. Warner and Kanter were usually treated as heroes. They were bailing out the politicians and the FHA, and they were building affordable housing besides.

Occasionally, they would run into delays in pushing their approvals through the FHA bureaucracy. But Marvin had become adept at pulling the right levers, and, if he had serious difficulties, he could play his political trump card, John Sparkman. Marvin recollects,

"You get into legislative and administrative snarls. You file an application, you got the land, you're paying interest on it, and then you don't hear anything for three to six months. Sparkman could find out what was holding things up. . . . It was a matter of getting things through so we could get started."

From their bases in Cincinnati and St. Louis, Marvin and Joe managed major projects in those cities, and in Indianapolis, Kansas City, Chicago, and Omaha. By 1951, they had become very confident of their building skills and decided to eliminate the general contractors. This increased their take considerably, because the general contractors usually earned a profit of at least 10 percent of the building costs. With their new contracting responsibilities and with operations going forward in several cities at once, the boys spent prodigious hours in the field—driving the building crews, expediting shipments, making deals with labor unions, negotiating zoning changes, running sales campaigns. Marvin remembers the problems with their first Cincinnati development, Stratford Manor:

> Here I couldn't find one who would do it as quickly and economically as I thought it should be done. So, I became the contractor, and I imported people to do the subcontracting—the plumbing, the electricity, and the heating. Carpentry, grading, and utilities were done locally.
>
> But these were all union jobs, and I had to get all my imports admitted. We were dealing with ten to fourteen unions—rodbusters, tile, glazers—and we had to get to somebody in all of them. So we just worked at it. You've got to be like a bulldog; you're under contract to the federal government, and you got to do it. . . .
>
> We had the rough lumber prefabricated in Fort Payne, Alabama, and had it shipped in. The custom building people didn't like it. We were the first here to use drywall, and naturally, the plastering contractors didn't appreciate that.
>
> But we had to do it. We had constant pressure on the unions to let us bring in outsiders, because either they couldn't supply or wouldn't supply, the people we wanted. Oh, I wasn't winning any popularity contests in those days. . . .
>
> Hell, I was out there riding my bulldozer, and somebody would say to me, "We can't pour that foundation, it's too wet." And I'd say, "The hell you can't, get up there and do it." I'd call those subs at night. I knew just when the plumbing had to be roughed in and the electricity and the wallboard.

Their intelligence and their "hands-on" zeal carried the day everywhere, and by the mid-1950s, Marvin and Joe owned more than three thousand rental apartments and had $1 million in the bank.

They also took advantage of opportunities outside the 608 program.

First, they broke out of the rental business into single-family housing where they sold the homes. With their competitive edge, they soon had 15 percent of the market in Cincinnati and St. Louis. Single-family homes were covered by Section 603 of the 1946 Housing Act, which provided for federally guaranteed mortgages for veterans. The FHA was so eager to push veteran-owned housing that they came up with "sweat equity" down payments for veterans who had no money. The builders were instructed to leave five to ten percent of the construction unfinished, and the veteran would earn his "sweat equity" by completing it. Marvin and Joe were among the first builders in the country to construct such projects.

Next, they moved on to large planned communities, where they built everything—the schools, the shopping centers, the parks, the firehouses. They got into this business by buying from the federal government in 1953 a 3,500-acre tract west of Cincinnati called Forest Park. The government had bought it as part of one of the most idealistic experiments of the New Deal days. Eleanor Roosevelt had wanted to build a fully planned community as a model for the nation. The project began with the small village of Greenhills but then ran out of money. And the 3,500 acres surrounding Greenhills on three sides lay fallow.

Warner-Kanter bought the land for the bargain price of $500 an acre, but the problems were formidable. Forest Park, at that time, was beyond the Cincinnati suburbs. There were no roads, sewers, water, or gas. Marvin and Joe put in their own sewers and mounted a successful political campaign to force the local utility to provide water and gas. They started building from an initial plan for a city of fifty thousand. They gauged their market well. Today, Forest Park has a population of sixty-five thousand.

By 1956, Joe had become tired of it. He was thirty-two and still a bachelor. He had been working at a breakneck pace for ten years, and he was very rich. He wanted to take it easy, move to New York, and perhaps find a bride. Marvin was shaken. He was in full stride, and he wanted to keep driving, keep pushing to wider horizons. He toyed with the idea of using Joe as a high level, part-time consultant. But that wouldn't work. Their kind of business needed a seven-day-a-week commitment. The only realistic solution was to split up.

To achieve this, they used a Talmudic method. One divides, the other chooses. Marvin would decide what was to go into the two piles of property, and then Joe would pick the pile he wanted. Marvin wished very much to stay in Cincinnati, so he put extra equity in the non-Cincinnati pile. Joe became suspicious. He thought Marvin was trying to put something over on him, and he chose the Cincinnati properties. Marvin was furious. He couldn't bring himself to talk to Joe for several years. The breakup occurred in 1958.

Joe went to New York, found his bride, and returned to Cincinnati to manage his properties. Marvin stayed in Cincinnati, too. He and Jane had put down roots there and had two more children: Alyson, born in 1950, and Mark, born in 1957.

Joe completed Forest Park and similar planned communities outside Washington, D.C., and Milwaukee. He retains several of the Cincinnati properties, but in 1975 moved his base to Miami, where he has continued in real estate and branched out into banking. In recent years, he has realized a long-held dream: he became a moviemaker. He was executive producer of the 1987 Meryl Streep–Jack Nicholson film *Ironweed*.

The Warner-Kanter breakup was a watershed in Marvin's career. After the split, he took a deep breath and assessed his position. He was thirty-eight, in robust health, and worth about $15 million. Until now, except for work for Jewish causes—he was on the board of Hebrew Union College and president of the Jewish Federation of Cincinnati—his career had been all business. Other self-made millionaires in his position, if they shift focus at all, usually move on to another overriding endeavor. Norton Simon amassed one of the world's great art collections; Bob McNamara devoted himself to public service; Joe Kanter made movies.

But Marvin was different. Unlike most of his peers, the ambitions of Rose's son seemed to extend in all directions at once: politics, thoroughbred racing, a jet-set life-style, philanthropy, professional sports, public service. Marvin was insatiable; he wanted everything. People have asked: Why would anyone who had so much want more? But astute Warner observers say that wanting more is what Marvin is all about. And whatever he wants, he pursues with unswerving zeal.

He never stopped pursuing dollars. No matter what else he was doing, Marvin was a businessman twenty-four hours a day. He has always appreciated money. He likes to know it's there and, of course, he enjoys what it can buy for him: jet planes, political influence, opportunities to give to universities and hospitals, lavish homes. And he seems enamored of the process of making it, getting a visceral thrill from besting someone in a negotiation. He loves to pull off a smart deal—however small, however big—from buying an under-valued thoroughbred yearling to selling a bank for a $30 million profit.

Marvin restaffed his organization in Cincinnati and was off build-ing again: a shopping center in Phenix City, Alabama, a $35 million "new town" in Mobile, Alabama, top-of-the-line mobile home parks in Florida, high-rise apartment towers in Cincinnati, single-family developments in Tampa, Florida, and Paducah, Kentucky.

Marvin's career has strong parallels to that of Shepard Broad. Both started as lawyers, shifted to real estate, and made their initial fortunes in the postwar housing boom. Now, thinking again like Shepard, Marvin reasoned that owning a savings and loan had great advan-tages for a builder. In 1958, he bought Home State, a fledgling thrift in the Cincinnati suburbs. Under his leadership, it became the biggest savings and loan in Southern Ohio.

Jane Blach Warner did not try to keep pace with Marvin. She became increasingly estranged from his activities, and the marriage started to show strains in the early 1960's. Jane initiated divorce proceedings in 1966, and the marriage ended in June 1967, twenty-five years after it began. In the wake of the divorce, there was considerable strife over the loyalties of the children. Marlin, who was married in 1966 to Steve Arky, remained close to her mother, but her sister Alyson has been completely estranged from Jane. Alyson has always been her Daddy's girl and has participated in several of his business ventures, serving on the board of Home State and other Warner corporations. Marvin, Jr., whom everyone calls Mark, lived with his mother till he completed his education. Then he did not see her for several years; they were reconciled in the early 1980s. Mark served on the American Savings & Loan board with Marvin and has worked closely with his father in other areas.

Since the divorce from Jane, young and beautiful women have been a fixture in Marvin's life. And they were there on many occasions—college reunions, business conferences, Kentucky Derby weekends, political conventions. When he was in his fifties, Marvin asked a Birmingham friend about the friend's daughter. He told Marvin that she was too old for him; she was twenty-two.

The center of Marvin's new bachelor lifestyle was Warnerton, a six-hundred-acre farm which lies among rolling hills about twenty miles east of Cincinnati; he bought it from an old local family. He thought it would be a good tax shelter idea to breed quarterhorses there as a sideline. But Marvin never does anything as a sideline. He got the best professional staff and began spending serious money. By 1971, Warnerton was a major breeding operation with Triple Chick, the greatest quarterhorse sire of that time, in residence. The main barn held sixty-six horses, and there was a special breeding barn and a full-time veterinarian. The equipment, which was state-of-the-art, included water troughs that stayed full automatically.

Marvin bought himself a helicopter, and the horses almost had nervous breakdowns whenever his chopper took off or landed. His usual destination was the pad he had built on the roof of the Home State headquarters building. Marvin was a nitpicker about office neatness, and the route from Warnerton to the headquarters passed over one of the Home State branches. When the copter flew over the branch, one of its employees would call the headquarters to tell everyone to tidy up because the boss was coming. The copter also made frequent hops to the airport to pick up Marvin when he returned from trips in the Sabre jet and to gather up girlfriends and other guests for the lavish parties he threw at the farm.

Warnerton has a New England look to it. Deep-green shutters stand out against whitewashed brick and white clapboard. The main house is two stories high and makes a long horizontal silhouette as it rambles across a pasture. Tennis courts sit behind it. The main barn is about two hundred feet away, and there are about a dozen smaller buildings scattered across the property.

Marvin likes the canvasses of LeRoy Neiman. His work and those of other modern artists burst with primary colors from the walls at Warnerton and contrast with the deeply hued furniture. There is a sense of comfort about the place—top-drawer comfort derived from the richest leathers, the finest crystal, the softest fabrics. The only jarring note is the telephones. They are everywhere—on tables, in wall niches, on floors. If there is a telephone at hand, Marvin can do business, and Marvin wants to be able to do business all the time.

In 1973, Marvin switched from quarterhorses to thoroughbreds. The change was dictated partly by geography. He was only seventy-five miles from the epicenter of the thoroughbred world in Kentucky, but he was over 1,200 miles from quarterhorse country in Colorado. And thoroughbred racing was the traditional "sport of kings." It was

fun to watch your quarterhorse compete in the $2 million sprint championship in Denver, but there was a special excitement in seeing your silks ridden in the Kentucky Derby or at Longchamps in France. There was glamour in bidding against the Queen of England at the British sales in Newmarket, in having your private box at Churchill Downs, or in rubbing elbows with the Ogden Phippses in the clubhouse at Belmont. It was a long way from the Bohemian Bakery.

By 1976, Marvin was a major force both in breeding and in racing. 1977 was a banner year for him. His horses were fourteenth in the nation in victories; he sold fourteen yearlings at the Keeneland auctions for almost $1 million; and one of his colts, Papelote, carried his bright red and white silks in the Kentucky Derby. This was a terrific achievement in so short a time. Marvin added other horse farms in Kentucky and Florida in subsequent years, and both his breeding and racing operations continued as major forces in the 1980s. A source of gratification to Marvin was the passion which Mark developed for the horse business. Marvin's son lives in Lexington, Kentucky, and is deeply involved in his own and his father's thoroughbred operations.

In the mid-1980s, Marvin's net worth was approximately $100 million. Of this, a surprisingly high total was invested in the thoroughbred business—$40 million. The farms were worth roughly $10 million, and the thoroughbreds $30 million.

In the early days, when he got Senator Sparkman and other officials to expedite his projects, Marvin used the political system to his personal advantage. After the Kanter split, he wanted to be part of the system, an active player. He entered active politics with his wallet. By the mid sixties, he was the largest single contributor to the Ohio Democratic party and a major fund-raiser for the national party. His benefactions did not go unnoticed, and, in 1968, Lyndon Johnson named him to the ten-member U.S. delegation to the United Nations General Assembly. While there, he concentrated on the problems of investment in the Third World. And, ever the salesman, he lobbied for the U.N. to move to Ohio.

In 1972, he was appointed by Governor Gilligan to the board of regents for the Ohio state university system. Marvin took his responsibilities as a regent seriously. He did his homework on the important issues and was identified as a fierce opponent of waste, particularly in building construction. He beefed up budgets for vocational education, saying, "There still should be pride in being able to use your hands as well as your brain. I want to emphasize the dignity and respectability of a technical education." He was elected chairman of the regents in 1975 and served until 1977. As chairman, he worked hard and successfully to bring the University of Cincinnati, which was having financial difficulties as a private institution, into the state system. One of his frequent allies on the regents was Cleveland businessman George Steinbrenner.

When George put together a group to buy the New York Yankees from the CBS network in 1973, he asked Marvin to join in, and Marvin became one of thirteen investors who put up $770,000 each. The Yankees had been floundering under CBS, and there was even talk of them leaving New York City. George and Marvin and their partners pledged to keep the team there and to return them to their former glory. George, it soon turned out, wanted total ownership and control. He started purchasing his partners' shares and, in 1975, took Marvin out at a handsome profit.

Marvin wasn't absent from professional sports for long. In 1976, Hugh Culverhouse, Sr., a boyhood friend from Birmingham, asked Marvin to invest in the Tampa Bay Buccaneers, one of two new teams in the National Football League that year. Marvin bought a 48 percent share.

Culverhouse also convinced him that they should buy a controlling interest in ComBanks, a holding company which owned banks in six medium-sized cities in Central Florida. The two men were attracted to ComBanks, because its branches were located in communities with excellent growth prospects and its management had not come close to exploiting this potential. Warner and Culverhouse replaced the existing management with people who were more aggressive, more imaginative, and more responsive to the market.

In January 1977, soon after Marvin bought into ComBanks, Steve Arky brought to his attention another Florida bank chain which wasn't realizing its market potential. It was called American Bancshares, Inc. (ABI), and it owned banks in nine communities. Marvin was fully extended at that moment and turned down the deal; so Arky took it to his friend Ronnie Ewton. The two had met ten years before when Ewton was Arky's commanding officer in the National Guard. Steve had worked as Ronnie's lawyer in organizing ESM in 1975, and he continued as counsel to the company.

Ewton talked the proposition over with his associate Bob Seneca, the "S" in ESM, and the two men agreed in February to buy 24 percent of the ABI stock for $3,369,750. The 24 percent represented the controlling interest in ABI.

The catch was that Ewton and Seneca were short of cash and needed to borrow $3 million to complete the purchase. They could handle the interim financing but needed a long-term loan. So Steve took them up to Ohio to meet Marvin and his associates at Home State. Marvin may have been overextended, but Home State wasn't, and the bank lent Ewton and Seneca the $3 million in April 1977. The two men pledged as collateral both their ABI and ESM shares. Ewton and Seneca then proceeded to do with ABI what Warner and Culverhouse were doing with ComBanks: they installed a more aggressive management team to improve the profitability of the branch banks.

As Marvin moved further into the worlds of banking and professional sports, he intensified his involvement in politics. The Democratic party was a shambles after the disastrous defeat of George McGovern in 1972. The task of reconstruction fell to Texan Robert Strauss, who was elected chairman of the Democratic National Committee (DNC) in early 1973. He inherited a demoralized organization, a divisive liberal-conservative split among the rank and file, and a $15 million debt. AT&T was threatening to cut off his telephones, several major airlines wouldn't sell him tickets, and scores of smaller creditors were baying at his heels.

Marvin Warner was one of a small group of party stalwarts who rallied behind Strauss in his rebuilding efforts. He was everywhere, helping Bob to raise money and to reduce friction among party elements. Marvin was elected to the DNC itself in 1975 and stayed on until 1977.

Strauss's term as chairman was a major success. By 1976, he had rebuilt the party to the point where it could contest and win a national election. The debt was down to $9 million, the organization was strong, and the troops were united.

In late 1975, Strauss and the party hierarchy were backing the presidential candidacy of Senator "Scoop" Jackson of Washington. If Jackson stumbled, they planned to turn to Hubert Humphrey. Marvin split with the hierarchy because he couldn't resist the siren song of another "down home" southerner, Jimmy Carter. Bob Strauss thought Marvin was crazy. In a recognition poll commissioned by the DNC, 75 percent of the Democrats interviewed could identify "Scoop" Jackson from a photograph, and less than 20 percent could identify Jimmy Carter. But Marvin's instincts were sounder than Bob's. He joined up with Carter in November 1975 and became one of his leading fundraisers.

After the Carter victory, Marvin thought he should get a major ambassadorship like France or Great Britain. The Carter appointment people couldn't swing that, but they could give him Switzerland. Even Switzerland was tough to pull off, because Carter, in one of his "good government" speeches, had promised to increase from a traditional 67 percent to 75 percent the allocation of ambassadorships going to State Department career people; the politicos had to be satisfied with a meager 25 percent.

Switzerland was okay. It was an important financial and industrial center and an intelligence hub. Its CIA outpost was one of the most important anywhere. It certainly beat being posted to New Zealand or Paraguay. When he testified at his Senate confirmation hearings, Marvin was flanked by Ohio Senators Glenn and Metzenbaum, who had benefitted handsomely from his campaign contributions. John Sparkman presided as chairman of the Senate Foreign Relations Committee, and the confirmation went through smoothly in July 1977. Marvin arrived in Bern, the Swiss capital, two months later.

Marvin does not like to give up anything he has latched onto. He tried tenaciously to retain his posts at the Ohio Board of Regents and the DNC and attempted to jet back and forth from Switzerland to attend their meetings. After about sixty days, this proved impractical, and he resigned both positions.

He never broke stride when it came to business. He designated Burt Bongard, Home State's president, and Steve Arky as his chief lieutenants. Marvin immediately had installed in Bern a special telephone line to which only he, his Ohio secretary, the chairman of Ohio's Democratic party, and Burt Bongard had access.

The wheeling and dealing went on. In early 1978, Marvin sold to Culverhouse his interest in the Tampa Bay Bucs and bought all of Culverhouse's shares in ComBanks. In June of 1978, Ewton bought Seneca's ABI stock. He then sold the full 24 percent ABI interest to ComBanks for $4,122,000 plus an option to buy 15 percent of ComBanks at a later date at a reasonable price.

As a result of this maneuvering, Marvin now controlled both ABI (which soon changed its name to Great American) and ComBanks. Ronnie was named to the boards and the executive committees of both companies, each of which responded to the aggressive Warner-Ewton management philosophy; their profitability picked up dramatically in the 1978–1980 period.

On the diplomatic front, Marvin caused controversy. He saw himself as a salesman and advocate for American business, and his brash ways shook up the staid Swiss. He ran a conference on investing in the United States and, at its end, asked those who wanted to put money into the American economy to raise their hands. This may work at a Democratic party fundraiser, but it rubbed his Swiss audience the wrong way. To them, investing is an almost priestly calling, and they like to make their decisions in private, after a good deal of rumination.

Another brouhaha erupted when Marvin decided to promote American cars by parking twenty-four of them all over the lawn of the U.S. Embassy. To the tradition-minded Swiss, embassy lawns are to be used for teas on summer afternoons, not for commercial displays.

And then there were the girlfriends—a steady stream, both local and imported. One of them was Susan Clough, President Carter's personal secretary. When she came to Switzerland, there was a mix-up on protocol. Marvin took her to a diplomatic dinner and, on arrival, was told that Susan couldn't attend because the only women invited were the wives of the male guests. Marvin protested that the mistake was an innocent one and that Susan had come a long way to attend, but the Swiss would not be moved. Marvin and Susan ate elsewhere that night.

Another girlfriend was Susan Goldwater. A sometimes fashion model, she was trying to make it as cohost of an afternoon TV magazine show in Washington, D.C., when she met Marvin. Susan lived literally in the fast lane; she was a race car driver and had a pilot's license. A leggy, attractive, suntanned blonde, she looked as if she had just stepped off a southern California beach. That is exactly where she came from—Newport Beach, California. She was separated from her second husband, Barry Goldwater, Jr., by whom she had a son, Barry III. Her first marriage had been annulled after six months.

Susan and Marvin had a jet-set romance. There were daily transatlantic phone calls and frequent flights to rendezvous in Washington, Switzerland, and Palm Beach. In the middle of it all, Marvin announced that he was resigning his ambassadorship to marry Susan and return to Cincinnati.

Susan was divorced from Goldwater on May 15, 1979, and she and Marvin were married on May 27. He was sixty, and she was thirty-three. They had a traditional Jewish ceremony at a synagogue in Cincinnati. Less than seven months later, the *Cincinnati Enquirer* reported that the marriage was on the rocks, and the pair filed for divorce on February 25, 1980.

Marvin's friends described Susan as ambitious, aggressive, even nervy. Some say she took advantage of him because she got a handsome settlement when they were divorced.

Susan was one of Marvin's two major disappointments of 1980. The other was Home State. Like American Savings & Loan and thousands of other thrifts, Home State had been thrown into a sea of red ink by the 1980 deregulation act. The losses were so severe that they threatened its existence.

With Home State, Marvin faced, for the first time in his life, a major business failure. He had several options to head off disaster, a couple of them conservative; he could have sought a stronger institution to merge with or he could have pumped in more capital. But he chose a third option, a more risky one. He decided to let Ronnie Ewton try to create the profits for Home State through speculation in the government bond market. He was on a winning streak with Ewton at ComBanks and Great American, and he decided to let Ronnie roll the dice for him at Home State.

4

The World of the Bond Daddies

Ronnie Restine Ewton was born in 1942 in Nashville, Tennessee, and raised in Donelson, a modest suburb of the city. He has always impressed people with his polite manner and his ability to talk the birds out of the trees. And he has a way of making you feel you are his best friend after you have only known him for fifteen minutes. Many folks who knew him predicted that he'd either be a salesman or a man of the church. As it turned out, he became both.

Ronnie never had clear goals or ambitions. He glided through life, usually following the paths opened to him by his great powers of persuasion. After three desultory years at small colleges in Tennessee and Kentucky, he left to make his mark in the world. He hadn't yet heard God's call, so he went to work as a salesman.

Ronnie's dad made a modest living selling life insurance. When Ronnie's mother died of cancer in 1965, it badly depleted the older man's resources and traumatized him emotionally. He moved with Ronnie and Ronnie's younger brother to Jefferson City, Missouri, where he had prospects for work. Ronnie remembers: "We left Nashville altogether because things were not running too smooth. We worked Missouri for a year, a year and a half, in the insurance industry, getting my family back stabilized."

Ronnie sold life insurance in Jefferson City and Sedalia, Missouri, and did well from the start. He was always beating his sales quotas and pleasing his bosses. And he was encouraged to do even better because he was in love with a strong, intelligent, and ambitious girl. They had met back in Tennessee when he was still in school. Her name was Darla, and they were married in 1967.

Darla has a commanding presence and always seemed to loom over Ronnie. She is two inches taller, at five feet, eleven inches, and her bone structure is much more rugged than his. Her features are strikingly beautiful, and her face is framed by shoulder-length brunette tresses highlighted here and there by touches of frosting.

Darla is a strong-willed, outspoken woman with lots of down-home country smarts. She was more than a full partner in Ronnie's life; Ronnie craved direction and she became his mentor.

They made an attractive couple. Darla was careful always to wear flat shoes when she was with her husband, and she encouraged him to wear well-tailored, understated clothes. Ronnie had conventional good looks much like 1950s TV idol Robert Stack, and he moved with the grace of a good athlete; he was, in fact, always an excellent horseman.

Ronnie liked life insurance, but the good salesmen seemed to top out at about $40,000 per year. He and Darla wanted to do better than that. When they checked out the Sunday newspapers, they began to read ads like this one from the *Memphis Press-Scimitar* soliciting salesmen in a newly booming business, municipal bonds:

> Your first year income should exceed the $20,000 a year level. Second year level incomes of $40-50,000 aren't rare! and $100,000 is a heard of figure during this same time span. Previous investment sales isn't a requirement. While you should be a first-rate, Hi-caliber individual, you should also be somewhat of a high-roller.

Soon after, the Ewtons actually met some of these bond salesmen. They were young, and they had come off used-car lots and farms and now they were making six-figure salaries. They favored fancy cars and luxury condos and liked to keep their friends lubricated with "Jack" (Jack Daniels on the rocks).

Ronnie and Darla decided that they had to give the bond business a try. They moved to Little Rock, Arkansas, where Ronnie joined a small municipal bond house called Delta Securities. That's when he entered the world of the "bond daddies."

Little Rock was on the periphery of this world. Its center was 140 miles to the east, in Memphis, Tennessee, where the term "bond daddy" was coined in the late 1960s. The aptly named Melvin Bogus, an early associate of Ronnie who served a sentence in federal prison for securities fraud, recalls: "Those were the days of the 'bond daddies,' a kind of a term of endearment. This is the guy who used to sell corrugated boxes or something, and somehow got into the securities business. He didn't have much training, but they'd stick him on a telephone. He had Rolex watches, he'd drive a Ferrari, but you were lucky if he could spell his name."

Memphis has been an important American financial center since the early nineteenth century, because it sits in the middle of the rich, black muck of the Mississippi Delta, one of the most fertile farm areas on earth. The brokers and bankers of Memphis financed huge quantities of the cotton and later, the rice and soy beans which flowed from the delta to buyers everywhere in the world. Over the decades, they acquired a high degree of financial know-how and sophistication. So it was no surprise that the municipal bond trade took firm root there.

Municipal bonds are sold by states and by governmental units within states—cities, counties, water districts, turnpike authorities—to raise money for projects deemed worthy by the sellers. Until recent years, none of the interest paid on municipal bonds was taxed by the federal government. Revisions to the federal tax code in the 1980s have made the interest paid on certain classes of these bonds taxable, but the vast majority are still tax-exempt. That is, the receiver of the interest pays no federal tax on his income.

The tax-exempt provision has saved governmental borrowers hundreds of billions of dollars, because it has allowed them to pay lower interest rates than their competition—the issuers of corporate and federal bonds whose yields are taxed. For a taxpayer earning $100,000, a 7 percent yield on a tax-exempt bond provides the same net income as a 10 percent yield on a corporate or a federal bond; the customer is as happy as he would be with a higher-yielding, taxable bond, and the municipal issuer saves a healthy 3 percent per year in interest payments.

To retain this enormous competitive advantage, the state governments and the multitude of local government entities have maintained a very powerful lobby in Congress. This lobby did not stop at freedom from federal taxation; it wanted freedom from federal regulation as well. And until well into the 1970s it succeeded. The market was wide open. Laissez-faire. No rules. No training requirements. No licenses. In contrast, the markets for corporate bonds and for stocks were under close federal regulation by the SEC.

The state of Tennessee also made it easy on the boys in Memphis. Unlike most states in the 1960s, Tennessee had no capital requirements for brokers. You didn't have to put up a penny to get into the business. All you needed was a desk and a telephone.

The bond daddy operations were a variation on an old concept in the American securities business, the "boiler room." "Boiler rooms" came into being as soon as the telephone became a part of American life. Basically, they consisted of a room full of con men calling naive and often greedy customers to sell them securities of dubious worth.

Boiler rooms have flourished in several American locales over the decades. They pushed land ventures in Florida in the twenties, penny mining stocks in Denver in the fifties, high-flying electronics companies on Wall Street in the seventies. Why, then, did the municipal bond boiler rooms flower so exuberantly in Memphis in the 1960s? The answer comes in two parts—George Lenox and the WATS line.

George Lenox was born poor on a houseboat on the White River near Roe, Arkansas in 1924. A small, wiry man, he had a steely determination to succeed and an unflagging capacity for hard work. His first job was digging mussel shells out of the White River bottom for sale to a button factory. He crisscrossed the globe as a Merchant Marine navigator during World War II, worked his way through the University of Arkansas and its law school, and started as a teller at the First National Bank of Memphis in 1953. He moved up to the bank's municipal bond department and quickly saw the potential for aggressive selling of these securities.

In 1959, he formed his own municipal bond firm, First U.S. Corporation. George was fascinated by computers and other new technology and sought constantly to apply them to his business. He was particularly attracted to Wide Area Telephone Service (WATS) lines, which AT&T introduced in 1961.

WATS lines greatly reduce the cost of long-distance telephoning for heavy users. A WATS subscriber does not pay by the call for long distance; he pays one monthly charge for an unlimited number of calls. Once the number of calls exceeds a certain threshold, the rest of them are, in effect, free.

WATS lines gave George Lenox cheap and immediate access to customers in every nook and cranny of the United States. There were plenty of them out there, and many had only sketchy knowledge about municipal bonds. George became a multimillionaire in less than a decade by connecting via WATS lines his bond daddy salesmen with these naive buyers. Many of the buyers were small banks.

Of the roughly 19,000 American banks extant in the 1960s, 15,000 were small. That is, their deposits came to less than $50 million each, and they had one or two branches. The small bankers were heavy buyers of municipal bonds for two principal reasons. They were attracted by the tax-exempt yields; and their perception of bonds as much less risky than stocks fit well with their conservative, non-speculative investment philosophy.

The bankers combined too much trust with too little knowledge.

They were conditioned to be trusting, because they were used to dealing with bond salesmen whom they had known for years and who often visited them in person. In the WATS era, when they heard a quiet, sincere country voice on the other end of the telephone with a bargain in municipals, they would more than likely give the caller the benefit of the doubt.

The bankers were naive because they did not understand fully the risks inherent in municipal bonds. Most municipal bonds are very safe because they have the taxing power of the issuer behind them. But bad judgment or bad management by elected officials can some-times make their bonds as risky as a high-flying stock. The holders of New York City bonds in the 1970s learned this lesson. The best way to insure against risk is to be fully informed about the entity behind the bonds.

The problems of the small bankers were compounded because accurate data about municipal bonds is much harder to come by than it is for other securities, such as corporate stocks. A buyer can get from any major brokerage house—Merrill Lynch, PaineWebber—well-prepared research reports on the history, current condition, and future prospects of an IBM or a General Motors. And accurate prices are always available, because there is an active market in these securi-ties with thousands of participants.

In contrast, the buyer would have great difficulty obtaining reliable data about the condition of entities like the York, Pennsylvania, Public Housing Authority and the Pueblo West Metropolitan Water District of Colorado, or the prices of their bonds. He would usually rely on the word of his salesman, his bond daddy.

And the word of a bond daddy was a very sometimes thing. The unconscionable mark-up was his principal money-making ploy. Taking advantage of customer ignorance, he would sell bonds for prices well above those quoted in the established centers of New York and Chicago. One veteran Tampa bond dealer recollects, "They'd get a $4 million issue of nursing home bonds out of Lubbock, Texas. Who knew what they were worth? Who knew what they yielded? They'd sell them for five or six points above the market."

And the bond daddy was not above lying about quality. The Kevil

Bank, of Kevil, Kentucky, was sold—for $9,600—ten $1,000 bonds issued by the Larue County, Kentucky, Water District. Before the bonds were delivered, the bank's president heard by chance that the water district had defaulted on its interest payments and that the bonds were worth only $5,000. He managed to cancel the order before his bank paid for the securities. Another banker thought he was buying Cleveland, Ohio, bonds, and then discovered that he had purchased Cleveland, Tennessee, sewer bonds which were worth much less.

Other oft-used bond daddy scams were the "stuffed pig," "twisting," and "scanning the obits."

The "stuffed pig" was simply the practice of the bond daddy using money left on deposit in the customer's account to trade for the bond daddy's own benefit. Of course, the customers were never informed that this was going on.

"Twisting" involved collusion between the customer and the bond daddy to raise yields at the expense of quality. To attract buyers, risky bonds must pay higher interest rates than quality bonds. Unscrupulous bank officials would sometimes work with bond daddies to trade quality bonds for riskier ones to raise the yields on their portfolios and increase short-term profits. Since quality ratings were often difficult to come by, the changes frequently went undetected by interested parties such as bank regulators.

Millions of dollars worth of bonds were unloaded at exorbitant mark-ups by bond daddies scanning the obituary columns. Salesmen would find obituaries of bank officials and then call their banks and claim falsely that the deceased had ordered a particular bond the day before he died. In the confusion following the banker's death, the surviving officials often paid for the bonds in question.

Bond daddies everywhere were shocked to read that George Lenox had been murdered on the morning of Tuesday, March 10, 1970, on the way to GLL Farms, his Tennessee Walking Horse operation. George's major passion outside his business was his collection of walking horses. Every morning he would rise at 5:00, and drive in his gold and black Fleetwood Cadillac from his 650-acre estate to GLL Farms, a few miles away. There he would check out his prize breeding stock, which included stallion Carbon Copy, the 1964 world champion.

George never saw Carbon Copy that Tuesday morning. He was forced off the road by two armed men, driven four miles to a lonely, wooded site, and killed by two shots in the left eye. Bobby Joe Fabian, a low-level Dallas hoodlum who police described as "cold-blooded as a rattlesnake and mentally unstable," has been convicted of the murder. His alleged accomplice was shot dead by police as he attempted a holdup two months after Lenox's death. Bobby Joe, who received $15,000 to kill Lenox as a "contract hit," is serving a life sentence for the murder plus 163 years for assorted other crimes.

Detectives have identified many enemies of George Lenox in the bond business and in the highly competitive world of Tennessee Walking Horses, and they feel sure that one of them ordered his death. The police were able to put behind bars the middleman who gave Bobby Joe the $15,000, but the trail went cold after that. Whoever it was higher up the ladder that engineered George Lenox' killing has gotten away with murder.

Even though he made millions, Lenox was vexed in his later years by the ease with which his formula was copied. There were numerous spin-offs of First U.S. Corporation; in 1970 alone, twenty new bond houses opened in Memphis. It was so simple. All you needed in addition to the desk and the WATS telephone were three men: a salesman, a trader to keep the bonds moving in and out, and a bookkeeper.

The most successful of the Lenox spin-offs was Hibbard, O'Connor & Weeks, Inc. (HOW). Founded in 1967, HOW zoomed to $231 million in sales in 1969. That was the year it hired Ronnie Ewton, who had made quite a name for himself at Delta Securities in Little Rock.

In his two years with Delta, Ronnie became a virtuoso of the WATS line. He learned all the wiles of a bond daddy, and he put them to use so well that he reached the coveted $100,000-plus income bracket in record time. The HOW people thought so highly of their new prospect that they made him a vice president and sent him down to Fort Lauderdale to start their operations in the southeast. Ronnie could feel confident that he had picked a winner; HOW went public in 1970 as its net worth exceeded $1 million for the first time and its sales made a spectacular spurt to $329 million.

When Ronnie arrived in Fort Lauderdale, he found a permissive live-and-let-live attitude towards securities trading. The head of the local historical society describes the place as "a frontier town where anything is possible. It's got that boom mentality, and people aren't as cautious here as they would be in, say, Akron, Ohio." And *The Wall Street Journal* reported, "Fort Lauderdale . . . is home to questionable business outfits of every sort, many operating high-pressure telephone sales offices known as boiler rooms. A local labor pool of voluble telephone solicitors supports the firms, which variously offer the unwary terrific deals on gold and silver, gems, second mortgages, oil and gas leases, thoroughbred horses, time-sharing vacations, or what have you."

Charlie Harper, chief of the South Florida SEC office, has called Fort Lauderdale "the white collar fraud capital of the country." Harper frequently is so swamped with cases that he shifts them to other SEC offices which are not as busy as his.

Some say it's the climate and the beaches, others say it's the abundance of new wealth and the proximity of Caribbean tax havens, but, for whatever reason, con men have been drawn to Fort Lauderdale for decades. Indeed, the city was founded on a scam. In 1911, the village of Fort Lauderdale, numbering a scant 150 souls, was suddenly invaded by 3,000 Midwesterners. The new arrivals had bought "prime" lots, sight unseen, from the legendary Florida Fruit Lands Company. When they got there, they discovered that their prime land was under water. Some went back to the Midwest in disgust; but others stayed, drained their land, and built a city.

Ronnie and Darla were happy in South Florida. They were absorbed in raising their daughter, Stephanie, who was born in November 1969 soon after their arrival, and they liked the casual lifestyle. They loved being near the water and became enthusiastic sailors. And they spent many hours on horseback; they introduced Stephanie to her own pony almost as soon as she was able to walk. They could afford expensive hobbies like boating and horseback riding, because by 1971, Ronnie was pulling down $250,000 per year.

They were uprooted in December 1971, when HOW moved its headquarters to New York and transferred Ronnie there to become national sales director. The Ewtons never adjusted to the Big Apple, and in less than a year were back in Fort Lauderdale where Ronnie again became manager of the southeast region.

The boys in the business didn't realize it at the time, but 1971 was the last big year for the Memphis bond daddy operations. Their scams were becoming too widespread, and publicity about the Lenox murder contributed to a growing national awareness of their activities. Although some cheated customers were too embarrassed to reveal the frauds which victimized them, more and more complained to government authorities and to the media.

The *New York Times* of August 1, 1971, reporting on "a bond boom in Memphis" said that "the fear of some major scandal has the municipal-bond-market establishment highly concerned, for it is worried that Congress may put the industry under tighter control." And the *Wall Street Journal* on December 3, 1971, ran a front-page story with the headlines "Memphis Blues—City Becomes a Center of Municipal Bonds—And Also Shady Dealing—Buyers Across U.S. Conned by Tennessee Salesmen." Federal and state bank regulators launched investigations of bond trading by member banks, and the FBI started questioning some of the bond daddies themselves.

In response to all this, the Tennessee legislature passed a bill in April 1972, which required licenses for bond houses and which mandated minimal capital requirements—starting at $35,000 for a one-man shop and increasing to $150,000 for a firm with thirty or more salesmen. A seven-man board was created to enforce the rules.

Most industry leaders felt that the Tennessee measure was too little, too late. Abuses continued in that state and elsewhere, the widespread publicity and continuing government investigations made customers increasingly wary, and business fell off for many of the bond daddies.

By 1973, the air had started coming out of HOW's balloon. Weeks left. And Hibbard, O'Connor, and Ewton got into trouble with the National Association of Security Dealers (NASD), an industry watchdog. Hibbard and O'Connor had committed serious offenses; they had used securities owned by customers as collateral to borrow money for themselves, had falsified financial records, and had disguised payments made to a salesman from another firm. Both were thrown out of the NASD and each was fined $15,000. Ewton's transgressions were minor in comparison. Ronnie was censured for allowing an unlicensed salesman to make transactions.

In November 1974, HOW decided to retrench. They closed the Fort Lauderdale office and consolidated all sunbelt operations in Houston, Texas. Ronnie was out of a job, and he had to scramble.

Between November 1974 and November 1975 he worked for three firms: Kidder, Peabody & Co.; Bevill, Bresler & Schulman; and Winters and Company. Today, Kidder Peabody is a large, respected securities firm which is a subsidiary of conglomerate General Electric. But Bevill, Bresler & Schulman and Winters and Company—both run by bond daddies who were HOW alumni—came to scandalous endings. Key operators of Bevill, Bresler admitted to a $240 million securities fraud and are currently serving prison terms. Winters and

Company went broke in 1977 after salesmen bilked numerous customers; at least one victim committed suicide as a result.

During 1973 and into 1974, Congress was starting to look seriously into bond daddy abuses, but it did not feel enough political heat to consider enacting new regulatory legislation. Then came the R. J. Allen case.

R. J. Allen & Company was housed just down the street from Ronnie's HOW office in Fort Lauderdale. Owner Robert Allen had obtained a list of Viet Nam prisoners of war who were returning stateside with large amounts of back pay accumulated while they were captives. He hired a salesman who wore a POW bracelet and who told the veterans that he had been a Korean POW, and the firm sold the veterans millions of dollars of worthless municipal bonds. One vet, who had been in Viet Nam prisons for seven years, lost $100,000 on Tuskeegee, Alabama, bonds issued to build a hydroponic tomato-growing operation. In 1974, Allen & Company was closed down, and Robert Allen confessed to Federal fraud charges and was sentenced to three-and-a-half years in prison.

The Allen case set off a storm of protest so strong that Congress was forced to act. It passed the 1975 Federal Securities Act bringing the municipal bond industry under the strict regulations of the SEC.

That didn't stop the bond daddies, however. When the municipal bond market was brought under regulation, they just looked for another venue where they could operate without SEC men peering over their shoulders. They were delighted when they discovered the market for securities issued by the U.S. government. Its history and structure, its buyers and sellers were completely different from those of the municipal bond market. But, it had one wonderful characteristic—it was totally unregulated. For the bond daddies it was a glittering last frontier.

Ronnie Ewton wanted very much to exploit that last frontier. As he skittered from Kidder, Peabody to Bevill, Bresler & Schulman to Winters and Company in 1975, he was making plans to get into the market for U.S. government securities. And Ewton sought as his partners fellow bond daddies and HOW alumni, Bob Seneca and George Mead.

With $75,000 in total capital, they launched, in November 1975, ESM Government Securities, Inc. (ESM), and two related companies. ESM was formed from the first letters of their last names. Ewton and

Seneca each owned 40 percent of the companies and Mead 20 percent. Seneca, who had built a reputation at HOW as a clever speculator, was the inside man running the trading operation; Ewton was the outside man, or salesman, and Mead assisted him. Ronnie retained his friend Steve Arky to set up the companies and to serve as their attorney.

He also hired Alan Novick—through a headhunter firm—to back up Bob Seneca as a trader and to supervise all the back-office financial and accounting work. The headhunters had found Alan at White Weld, a prestigious old-line New York investment banking firm which was later purchased by Merrill Lynch. Alan had done very well there and was president of a leasing subsidiary when he was brought together with Ewton.

Ronnie could not have been impressed by Alan's appearance. He was a chubby, short fellow with the kind of features you would have difficulty remembering a week after you'd met him. But when he talked, you sat up and took notice. He dealt with numbers with great rapidity and complete self-assurance. He displayed an ability to perform large calculations in his head as quickly as other people do them with a pocket calculator. And he showed a near-encyclopedic knowledge of Wall Street's latest techniques and products—commodity futures, straddles, real estate investment trusts, hedge funds. Immediately, Ronnie could see that Novick was the right man for the job. He was familiar with the terrain, he appeared creative, and he would fill a gaping hole in ESM's back-office operations.

Alan was happy to exchange the mock-Chippendale furniture of his office at White Weld for the battered, metal desk at the edge of the noisy trading room at ESM. He felt he was born to be a trader. He delighted in matching wits against the thousands of other traders peering into their computer monitors around the world. Deep in his bones, he felt he was a winner. At White Weld, they would never give him the chance to hone his trading skills. At ESM, by working closely with Bobby Seneca, he would enter the trading world at last.

In December 1974, Ronnie had needed help with his tax returns. He had just left HOW and he was so busy getting started at Kidder, Peabody that he didn't have time to make an organized search for assistance. As he remembers, he wandered into the lobby of his building: "Our offices were in the Landmark Building and I was looking on the marquee and they were A on the marquee, Alexander Grant, Certified Public Accountants. I caught the elevator and walked

in the front door. I went to Alexander Grant just by happenchance."
Ronnie didn't know at the time that Grant was a major firm, the
eleventh largest in the United States.

A year later, when ESM was picking its own accountant, the size of
Grant would work in its favor. Ronnie was pleased with what they
had done for him personally, but he had no strong feelings about
whom ESM should hire. His associates, and Novick in particular,
liked the prestige which a major firm would bring, and that tipped
the scales in Grant's favor. They became ESM's auditors in January
1976.

When Ewton, Seneca, and Mead were studying how the U.S. government securities market worked, they made a discovery whose
potential promised millions of dollars; enormous leverage was a time-
honored practice there. To buy $100 million in U.S. bonds, you can
borrow $99 million and need put up only $1 million. This is a highly
risky level of borrowing. In the regulated markets where excessive risk
is discouraged, you would have to put up $50 million to buy $100
million in securities—not just $1 million. The reason for the scary
level of leverage in the government securities market: the U.S. government needs maximum flexibility in its difficult task of finding lenders
for its ever-growing mountain of debt, now valued at more than $2.6
trillion. The government is a little like a car dealer whose models are
selling too slowly. It must give easy credit terms, or it can't move its
bonds off the shelf.

What the leverage meant to the bond daddies, and particularly to
the more speculative ones, was the promise of quick and tremendous
profits if you guessed right. Of course, if you guessed wrong, you
could be wiped out overnight. It worked like this: if you put up $1
million to buy $100 million in bonds, and the bonds went up only 1
percent, you doubled your money. You would sell the bonds for $101
million, pay off the $99 million you borrowed, and walk away with $2
million. On the dark side, if the market slipped 1 percent, you had $99
million to pay off your lender and nothing left for yourself; you had
lost your million. The U.S. bond market frequently moves 2 percent to
3 percent in one day, so the figures cited above are not unrealistic.

The arena that Ronnie and his associates were getting into was
immense. Virtually unknown to the general public or even to the
sophisticated investor, the U.S. government securities market is the
world's largest of any kind. It dwarfs its nearest rival, the New York
Stock Exchange (NYSE), by a factor of twenty to one. The average

daily volume of the NYSE is $6 billion; the average daily volume of the government securities market is $120 billion, and $200 billion days are not uncommon.

Unlike the municipal bond market with its thousands of issuers, the government securities market has only a dozen of any consequence, and is dominated by one, the U.S. Treasury. The others are specialized agencies of the U.S. government, such as the Government National Mortgage Association (GNMA or Ginnie Mae), the Federal Home Loan Mortgage Corporation (FHLMC or Freddie Mac), and the Tennessee Valley Authority (TVA). Of the $120 billion in daily trading, the Treasury represents $100 billion and the other agencies $20 billion.

The Treasury sells its securities to finance the national debt, which stands at roughly $2.6 trillion. The other federal issuers owe $700 billion, but this is not included in the national debt, because it is backed by specific types of assets such as home mortgages (Ginnie Mae) and dams and electrical supply systems (TVA). Treasury securities are backed by the taxing power of the U.S. government and implicitly by its vast holdings. It owns, for example, approximately 32 percent of America's land.

Treasury securities represent interest-paying IOUs of our government to the purchasers. In other words, the buyer is earning interest by lending the Treasury money to finance the national debt. These securities come in three forms: bills, which are due in a year or less; notes, which mature between one year and seven years; and bonds, which mature between seven years and thirty years.

In contrast to the municipal bond market with its many degrees of risk and obscurity, there is only one level of risk in the U.S. government market, and it is far from obscure. U.S. securities are the least risky in the world because they have the enormous taxing power of the federal government behind them, and essential information about them is available everywhere. Their prices can be obtained from brokers at all times, and they are printed in every major newspaper.

The Treasury and the Federal Reserve Board (the Fed) each need an efficient government securities market to accomplish two vital objectives.

For the Treasury, the market is a lifeline of funds to finance the $150 billion annual federal deficit and to refinance the older debt as it comes due. The Treasury must sell roughly $350 billion in bonds every year to keep the government afloat.

The market is also the Fed's basic instrument for changing the money supply and is therefore essential to its fight against inflation, recession, and other economic ills. The Fed adds to the money supply by pumping out cash to buy government securities, and shrinks it by selling government securities for cash and then taking the cash out of circulation.

Others besides the Treasury and the Fed benefit from this huge, hectic market. There are hundreds of dealers and tens of thousands of customers. Corporations and municipalities invest short-term cash conveniently, foreign governments manage currency reserve positions, investment managers earn extra returns on their portfolios, and banks and savings and loans can borrow or lend funds as needed.

Trading in government securities started after the Civil War and was a clubby, insiders' game into the 1970s. The government dealt exclusively with a coterie of primary dealers for its underwriting and money supply operations. The primary dealers, which numbered thirty-five in the 1970s, were solid old houses which included such broad-gauge organizations as Merrill Lynch, Citibank, and Goldman Sachs and specialty firms such as Aubrey G. Lanston and Co., and Briggs, Schaedle and Co. Quietly, and in an atmosphere of trust, they sold the government's obligations to big sophisticated customers such as banks, pension funds, and foreign governments. The amount of activity outside the primary dealers was not significant.

During the last decade, strong forces have transformed this almost nineteenth-century gentleman's world into the arena where Ronnie Ewton flourished, and where fraud and abuse have taken place on a grand scale.

The most important of these forces has been the explosion of volume. Treasury debt outstanding in 1970 was $400 billion. It hit $1 trillion in 1981, and now exceeds $2.6 trillion. Daily trading volume has followed an even steeper upward path, growing from $3 billion in 1970 to $22 billion in 1980 to $100 billion today.

Even in Jimmy Carter's day, an annual deficit of $40 billion was considered a debauch. Now the government routinely runs $150 billion in the red each year. This avalanche of new debt overwhelmed the financial capacity of the primary dealers and their customers. They just didn't have the money to take the bonds off the Treasury's hands. The chief of government trading at Goldman Sachs says, "The market is suffering from a crisis of oversupply of securities. That places enormous pressure on this market and its participants."

One way for the primary dealers to relieve this pressure was to rely on newcomers such as ESM to find new customers. The newcomers were called secondary dealers. Goldman Sachs is geared to sell $100 million bundles of U.S. bonds to huge buyers such as the Japanese government, Metropolitan Life, or the General Motors Pension Fund. Its sales force is not trained to deal with the president of a small bank in central Iowa, or officials of Tamarac, Florida, and Beaumont, Texas.

That is where ESM came in. Ronnie and his staff sold hard to this untapped market of smaller customers. They went to city manager conventions; they traveled to Beaumont and Spokane; they entertained small-town bankers at the Kentucky Derby. Ewton and the other secondary dealers found buyers for the bloated inventories of the primary dealers. As Tom Tew put it, "They were the link between Main Street and Wall Street."

5

Anatomy of a Scam

Ronnie may have beaten the bushes effectively to find the new "Main Street" buyers for U.S. government securities, but once they became ESM customers, he didn't treat them very well. He couldn't keep his bond daddy instincts in check.

Lou Frank had run up against bond daddies many times during his career as an investigator for the U.S. Controller of the Currency, the agency which regulates all federally chartered banks. In 1976, during a routine inspection of the books of the National Bank of South Florida, he found a familiar pattern of Memphis chicanery in ESM's handling of transactions for the bank. He accused ESM of:

- giving the bank a phony, inflated profit on a small transaction to lure it into a series of unprofitable transactions which earned ESM fat fees.
- pressuring the bank into trading a very speculative form of Ginnie Mae security. Lou Frank believed that "only a very inexperienced and unlearned banker coerced by an unscrupulous and unethical bond broker would try to trade such issues."
- deceiving the bank by overstating the price of a security the bank had bought. The difference between the real price and the inflated one went to ESM, not the customer.
- jumping the gun on getting into business. ESM was licensed by Florida to begin operations on December 23, 1975, but executed the trades for the Bank of South Florida between December 2 and 8, 1975.

Lou wrote to his boss about Ewton and Seneca:

Everyone seems aware of their names and they are known as suede-shoe types, slickers, high-pressure salesmen, i.e., the usual high-pressure bond salesmen. They are known and feared because they once operated in Memphis and Little Rock, as well as Houston, Texas, prior

74

to coming to Fort Lauderdale and are branded as "Memphis Bond Bandits."

As a result of Lou's investigation, his office banned the Bank of South Florida from doing business with ESM, and forced ESM to make up the losses the bank had suffered.

In February 1977, Ewton and Seneca again alarmed Lou Frank when they showed an interest in buying a control block of stock in the bank holding company, American Bancshares, Inc. (ABI). Lou was concerned because, of the nine banks owned by ABI, six had federal charters. He went to work and forced ABI to sign an agreement prohibiting any dealings among the six banks and ESM.

Later, after Ronnie and Bobby bought control of ABI, the company nullified the ban by changing the federal charters of the six banks to Florida state charters. Florida was much more permissive than the federal government and allowed the banks to deal again with ESM.

Lou Frank's boss wrote to Charlie Harper at the SEC about the National Bank of South Florida case and said that "it is clear that an intent of fraud was perpetrated by the ESM Government Securities, Inc., and, but for the fact that we intervened, substantial loss could have occurred." He wrote a similar letter to Gerald Lewis, the state of Florida's securities regulator.

Lewis did nothing, but the SEC took action. It had no day-to-day jurisdiction over ESM in the unregulated government securities market. Federal law, however, made one exception which allowed SEC involvement; the agency could intervene if it had strong suspicion of fraud. The letter from Lou Frank's boss made fraud an issue, and the SEC put out a formal order of investigation into ESM in June 1977. In an interoffice memo, Charlie Harper wrote: "The staff believes that it may have uncovered the tip of an iceberg involving the fraudulent trading of Ginnie Mae's and other securities issued by the United States and its agencies."

Ronnie Ewton turned to Steve Arky to fight off the SEC. When Steve and Ronnie met in 1969 as "weekend warriors" in the National Guard, Steve was in fact an SEC staff lawyer. Arky had a sergeant's rank in the Guard, and Ronnie, a lieutenant, was his commanding officer. Ronnie had been looking over the resumes of his troops, was impressed by Steve's SEC credentials, and went searching for him on their Army base. He found Steve washing a jeep. They hit it off immediately, talked about the securities business, talked about Ewton's start-up of HOW's Fort Lauderdale office. Steve remembered, "I liked Ronnie right away. I thought he was smart and he was the only guy to show up at National Guard meetings in a new Cadillac."

The SEC did not issue a formal subpoena when it started looking into ESM's records in November 1977, because the ESM people were being so cooperative. Their attitude was open, cordial, informal. On their first visit, the SEC examiners got into some compromising areas. They uncovered "at least sixteen transactions with six customers in which ESM made a profit which greatly exceeded the profits made by its customers." On one transaction, ESM made $66,000 and its customer, an Illinois savings and loan, netted only $2,500.

Arky heard about the discoveries and decided to play it tough. This was vintage Steve. He was always the belligerent litigator who believed that a good offense was the best defense. He had Ewton close ESM's doors to the SEC, forcing them to issue a subpoena. Then he challenged the subpoena. He stated in a brief that the SEC had used "fraud, trickery or deceit" to get to ESM's records, claiming that the investigators told Ewton they were only visiting his offices to gain an "education about the government securities business in connection with another investigation." Steve wrote that "only when the investigators went so far as to demand Xerox copies of all of ESM's salesmen's commissions did Ron Ewton . . . realize that the 'education' they desired had nothing to do with another investigation." The SEC men denied these charges categorically.

Arky knew that the wheels of justice grind slowly, and he reasoned that an additional lawsuit would slow them down even more. So, in another offensive thrust, he sued one of the SEC agents for trespassing on ESM property. He now had two interlinked actions on which to file briefs, argue fine points of procedure, request postponements, and make motions and countermotions.

The arguments dragged through the courts for almost eighteen months; finally in April 1979, a judge ordered ESM to comply with the SEC subpoena, rejecting ESM's claims that the SEC had used "fraud, trickery or deceit" to gain access to its books.

Arky was far from finished. He appealed. He knew that the appeals process was more maze-like, more excruciating than the process of bringing suit in the first place. And he went all the way to the U.S. Supreme Court. More than two years later, in May 1981, he got the case sent back to the original court for consideration of three questions about SEC intent. It had been a virtuoso performance in stonewalling. The SEC had sweated and strained for four years, and it couldn't even enforce a simple subpoena! The agency's lawyers were exhausted, demoralized. Over Charlie Harper's strong objections, they decided to drop the case.

Steve Arky had built a strong shield around ESM from 1977 to 1981. Behind it, Ewton and his cohorts constructed a massive fraud. During those four years, they stole more than $140 million.

The foundation for this enormous theft was laid when Novick, Ewton, and Seneca sat down on December 17, 1976, to plan ahead for 1977. The boys were happy about their 1976 results. Their companies had earned a posttax profit of $792,760—after paying out healthy salaries to themselves and to other key players.

And 1976 was a relatively clean year. There were the everyday boiler room scams like the ones that Lou Frank had so easily discovered, but no one had done anything seriously crooked. Alan Novick was planning ahead, however. He wanted to put an essential smoke-screen mechanism in place in case it became necessary to conceal wrongdoing in the future.

As Laurie Holtz discovered in the first hours of his investigation on Saturday, March 2, 1985, an essential element of the fraud involved transferring losses via a dense, confusing footnote from the operating companies to an inactive affiliate, ESM Financial Group, Inc. There were three operating companies, but only one, ESM Government Securities, Inc. (called ESM throughout this account), was truly active. Each year, the world saw a healthy audit of ESM after it had shed its losses to ESM Financial Group, Inc. The world never saw an audit of loss-ridden ESM Financial Group, Inc.

In a December 20, 1976, memo concerning the December 17 meeting, Novick set forth the basic scheme to cover up "unusual items," a euphemism for questionable transactions:

> It is my recommendation that at the present time we should prepare . . . a financial statement without ESM Financial Group. This will offer the following advantages:
> 1. Flexibility in charging the Financial Group with expenses incurred during the year that was paid by ESM.
> 2. All the unusual items that we have been involved with will not show on the balance sheet. . . .

Novick's concept was at the core of the accounting fraud which served

ESM so well from 1977 until its collapse in 1985.

Bobby Seneca charged into 1977 with a full head of steam. He had reason to feel that finally, at age thirty-two, he had arrived in the big leagues. He always believed that there was something special about himself, even when he was hustling pool and kidding and fast-talking people as a teenager in South Philadelphia. In those days whenever Bobby Seneca was on the scene, it was party time. People liked his laughter, his good looks, his energy, and they felt he would ride them to success one day. But it was a long time coming. He barely got by for several years. But in his late twenties, he discovered the world of the bond daddies and was off and running.

He loved the swift, wide-open bond business he was in. He had bought 40 percent of ESM for only $30,000 in 1975, and the new company made more than $790,000 in 1976 after giving him over $200,000 in salary and expenses. They had left the $790,000 in the business for working capital, but technically 40 percent of it was his. What a year! Bobby could not have never dreamed that the big money would come so quickly.

He couldn't wait to enjoy it. He spent fistfuls of it on good times, on his friends, and on his British dream girl. Her name was June Bellas, and he had picked her up in the bar of the Regency Hotel in Manhattan. She had come out of swinging London where her undraped classical figure had been featured in the pages of girlie magazines and where she had tried her hand at hairdressing and acting.

Bobby became obsessed with June. They played up and down the East Coast, cavorting in the most lavish suite at the Waldorf-Astoria in New York, burning through $30,000 in one week at Paradise Island in the Bahamas. June loved to snuggle next to Bobby in her new $12,000 hooded mink cape as they travelled in chauffeur-driven limousines or in the 1953 Bentley which had caught Bobby's fancy. She remembers, "He bought me shoes from Maria Valentino. He bought me clothes at Bloomingdale's, he opened a bank account for me. He gave me money and everything . . . (he) always picked up the tab in every restaurant we went to, for all his friends, for everybody. It was too generous."

She also remembers the cocaine. June said that Bobby had used it the night they met in New York and almost daily after that. "He doesn't stop. I've never seen as much in my whole life."

Barely four months after they had met, Bobby married his dream girl. And he did it twice. A simple wedding on September 23, 1976, in Fort Lauderdale, wasn't enough. They had to be married in the

Vatican. And by the Pope, himself. Bobby flew sixty guests to Rome for the ceremony on October 9. The whole thing cost him $70,000. And that didn't include the gifts for his bride—the $35,000 mink coat, the $8,000 Rolex watch, the jewelry worth $10,000. The couple settled into a $375,000 home when they returned from Europe.

The first order of business for Bobby and Ronnie in 1977 was the ABI deal. Steve Arky had found it. He knew that the owners of the control block of stock in this bank holding company were looking to cash out, and quickly. Steve's first prospective buyer was Marvin Warner. Marvin thought it was a decent purchase, but ABI just didn't fit into his plans at that moment. He turned it down on January 30, and Steve turned to Seneca and Ewton. The asking price was $3,369,750.

Less than two years before, Bobby had scraped hard to round up the $30,000 to put into ESM. Now, he was seeking $1.7 million to buy half of a control block in a company which owned nine banks. The change was fantastic.

And he was amazed to discover how easy it was to find the big bucks if you had ideas and connections. Alan Novick had a great idea, and Steve Arky had the connections. The problem with the ABI financing was urgency; the sellers wanted their money right away. If Seneca and Ewton could solve the problem of urgency, it seemed reasonable that they could find long-term financing by borrowing from a bank against the ABI stock itself; it had considerable value. The catch was that they didn't have time to work through the lengthy check-out processes involved with bank borrowing.

That's when Novick came up with his idea: until you get the money from the bank, you just borrow against securities of ESM customers. This simple stratagem would solve the problem, but its legality was dubious.

Better than 99 percent of all U.S. brokerage clients leave their securities with the brokerage house and in the broker's name. The average customer doesn't want to be bothered with finding a safe place for his stocks or his bonds, or with the tedious process of transferring them to his own name. As a consequence, brokerage firms usually hold large quantities of securities in the names of their firms "in trust" for their customers. For convenience sake, the brokers hire specialized institutions called custodians who guard the securities in their vaults and who perform the paper work involved in delivery and retrieval.

So Alan Novick took about $4 million worth of government securities left by customers in ESM's name at its custodian and used it to borrow the $3,369,750 for Bobby and Ronnie to buy the ABI stock. They made the transaction on February 4.

Now it was time to go for the long-term financing and Steve Arky introduced Bobby and Ronnie to his prime banking connection, father-in-law Marvin Warner at Home State. They met on February 15 and talked for a couple of hours. Marvin really liked the boys from Fort Lauderdale. They were kindred spirits, men like him who fed off the excitement of life in the fast lane, men who took chances with their money, men who played hard. He admired their entrepreneurial flair in taking on the risk of running ABI, and he quickly saw that there could be profit opportunities in merging the ABI operations with those of ComBanks, which he controlled with Hugh Culverhouse.

In addition, Marvin was intrigued with the possibilities of making big money with Bobby and Ronnie in the wide-open government securities market. By April 1, both Warner and Home State had opened trading accounts at ESM.

Marvin had already done his homework on ABI, so he was able quickly to decide to lend Bobby and Ronnie $3 million from Home State; he had them put up both ABI and ESM stock as collateral. The loan went on the books on April 26.

Seneca and Novick saw to it that things started auspiciously at ESM. During April 1977, they made trading profits of $510,000 for Warner and Home State.

Marvin appeared to be very pleased. He invited the Senecas and the Ewtons to Lexington for the Kentucky Derby weekend of May 7. They went to all the big parties and had a roaring good time.

The more Marvin studied the synergy between ComBanks and ABI, the more he liked it. He told his ComBanks partner, Hugh Culverhouse, that he wanted to work more closely with Ronnie and Bobby, but Culverhouse raised questions. He wrote Marvin:

> Please obtain and send me a resume on Ronnie Ewton and Robert Seneca. I would like to know the names of the companies they worked for in Nashville and Memphis so that I can have Hugh, Jr., check them out. Certainly the company they were formerly with in Fort Lauderdale did not, nor does it, enjoy a very good reputation. I think that since so much of your investment is being turned over to them that we should do

all possible to ascertain their reputations. Hugh, Jr., believes he can do this without anyone knowing.

Culverhouse's son, Hugh, Jr., had been a lawyer with the SEC and he asked former SEC colleagues in Memphis about Ronnie and Bobby. Their responses were decidedly negative, and Hugh, Jr., wrote his dad, "Their employment past is suspect. Their employment in Tennessee should be explored. . . . I would be on the alert for speculative purchases."

Marvin brushed aside the SEC misgivings as bureaucratic carping, and in July he talked Hugh Sr., into striking a deal with Bobby and Ronnie. Warner and Culverhouse gave them ComBanks shares in exchange for their ABI shares and as a result now had effective control of both bank chains.

It was the kind of transaction that could be counted on to give Marvin special pleasure, because he had used a Home State loan to make a legitimate deal for his own personal advantage. He couldn't have swept ABI into ComBanks without the resources provided by those thousands of Home State depositors whose savings he had lent to Bobby and Ronnie. That was power; that was leverage.

Bobby Seneca went down in flames in September 1977. Maybe his judgment was clouded by drugs, maybe he just got too cocky. Whatever it was, he made a huge buy—$29 million in Treasury bonds—for ESM's account in a market noted for wide price swings; the bonds promptly plummeted in value. When the dust had settled, ESM had lost $2.3 million. The debacle had wiped out all of ESM's accumulated profits and initial capital and left it flat broke, over $1 million in the red.

Bobby fell apart totally in October. He left June, who was having a cocaine-fueled affair with a twenty-three-year-old beach boy, and his dissipation use increased. Burnt out, he checked into a hospital on November 1 and stayed there for the rest of the year.

Ronnie had to make a crucial decision, perhaps the pivotal decision of his life. He had to decide whether or not ESM should file for bankruptcy. That would have been an honorable ending to a brief but spectacular chapter in bond daddy annals. You just go up to the federal bankruptcy judge, tell him that you made some terrible errors in judgment, and promise to do your best for the creditors. A sense of failure, a sense of regret, some feelings of guilt. But no crimes. You walk away clean.

Before he made the decision, Ronnie felt he must talk it over with Alan Novick. Ronnie had found himself relying more and more on Alan's judgment, checking with him on every major move. He recognized that Alan was a different order of intellect than the other fellows at ESM, himself and Mead and Seneca included. The other guys weren't thinkers; they were basically salesmen, smooth-talkers who frequently had trouble adding up a column of figures.

Ronnie had good reason to believe that Novick truly understood the business. Alan had held it firmly together while Seneca was careening out of control and, slowly and quietly, he had taken over. Alan loved to trade, he now had all the books and records firmly in hand, and, to Ronnie's delight, he had a way of putting customers at ease. His market strategy discussions made them feel that their securities were in the hands of a shrewd winner who always did his homework.

When Ronnie asked Alan whether ESM should file for bankruptcy, Alan replied, "If you get rid of Seneca, I'll get rid of the losses." Alan believed that, with any luck at all, he was clever enough to hide Seneca's losses by shuffling them off to ESM Financial and by using customer securities for essential borrowings. And he was absolutely sure that he could make back the $2.3 million in a hurry through skillful and daring trading.

Alan was so convincing that he could talk almost anyone into believing that he could "beat the casino," that he had the temperament and the intellect to win big in the trading world. And if Alan didn't succeed, Ronnie would have to start over again from rock bottom with a failure on his record. Until this single massive blunder by Seneca, they had been on a roll. Profits were excellent. The ABI-ComBanks deal promised to make them millions. And they were starting to work well with some true power brokers, people who could lead them on to megadeals. Marvin Warner, newly ensconced as ambassador to Switzerland, was one of them. There would be others. Alan just needed time to win back the $2.3 million. Then they would continue rolling.

Novick had convinced Ewton. Ronnie would get rid of Seneca.

While Bobby was still in the hospital, he told Ronnie that he was going to divorce June. Ronnie was shaken. A highly publicized divorce case spotlighting cocaine use and lavish spending could quickly scuttle the plan he and Alan had concocted to hide Bobby's market blunder. June would attack hard, trying to grab the big money she felt sure was filling ESM's coffers. She had to be defeated, and with a minimum of fuss. Ronnie knew he had to hire lawyers whom he could trust and who were skillful and tough. Above all, tough.

He turned to Steve Arky, who assigned Arky, Freed partner Gene Stearns to represent Bobby. Arky, Freed didn't normally handle divorces, but it was imperative that this case be kept within ESM's inner circle. Bobby Seneca filed for divorce on January 6, 1978.

The next move was to get Seneca out of ESM and Fort Lauderdale. On January 12, they sent him to New York City to run Foxton Securities, a small subsidiary which ESM had acquired a year earlier. Foxton was in a very specialized business—buying certificates of deposit (CDs) wholesale, and selling them retail. It was doing poorly because sales were anemic.

Seneca was happy to leave everything in Fort Lauderdale behind him—and especially June. He remembers, "She was causing tremendous problems at the office. Charging all her things on company credit cards, falsifying things in my name, coming up to the office and creating scenes; a lot of things. I was happy to get away, but then at that time, I was not privy to anything that was going on . . . they were having board meetings that I was not even aware of and decisions were being made that I was not aware of."

On February 1, Seneca was forced to give up 64 percent of his stock in the ESM companies. These shares were then distributed to Ewton, Mead, Novick, and two other officers, Nick Wallace and Pete Summers. This marked the first time that Novick, Wallace, and Summers had an ownership interest in ESM.

Seneca was stripped of the rest of his stock and fired on June 21. At the same time, Foxton, which had stayed resolutely in the red, was closed. Bobby signed a "Quiet Statement," in which he agreed to keep confidential everything he knew about ESM. He also entered a financial settlement with Ewton whereby Ronnie assumed his debts and took over the ownership of both his ABI stock and his remaining ESM stock.

Jose Gomez first became involved with ESM when Bobby Seneca was riding high. That was in January 1977, when Jose was given the assignment of reviewing the work of the Alexander Grant team which audited ESM's 1976 results. Seneca and Ewton liked him, and Jose spent a lot of time with them in 1977 doing profitability analyses for the ABI stock purchase and financing. At Ronnie's request, Grant put Jose in full charge of the ESM account in December 1977.

Alan Novick moved Seneca's 1977 losses over to the affiliate, ESM

Financial, and he handled it so skillfully that when Jose Gomez did his audit in the spring of 1978, he missed the losses completely.

Novick was less successful at making back Seneca's losses than he was at hiding them. In fact, he made Seneca look like a penny-ante player. Alan dropped more than $5 million in market speculations in 1978. But there was plenty of customer collateral to grab, so he sailed right on. He told Ronnie that he'd just run into a rough patch of market luck and that they would win big soon.

Borrowing with customer collateral became second nature to Alan. He had discovered a huge cookie jar, and he was amazed at the ease with which he could hide what he was taking from it. He had no trouble finding places to invest the money he was stealing for himself and Ronnie and their cohorts. There seemed to be opportunities everywhere. An intriguing one was the energy shortage, which had turned into a constant crisis for America during the late 1970s.

Alan and Ronnie believed they could take advantage of the crisis in a big way. The cookie jar was filled with millions; all they needed to do was find promising energy properties. With oil prices soaring, coal seemed a good bet. They started small in 1976 with an investment of $426,000 in a coal partnership called S-J Minerals. They were in glittery company. Other investors included Elvis Presley, Margaux Hemingway, and rock star Alice Cooper.

Alan and Ronnie stepped up the pace in 1977 and 1978, borrowing against customer collateral for a total of $6,047,000 for energy investments. They poured this money into 5,200 acres of coal land in Marion County, Tennessee, and a natural gas field and pipe line near Greutli, Tennessee. The promoters of the energy properties dazzled Novick and Ewton with glowing geological surveys. The Marion County mine was supposed to throw off $1 million per month for at least three years, and the Greutli property had a claimed profit potential of $19 million.

It was a classical case of con men being conned by slicker con men. The key promoters of S-J Minerals, the Marion mine, and the Greutli gas property served time in jail for frauds connected with these ventures.

With an unquenchable optimism that obliterated memories of past failures, Alan and Ronnie went for an even bigger win in 1979. They invested $8,755,000 in AIMEE, a coal operation in Alabama, and committed an additional $11 million to it for future years. AIMEE was promoted by the same con artist who sold them the Marion mine in Tennessee.

The geological surveys which mesmerized Alan and Ronnie were for the most part glorious fictions. Their oil and gas properties were worthless, sinkholes into which they eventually dropped $20 million. They were the Laurel and Hardy of the energy business.

Darla Ewton had no idea that her husband was stealing tens of millions of dollars. She just thought that Ronnie was a typical yuppie overachiever, a natural salesman who had found his true metier. Despite the apparent success and the money, she didn't like what was going on. Her days felt gray and empty; she was stifled by the luxury. She rattled around her big house where servants did everything for her, and when she got too bored, she went over to a girlfriend's home and helped her scrub her floors.

Above all, Darla was disturbed—for herself and for her daughter Stephanie—by Ronnie's values, his vacuous materialism. She was a realist. When she married Ronnie, she knew he was no mental giant. But she expected some growth, some intellectual stimulation. And Darla wanted a career of her own, but Ronnie couldn't have cared less. All Ronnie could think of was the next Mercedes, the glitzier diamond choker, the more fabulous party. Darla told him, "Ronnie, you've lost your perspective, and when you lose your perspective, you lose your ass."

They saw a marriage counselor but that didn't help much. Then Darla discovered that Ronnie was having an affair with a secretary at ESM. He agreed to end it, but couldn't bring himself to tell the lady in question. So he had one of his underlings do it. This wimpy behavior was the last straw. Darla walked out with Stephanie and moved to California.

Ronnie and Darla were divorced on May 29, 1979. It devastated Ronnie. Darla had been his anchor and now he was adrift. He slipped into an alcoholic depression. He would sip brandy and cry for hours at a time. He came into the office only two or three times a month.

Darla remarried and has built a busy and successful career as a set designer in the movies. She has earned a screen credit for her designs for the Geraldine Page Academy Award film, "A Trip to Bountiful."

Back at ESM, Alan Novick continued to rack up the losses and hide them away. He fooled Jose Gomez for a second time in the spring of 1979 with skillfully doctored books covering 1978 operations.

On August 1, 1979, Jose was made a partner in Alexander Grant. At age thirty-one, he was one of the youngest people ever admitted to the partnership. And he was a unique Cuban-American success story. He had come out of Miami's "Little Havana," and he had made it in the

most straight-laced Anglo segment of the American business community, the world of the major accounting partnerships. Grant was just
the opposite of Laurie Holtz's informal, loosely structured firm where
the seven partners worked in shirtsleeves and most of them went
without ties. Grant had over four hundred partners and the uniform
of the day was a dark blue suit, a white shirt, and a muted tie. The
chain of command was rigid, and a thick procedures book dictated
how things were done.

Jose was a business-getter, and worked long hours on charitable
boards to broaden his circle among Miami's power elite. He was also
constantly looking for the promising business whose executives would
likely enter the power elite a decade hence. ESM seemed to him to
carry that promise. Its young leadership appeared to be building a
dynamic and growing company. You didn't need many ESM's to build
a solid practice.

Gomez had one serious problem; he had adopted a life-style geared
more closely to the income of a senior partner than a junior partner.
He was $15,000 behind in his credit card payments, and he had other
serious debts as well. Jose had gotten pretty friendly with Alan Novick
and felt he could let down his hair with him. Over lunch one day, he
told Alan about his debt burdens.

Soon after Gomez had made partner, Novick revealed to Jose that he
had fooled him with phony bookkeeping on ESM's operations for
both 1977 and 1978. Alan then tried to shame him into accepting the
situation. As Gomez tells it: "He must have said it four or five times:
'How's it going to look? It's going to look terrible for you, and you just
got promoted to partner. Just give us a chance. It just takes time. We're
not going to have those losses.'

I really wanted to believe that they could do it. So I just made up my
mind: OK, I'm going to let them do it. . . ." Then Novick suggested
that ESM help Jose out with his debts. Jose remembers, "He indicated
they would . . . arrange for a loan at Florida Coast Banks . . . and they
would put up the collateral and they would do it in such a way that it
wouldn't raise any suspicions or cause me any discomfort." A $20,000
check helped Gomez meet a December 1 deadline on his credit card
payments. He had been corrupted.

Gomez continued to feel uneasy about his creditors. He wanted to
clean up all his debts, which now amounted to about $60,000, and
throughout 1980 he bothered Alan and Ronnie to help him. They set
up a complex money laundering scheme through AIMEE, one of their

Alabama energy companies, and got the $60,000 to him on December 1, 1980.

Jose and Alan worked together to cover up ESM's 1979 losses, which had ballooned to $14,422,605. In addition, they had to take care of the $8,755,000 which Alan and Ronnie had borrowed to invest in energy projects in 1979. The numbers were getting bigger and bigger.

Swiftly, Alan and Ronnie had burned through almost $48 million. The cumulative figures looked like this at the end of 1979:

Operating losses	$21,500,000
Energy investments	15,300,000
Officer Loans	11,000,000
Total	$47,800,000

The loans, piled on top of the generous salaries, were feeding a lifestyle that was increasingly ostentatious. There were luxury homes, lavish parties, Mercedes and Jaguars, lots of jewelry for the wives. The boys were losing money in carload lots, but to the outside world it looked as if they had hit a vein of pure gold.

June Seneca wanted to get her hands on some of that gold. She saw how the other ESM wives were living, and she remembered the $70,000 Vatican wedding, the countless grams of cocaine, the mink capes, and the $8,000 Rolex watches. She was sure that the ESM gang had millions stashed away. She sued Bobby for support payments and as codefendants brought in Ewton, Mead, and ESM and its affiliates.

The case came to trial in July 1980. The main thrust of the defense, which was led by Gene Stearns of Arky, Freed, was that the ESM principals and their companies were dead broke, and there wasn't a penny for June. Stearns trotted out enough expert witnesses and revealed enough about ESM's books to win over the judge. Then Stearns argued that it was vital to the smooth operation of ESM's business that the company's financial records be kept confidential after the trial. The judge agreed with him again. This decision was of prime importance to the continuation of the scam. The world at large got a quick snapshot of the reality of ESM, and then it was whisked away. The boys from Fort Lauderdale had dodged another bullet.

It is reasonable to assume that Stearns, Arky, and their associates at Arky, Freed noted the discrepancy between the picture of financial disaster which they painted in court and the portrait of robust financial health put forward to the public in the phony audited statements concocted by Novick and Gomez. It is hard to believe that at this point, the Arky, Freed people did not realize that their clients were engaged in some dubious financial practices. There is no record that they made an issue of this situation at ESM or elsewhere.

In 1980, Alan was running the show. Ronnie was still in his post-Darla funk, and came to the office only a couple of times each month. He had bought a farm in the Aiken, South Carolina, horse country and was spending almost all his time there. Alan only needed him for spot duty—getting a small number of large institutions to do business with ESM and somehow convincing them to leave large bundles of collateral there. As long as he could keep his hands on those millions in customer securities, Alan believed he had a chance to pull ESM out of its hole. Ronnie was more than content to limit himself to the occasional foray out of Aiken to sweet-talk a big customer. And he was extremely happy spending the bundles of cash that Alan kept sending him.

Alan could not run his massive fraud in Fort Lauderdale with the help only of Jose Gomez. He needed more lieutenants, and he got six other men to join him in the conspiracy. They were George Mead, who continued in his salesman's role, George's assistant Charlie Streicher, traders Nick Wallace and Tim Murphy, and accountants Earl Riddell and Tom Saunders.

Alan had hoped that the energy investments would offset the securities trading losses of 1977–1979. But by early 1980, he knew that the coal mines and the gas wells were losers too. He had started out two years before attempting to make up a $2.3 million loss. He now saw clearly that he had swiftly dug a $48 million hole for himself and his cohorts. He decided to try to win it back with some truly high-stakes bets.

Alan was dazzled by leverage, the opportunity to gamble for big stakes with large amounts of borrowed money. That was the main reason why he had been attracted to the government securities market. Alan felt he knew the ins and outs of the stock market, but there he could only become rich. In the government securities market, where immense leverage was the order of the day, he could become very, very, very rich; and he could do the same for his partners.

He grabbed $100 million in customer securities, and in a series of transactions leveraged it to buy $1 billion in Treasury bonds; a lender gave Alan the $1 billion, but kept the Treasury bonds and the $100 million in ESM customer securities as collateral. Thus, he had $1.1 billion in collateral against the $1 billion he lent to ESM. Then Alan bet the billion on the speculation that interest rates would decline.

They skyrocketed, and he dropped $80 million! Alan knew how to steal, and he knew how to cover it up, but he certainly didn't know how to invest. He lost another $13 million in 1980 for a total of $93 million.

It had all happened with sickening speed. After the initial shock, Alan bounced back with all his optimism intact. He told Ronnie that their trading concept was right; it was their timing that was off. Besides, Gomez was continuing to do his part. The Grant audit showed the world a $12 million ESM profit for 1980. If Ronnie could use Jose's healthy numbers to keep the big customers in the ESM corral, they might still pull it off.

By far the biggest ESM customer in 1980 was Unity Bank and Trust of Chicago, a client carefully cultivated by Ewton. The bank was doing a brisk business with ESM and was leaving tens of millions of dollars in excess collateral there. But Ronnie and Alan felt insecure relying so heavily on one principal customer. They needed the support of two or three Unitys. In their search for other large clients, they were struck by the promise that Home State offered. And for one major reason: it was in terrible financial condition.

Marvin Warner had come back from Switzerland to find his flagship enterprise bleeding red ink; he needed desperately to turn Home State around. Alan and Ronnie reasoned that, if Alan could produce for Marvin the profits to put Home State in the black again, then Home State might take its place beside Unity as one of ESM's major pillars of support. They realized that an important asset in winning Warner's cooperation was Warner's delight with his successful partnership with Ronnie at ComBanks.

Ewton and Novick quickly recognized that, in order to rope Home State in, staying close to Marvin Warner would not be enough. They would also have to gain the cooperation of Burt Bongard, the bank's president and chairman of the board. They had known Burt since the 1977 ABI negotiations and were on cordial terms with him. When Marvin returned from Switzerland, he continued to watch closely over Home State, but his role was unofficial, informal. Despite his 84 percent ownership position, he did not again become an officer or a director. This was largely because he had developed confidence in Burt Bongard's abilities.

Bongard looked to Warner for policy direction but ran the show day-to-day. Burt, a Cincinnati native, was a slow starter who had difficulty finishing high school but picked up speed when he took a job with a savings and loan at age twenty-three in 1963. Marvin hired him from a rival bank six years later, and Burt moved to the top at Home State in just four years. Other than Marvin, he was the only significant stockholder in the bank and held a 13 percent interest.

Burt's responsibilities extended beyond Home State. He was Marvin's right hand man, some say his lackey. He bought presents for the boss's girl friends, helped manage his real estate investments, dealt frequently with his accountants and lawyers, coordinated his travel plans. His salary was $233,000 a year, and he earned impressive perks. One of them was the opportunity to participate in lucrative Warner deals such as ComBanks.

Despite his very healthy income, Bongard was in serious financial trouble in March 1980 and couldn't meet payments on a bank loan. The reason: he had lost $1 million in 1979 in a restaurant venture. He mentioned his financial difficulties to Novick, and Alan suggested that he open an account at ESM. This occurred on March 21, 1980. Burt went to great lengths to keep the account secret. He ran all the monies through a bank other than Home State and made the ESM people promise not to tell Marvin what was going on.

By June 30, Novick saw to it that Bongard had made $413,332. Burt was able to satisfy the creditors who were baying at his heels, and he could breathe easily again. Burt's ESM profits were fictitious; they were really a present from Novick, and Bongard had been sucked in. As with Gomez, debt had led Bongard to become part of the ESM conspiracy.

Novick turned Home State into the black, and with startling swiftness. The bank, reeling from the effects of bad loans, deregulation, and unwise investments, had a 1980 operating loss of $7,927,654. But Novick turned that into a profit of $923,346 by making Home State a present of $8,851,000.

The present came in two parts: interest subsidies and fictitious trading profits. During a period when commercial interest rates were ranging between 11 percent and 19 percent, ESM lent Home State $150 million at 7.75 percent. This loan and other interest rate favors netted Home State $6,209,000 in 1980. Fictitious trading profits came to $2,642,000, making Home State's total ESM benefit $8,851,000.

Novick also churned out handsome profits on a steady basis in Burt's and Marvin's private accounts during 1980, and the two men must have been delighted.

The piper had to be paid. ESM needed excess collateral for its very survival; it would send profits up to Ohio, but in return it was looking for collateral to move to Fort Lauderdale. During 1980, Home State's excess collateral level at ESM grew from $15 million to $58 million.

ESM was drained of more than $96 million in 1980—$93 million in losses and $3.6 million to the energy projects. Adding this to the $48 million lost by the end of 1979, the company was now in the red by more than $144 million. Notwithstanding Novick's optimism, he and Ronnie needed a miracle to pull them out of the hole they had dug for themselves. A single expense item, ESM's interest bill on the $144 million, now ran at a staggering $20 million per year. They had traveled a long road from the day five years before when Ewton, Mead, and Seneca pooled $75,000 to start the business.

Undaunted by their reverses, they decided to party. Ewton and Novick took all the employees for a pre-Christmas, three-day holiday in the Bahamas.

Soon after their return from the Bahamas, Alan and Ronnie found that their number one customer, Unity Bank and Trust, had been shot out from under them. Unity is a federally chartered savings bank and as such is regulated by the Federal Home Loan Bank Board (FHLBB). When they went over Unity's books for 1980, the FHLBB officials were appalled to find that the bank's officers had left $93 million worth of securities in the tender hands of Alan Novick.

The FHLBB people had no idea that ESM was broke and perpetrating a fraud; the Gomez cover-up was keeping them in the dark about that. They did know that Unity was exposing itself to a massive risk. The $93 million was in effect an unsecured loan to ESM, and the FHLBB didn't like risking depositors' money on unsecured loans. Period. Forget that $93 million was a huge amount of money. Forget that the borrower was a little-known broker in Fort Lauderdale. The FHLBB intervened. On February 27, 1981 they issued a "cease and desist" order stopping Unity from doing business with ESM.

Novick bought time by telling the FHLBB that he would need a few months to extricate Unity from all of its ESM commitments. Then there was a frantic scramble to replace Unity's $93 million with securities from other customers. The entire ESM team went to work on the problem, and by autumn they succeeded. They got Bongard to chip in $30 million worth of securities from Home State.

While they were sweating to replace the Unity collateral, the morale of the ESM boys was boosted by a strong positive report from the courts. The SEC cloud was lifted from their heads. On May 18, Steve

Arky won ESM's appeal against the agency, and on August 19 the SEC abandoned its investigation of the company.

With Unity gone, ESM was forced to look to Home State as its main benefactor. Novick simply had to make Warner and Bongard continuously happy in order to keep ESM alive. He geared up his phony profit machine and in 1981 steered $13,433,776 to Home State. He increased the interest rate subsidy to $6,360,000, and more than doubled 1980's fake trading profits to $5,570,000. In addition, he did Home State a favor by buying from them $200 million in Treasury bills at a price $1,503,779 above market. None of this was enough to make Home State profitable in 1981, because its operating deficits were a horrendous $14,686,833. Netting this out against the ESM benefits resulted in an annual loss of $1,253,057.

Alan also took care of Warner and Bongard personally, steering $560,000 to Marvin and $964,000 to Bongard. Neither man put up any cash for these transactions.

ESM's gifts to Home State, Bongard, and Warner made its operating results considerably worse than Home State's. It's true 1981 losses were $20,628,629. However, Gomez did his annual manipulation and produced an audited report showing profits of $26,058,743.

It had been a scary year. ESM had dodged three bullets in 1981, and it was still alive. There had been two cannon shots, the ones fired by the SEC and by the FHLBB in the Unity Case. And there was a small-bore rifle shot—fired by Pete Summers.

Pete decided to leave ESM in April 1981. His departure presented a problem because he was a stockholder and he had to be bought out of his position. To help Pete bargain with ESM, Charlie Streicher dictated for him a memo explaining how he understood ESM's loss-covering mechanism worked. It described a hypothetical transaction in which ESM lent money at an extremely favorable interest rate to a customer in order to get its hands on a large hunk of the customer's collateral. The memo read in part:

> Example: Customer owns $50 million worth of collateral. ESM tells them they will give him $25 million for the collateral. ESM in turn puts the collateral out and receives $40 million. ESM nets out $15 million which they use to cover the loss ESM Government Securities took.
>
> They do this example three times to raise money to cover losses taken in the market.

After explaining that ESM Government transfers its hypothetical losses to an affiliate, the memo says: "Therefore ESM Gov. does not show any loss, but somehow has a payable & receivable between the companies. The whole operation is capitalized by borrowed money from customers without their knowledge. . . ."

Summers negotiated his parting settlement with ESM during the latter half of 1981. He signed it on January 5, 1982, together with an agreement not to disclose to the outside world anything he knew about ESM's operations or finances.

As the losses and the difficulties in maintaining the cover-up mounted for Alan, so did the tension. He became increasingly rude and irritable, and frequently abused his subordinates over trifling errors. He also became more boastful. He would tell listeners that he could create millions in an instant and make them disappear just as quickly.

To break the tension, he and his traders would frequently play childish games. They would have water fights, chase each other over and around the desks in the trading room, throw darts at one another, and do mock combat with whips.

Alan found respite with his family. He was devoted to his wife and three children and retreated with them on weekends to a rural hideaway. He would frequently appear bleary-eyed at the office Monday mornings after making the grueling return trip.

His main diversions were his thoroughbreds and his show dogs. The Novicks lived at Rustic Woods, a thirty-one-acre estate for which he paid $1.2 million. It was in Plantation, a community west of Fort Lauderdale, and it boasted the most luxurious stables and kennels that money could buy.

He also had a major thoroughbred operation in Nicholasville, Kentucky. It was a 248-acre spread, and it was also called Rustic Woods. The land alone cost $2.3 million, and Alan sunk at least that much in the training and breeding facilities for the race horses. When he died, he owned thirty-nine thoroughbreds worth $2.9 million.

The cost of running these operations was staggering. During the last few years of his life, Alan was spending $100,000 per month to maintain them and the other elements of his life-style.

Novick's thoroughbreds won only moderate success at the track, but his dogs were exceptional, and one of them was the greatest competitor in canine annals. She was Ch. Braeburn's Close Encounter, a Scottie better known as Shannon. She had cost Alan $78,000, and he must have felt that she had repaid him many times. Shannon won best in show two hundred times, an all-time record that may never be equalled. Aficionados compare it to Joe DiMaggio's fifty-six-game hitting streak in baseball. In 1985, a few months after Alan's death, Shannon won best in show at Madison Square Garden, which meant that she was world champ, the top dog that year of any breed.

If the Unity crisis and the Pete Summers settlement had caused Novick great anxiety during 1981, the growing closeness with Home State was a source of satisfaction to him. Bongard was firmly bought off and had performed well in the Unity affair; he and Warner were pleased with their profits and with the prodigious gains which Alan had produced for Home State. It had become a marriage of convenience, and both sides seemed happy with the relationship.

There was another marriage in 1982, that of Ronnie Ewton and Jerilyn Moroney.

Aiken's bracing air, rolling countryside, and most of all, the opportunity it afforded Ronnie to spend hours each day on the back of a horse, had a tonic effect on his psyche. Aiken boasts one of the most active and prestigious hunt groups in the United States. Ronnie joined, and he was such a good horseman that he soon won the coveted title of master of fox hounds. As he threw himself into riding to hounds, the intense concentration and vigorous exercise helped free him from the depression which had gripped him after Darla's departure.

He also found solace in a frequent visitor to Aiken, his secretary, Jerilyn Moroney. Ronnie looks to his women to provide direction in his life, and Jerilyn was soon doing that. She is not as dynamic as Darla, but she knew where she wanted to go. And Ronnie was happy to follow her. She preferred the reserved, tweedy, old-money life style of Aiken to the glitz of Fort Lauderdale, and she encouraged Ronnie to make his home there. He soon expanded his holdings in Aiken to 5,600 acres. She also encouraged him to take up polo, a favorite sport of both the old- and the new-money set. Ronnie amassed a troop of seventeen polo ponies, and he and Jerilyn became fixtures at the clubs along the east coast polo circuit.

Jerilyn is as tall and as beautiful as Darla, but her presence is less commanding. Her bone structure is much more delicate, and she is very slender. She is gregarious, and Ronnie was pleased that she mixed so well with the attractive friends he had made in Aiken.

Jerilyn comes from a large Irish-American family, and is close to her father, who sells Roman Catholic religious articles and books. She and Ronnie were married in a Roman Catholic ceremony in Fort

Lauderdale in February 1982. They signed a prenuptial agreement providing Jerilyn with a $475,000 trust fund.

When Ronnie returned from his honeymoon, he faced intensified pressure from Bongard and Warner to insure their Home State profits, because they faced a harrowing problem a couple of years down the road. The problem could be stated simply: Home State had a $29 million debt coming due in October 1984, and it didn't have the money to pay it. In fact, it was Home State Financial, Inc. (HSFI), a Warner holding company which owned 100 percent of Home State's stock, that needed the $29 million. But Home State was totally in jeopardy because if its parent, HSFI, failed, it would go down, too.

In 1979, HSFI had issued $29 million in debentures which had to be paid off in October 1984. A debenture for a corporation is similar to an unsecured loan for an individual; it is a debt obligation which must be repaid. Since HSFI didn't have the money, its plan was to sell $30 million in new debentures and use the proceeds to retire the old ones; it would put the extra $1 million in its treasury.

Bongard and Warner simply could not afford losses at Home State for the 1982–1984 period. Such losses would doom their efforts to sell fresh debentures. Prospective buyers would be loath to purchase them from a company which seemed to be forever mired in the red.

In 1982, Novick came through. Home State's operating loss was only $800,198, so that when Novick provided $5,362,000 in phony trading gains and $118,000 in interest rate subsidies, they produced a healthy profit of $4,678,802. Alan, however, had racked up a loss of $12,678,594, so his need for collateral was greater than ever. Bongard cooperated by moving fistfuls of securities to Fort Lauderdale. By June they totaled $125 million—$32 million more than Unity had provided.

While Novick and Ewton were keeping Home State alive for Marvin and sweating out their losses and their cover-up, Warner was making a spectacular series of deals with Florida banks.

First he found another undervalued chain, Century Banks. He bought about 7 percent of Century's shares privately and then, on May 5, 1981, sought control through a public offer for an additional 25 percent. Century executives feared Marvin, because they knew how he had shaken up management at ComBanks and Great American, and they sought a friendlier takeover.

On May 19, Century signed a merger agreement with Sunbanks, a major Florida chain. Steve Arky immediately filed a lawsuit challenging the merger on the grounds that Marvin was not being given a fair opportunity to present his case to the Century shareholders. Negotiations continued into early 1982, and on March 19, Marvin agreed to sell his Century stock to Sunbanks for a profit of $12.5 million. He also got $5 million for calling off his lawsuit.

It was a terrific coup. Even in a losing effort, he had made $17.5 million. Arky, Freed, which had made $602,000 from its work on the purchase of ComBanks and ABI, received $650,000 for its role in the Century negotiations.

Marvin seemed always to be in motion in the spring of 1982. At the same time that he was wheeling and dealing with Century, he threw himself into negotiations with the Broads. In December, he consummated the deal to buy American Savings & Loan stock and to share control of this major bank.

There was other good news in 1982. The strong earnings gains at ComBanks and Great American had caused the prices of their shares to shoot up to a very high level. Marvin took one look and decided to sell out. This elated his ComBanks partners, Ewton and Bongard. Marvin easily found a buyer for Great American. It was Barnett, Florida's largest bank holding company. When the deal was closed in February 1983, Marvin made $18 million, a 325 percent gain.

Finding a purchaser for ComBanks was not as easy. Marvin's candidate was Freedom Savings & Loan of Tampa. But the Freedom shareholders were recalcitrant. They voted down the takeover three times. Just before the fourth vote on January 4, 1983, Marvin made a daring move. He had Home State buy two hundred thousand Freedom shares for a premium of $1.2 million above the going market price. When those shares were voted in favor of the ComBanks purchase, Marvin's side had won by a slender two-tenths of one percent.

The vote represented a big payday for the four shareholders, who would divide up $72,594,870 in proceeds. Marvin Warner was the largest beneficiary, receiving $42,615,877. Ronnie Ewton's take came to $11,158,101. Burt Bongard pocketed $1,882,089, and Home State received $16,938,803.

Marvin's profit was over $30 million, and Burt's was $1.4 million.

Ronnie made roughly $7 million and his joy was compounded by the birth of a son, Brandon, on March 10.

The ultimate toy for America's swinging newly rich is a professional sports team. Marvin had been there before with the New York Yankees and the Tampa Bay Bucs, but the boys in Florida had never played in this glamorous arena.

With 1982 came the birth of the United States Football League (USFL), a rival to that giant of American sports, the National Football League (NFL). The NFL had easily beaten down leagues which had challenged it head-to-head in the fifties, sixties, and seventies. But the USFL believed it could survive, because it started with an asset that previous NFL competitors never had, a lucrative TV contract.

Marvin bought control of the Stallions franchise in his native Birmingham. Following his lead, Arky and Novick became owners of the Tampa Bay Bandits—Steve as a general partner and Novick as a limited partner. A year later Ewton bought out Novick's share.

Marvin not only led the ESM boys into professional sports, he got them involved in politics as well. He had become the leading fund-raiser for Ohio gubernatorial candidate Dick Celeste, and was credited with saving Celeste's campaign when it desperately needed media money. Marvin gave $38,000 personally, cosigned a note for $75,000, and got Ewton and Novick to contribute $10,000 and $5,000, respectively.

Celeste rewarded Marvin with the chairmanship of the Ohio Building Authority, an agency which spends tens of millions of dollars each year constructing and maintaining state office buildings, prisons, and storage facilities.

But Marvin's greatest reward of the campaign was meeting Jody Piehowicz. They fell in love almost immediately. Jody is dark, slender and attractive, with an easy smile punctuated by striking blue eyes. When she met Marvin she was twenty-seven, thirty-six years his junior, and was working as legal counsel to his long-time political ally, Ohio Speaker of the House Vern Riffe.

While sunshine was filling Marvin's personal life, dark clouds were brewing for him in Ohio's state bureaucracy.

Sylvester Hentschel is the senior field examiner for Ohio's Division of Savings and Loan Associations, and he is just the kind of man central casting would send if you were looking for a bank regulator. There is no flash about him. His analytical skills, honed during six years in a Jesuit seminary in his youth, are excellent. He is precise, dogged, and deliberate, and he was right on the money about Home State and ESM. In July 1982 he was performing a routine examination of Home State, and he discovered that $125 million in excess collateral had been sent to Fort Lauderdale. He immediately recognized the great risks involved and wrote to his boss:

Securities with a book value of $208,200,000 are assigned to a securities dealer in Florida under repurchase agreements. (Home State) has borrowed $83,800,000 on those securities and is therefore vulnerable to a potential loss of about $125,000,000 should the dealer be unable for any reason to redeliver the securities upon expiration of the repurchase agreements . . . this situation must be considered as an unsafe and unsound practice.

Home State in effect had put up $208 million in collateral to borrow $83 million—$208 million is 251 percent of $83 million. In other words, the $125 million over-collateralization at risk was 151 percent of the amount borrowed.

Hentschel understood that the Home State depositors would suffer most of the damage if things went wrong at ESM. The stated equity of Home State's owners was less than $12 million at the time; subtracting that number from the $125 million meant that $113 million of the depositor's money was at risk. Hentschel remembers:

> The large amount of securities that Home State had assigned to ESM, I had never seen any massive amount such as that. The amounts that I had been accustomed to would be perhaps in the range of $1,000,000 up to perhaps $25,000,000 . . . in an institution that had only $12,000,000 net worth, to have an exposure of $125,000,000 was completely beyond my experience.

Then he looked further and discovered that Home State had made $5.6 million in profits on twenty-two straight winning trades engineered by Alan Novick. Twenty-two straight winning trades in the highly speculative, highly volatile Government securities market would be almost as rare as picking twenty-two straight winners at the race track.

Hentschel struck close to the heart of the Home State/ESM marriage of convenience when he conjectured that ESM was manufacturing the profits for Home State in order to hold on to a customer who would leave huge amounts of securities lying around. He reported to his boss, "It is not inconceivable that ESM, which like all government securities dealers, is not regulated by the SEC, is protecting (Home State) against losses on its . . . trades in order to retain Home State's business."

Sylvester's analytical cast of mind led him to suspect that Bongard and Warner were also getting manufactured profits from ESM. Regulations allowed him to question only bank employees or board members, and at the time Warner was neither. So he was forced to ask

Bongard if Bongard and Warner had ESM accounts and Bongard said "absolutely not," which was an out-and-out lie.

Hentschel asked that the state of Ohio issue a "cease and desist" order banning all business between Home State and ESM, but his recommendation got lost in a political shuffle after election day 1982 when the Democrats wrested the statehouse from the Republicans. Sylvester's Republican boss left to become a lobbyist for Home State, and everything was put on hold until the new Celeste administration took over in 1983.

Hentschel finally got action through another organization which he worked closely with, and which was seriously interested in Home State's condition. This organization was the Ohio Deposit Guarantee Fund (ODGF), a private insurance cooperative.

Almost every American who saves at a thrift institution has his or her deposits insured by the federal government through the Federal Savings and Loan Insurance Corporation (FSLIC). This was not the case, however, for depositors at Home State and sixty-eight other savings and loans in Southern Ohio. Because these S&Ls did not like the regulation and the red tape that went with federal insurance, they formed ODGF in 1955 as a cooperative venture to insure the assets of their depositors against catastrophe. Each member bank pledged 2 percent of its deposits to the fund.

Armed with Hentschel's numbers showing the 251 percent collateralization level, the ODGF on February 25, 1983, directed Home State not to exceed national guidelines on excess collateral in its dealings with ESM. The guidelines were known by all lenders and borrowers of U.S. government securities; they stated that collateral should not exceed 105 percent on money borrowed against Treasury securities and 110 percent on money borrowed against Ginnie Mae and other agency securities.

The guidelines were designed to protect lenders against price declines. Daily price movements rarely exceed 3 percent for Treasury securities and 6 percent for agency securities, and the guidelines work in the following way: If a Treasury bill which is being held as collateral declines by 3 percent in one day, at the end of the day the lender would still have a 2 percent cushion (5 percent excess collateral less the 3 percent decline). Before the next day's trading, he would ask the borrower to throw in 3 percent more to bring the collateral back to a comfortable 105 percent level. If the borrower couldn't come up with the 3 percent, the lender, to protect himself, would sell the collateral.

The ODGF pressed hard for the collateral limits and at a March 31 meeting, Home State's board discussed the February 25 directive at length. They took no official action, however, because Marvin Warner and Burt Bongard did not attend the meeting. They were in Florida picking up their checks for the sale of their ComBanks stock.

Ewton thought it would be a fine idea if a large portion of Warner's and Home State's ComBanks proceeds were reinvested at ESM, and he asked Novick to concoct a proposal to convince Warner to do that. Alan came up with a multipurpose proposition. It would provide a totally predictable income stream; it would be virtually free of risk; and, most importantly, it would help solve Home State's overcollateralization problems with the regulators and ODGF.

The proposal, as approved by Warner at an April 13, 1983, meeting, involved a huge buy, the purchase of $800 million in securities: $100 million in long-term Ginnie Mae's for Warner and $300 million in long-term Ginnie Mae's and $400 million in Treasury notes for Home State. Leverage would be high. Warner would put up only $17 million and borrow $83 million, and Home State would advance only $60 million on its $700 million dollar purchase. The spread between interest paid and interest earned would be fixed to provide a return exceeding 20 percent.

There was one catch: the Ginnie Mae's, like all long-term bonds, could gyrate wildly in price and thereby subject the buyers to substantial risk. Novick proposed to eliminate virtually all of this risk by entering into what is called a "hedge" transaction. Alan studied the market carefully and he felt sure that if long-term Ginnie Mae's went down in price, short-term Ginnie Mae's would rise; and vice versa. He would "hedge" his bets on the long-term Ginnie Mae's by wagering in the Chicago futures market that short-term Ginnie Mae's would move in the opposite direction.

The hugeness of the deal, the commitment to hundreds of millions, was designed to help solve the overcollateralization problem. Home State's collateralization in April 1983 was $370 million on borrowings of $292 million, or 127 percent. In other words, overcollateralization was $78 million. When that same $78 million overcollateralization was applied to the $700 million value of the new transactions, then the collateralization percentage shrank from 127 percent to 111 percent, and Home State was almost within the guidelines. Bongard would have an easier time with the regulators.

The deal was approved on April 13 but wasn't put on the books until late May. In the meantime, Home State's board responded on April 28 to inexorable pressure from ODGF and voted to bind the company and its officers to the 105 percent–110 percent guidelines.

For a few weeks the hedge transaction worked as expected. Then suddenly the market, according to Novick, "went out of sync and produced an aberration." What he meant was that his predictions had turned sour. The long-term Ginnie Mae's were declining and so were the short-term Ginnie Mae futures. They were moving in tandem, not in opposite directions. This happens very rarely; that is why Alan had presented the deal as virtually, not totally, riskless. The one happening in a hundred, "the aberration," had occurred and the hedge transaction turned into a disaster.

And it was costing Home State and Marvin a bundle. Because they were so highly leveraged, they had to keep sending collateral to ESM to cover their loans on their Ginnie Mae's and Treasuries which were declining in value. By the end of July, Home State had transferred almost $72 million in collateral, and Warner almost $10 million.

Marvin was on vacation, and at first Bongard was afraid to tell him the awful truth. But the hemorrhaging was so bad that, on August 3, he let Warner know what was happening.

Marvin blew up. He summoned Ewton and Novick to Cincinnati on August 9, and demanded that they help cover the losses and return some of the collateral. Ronnie and Alan convinced him that ESM was tapped out, and Marvin reluctantly agreed to continue sending down securities. After Bongard had sent a total of $101.9 million from Home State to Fort Lauderdale, Marvin decided on August 29 that all payments had to be approved by him. On that day he OK'd a $2.5 million transfer.

He had become, de facto, an officer of Home State again; this was to become a significant factor in assessing responsibility in subsequent controversies. The next demand from ESM on Home State came on August 31; it was for $1.7 million, and Marvin approved it.

Home State's paper loss on the hedge was now $30 million and the company had sent ESM $106.1 million in collateral to cover related borrowings. Marvin's loss was $5,718,000 and he was out $15 million in collateral. There seemed no end in sight.

Marvin again summoned Ewton and Novick to Cincinnati. They flew up on September 6 and it was a draining meeting, an emotional shouting match which went on for four hours. Marvin focused first on his own account. Ewton remembers Novick lecturing Marvin:

Alan is giving him this technical explanation, and it was real technical and it probably was true, but he didn't want to hear that.

And he just got up in Alan's face and jumped on him. "I don't want to hear that. I don't want to hear that. I don't want to hear that anymore. That wasn't supposed to happen. . . ."

"You got to do something about this," he says. "I want my money back. I want out of this transaction. . . ."

After him beating us all up I finally said, "OK, Marvin. Look, we'll try to get you out."

Marvin then wrote out the following note and got Ewton to sign and date it to ratify it as an agreement:

GNMAs—Freeze loss @ *5,718,000.00*
Meet all calls—*calls—both sides*—NET
Sell position—liquidate GNMAs &
substitute Treasuries—soon as you think
practical
Right to do so at all times.
Make up my losses—
Most favorable rate on repo that
can be justified.

The note was later used as the basis of a formal agreement under which ESM made up Marvin's losses with interest.

Marvin never asked Ewton and Novick to apply the $5,718,000 to the losses of the Home State depositors. He took care of himself first and then turned to Home State's problems. Ronnie and Alan convinced him that ESM couldn't help make up Home State's losses, because after doing him a $5 million plus favor, the well at ESM was dry. Alan kept insisting that "the aberration" would end and that the hedge would eventually work and bail Home State out. Six months later, after the hedge began to pour cash into the coffers of Home State and ESM, Warner did get Ewton to help Home State through a sizable interest rate concession.

During September and October, Marvin approved four more Home State collateral transfers to ESM totaling $8 million. Then the hedge finally kicked in, and cash started flowing back to Home State.

Burt Bongard was not at the September 6 meeting. He was on vacation. But it didn't matter, because at this point he was fed up; he had decided to quit. He was tired of the pressures—the law-breaking, the nosy regulators, the failed hedges, the endless struggle to keep Home State afloat. He was tired of being at Warner's beck and call, and he was angry at him because Marvin had refused to give him a finder's fee when he had turned up the buyer for ComBanks. Marvin had promised him $500,000, but then reversed himself, arguing that Burt had made more than enough money on ComBanks and other Warner deals.

Burt would sell his Home State shares to Marvin and, at age 42 with a total net worth of $4 million, start a new career as a financial consultant in New York.

Warner pleaded with him to stay around to help clean up the ESM mess, arguing that they both had too much at stake to let it fester. Burt agreed. With overcollateralization at $158 million, the cleanup was a tall order. But the hedge worked reasonably well in Home State's favor, and when Burt left early in May 1984, the excess collateral was down to $70 million. He also got Novick to give Home State $2,346,000 in phony trading profits for 1983, reducing the bank's losses from $3,265,157 to $919,157.

Novick made sure that Bongard's parting memories of ESM would be happy ones. On October 5, 1983, he put together a final phony trade for Burt which netted a $50,000 profit. And when it came time to close Burt's account on March 9, 1984 and it showed a balance of $37,250, Novick sent him $285,000—a going-away present of $247,750.

Since Bongard was preoccupied in early 1984 with setting up his new business, he was not much help to Marvin in dealing with one of Home State's major problems of that year—selling its $30 million debenture issue. There were two main obstacles to overcome: getting the SEC to approve the sales prospectus; and insuring that the prospectus would show profits healthy enough to attract buyers.

The SEC had to be dealt with first. The key words in its vocabulary are: "full disclosure" and "buyer beware." As long as the seller discloses all the essential facts about his company in his prospectus, the SEC is satisfied. It is up to the buyer to read the prospectus and determine whether the risks and rewards described justify a purchase of the securities in question.

The way it works is this: the seller sends a draft of his prospectus to the SEC, and the SEC reviews it and sends it back with requests for corrections. This process is repeated until the SEC is satisfied that the seller has fully and clearly set down all the relevant data about his company.

On January 19, 1984, Home State submitted its draft prospectus to the SEC and on February 27 the regulators came back with fourteen single-spaced pages of suggested changes. They questioned "the company's viability as a going concern" because of the continuing branch operating losses and they zeroed in on the risks inherent in the ESM relationship. The debentures would be a very difficult sale if these issues were going to get top billing in the prospectus.

Marvin was stymied. He called in his best securities lawyers and ordered them to get the SEC off his back. Their struggles with the Federal watchdogs would prove to be long and arduous.

Bongard was something of a lame duck in the winter of 1984, and Warner had to become more directly involved in Home State's dealings with ESM. After 1983's loss, Home State desperately needed ESM-generated profits to make the fast-approaching October debenture offering salable. And ESM's appetite for collateral was more voracious than ever. Their interest bills were enormous, the principals continued to grab millions to maintain their sheik-like living standards, and the presents to Home State insured that ESM's operating losses would continue.

Home State's first order of business was to better the hedge deal. Warner summoned Ewton to a meeting with himself and Home State executive V.P. David Schiebel at a private suite at the Waldorf-Astoria in New York on March 12, 1984, and asked Ronnie to give Home State a two-year 2 percent interest rate subsidy, or $12 million, on the $300 million dollar Ginnie Mae position.

In a reprise of the September 6, 1983, scenario, Marvin demanded, Ronnie whined and complained, and Ronnie acquiesced in the end. Ronnie maintains he said that ESM was in such bad shape, it "was bleeding out of both ears," but Warner and Schiebel deny this. Novick later protested that Ronnie had given away the store, but when you are more than $300 million in the hole, $12 million doesn't seem so much.

And by early 1984, Novick needed $300 million in other people's securities just to keep his circus going until he made the big win that was always on his horizon. ESM had lost $300 million in its giddy nine-year history, and the money had gone in five directions, as follows:

	$ million
• Speculative and operating losses	$ 85
• Energy losses	20
• Officers salaries and loans	60
• Profits given to Home State, Warner, and Bongard	47
• Interest on the above	88
	$300

In early 1984, Home State's excess collateral at ESM was roughly $90 million. This meant that Novick was using $210 million of other customers' securities to cover ESM's losses. The great majority of these other customers were public bodies: municipal and county governments. They were lending excess cash against collateral supplied by borrowers who were other ESM customers.

Ewton convinced the public bodies that it was just a bit of unnecessary paperwork to actually take possession of their borrowers' collateral. Ronnie told them that these securities were segregated for them with the custodian in New York. The securities were in fact in the custodian's vaults, but they were sequestered in an ESM account, not the customers' account. Novick moved securities in and out of the ESM account to borrow money when he needed it. The public officials who bought Ewton's explanation were, for the most part, very unsophisticated.

To Ewton and Novick, Home State and the public bodies provided a barely adequate cushion against disaster. ESM's ravenous appetite for cash and the vicissitudes of the market meant that the boys were constantly walking a tightrope. To get their feet on solid ground, they needed more friendly customers with large amounts of available collateral. Three months into the new year, they were delighted because they believed that Marvin's acquisitive drive had brought them such a helpmate. It was American Savings & Loan.

6

The Stags Lock Horns

After the vote was taken, Marvin stopped drumming his fingers on the table and unclenched his jaws. He was in charge at last. It was March 22, 1984, and the board of directors of American Savings & Loan had finally elected him chief executive officer. He had a full head of steam, and he was going to energize this old maid of a savings and loan, make it over in his own image.

The "damned bureaucrats," the federal and state banking authorities, had fiddled between December 1982 and November 1983 before approving his deal with the Broads. And then Shepard and his son Morris said that they wanted to work in tandem with Marvin for a while to become comfortable with his management style. Finally, they were satisfied. With Marvin's election as CEO, the Broads would seriously cut back their role in day-to-day management. They retained a voice in all vital policy decisions, however, through their membership on the board and its executive committee.

Marvin had Steve Arky by his side. Steve wasn't a director, but Marvin asked him to attend the meeting because he wanted to show his associates what his son-in-law meant to him. In Shepard Broad's opinion, Steve was more than a lawyer to Marvin. Shepard said, "He counseled with him on business matters apart from the law. It was more like a lawyer who was also a business consultant or adviser, and participant. And he held Marvin's power of attorney. Every document that gave rise to our arrangement was signed by Mr. Arky as attorney in fact for Mr. Warner." Marvin's first act as CEO was to define for his fellow directors the responsibilities of his principal operating managers: Bill Cooper and Ed Mahoney.

Marvin had hired Cooper, who had worked his way through college as a Detroit policeman, away from the presidency of a major Ohio bank. He directed Bill to take over the general operations of American—the branches, data processing, advertising and promotion, soliciting major customers, supervising the loan portfolio. Cooper's title was chief operating officer, and his job was considered important

enough to warrant a seat on the board of directors. He was elected as a
Warner nominee on March 22.

Cooper's election resulted in a 7-to-6 imbalance in favor of Marvin.
This violated the Broad-Warner voting trust agreement which stated
that each should name the same number of directors.

To redress the balance, Ed Mahoney was elected as the seventh
Broad director and given the titles of vice chairman of the board and
deputy CEO. Mahoney had joined American in 1978 and had been
chief operating officer under Shepard and Morris. Before that, he had
been Florida's deputy banking commissioner. A University of Alabama graduate, he is caught up in the mystique of its Crimson Tide
football team. His office is decorated with imposing photographs of
the team in action and of himself participating in his favorite sport,
skydiving.

Marvin told Mahoney to handle all state and federal regulatory
matters. He also wanted Ed to be the conduit for the many detailed
changes that he planned to make. And Marvin really got into the
details. Cooper remembers, "Warner, either in person or by phone,
would discuss the organization of the bank, its monthly profits, its
quarterly statements, its annual report, and major loans. He asked us
to create a book for his review that contained every form in the bank;
he asked us to maintain an organization chart on a wall that contained not only names but was updated daily with everybody's salary
on it, so that he could be constantly aware of how many people there
were, how much they were being paid, and what jobs they had."

Marvin was very clear about who would make investment policy.
He told Cooper and Mahoney, "I don't want the two of you to be
worried about the investment portfolio. You've got your thing to do,
and I will handle the investment decisions with Ronnie Ewton."
Marvin talked with gusto about the wonderful things that Ronnie
had done for Home State. He didn't mention his personal trading
successes at ESM, however, or even that he and Arky had accounts
there.

Ewton bowed his head modestly as Marvin told his fellow directors
that Ronnie was "a very sophisticated financial man and the best
partner I ever had. Ever. Period." He closed the meeting on that note.
The board would meet again in July, and until then, its executive
committee would deal with important policy matters.

Later, Shepard and Morris showed Marvin the large corner office
they had reserved for him. But he vetoed the idea. Marvin expected to

be constantly on the run managing his several businesses, and he would only be in Miami two or three days a month—so why waste space with a permanent office? He could work in a conference room or a vacant office when he alighted at American. As long as he had a telephone, a chair, and a tabletop, he was happy. The telephone was Marvin's principal business tool, and he used it so much that it occasionally caused a callous to form on his right ear.

It was business as usual during April 1984 as Marvin practically lived in the Sabre jet. He made more than a dozen trips and touched down in New York; Washington, D.C.; Birmingham; Jacksonville, Florida; Columbus, Ohio; Detroit; Lexington, Kentucky; Denver; and Miami. He bought and sold thoroughbreds, drummed up business for AS&L, worked on the Home State debenture problem, reviewed a couple of Ohio Building Authority projects, and helped the Birmingham Stallions clear some difficult financial hurdles.

On May 6, Home State received a panicky phone call from ESM. A government bond dealer named Lion Capital Group had collapsed four days earlier and its failure was sending shock waves through the industry. Lion was in the same business as ESM, and its leaders had been perpetrating a remarkably similar fraud. Lion's failure severely shook the public's confidence in the government bond market, and customers everywhere pulled securities away from their brokers and stuffed them into their safe deposit boxes.

Ewton and Novick were hit with a blizzard of demands, and millions of dollars in collateral were leaving each day. Ronnie's message to Home State: "Send us securities, more than you ever have before. We are hemorrhaging. It looks like we'll need $100 million." Home State had no choice. If ESM went down, Home State went down. But Home State didn't have $100 million to pile on top of the $90 million already resting in Fort Lauderdale. With a lot of pushing and sweating, it was able to squeeze out another $55 million. If ESM were to get additional significant help in the crisis, AS&L would be the logical source.

Marvin's first major opportunity to push American in ESM's direction occurred on May 16, when he attended an AS&L executive committee meeting with the two Broads. Ewton, the fourth member, was absent. After the formal meeting was over, Marvin pulled from his briefcase a two-page document which had been prepared for him by Alan Novick; the two had discussed it the day before in Fort Lauderdale.

The document described a complicated six-step transaction which involved U.S. Treasury securities. The essence of the deal was that American would put up $108 million of its Treasury securities as collateral to borrow $1 billion for one year from an assortment of local governments. Then American would loan the $1 billion to various borrowers. It would make roughly $5 million because, for several technical reasons, the municipal governments would accept a lower rate of interest than prevailed elsewhere in the markets.

Marvin assured the Broads that Novick had structured the deal as a "back-to-back arbitrage," a kind of transaction that would be absolutely riskless to American. In securities parlance, "back-to-back" meant that ESM would always keep for American enough cash in hand to cover the $108 million in Treasury securities American would put up to start the transaction; the presence of the cash would eliminate the risk.

Marvin insisted to Shepard that this was the kind of creative, aggressive financing which would put American firmly in the black. Shepard replied, "If it's really riskless, I would do this deal seven days a week." Marvin took this as tacit approval and implemented half the transaction, or $500 million, that day.

The $1 billion deal had never been ratified at the formal May 16 executive committee meeting, so it was put on the agenda for the next one, which took place on June 7. Again, one of the four members was absent. This time it was Shepard, who was in Toronto working on a real estate financing for American. Cooper, Mahoney, and Steve Arky were present by invitation.

Ronnie Ewton told everyone how pleased he was that the first half of the $1 billion transaction had been completed and proposed that the second half be consummated immediately.

Arky cheered him on. He said, "This is a great move that I think you guys should do. This is the right direction for American."

Bill Cooper dissented. "Even if it's riskless, I don't like the size. I don't like the idea of doing a billion dollars with anybody."

Ewton replied, "If you're going to make real money, you've got to go big. Tell me where else we can make $5 million with no risk."

Marvin was impatient to move on. He interrupted, saying, "Come off it, Bill. I've done these no-risk transactions at Home State and other places and never had any problems." He asked for a vote on the full $1 billion, obtained approval, and put the second $500 million transaction on the books that day. ESM had its hands on another $108 million in collateral and had put the Lion Capital crisis behind it.

Cooper and Mahoney were excused, and Marvin called for Steve Arky to make a presentation. Steve said that he had a pleasant surprise for the group; he and Marvin had worked out a deal to buy control of Freedom Savings & Loan, the large Tampa bank which had bought ComBanks from Marvin in 1983.

The two of them had lined up four shareholders who wished to sell their stock in Freedom for shares in American. Together, the four owned 30 percent of Freedom, and this, said Arky, constituted a control block. The shareholders were: Harold Vernon, Allen Singer, Home State (which had purchased its shares in 1983 to vote for Freedom's buy out of ComBanks), and Juan Perez-Sandoval.

Ferez-Sandoval was a client of Steve's with a controversial past; he had constantly been in scrapes with the government of his native Venezuela. Later his country would indict him for embezzlement and bribery. In 1985, he moved to Switzerland as a fugitive.

Steve then passed out drafts of contracts which he had prepared and which defined the terms by which American would buy out the Freedom shareholders with American's stock. Steve explained that, because the circumstances of ownership varied, the contracts were different, and he described the main points of each.

Ewton's response was mildly positive, but Morris Broad disagreed with him. He said, "I don't like it, Marvin. You and Steve have been working on this for weeks or months, and it's a very large deal, and you pop it on me from out of nowhere. From what Steve has said, there are things I don't like about the contracts. I hope you won't do anything until my father and I have a chance to make a thorough review of this thing."

And he remembers Marvin's reply, "I don't know, Morris. I've got to move on this deal quickly."

After the meeting was over, Morris went to Ed Mahoney and described what had happened, in detail. He asked Mahoney to prepare a set of executive committee minutes reflecting a deadlock on the Freedom takeover and instructed Ed to get Warner and Ewton to sign off on its contents.

Mahoney telephoned Warner and Ewton several days later. Marvin told him that Morris was wrong, that the executive committee had given him specific authority to proceed on Freedom. Ronnie said, "Look, I really don't want to get in the middle of it, but I believe that the executive committee approved proceeding. But that's a dispute between Morris and Marvin, and let them resolve it. The minutes should reflect that the executive committee had given authority and that Morris wants time to review the contracts."

To Marvin, it was a done deal. Forget about Morris's concerns, forget about the fact that, if Shepard had been there, the vote would almost certainly have been two to two. He had won the vote; he would get the contracts signed.

There was one minor hitch. Marvin needed someone else's signature on the Home State contract. It would look bad, it would smack of conflict of interest, if he—now the sole owner of Home State—signed that one.

Marvin called Bill Cooper and asked him to meet him out at Opa Locka Airport, just north of Miami. Cooper remembers, "When I got there, sitting out there was his jet airplane with the engines running, and his wife or wife-to-be loading luggage up, and Marvin told me that the executive committee had agreed to buy Freedom and that he had negotiated the contracts for the other shareholders. However, since it was a potential conflict of interest for him to sign the contract to buy the Home State shares, he wanted me to sign that contract. While the engine was gearing away, I briefly reviewed the contract and signed it. That's the first I heard about the Freedom transaction."

Cooper brought the Home State contract back to American, and soon after, the Perez-Sandoval contract signed by Warner arrived by mail. At about the same time, Arky called Mahoney about the Singer and Vernon contracts and said, "They're on the way up to you. I spoke with Marvin. He's tied up on the road or in the air or whatever. He's signed one, and he wants you to sign the other." Mahoney followed orders and executed the Vernon contract.

When Shepard came back from Toronto and reviewed the contracts, all hell broke loose. He was furious about the manner in which they had been handled. He didn't like the way Warner and Arky went and got the contracts signed after Morris had objected so strongly and had asked for time for Shepard to make his review. And more importantly, the contracts stated clearly that they were approved by American's board of directors. This simply was not the case; that step hadn't even been attempted yet.

In addition, Arky, who was representing the sellers, had inserted clauses calling for heavy penalties for American if the company failed to complete the purchases. And Warner had not even provided for an American lawyer to go over the contracts to protect its interests.

But the thing that got Shepard most angry was the issue of power;

the deal was a crude power grab on Marvin's part. Paying out American shares to Home State was the same as giving them to Marvin because he owned Home State. This would undo the carefully constructed voting trust and tip the balance of power at American to Marvin. To add insult to injury, the contract with Arky's client Perez-Sandoval provided for Perez-Sandoval to name two directors to American's Board.

Shepard had studied Freedom for years and was friendly with its management. His knowledge of the company gave him concern that the 30 percent block would not be enough for complete control and would involve American in a costly and unfriendly takeover battle with the rest of Freedom's shareholders. He did not want to fight that battle.

And, to top it all off, the price was wrong. It was too sweet for Perez-Sandoval, Vernon, Singer, Home State and Marvin, and too sour for American. Shepard knew that Freedom was losing money rapidly and might never be able to pull itself out of its tailspin. The price that Warner was willing to pay himself and his cohorts did not reflect Freedom's serious problems. In the end, Shepard's misgivings were proven correct; Freedom went bankrupt in 1986.

Shepard was also angry that the $1 billion ESM transaction had been approved while he was in Canada on June 7. Somewhere in the back of his mind, there were doubts about the deal that he couldn't dismiss. And they were doubts that went to the very heart of the transaction—its purported risklessness. The explanations given by Novick, Ewton, and Warner were too glib. Shepard knew that American had delivered $108 million of its own Treasury notes to ESM, and he wanted to be sure that American always had enough of ESM's hard cash to cover the value of the securities.

On June 29, Broad had a chance meeting with Ewton in a hallway at American's headquarters, and he asked Ronnie to go over the complicated transactions step by step. Shepard explains:

> I wanted to know, to trace these securities enroute from acquisition to return, this round trip that was going to take place. For the same reason that people put things in a vault box. It's important to make sure that this valuable asset doesn't somehow evaporate or get into weak hands or other such things that could occur that could cause loss.
>
> It's important to achieve the worthy designation of "riskless." Really, essentially nothing in life is riskless, but as close as you can make things, that's what's important to do.

I understood the term "back-to-back" as used by Warner to mean that the Treasuries we gave them are backed up either with cash or other securities. That which we part with is collateralized right then and there at market value. When Ewton explained to me in the hallway how he worked those Treasury notes, it didn't sound like he had done that. It was the first time that the "back-to-back" that Marvin Warner talked about began to look a little fuzzy to me.

Shepard decided to engage Kelley Drye & Warren, a respected securities law firm which had done a lot of work for American, to review the $1 billion transaction and to provide an opinion concerning the risks surrounding American's $108 million in Treasury notes. When Shepard called there, a Kelley Drye partner told him that he couldn't accept an assignment from him. Marvin, in a drive to cut lawyers' bills, had given strict orders that only he could authorize legal work. Shepard bit his tongue before he called Marvin to obtain his assent to hiring Kelley Drye. Marvin offered no opposition.

At the time, Marvin was concerned with something much closer to his heart than okaying what seemed to be a routine legal assignment. Novick was putting the finishing touches on an important Home State–ESM transaction, one which would significantly enhance the picture of Home State painted in the prospectus to be used in selling its debentures to the public in September.

Home State was going through a bad spell again and was facing a $1.8 million loss for the twelve months ending June 30, 1984. Such a result, if reported, would have had a chilling effect on potential buyers of the debentures. So Home State got ESM to pull it into the black by absorbing a $2.1 million loss in a Home State Treasury note position. Marvin's banks, AS&L and Home State, had saved ESM's hide with their generous contributions of collateral following the Lion Capital collapse, and Ronnie and Alan could not turn the deal down.

The $2.1 million brought to more than $36 million the benefits which ESM had given to Home State between 1980 and 1984. Since Home State's stated net worth in the prospectus was $19.7 million, it would have had to report a $16.7 million deficit without Alan Novick's largess.

Subsequent events showed that the $19.7 million figure grossly overstated Home State's position; if a strict, conservative accounting had been made, even Alan's magic would not have produced a positive net worth.

Marvin turned from his Home State concerns to discover that the

Freedom deal had created an unbridgeable chasm between himself and the Broads. The proposed takeover had made clear to everyone that Marvin never intended to share power with Shepard and Morris for very long. The Freedom contracts, brought crudely to the fore less than ninety days after Marvin had become CEO, would have shifted power irrevocably in his direction if consummated. The fierce opposition of Shepard and Morris to Marvin's attempted backdoor coup d'etat led American's board members and executives to believe that Marvin would be inexorably driven to take the gamble of initiating the buy-sell agreement.

And it was a gamble, because although the initiator set the price, the other party had the option to be the buyer or seller. Shepard had told everyone that he would never be the initiator. He always wanted to preserve his option to buy or to sell.

After the June 7 executive committee meeting, Bill Cooper became disenchanted with both Marvin's power moves and his business judgment. Cooper is a tough, wiry fellow who fought his way out of one of Detroit's meanest neighborhoods into top executive echelons, and he has developed keen instincts about power and its uses.

He had never liked the $1 billion ESM transaction, and when Shepard explained his misgivings about risk, he became an open opponent of the deal. Bill believed that Freedom was a very sick company and, on those grounds alone, opposed the purchase of the Freedom shares. And he resented the fact that the contracts drawn by Arky represented that American's board had authorized the takeover when in fact it hadn't. In addition, he was angry that Marvin had not leveled with him at the Opa Locka Airport when he had said that the executive committee had approved the Freedom purchases and made no mention of the Broads' opposition.

Barry Winslow deepened Cooper's doubts about Warner's judgment. In early 1984, when Marvin recruited Cooper for American, he was also looking for someone to replace Burt Bongard as president at Home State. Marvin mentioned this to Cooper, and Bill suggested Barry, who had formerly worked for him as a senior vice president. Warner was impressed by Winslow and hired him to succeed Bongard.

Barry came on board in early April and spent several weeks making a personal study of Home State's operations. He was disturbed by what he found. He was particularly upset about the Home State–ESM relationship. In a May 18 memo to Warner, he wrote:

> The ESM . . . situation is distorting our balance sheet and creating unnecessary but troublesome concerns (which we must constantly address) from accountants, the regulators, and the SEC. . . . We must constantly be concerned about the credit worthiness and viability of ESM due to our large concentration.
>
> [We must] reduce the size and structure of our . . . arrangement with ESM as soon as possible and by whatever means possible.

Winslow called Cooper about their new boss and thanked Bill sarcastically for getting him into such a mess. He told Cooper that he was scared about the risks that Marvin was taking with Home State's assets and, in particular, the risks inherent in Home State's massive and growing loans to ESM. He was totally frustrated, because he felt Warner was really running the show and had frozen him out of the crucial investment policy area where decisions about ESM were being made. He sent Cooper a copy of his anxious May 18 memo.

Cooper showed Shepard Broad the memo and relayed Barry's comments that the Home State–ESM situation had grown scarier and riskier since then. This deeply intensified the concerns of Shepard and his allies.

During the month of July, there was open dissension among American's directors. A board meeting was scheduled for July 31, and emotions were running so high that the Broads called a "workshop" meeting for July 30. Its purpose: to give the directors plenty of opportunity to blow off steam so that the formal meeting of July 31 wouldn't descend into chaos. Steve Arky was invited to attend both meetings to discuss the Freedom contracts.

Shepard felt that he could take the risk of not attending the meetings because Bill Cooper had made it clear to him and Morris that he would vote against board ratification of the Freedom contracts; Bill told no one else. On July 15, Shepard and his wife Ruth departed for a European vacation, and he left Morris to represent the interests of the family.

Morris began the workshop by saying that the executive committee had not approved the Freedom deal, because he and his father had not agreed to it. Then he recited the long litany of their objections to the four contracts and read a letter from Shepard which repeated the same points. Marvin replied that he had struck a brilliant deal for American and that Morris simply didn't remember what had happened on June 7. Steve Arky backed him up, and both sides argued for several hours.

Marvin appeared happy that everyone had had a chance to air their differences at the workshop. It would make everything easier the next day. Because of Shepard's absence, Marvin could feel pretty relaxed about the upcoming vote; a seven-to-six victory looked to be in his pocket. But he didn't want to leave anything to chance. So after the workshop ended, he took Mahoney aside and told him, "When Shepard and I got into this voting trust, it was never contemplated that you and Cooper would be in the middle. There's really no need for both of you to be involved in this fight, so if you want to abstain in the vote tomorrow, that's OK with me."

Mahoney asked Warner to let him think about it, and then he told Cooper of Marvin's proposition. Mahoney remembers, "Both of us had the same reaction, which was, maybe they didn't intend to appoint us to the board, but like it or not, we're on the board. Unless it's a matter that directly involved our own personal interests, like our own salaries or a transaction with a company that we owned, we're not ever going to abstain from a vote."

The next morning, before the board meeting started, Marvin called Mahoney into a small office adjoining the board room and, as Mahoney recollects, the dialogue went like this:

WARNER: I need your vote on this Freedom deal. I signed those contracts. I know Morris and Shepard don't like them. And I know you're good friends with them and all that, but I'm the CEO of this company.

MAHONEY: Marvin, that's a real problem. I agree with Morris and Shepard. Furthermore, the contracts say that we represented that the board approved it.

WARNER: If the board approves it today, that issue is basically moot.

MAHONEY: I understand that, but I can't vote for these contracts the way the deal is structured.

WARNER: But, you know, you work for me. And I need your vote.

MAHONEY: Marvin, I'm going to vote against you, even if it means my job. And don't take it personally.

WARNER: Well, I take it that way.

Marvin was silent for a while, just stared into space, and then asked Mahoney to get Cooper to join them. When the two men returned to the room, Warner told Bill that he expected him to vote for the Freedom takeover since he was a Warner appointee to the board. Cooper said "No" and Marvin must have felt a hand cold as ice wrap around his heart. He had lost control. American was not his. Freedom would not be his.

Cooper remembers what happened next: "We had a confrontation. He stood up, and I stood up. I was bigger than him, so he sat down. Then he became angry and stalked out. Mahoney and I got up and followed him and entered the board meeting together."

Mahoney felt that these corporate confrontations were a lot tougher than skydiving.

At the meeting, Morris Broad hammered at the fact that the board had not authorized the Freedom stock purchases even though Arky's contracts had attested to this.

Arky tried to save the day with a hard sales pitch. He rolled on like a used-car salesman. He said that he was an expert in bank takeovers, that he knew more about them than anyone at the table, and that he had never seen a better deal than this. He even told the board that he had people waiting in his office at that very moment who were willing to make the Freedom deal if American turned it down.

It was a good try, but Marvin knew they were licked. He never brought the contracts to a vote. Instead, he suggested that an attempt be made to meet with Shepard in Europe to iron things out.

Shepard scotched that idea. He had won a crucial victory, and he wasn't going to give his opponents an opportunity to harass him on his vacation. In the end, a special board meeting was scheduled to deal with the Freedom issue on September 10, more than a week after Shepard's return from Europe.

While he was going mano a mano with Shepard, Marvin still had to deal with those SEC pests who were harassing Home State. Since February, they had tossed the prospectus back four additional times. They were digging deeper and deeper into Home State's transaction with what they called "a small government securities dealer in Fort Lauderdale." And of course, Marvin couldn't be expected to parade the horrendous risks inherent in the ESM relationship across the pages of the prospectus. Potential debenture buyers would "head South" once they understood the risks.

As the stalemate with the SEC dragged on into the summer, one of

Warner's lawyers made a brilliant suggestion. It was well known that Ohio's securities regulators were much less demanding concerning prospectuses than the SEC. Home State was an Ohio-chartered bank, and, as such, any sale of its own securities would only need the approval of the state regulators. In other words, the SEC had no jurisdiction over the savings bank.

The lawyer's idea was to merge Home State and its parent, HSFI, with Home State as the surviving corporation. Then Home State could sell the debentures using a prospectus approved only by the Ohio regulators.

The Ohio regulators, who were very concerned about Home State's financial weakness, extracted a high toll from Marvin before they would approve the merger and the debenture offering. The price: Marvin would have to deed over to Home State 1,100 apartments, located in four states, worth $24 million. When it came to the prospectus, they were very lenient. The SEC had demanded a 150-page document with strong language concerning the risks of the ESM relationship. The Ohio regulators approved a four-pager which didn't mention ESM at all.

Marvin put a major task behind him on August 27, 1984, when the merger went through. Now he could relax. He could attend to something that was truly important; he would marry Jody Piehowicz, the woman he fell in love with on the campaign trail in 1982. It wouldn't be a big splashy event like the Goldwater wedding, which after the fact had provided rich grist for the gossip mills. They would simply find a judge and then take off for a quiet Caribbean honeymoon. They set Sunday, September 2, as the date.

Shepard Broad returned from Europe on August 30 and was back in his office the next day. The Kelley Drye report on the $1 billion ESM transaction had just been received, and Cooper saw to it that it was on the top of Shepard's stack of mail. Shepard read it, and his worst fears assailed him.

This carefully reasoned ten-page analysis of the transaction stated unequivocally that the $108 million in Treasury notes in the hands of ESM was an unsecured loan. If, for any reason, ESM was unable to meet its obligations to American, American would lose the $108 million. Shepard immediately called for a September 5 meeting of the executive committee, senior American management, Alan Novick, and a representative of Kelley Drye to deal with this crisis.

Shepard was killing Marvin's honeymoon, but Warner went along with the old boy and showed up in Miami; the $1 billion deal was crucial to his program at American. In addition, if Shepard over-turned the deal, there could be problems for ESM. And ESM and Home State were in such a delicate embrace, that trouble for ESM would mean trouble for Home State.

Shepard started the September 5 meeting by passing out copies of the Kelley Drye study, together with explanatory worksheets which Cooper had prepared. Then he banged his fists on the table and said, "I want to know now. Where are the securities? I want to make absolutely certain that when the time comes for unwinding, we get back our securities plus the profit promised us."

Shepard remembers Marvin's rejoinder: "Mr. Warner half rose from the chair, appeared very angry at me, shook a finger as close to touching my nose as one could, and firmly and angrily said, 'Are you questioning Ronnie's integrity?' My response: 'It's not a question of integrity, Marvin. It's over a billion dollars. It's a huge transaction. We need to take these safe-guards to make it riskless like it's represented to us.' "

Ewton tried to calm things down. His position was that, even though the loan was unsecured, American wasn't taking much of a risk. ESM was solid, he said, and so were the other parties involved in the transactions. Marvin chimed in that he didn't consider the loan unsecured at all, because the parties holding the securities were so strong.

Novick supported them. He spoke rapidly and with great self-assurance, asserting that this kind of deal was made hundreds of times each day by institutions all over the United States, and no one felt they were exposed to excessive risk.

But Shepard hammered away. He kept saying, "I want to feel comfortable about my merchandise. I want my hands on my $108 million again."

Finally, the discussion became a conversation between Shepard and Novick, and the executive committee designated them a sub-commit-tee of two to work out the problem. Shepard and Alan tentatively agreed to a procedure to put the $108 million in Treasury notes in the hands of a solid escrow agent.

But Alan saw that this was not really making Shepard happy. He finally said, "Shep, I think you really want to get out of this transac-tion. Why don't we do that?" Shepard answered, "You're right. Get me out of this." And Alan replied, "I will, but it will take time to unwind. This large deal is made up of lots of small deals with different institutions, and the small deals each have separate unwinding dates." The meeting ended as they agreed to work closely together to bring the $108 million back to American.

Marvin didn't bother to return to Ohio because the September 5 meeting was on a Thursday, and the full board was getting together the following Tuesday for the showdown on the Freedom contracts. Representatives of Kelley Drye and another law firm attended by invitation, but, for the first time in the Freedom controversy, Steve Arky was absent. Steve's all-out sales effort had not changed any votes at the July 31 meeting, and it didn't appear that he could provide much help to Marvin now.

After long debate on both the business and the legal issues, it was decided to renounce the Home State and the Perez-Sandoval contracts and to proceed with Singer's and Vernon's. The last two were ratified because the nonperformance penalties that Arky had written into them were so severe. In the end, American did not have to buy the Singer and Vernon shares because, for technical reasons, the federal regulators disallowed the purchases.

In terms of control, the Home State and Perez-Sandoval purchases were the vital ones because, if consummated, they would have tilted the balance of power at American in favor of Marvin and his allies. With the help of Bill Cooper, whose switch to the Broad camp was crucial in the voting, Shepard had prevailed again.

But the struggle would continue. Marvin had decided on his next move quickly. He would invoke the buy-sell agreement. He would attempt to buy Shepard out, make him an offer he couldn't refuse.

Marvin could feel confident that he would come through the latest crisis in triumph. He would get rid of Broad and take full control of American. Then he could merge it with Freedom to form a $5 billion institution, an institution that would have more than enough collateral to satisfy ESM. He would sell his Home State debentures and continue to count on profits from ESM to keep it alive. Eventually he might merge Home State into the Freedom-American giant and bury its problems there.

When Ewton and Novick heard of Warner's plan to buy out the Broads, they were overjoyed. All the aggravation they had taken from Marvin seemed to be paying off. He was leading them to larger and larger customers with billions in collateral. The cover-up with Gomez would continue. They would be safe until Alan made the really big market wins he was sure he was capable of. They could enjoy themselves—refurbish their estates, buy more thoroughbreds and show dogs, festoon their wives with more jewelry. The future looked bright.

7

Masterful Maneuvers

As Marvin worked over the buy-out strategy in his mind, the main consideration was price. The offer couldn't be ridiculously generous, but it had to be pretty rich. For two reasons. It had to be sufficiently high that Shepard would be unable to raise enough money to turn the tables and become the buyer. And it had to be tempting enough to get Shepard to opt for a very, very affluent retirement.

Marvin decided on a price of $14 a share. Since American's shares were trading on the New York Stock Exchange at $10.50, this represented a hefty 33 percent premium over market. It meant that the Broads would walk away with $15 million. When Warner had committed his capital two years before, American's future looked dim, its financial condition was shaky, and the Broads' position was worth only $7 million. So Marvin could feel that his offer represented a major turnaround in the fortunes of his seventy-eight-year-old adversary.

The number of shares Marvin owned gave him a major advantage in the buy-sell chess game. The voting trust provided for a fifty-fifty sharing of power, but it contained a lot more Warner stock than Broad stock. Shepard would have to come up with more than $26 million to buy Marvin out.

While Marvin was refining his buy-out strategy, Federal Home Loan Bank Board (FHLBB) examiners from Washington were digging into American's records in Miami. They had arrived on Wednesday, September 4, for one of their routine, periodic reviews of all of American's operations and finances. These examinations took place every twelve to eighteen months. American had a state charter, but its deposits were insured by the Federal Savings and Loan Insurance Corporation (FSLIC) and like all other FSLIC members, it was regulated by the FHLBB. The FHLBB field team at American was led by Trish Morgan, a petite, no-nonsense accountant in her late thirties.

Ed Mahoney explains how the examiners dealt with management

121

saying, "What normally happens is that when they first get here . . . they do their own checking into lots of things, but they ask, 'What are the sorts of things we ought to know about; what's unusual.' Bill Cooper and I filled them in on the ESM transaction and the Freedom matter. Those were the two key things that were unusual." They also told the examiners about the management changes. How the Broads had pulled back and Warner and Ewton had moved in. And how Cooper had been hired.

The $1 billion ESM transaction both surprised and disturbed the examiners. It was very different from anything that they had dealt with during Shepard's thirty-four-year reign.

The way he ran things had never troubled them. Management controls were tight, expenses were kept at an almost miserly level, and regulations were followed scrupulously. And there was always a healthy attitude towards risk.

Shepard had treated risk like a Las Vegas blackjack dealer. It was part of your business, but you constantly took its measure, and you used all your wiles and energies to minimize the hurt it could cause you.

Now Warner had come in and almost invited the hurt, and the numbers were huge. Shepard had started American with $7,500 in 1950 and thirty-four years of hard striving had built up the equity of the owners, the shareholders, to $155 million. Now, as the Kelley Drye report made clear to the examiners, one wild decision had put $108 million of it at risk.

The FHLBB people did not need this sort of thing. Over half the net worth of the savings and loan industry had been wiped out by the deregulation firestorm of the early 1980s and hundreds of institutions were critically ill. The regulators were fighting a seemingly endless battle to keep the industry afloat and unnecessary, high-risk gambits only made their struggles more gut-wrenching and exhausting.

Risk was not the only thing which bothered the FHLBB about the ESM transaction. There was a blatant conflict of interest. Ronnie Ewton was an insider making money two ways, as an American director and as an ESM principal, and this violated FHLBB rules. In addition, they didn't like the way the $1 billion transaction had been put on the books. It was a huge deal putting a high percentage of American's net worth at risk, and Warner had pushed it through without bringing it to the board of directors for a discussion or a vote. The deal had only been approved by the executive committee, and, to make matters worse, this group had ratified half the transaction a full month after it had been consummated by Marvin.

Trish Morgan took some comfort from the fact that Shepard Broad had forced the unwinding of the transaction at the September 5 meeting. She decided that she would monitor the unwinding process carefully.

Two other major concerns emerged from the FHLBB field study: the Freedom deal and Marvin's expense accounts.

The FHLBB had to approve the Freedom purchases because they were not casual investments. They were of considerable size (Vernon and Singer together owned about 15 percent of Freedom's shares), and both banks involved—American and Freedom—came under FHLBB regulation.

Trish Morgan was relieved that American's board had rejected the Home State and Perez-Sandoval contracts. The FHLBB had spent almost a year working over and modifying the Broad–Warner voting trust agreement before approving it, and she was happy that they would not have to deal with purchases which would have vitiated that agreement. The Vernon and Singer contracts were sent to regional headquarters in Atlanta for approval.

Marvin charged his companies $1,370 per hour for the use of the Sabre jet. When you added in an 8 percent excise tax, the companies were paying $1,479.60 per hour for the plane. With a rate like this, a routine trip could became very expensive. For example, Marvin's visit to Miami for the May 16 executive committee meeting was billed to American at $6,764.36, and the trip for the September 5 and 10 meetings had a price tag of $8,095.61.

The contrast with the Broads' expense accounts, which the FHLBB was so accustomed to dealing with, was quite startling. The Broads always traveled via commercial airlines and, more often than not, used tourist class seats. When the examiners added up Marvin's 1984 charges to American, the total came to roughly $300,000. Trish Morgan was to recommend that Marvin return almost all of this to the company.

One of the keys to Marvin's success was his ability to keep several projects going forward at once while maintaining the discipline of mind to deal with the most urgent. Whatever occupied him at a particular moment drew his undivided attention. In the latter part of September 1984, Marvin focused on Home State.

First there was the debenture issue. After the Home State–Home

State Financial merger was approved on August 27, Marvin immediately directed his lawyers to write up a prospectus. They worked fast
and submitted a draft to the Ohio savings and loan regulators in early
September. The bureaucrats were very cooperative with Governor
Celeste's leading fundraiser, and final approval was obtained in near-
record time. It came down on Tuesday, September 25.

The debentures went on sale at once at all Home State branches.
The four-page prospectus, which made no mention of the Home
State–ESM relationship and its attendant risks, was available to
anyone interested in making a purchase.

The Ohio authorities had been very helpful in expediting the
issuance of the prospectus, but they were not being cooperative about
Home State's unsecured lending to ESM; it had reached a level of
roughly $150 million by the end of the summer. Larry Huddleston,
superintendent of Ohio's Savings and Loan Division, had demanded a
drastic reduction in a September 6 report, and he and his associates
followed up with constant pressure on Warner and David Schiebel.
Barry Winslow had resigned out of frustration as of September 24, and
Schiebel had taken over his responsibilities as CEO.

The debentures would become a difficult sell indeed if Huddleston's
concerns became public. Marvin called Ronnie Ewton and told him
that this was a crisis, that ESM had to help get these regulators off
Home State's back.

Ewton and Novick flew up to Cincinnati on September 26 to find
Marvin very angry. ESM had $250 million in excess collateral from
Warner's two banks, $150 million from Home State, and $100 million
from American, and Ewton remembers that Warner demanded that a
chunk of it be sent back to Home State. Home State's debenture issue
could be in jeopardy and that meant trouble.

Novick explained that ESM was in trouble, too. It was in a terrible
cash bind caused by the agreement to return securities to Broad at
American. It was hard to satisfy both American and Home State at
once.

Marvin couldn't control the anger and frustration that were boiling
inside him. He threatened, he pounded the table, he yelled for ten
minutes nonstop. Alan was so unnerved he had to leave the room.
Ronnie followed him, and Alan told him that he didn't know if he
could take this anymore. He was down in the trenches in the trading
room every day trying to keep all the balls in the air, fighting off the
creditors who could put ESM under. It was wearing him down, and on

top of this he had to come up to Cincinnati and take this abuse from Warner.

Ronnie went back to Marvin, and got him to calm down and promise he wouldn't yell at Alan again. Novick returned to the room and he and Ronnie agreed to slow down the American payback although it meant facing Shepard Broad's wrath every day. It wouldn't help much; it wouldn't produce a great deal of collateral, but at least it would be a move in the right direction, one that might placate Huddleston and his crew.

Huddleston was told that Home State's collateral would be coming back and that the savings and loan division would be given periodic progress reports. With the regulator mollified, Marvin could redirect his attention to American.

During the early part of October, Warner and Arky worked intensely to prepare the buy-out proposal for Shepard. Everyone at American knew what was in the wind and expected that the proposal would be presented at the regularly scheduled board meeting on Monday, October 29.

When Trish Morgan and her team left American on October 19, she asked Mahoney and Cooper to keep her informed about the buy-sell situation and other important developments. The fact-gathering field work phase of her study had ended, and the team returned to Washington to begin the interpretive work which would lead to her action recommendations. During the interpretive phase, she would be in almost constant touch with Carl Kamp who, as principal supervisory agent for the FHLBB in Atlanta, had direct authority over American.

The buy-out agreement was dated Friday, October 26, and was delivered to Shepard over the weekend. As Shepard read the cover letter, he found no surprises. Its main message was contained in its first four paragraphs. They read:

Dear Shepard:

Unfortunately you and I have reached a stalemate regarding what is best for American Savings and Loan Association of Florida (ASLA) and its shareholders. It is imperative that this stalemate be resolved as soon as possible.

I have therefore concluded that it is in the best interests of ASLA, its shareholders and employees for me to submit, herewith, my buy-sell Notice pursuant to our Voting Trust Agreement even though this gives you the advantage of choice.

Under the Voting Trust Agreement you will have up to sixty days from your receipt of the Notice to elect to be a Seller or a Purchaser. It is assumed that during such period you and your associates will refrain from any action which could adversely affect the Company or my best interests in the event I am eventually the Purchaser.

Although the Voting Trust allows you personally sixty days to make a decision, the Company during such a comparative long period of time, with the current volatile interest rate market, can suffer losses by the continuation of our stalemate. The Company must be in a position to move and to move adroitly. Accordingly, for the benefit of the Company and the shareholders, I beseech you to make a decision as soon as you possibly can. The ball is in your court—timing is now your responsibility.

The agreement proper did contain a major surprise. Marvin had structured the buyout on the installment plan: 25 percent on closing, and 25 percent a year for three years. The interest rate on the outstanding balance rose from 10 percent during the first year to 11 percent in the second and 12 percent in the third.

Marvin distributed a press release about the buy-sell before convening the board meeting at 10:00 A.M. He started by going over the cover letter and the main points of the agreement with the directors. His tone was relaxed, friendly. He told them that he had enjoyed working with them and that he harbored no personal animosities. He finished by saying that the Warner-Broad partnership could not continue because of unbridgeable differences in management philosophy, and in sixty days, one or the other of the partners would have sole control.

Shepard was equally polite and assured everyone that he harbored no hard feelings and that he would respond appropriately to Marvin's proposition. Then he asked Ewton for an update on the unwinding of the $1 billion transaction. Ronnie replied that he still didn't believe the transaction was risky, but since Shepard was so adamant about it, ESM was reducing American's exposure. Roughly $15 million in Treasury notes had been returned to American, and the process would continue.

Shepard couldn't wait for the meeting to end, because he knew what he wanted to do and he was impatient to get started. He wasn't going to walk off into the sunset with $15 million; he would fight. He would try to move Marvin out. Marvin, with his high risk gambits and his jet-set ways, Shepard thought, could bring American down in a hurry. And Shepard had put too much of his sweat and spirit into the company to let that happen.

The catch was that he didn't have the $26 million at hand to buy Warner out. Sixty days was a short period of time to line up this kind of money, but he would try.

As soon as he left the meeting, he was on the phone to bankers and investment bankers. He kept at it all week but with little success. The lenders told him that he wanted too much, too soon. He started to feel desperate. Then, over the weekend, it came to him: the cash was close at hand, in the coffers of American itself. He would try to use the stockholders' money to buy Marvin out. With a net worth of $155 million, the company was strong enough to handle a $26 million investment in its own stock.

It was a daring move, but there was an important obstacle in Shepard's path. He would have to convince the FHLBB to approve the deal. He called Atlanta and set up a confidential meeting with Carl Kamp the following Thursday, November 8.

On October 15, Kamp had received a short interim report on American from Trish Morgan. She had stayed in touch with Cooper and Mahoney and was able to brief Kamp several times subsequently. Her findings caused him genuine anguish. Here was a bank which had been a regulator's dream for thirty-four years. Everything tidily in place. No conflicts of interest. A prim, old-maidish attitude toward risk. Now, with Warner in the saddle, things were out of control and the institution seemed headed for serious trouble.

When Shepard met with Kamp on November 8, he reemphasized the need for confidentiality. He told Carl, "What I'm going to propose to you will only work if it's kept under wraps." Kamp reaffirmed his commitment to secrecy, and then Shepard put on the show of his life. The passion was in him, and he spoke heatedly about what he called "the $108 million unsecured loan" to this small-time outfit in Fort Lauderdale with only twenty-seven employees. He said:

> I wouldn't give Paul Volcker himself an unsecured loan for $108 million; I certainly wouldn't do it with a couple of bond brokers like Ewton and Novick.
> And look at the "sweetheart" deal Warner was proposing on the Freedom takeover. American's shareholders would have paid through

the nose on that one, and Warner, Arky, and Perez-Sandoval would have emasculated the voting trust and taken de facto control of our bank. I stopped them dead in their tracks.

Warner has made me this offer and I could walk away very rich and happy. But I don't want to. I've thought about American all day, every day, since 1950. I sweated every detail, built this from scratch with $7,500. I'm totally identified with this institution in the community, and I've lived in the community, in the same three-bedroom house, for thirty-six years. I don't do my business out of a jet airplane.

I'm too old to go into debt to buy out Warner. I want you to let American itself buy him out. The company's got plenty of money to do so. It's up to you. You can have Broad management or Warner management.

Shepard had gotten Kamp's attention. Carl told him that he would take a hard look at his proposal and would quickly get back to him.

Kamp felt like a doctor in the middle of an epidemic. There were at least one hundred basket cases in his district, and he was struggling every day to keep them alive. He did not need to have American, the fourteenth largest savings and loan in the United States, go down the drain. It would be the biggest catastrophe of his career. The irony was that American was not like his other sick patients. It was fundamentally sound and could only be put under by a management intent on taking crazy risks.

To Kamp, the danger was clear. It was Marvin Warner. He should be removed from American's management. Kamp had no statutory authority to depose him, so the buy-out proposal seemed like manna from heaven. Kamp felt that Warner would walk away with a profit of $12 million as a reward for mismanagement, but this wasn't a perfect world. On the credit side of the ledger, an institution with $2 billion in deposits would be removed from the danger list.

Kamp felt comfortable with his desire to get rid of Marvin. But he didn't like the way Shepard was slipping away from his obligations under the buy-sell agreement. He had to hold Shepard's feet to the fire. He telephoned him and demanded that Shepard guarantee the repayment of the $26 million to American's treasury. Shepard balked but kept the dialogue going. He asked Kamp for a written proposal and took it home with him to review it over the Thanksgiving weekend.

Alan Novick felt terrible on the morning of Friday, November 23, the day after Thanksgiving. He thought he had the flu. He couldn't shake a feeling of nausea, his joints ached, and his skin was sweaty and clammy. But he dragged himself to work because this particular Friday presented a golden opportunity to catch up on the mountains of paperwork that seemed a permanent part of the scene at ESM. Traders all over the United States were taking a four-day weekend and market activity was minimal that Friday. Alan and the staff took advantage of the lull to work on customer records which were two to three weeks out of date.

George Mead dropped by Alan's office, took one glance at him, and said, "You look like death warmed over. You ought to get out of here. Go home and get some rest over the weekend. It's just the flu. You'll be OK on Monday." Alan was determined to stick it out. If he could just get something to calm his stomach down, he could get through the day. One of the secretaries knew a Dr. Mollinet just down the street, and she arranged for Alan to visit him right away.

Alan got there at noon. During the examination, Mollinet probed for evidence of a heart condition. Alan told him that he had no chest pain or shortness of breath and that he had passed a recent stress test which was part of a company physical. Mollinet found that Alan's pulse rate and blood pressure readings were healthy, and he could identify no symptoms of serious illness. He decided to help Alan with his stomach upset and injected him with 10 cc of Compazine, an antinausea drug.

When Alan got back to ESM, he told his secretary that he wanted to take a short nap on his sofa. George Mead put his head in the door about fifteen minutes later and was shaken; Alan's skin had turned blue. He tried to wake him and failed. Then he ran out into the hallway and shouted for help. One of the secretaries was a trained nurse, and she tried frantically to revive Alan with mouth-to-mouth resuscitation and other survival techniques. Nothing helped. Alan was gone at 1:30 P.M., age forty-four.

Paramedics took him to a local hospital where he was pronounced dead and where an autopsy was performed the next day. It described him as slightly obese; he was five feet, eight inches tall and weighed 178 pounds. The autopsy showed severe heart disease with calcified plaque material clogging up the three main areas of the heart as well as the coronary arteries. Old and well-healed scar tissue was found in the heart itself. This indicates that Alan once had a heart attack which was so mild that he mistook it for indigestion or the flu.

Alan was a near perfect candidate for heart disease. He was a heavy smoker and got very little exercise. And, of course, the most imaginative cardiac researcher would be hard put to invent working conditions more stressful than those Alan subjected himself to at ESM every day.

Mead called Ewton at Ronnie's farm in Aiken to tell him the awful news. It was a severe, almost physical, blow to Ronnie, as if he had been slammed in the chest and had all the air knocked out of him. He wandered sadly through the house during the rest of the afternoon.

He and Alan had been in so many scrapes together and Alan had always come through. Whatever the problem, he had the solution. Who could replace him? Who else could take the heat of the trading room day after day and then, in the evenings, juggle the books to hide the $300 million loss?

Novick was buried on Sunday, November 25. The next day, Gomez and Arky went up to ESM to sort out Alan's personal papers. Steve suggested to Jose that he might take Alan's place, but Gomez wasn't interested. Arky called Ronnie and told him about Jose's rejection of the idea.

If Ronnie couldn't have Jose as a partner, he certainly wanted to keep him on his team. A few days later, he and Jose agreed that Ronnie and George Mead would each wire $50,000 into Gomez's account to help make life sweeter for him.

Ronnie went back to the farm and brooded. The bleak late autumn landscape could only have added to his feelings of depression and panic. There was no way that he or Mead or Wallace or any of the other guys at ESM could fill Alan's shoes. As he later told Charlie Harper, "Alan was a financial wizard; the rest of us were merely salesmen. Whenever I had dirty laundry to wash at ESM I would bring it to Alan and in a few days he would return it all cleaned and pressed. I didn't want to go down into that laundry. I couldn't run it."

He had to unburden himself to someone. On December 4, he called Steve Arky and told him that ESM had serious financial problems, that without Alan he wasn't sure they would make it through, and that he might have to talk to a bankruptcy lawyer. Steve tried to be helpful with management and personnel suggestions.

Ronnie must have thanked God that Marvin had made the buy-out bid to Broad. If they could get Shepard out of the way, and American firmly under control, there would be plenty of money to keep ESM alive, and there would be time to try to fill Alan's shoes. Maybe Marvin could talk a knowledgeable guy like Bongard into moving down to Fort Lauderdale. Maybe there were other guys out there he'd never heard of. After all, Ronnie had found Alan through a headhunter.

The key thing was getting rid of Broad. Ronnie respected the old boy. It would be just like Shepard to pull off some kind of a miracle and turn the tables on Marvin.

Ewton's worst fears about a Broad miracle were being realized in Atlanta. Kamp was hammering out a deal with Shepard. After a lot of backing and filling, he had gotten Shepard to agree to guarantee the repayment of the $26 million to American in two annual installments. The lawyers worked overtime on the documents, and, on December 17, Kamp approved them. Both parties had succeeded in maintaining complete secrecy about the negotiation and its outcome.

Thursday, December 20, marked the fifty-fifth day after Marvin had invoked the buy-sell agreement and had given Shepard sixty days to reply. On that Thursday, Shepard sent by three different means— express mail, certified mail, and registered mail—a two-paragraph letter to Marvin. The key sentences were simple and direct: "Pursuant to the above referenced agreement (the Voting Trust Agreement), I hereby elect by this notice in writing to purchase. Henceforth, I shall be known as the 'Purchasing Shareholder' and you shall be known as the 'Selling Shareholder.'"

The next morning, American held a board of directors meeting. Cochairman Morris Broad presided, because Warner was absent. Morris started the meeting by reading the following December 20 telex from Marvin: "Kindly advise directors that I request deferment of board meeting from Friday, December 21, to right after first of year because of difficulty of out of town directors getting to and from Miami this weekend before Christmas; because of the illness of my son; and moreover, there is a stalemate until the Broads make their selection." Then Morris read his reply: "While I wish your son, Mark, a complete and speedy recovery, and wish you seasons greetings, there is no valid reason why the meeting should be postponed. A quorum is assured and you are cordially invited to attend as was communicated to you by my father by telephone yesterday morning."

The group was polled and it was determined that a quorum of ten was present. In addition to Marvin and Mark, two other Warner directors had not shown up.

Shepard then read his buy-out letter and asked for a recess so that the corporate secretary could call Marvin about his response. Ronnie

Ewton and another Warner director joined the secretary in the conversation. The three men reported that Marvin was stunned but accepted his new position as seller. However, Warner had pointed out that there were important differences to resolve before the purchase could be consummated. The most important of these concerned the number of shares the Warner group held in the voting trust. There had been some ambiguity about this when the trust agreement was written in 1982.

The meeting ended with a decision by the directors to get together a week later to reorganize American's board and management to reflect the return of control to the Broad family.

Warner and Arky immediately began a campaign to undo Shepard's masterful maneuver. It was reminiscent of the Century deal where Arky's tactics had resulted in a $5 million payment to Marvin to call off his harassing lawsuits. Steve made a big fuss about the ambiguity concerning the number of shares in the voting trust, he demanded that Morris and Ruth Broad endorse Shepard's note guaranteeing the four-payment buy out, and he raised several technical legal points.

At the December 28 board meeting, attended by the same ten directors who were present on December 21, Marvin was replaced by Morris Broad as chairman of the board and CEO. Cooper and Mahoney took the places of Warner and Ewton on the executive committee, and lower level management changes were also made.

Marvin counterattacked in a letter of December 31 to Shepard in which he challenged Shepard's election to be the buyer rather than the seller. Its message came through clearly:

On December 21st, after learning of your election, and again on December 24, 1984, I wrote to you regarding unresolved issues and asked for immediate written response to determine whether your election was valid. . . . I have received no such responses.

Based upon your course of conduct, it is apparent that your election was a counter-offer and, as such, is invalid. Consequently, under paragraph 11A.(2) of the Voting Trust Agreement, you are conclusively deemed to have agreed to sell the Broad shares to me.

I intend to purchase the shares of American Savings set forth on Exhibit A of my Notice dated October 26, 1984. . . .

Please submit your resignation and Morris' as directors of American Savings immediately as required by the Notice.

The Warner-Arky counterattack continued into the new year.

Within days, Shepard and his lawyers were able to conclude that Marvin's charges had no real merit. Shepard decided, however, that he did not want to be harassed any further by Steve and Marvin. He would get rid of them at once. Instead of paying Marvin on an installment basis over three years, he would give him the $26 million in a single payment.

Marvin received the money on January 10, 1985. He did not discover until the next day that it had come from American and not from Shepard. He had made a profit of $12.4 million, but that was small compensation for the prize he had lost. If he had been able to put American and Freedom together, he would have had $5 billion in assets to work with. You could solve a lot of problems with $5 billion, and Marvin must have felt that 1985 would present its share of problems.

8

The First Domino Falls

Ronnie Ewton mulled over the bad news as he drove to Jose Gomez's office on Friday, December 21, 1984. The previous day, Shepard Broad had pulled American from Marvin Warner's grasp, and by doing so had dashed Ronnie's last hopes for ESM. It was a crushing defeat. Ronnie had to know that, without the help of American and its piles of securities, ESM was doomed. Broad's brilliant strategic move, coming so soon after Alan Novick's death, had sealed the company's fate.

Ronnie went to see Jose to get a clear and current picture of ESM's financial plight. Gomez spent more than an hour detailing the losses, which he put at about $180 million. This estimate proved to be more than $100 million short because Jose, at that time, had not understood all the nuances of Alan Novick's obfuscating techniques.

Jose told Ronnie that he had been thinking about ESM's problems and had come up with a plan which he thought could save the company. It involved obtaining perhaps $50 million in fresh capital, stretching out payments on ESM's debts for several years, and gradually paying off the debt out of profit. ESM had made money in recent months, and Jose presupposed that this would continue. He thought Marvin Warner would be a good candidate to put up the $50 million, because Marvin had such a big stake in Home State's survival and that appeared now to be dependent on ESM's survival.

Jose's bailout plan was not rosy enough to dispel Ronnie's pessimism, however. When Ewton returned to his office, his first instinct was to call Steve Arky, but he wasn't ready to face Steve with the enormity of ESM's losses. Instead, he called Gil Haddad, a longtime ESM lawyer who had recently won a $3 million judgment for the company. Ronnie gave Haddad no specifics, but he told him that he had problems that might lead to a bankruptcy, and he asked Gil for the name of a good bankruptcy lawyer. Gil said he would get back to him soon.

The next day, Steve and Marlin Arky, their two children, and two of their nephews spent a quiet day at the Ewtons' home with Ronnie, his wife, and their infant son. Ronnie gave no hint to the Arkys that he was struggling with feelings of sadness, shame, defeat. He bantered cheerfully with them and let the day wind down quietly as they sat around the pool in their sweaters in the cool winter sun.

On Monday the twenty-fourth, Haddad told Ronnie that he had found a damned good bankruptcy specialist for him—Bobby Schatzman. He added that Ronnie could probably get a good reference on Bobby from Arky, Freed. Arky, Freed had no bankruptcy department; they had passed several such cases on to Schatzman and had been happy with his work.

Bobby was away for the holidays and Ronnie didn't catch up with him until January 12. They scheduled a meeting for January 14.

When Ronnie was upset, if he wasn't brooding, he was out shopping. ESM's setbacks launched him on a spectacular spending spree. On December 18 he bought a $152,000 Aston Martin Lagonda sports coupe. On December 27 he purchased a couple of polo ponies for $29,000, and bought a boat slip—a kind of condo for a yacht—for $90,000. He gave a New Year's Eve party and decided it had to take place on the water. So he chartered a boat and a crew; it cost him $7,328. And, on January 3, he went and bought his own yacht, a $1.3 million, top-of-the-line Hatteras. He named it "Jerilyn," for his wife.

Ronnie returned from the glittering world of polo ponies and yachts to a much grimmer reality when he met with Schatzman on January 14 and again on January 17. They needed two meetings because the story of ESM and the issues surrounding it were so complex that Schatzman couldn't absorb it all in one session. Ronnie related ESM's history year by year and tried to explain the $180 million loss and the Novick-Gomez scheme to disguise it. And he said that ESM needed fresh funds immediately because Shepard Broad was fast pulling out the working capital that had kept the company alive; if that old shark kept coming after them, within a month they wouldn't be able to meet a payroll.

Ronnie then told Bobby about the Gomez plan to save ESM with Warner's money. Schatzman was skeptical, because he thought the plan represented nothing new, just a way to use Warner's capital to replace the money which Broad was taking back from ESM.

As his understanding of the situation grew, Schatzman saw a need for speed. He urged Ronnie to determine quickly whether Warner was interested in helping. Schatzman was worried about the criminal aspects of the situation. He wasn't sure yet whether crimes were being committed, but if they were, he didn't want to perpetuate them. And he suggested that Ronnie seek criminal counsel.

Ronnie replied that the next logical step was to talk with Steve Arky; Steve was ESM's main lawyer, he understood how its business worked, and he could give them a quick reading on Marvin's state of mind. But then Ronnie became flustered, almost incoherent. He remembers, "The depths and breadths of what we had done, I'm beginning to really come to grips with. I'm having to verbalize it for the first time, actually sit down and say, 'Here's what I did.' He [Schatzman] is looking at it from a legal point of view. . . . He is seeing big-time monsters. I'm having to look at those square in the eyes. The impact of my actions is frightening to me." Ronnie couldn't face the idea of sitting down and telling Steve about the horrendous losses. The fear and the shame were engulfing him.

Schatzman agreed that Ronnie was in no shape to meet with Steve. He suggested that he, Schatzman, meet with Arky and that Ewton should also be represented by Mike Josephs, a partner of Gil Haddad. Josephs knew Arky a lot better than Schatzman did, and Schatzman thought that would make Steve feel more comfortable.

Schatzman, Josephs, and Arky got together at Josephs's office at 5:00 P.M. on Monday, January 21. Schatzman started the meeting by describing how ESM had lost an estimated $180 million and how it was using the securities of Home State, American, and other customers to survive. He recollects, "Steve was speechless. He was shocked. He wasn't prepared to hear any of this, I presume. I then told him that Ron had a plan and I wanted to see if it made sense. I generally talked about the plan, and we both acknowledged that I was correct, that it was perpetuating a problem that couldn't be resolved. I told him that I had recommended Ronnie to criminal counsel and he agreed."

Arky wanted to distance himself immediately from any criminal activity. He announced that, as of that moment, he was resigning as counsel to ESM. It was a good defensive move. By resigning, Steve was insuring that he wouldn't have to relate to others what Schatzman had just told him about skulduggery at ESM. The legal doctrine of attorney-client privilege states that the attorney must remain silent about past crimes revealed to him by his client unless the client releases him from that obligation. However, if he stays on as counsel and the crimes continue, then the attorney is obligated to tell everything. Steve had created a vow of silence about the past and had also immunized himself from anything the ESM crew might do from that time forward. After Steve's announcement, the meeting broke up. It had lasted less than thirty minutes.

Arky was truly shocked by the enormity of the ESM losses and their dire implications for Home State, and he couldn't wait to call Marvin. Steve lived near Josephs's office and within fifteen minutes had driven home. He immediately telephoned Marvin, the first of sixteen calls that night among him, Warner, and Ewton. There were both two-way calls and three-way calls. They consumed five hours.

What was actually said that Monday night is a matter of some dispute. Marvin and Steve claim that, because of the attorney-client privilege doctrine, Arky could not reveal to Marvin the details of ESM's difficulties until he obtained a written release from Ewton. Marvin and Steve have said that the only thing Steve told Marvin was that ESM had problems and that Steve had resigned as counsel.

Ewton says that it was obvious from their conversations that night that Warner knew more than "ESM had problems." He asserts that the $180 million loss estimate had shaken Warner badly, and he claims that his discussion with Marvin went like this:

WARNER: Ron, I've just got off the phone with Steve. I can't believe these numbers. How did this happen?

EWTON: Marvin, the accumulated losses just got larger than life.

WARNER: Do you realize this could be the end of Home State?

EWTON: Yes, I do realize that.

WARNER: What are you going to do? Who have you talked to? Who is this Schatzman?

EWTON: Schatzman is just a friend and a lawyer I did talk to.

WARNER: Don't talk to anyone about this. Nobody. And I want you to get me out. Ron, can you do that? You get me out of my account? Get me out?

EWTON: Marvin, I'll do the best I can.

Warner claims that it was not he, but Ewton, who suggested that Marvin's account be closed. Marvin says that, Ronnie, who was usually a very talkative fellow, was very uncommunicative that night. He didn't want to talk about ESM's losses, his personal situation, anything. Marvin recalls, "It was completely unlike any conversation I had ever had with the gentleman. He was just a completely different individual and I was greatly disturbed."

In the midst of his telephone round-robin with Ewton and Arky, Marvin took time out to call Schiebel. He asked him exactly how Home State stood with ESM. Schiebel recalls, "He was asking me all kinds of questions as it related to ESM and what our dealings were, what our position is, and what we were going to do and what my game plan was, and so forth. And I indicated to him . . . I'll be happy to send you an update of what our position is. And somewhere in the conversation, I asked Mr. Warner, 'Is there something that you know about ESM that I don't know?' And then Mr. Warner replied, 'Not really.' "

The next day Schatzman took Ewton to meet with a criminal lawyer, Jay Hogan, and the three men agreed that Hogan would deal with Ronnie's criminal problems while Schatzman would continue to handle the bankruptcy issues. Hogan told Ewton that the first thing he must do is resign from ESM.

Marvin kept calling Ronnie. Ronnie's version is that Marvin wanted him to stay on at ESM, keep his mouth shut, and try to solve the problems. Marvin says that he was trying valiantly to coax more details about the ESM mess from Ronnie and that Ronnie kept stonewalling him.

On Wednesday, January 23, Schatzman called Arky and told him that Hogan had taken Ewton's case, that Ewton was resigning from ESM, and that George Mead, who was knowledgeable about the ESM losses, was going to replace Ronnie. Schatzman said there was a problem with Hogan: one of Hogan's partners, Evelyn Greer, was married to one of Arky's partners, Bruce Greer. Schatzman wanted Arky to tell Bruce immediately, because he wished to eliminate the possibility that Evelyn would reveal anything to Bruce about Ewton's situation.

Arky tried to stall. He said that Marvin wanted a chance to help Ronnie solve ESM's problems; he didn't want to talk to Bruce Greer while there was still a possibility that Marvin and Ronnie could work things out. Schatzman told him that delay was unacceptable, that Arky must speak to Greer immediately. Besides, Marvin wouldn't be able to deal with Ronnie anyway, because Ronnie was definitely resigning from ESM. Marvin would have to work with George Mead in the future.

Schatzman told Ewton what Arky had said, and Ronnie called Mead and told him that he had to meet with Warner about the bailout plan because Ronnie and Warner couldn't communicate anymore. Ronnie suggested that Mead talk first with Gomez to make sure he had a good grasp of all the numbers. He also told George to close out Warner's account.

Ewton walked into Mead's office on Friday, January 25 at 9:00 A.M. and surprised George by handing him his resignation letter. While the two men were chatting, Marvin called and asked to speak to Ronnie. Ronnie said "You're in charge now, George. You better take care of him. You might need him." He dropped the keys to his company car on Mead's desk and left.

Mead arranged to meet Warner the following day at Marvin's ocean-side condominium in the Kenilworth Apartments at Bal Harbour, a Miami Beach community just across the bridge from Shepard Broad's Bay Harbor Islands. Then George got together with Gomez to go over the numbers for the next day's meeting. Jose still hadn't gotten the details right; this time he estimated the losses at $256 million.

George arrived on Saturday at midmorning. Working from a spreadsheet prepared by Gomez, he went through the litany of ESM's problems leading up to its current $256 million deficit. Then he tried to reassure Marvin by saying, "That was in the past. Things are changing for the better." He painted a glowing picture of the company's current and future profitability. He concluded by saying that he was looking for a friend who could help with a major investment which would put ESM back on its feet again. He had been speaking for an hour and a half.

Marvin replied that he would always be George's friend. He couldn't say that about Ewton and Novick, though. He asked George plaintively, "How could they do this to me? Home State is in jeopardy and if it goes down, the entire Ohio banking system could be hurt."

Then Warner addressed the question of investing in ESM. He just couldn't buy the idea—first, it didn't look like a good deal, and, second, it might involve him in some kind of conspiracy. According to George, Marvin was so cautious about the conspiracy element that, although he read the Gomez spread sheet, he wouldn't pick it up. Fingerprints can be powerful evidence at a criminal trial. Marvin denies that Mead even showed him the spread sheet.

Next on George's agenda was closing Marvin's ESM account, and they cleared up a final detail about transferring money. Mead closed out the account the next working day, Monday, January 28, and wired the $4,885,990 proceeds to Warner; $300,000 was profit.

Marvin became restless and he led George outside past the pool, onto the beach, and to a nearby restaurant for lunch. There he focused on Gomez's knowledge of the situation and on the progress Jose was making with his audit of ESM's 1984 year. He asked Mead if the numbers on the 1984 statement would be similar to those for 1983, which reflected a profit of $4.3 million and a net worth of $29.7 million, and George said yes.

Marvin ended the conversation by asking Mead to meet with David Schiebel in Cincinnati once a draft of the 1984 audit statement was ready. According to George, Marvin suggested he not tell Schiebel of the huge losses which the statement so effectively covered up. Marvin has said he made this suggestion, because he felt Mead was so new to the financial details of the CEO job at ESM that he should discuss only final certified audited figures with outsiders.

Once he had concluded that it was folly to deal with the crisis by investing in ESM, Marvin's actions reflected a simple, clear-cut strategy—pin as much blame as possible for any impending Home State problems on Grant. If Grant had committed fraud by deceiving Home State and other ESM customers with phony audits, he reasoned, then Grant would be vulnerable to lawsuits brought by the deceived customers.

Marvin instructed Schiebel to conduct an all-out blitz to get the 1984 audit from Gomez and Mead. During the next two weeks, David harassed them daily with phone calls. Finally, on February 12, Mead came to Cincinnati with a draft version of the audit. He reviewed it in some detail with Schiebel and assured him that the final certified version, which he expected to deliver by the end of the month, would not differ significantly from the draft.

Marvin Warner revered the legal and business judgment of Clark Hodgson, an old associate and a partner in the Philadelphia law firm of Stradley, Ronan, Stevens, and Young. He thought so highly of Clark that he had named him one of the seven Warner directors on the board of American Savings & Loan. Marvin wanted Hodgson by his side as the ESM–Home State crisis ripened, and arranged for Clark to come to Warnerton on Wednesday, February 15, for an all-day strategy meeting.

When Hodgson arrived that morning, Warner immediately ushered him into a small downstairs study, and after about thirty seconds of pleasantries, got down to business. As Hodgson recalls, "Marvin was more concerned than I had ever seen him. He spoke with an intensity in his voice that left me transfixed. I felt that what Marvin was telling me was so important to him that I shouldn't even take notes, because by doing that I might break his concentration or give the impression that I was not listening as intensely as he was talking."

Marvin started by saying that he might be in the worst crisis of his life, and then went over the whole, sad ESM chronology. He told Clark that after the January 26 meeting with Mead, he had concluded that if Home State could get the certified audit from Grant, its exposure would be greatly lessened and it would have a strong claim against Grant. Hodgson thought that the issues were much more complex than that, but he agreed that it was good strategy to press hard for the certified audit. Possession of the audit wouldn't solve all of Home State's problems, but it would strengthen its hand considerably.

Marvin said that once he got hold of the audit he would immediately sever all ESM–Home State ties. Home State would close out its business with ESM and let the chips fall where they may. Hodgson agreed that this would be Home State's best option.

Then he addressed the issue of disclosure. Marvin had knowledge that could seriously affect the lives of Home State's ninety-two thousand depositors and those of ESM's other customers, and Clark believed that Warner could not legally keep that knowledge to himself. Marvin didn't want anything to interfere with getting that audit. He was afraid that disclosure would scare Gomez so badly that Jose would not issue the document. Marvin rationalized that any disclosure before receipt of the certified audit was based only on conjecture; besides, it might lead to an unnecessary panic run on Home State which "could blow the entire Ohio banking system."

Hodgson disagreed. He argued that at the very least Warner must talk to David Schiebel, as CEO of Home State. He advised Warner not to tell Schiebel everything he knew, but to say that the Grant audit was suspect and that ESM had financial difficulties which might result in big losses for Home State.

Schiebel was then summoned to Warnerton to join the meeting. Marvin told David what Hodgson had suggested he say, and then Clark advised Schiebel to disclose his knowledge only to directors of Home State who were not employees of the company. Employees must be told nothing, because knowledge on their part would inevitably lead to leaks and rumors and that could generate a panic.

In the days following, Schiebel kept prodding Mead. "George," he said, "I'm getting tired of this. I'm your biggest customer and you owe me that audit. I'm not asking for it; I'm demanding it." Mead was shaken, more by Schiebel's tone than by what he said. There was a hard aggressiveness in David's voice. Home State, ESM's old friend and ally, seemed to be turning hostile.

George was being worn down. One moment it was Schiebel demanding that damned audit. Next, it was Broad hounding him to return those Treasury notes. In January alone, Shepard had pulled $20 million out of ESM's coffers. He was bleeding ESM to death. George knew he was only a salesman, not a financial wizard like Novick who could create cash out of thin air. He concluded that he couldn't handle this alone.

Like Ronnie Ewton before him, George turned to Gil Haddad for help. He said he wanted to speak to a criminal lawyer, and Gil recommended Bill Cagney. Cagney is a criminal lawyer of the old school; a pugnacious product of Chicago's streets, he is a master of the dramatic gesture, the disarming question, the piercing aside.

On Friday, February 22, Mead told Schiebel he would have the certified audit on Thursday, February 28. Schiebel replied that he wanted to fly down to Florida to pick it up and to discuss future business relationships between ESM and Home State.

After his conversation with David, Mead called Cagney and asked for a meeting. Cagney suggested that Mead come over to his office, but George said "I can't do that. I don't want to be seen with a criminal lawyer. Meet me in the Howard Johnson parking lot off Route 95 in North Miami. I'll be sitting in a dark green, four-door Jaguar. You can't miss it."

Cagney spotted the Jaguar in the parking lot and tapped on the window. George told him to get in. Then he drove the two of them around North Miami and North Miami Beach for an hour and a half. He told Cagney that he needed advice for "a friend" who was in trouble in the securities business. To Cagney this was old hat; "a friend" was usually the initial subject of such conversations. At first Cagney was confused by the technical phrases and the welter of detail which George threw at him, but he eventually figured out that, one, there was a large imbalance between ESM's credits and debits, and two, ESM could continue to survive only if it could hold on to a big bundle of its customers' securities.

When he dropped him back at the Howard Johnson, Mead told Cagney he would be in touch with him soon and asked him to present a bill for the afternoon's work.

On the night of February 27, Schiebel, Hodgson, and Hodgson's partner, Don Collins, flew in to Fort Lauderdale.

Schiebel met with Mead at ESM late in the morning of February 28 while Hodgson and Collins remained at their hotel. Mead gave Schiebel the grail he had been pursuing for those many weeks, a copy of the Grant certified audit. George expected Schiebel to be elated, but the only response he got from David was a series of questions about specific numbers in the audit. George said that he didn't know anything about accounting and referred David to Gomez.

Schiebel telephoned Jose and asked his questions. He zeroed in sharply on the footnote which shuffled ESM's losses over to its affiliate. This disturbed Gomez greatly. He remembers, "I concluded that if Mr. Schiebel had the financial statement draft . . . since February 15, the draft delivered to Home State officials up in Ohio, if Mr. Schiebel waited fifteen days to ask me that . . . he was doing so because he was aware of the condition of ESM, and that he was merely waiting for the signed report to be delivered to him and he was trying to set up some kind of a law suit." Gomez couldn't work for the rest of the day. His thoughts were continually fragmented by the anxiety which Schiebel had triggered.

After Schiebel got off the telephone, he told Mead that a couple of Home State lawyers were in town, and he wanted George to meet them. He called Hodgson and Collins at the hotel, and they came over immediately.

The four men sat down in George's office and Schiebel told Mead that he wanted to close out all Home State transactions that day. Mead turned pale. Hodgson recalls, "He was tense, concerned, surprised. He did not know us, that is Collins and myself, did not know why we were there. He obviously thought that the report would allay our fears; it did not. We wanted to test the report by seeing if Mead could unwind these transactions."

George said that it would be impossible to unwind the transactions quickly. Home State was involved in complex deals at ESM and undoing them would take some time. He said he would do the best he could, would study the matter overnight, and would meet with them again the next morning. Collins and Schiebel said they would be there; Hodgson had to fly back to Philadelphia that night.

George called Gomez as soon as his three visitors left and told him about the demand to close out Home State's account immediately. For Jose, that was it. ESM couldn't survive Home State retrieving its $145 million. The game was over. He told George he was pulling the audit, and he was going to tell his partners of his seven-year cover-up.

He had given George twenty-four copies of the audit the previous day, and he wanted them all back. George only had twenty-three because Schiebel and his cohorts had walked off with one. Late in the afternoon, Jose drove over to ESM and retrieved the twenty-three copies.

Mead then called Cagney. His voice trembled in panic. He said, "I've got to see you right away. How soon can we meet?" Cagney replied that he could meet with Mead that evening, but didn't feel comfortable about going it alone, because he didn't know enough about securities. He said, "Let me phone a friend of mine who knows a lot about your kind of business. His name is Tom Tew."

After a flurry of phone calls, it was agreed that Tew and Cagney would drive up to Fort Lauderdale after work to meet with Mead and with Nick Wallace, the other principal ESM officer. Wallace knew very little about Mead's travails of the previous weeks and did little more than listen that night.

Mead told Cagney and Tew about his traumatic day and the events leading up to it. He said, "This has been the worst day of my life. I'm exhausted, totally beat, and I'm way over my head; I've got to rely on you guys to guide me. I won't hold anything back. You can look at all our records." He asked them to represent ESM and him and Wallace legally and said he would wire $2 million to Cagney the next morning; $1 million would be held in an escrow account for contingencies and Cagney and Tew would each get $500,000 as a retainer. The two lawyers accepted the assignment.

The next morning Gomez called Schiebel and asked him to return his copy of the ESM audit, the twenty-fourth copy. Gomez said he wanted it back because "it could no longer be relied upon." Schiebel refused. He wanted to keep the document as evidence for subsequent legal struggles.

After his confrontation with Gomez, Schiebel called Mead, and George said that he did not want to speak with David about the withdrawal of the audit. He wanted to be cooperative, however; he referred David to his newly retained securities lawyer, Tom Tew. Schiebel and Collins drove down to Miami and met with Tew at his offices shortly before noon.

Tew told them that he had only been on the case since the previous evening and was doing his best to come up to speed. Because George Mead had assured him that all of ESM's records would be available to him, he felt that their next step should be to examine those records to determine why Grant had pulled the audit.

He didn't want to do that alone, however. He needed expert accounting help. The sharpest accountant he had ever worked with was Laurie Holtz, who ran a small firm in South Miami. He suggested to Schiebel and Collins that the three of them meet with Laurie and ask him whether he could take on an immediate investigative assignment. Tom placed a call to Holtz, and Laurie's secretary said Laurie was out for the day, but she thought she could reach him. Tew told her to try very hard, because the matter he had to discuss with Laurie was urgent.

This was the beginning of the end for ESM. The weekend would bring its swift demise. The company had dodged many bullets. Those fired by Lou Frank; the SEC and Charlie Harper; Hugh Culverhouse, Jr.; June Seneca; Pete Summers; Unity Bank and Savings; Sylvester Hentschel; Lion Capital. But finally, it couldn't elude the one fired by the patriarch of Bay Harbor Islands, old Shepard Broad.

The collapse of ESM caused pain and hardship to its clients throughout the U.S., from Washington and Nevada to Texas to Pennsylvania. Nowhere was the hurt more severe than in the state of Ohio.

9

Devastation in Ohio

Marvin Warner, dressed casually in an open shirt and slacks, was grim as he talked with the group in his second floor study at Warnerton on the morning of Saturday, March 2, 1985. The men sipped their coffee and nibbled on their sweet rolls as they sat glumly awaiting the word from Don Collins in Fort Lauderdale. Their meeting had been arranged after David Schiebel and Collins had received the ominous news the day before that Alexander Grant had withdrawn its 1984 ESM audit. They understood that if ESM had serious trouble, there could be disaster for Home State.

Seven men had joined Marvin at the farm. Five were from the Cincinnati area: Schiebel; Nelson Schwab (a Home State director and long-time Home State lawyer); a law partner of Schwab; a partner from Arthur Andersen (Home State's auditors); and Home State's in-house attorney. Two—Don Collins's law partner Clark Hodgson and an associate—had flown in from their home base in Philadelphia.

Collins called early in the afternoon and told the group that ESM was hopelessly insolvent and that losses could total $300 million; the investigating accountants in Fort Lauderdale had made their determination in less than two hours, and felt very confident about their conclusions.

Collins didn't know if Home State could lose its entire $145 million excess collateral, some portion of it, or none at all. It depended on whether ESM had consumed the collateral to cover its own losses or had segregated it for Home State at a custodian bank. Since Home State's assets represented roughly half the losses, it was likely that ESM had used them for its own purposes. But there was an outside chance that the collateral was segregated. Since the custodian bank was closed for the weekend, no definite determination could be made until Monday.

Collins also reported that Tew and Holtz were almost positive that Gomez had been bribed and that this was the likely explanation for the Grant audit withdrawal. This news made Warner insist that immediate action be taken against Grant, and he instructed Hodgson to have his firm prepare charges at once.

Hodgson felt that Home State's situation was so explosive that it dictated that someone should meet immediately with officials of the Ohio Deposit Guarantee Fund (ODGF), the private cooperative which insured Home State's deposits.

Warner agreed and had Nelson Schwab call Donald Hunsche, executive vice president of ODGF. Schwab arranged for Warner, Schiebel, and himself to meet that afternoon with Hunsche and ODGF's lawyer at the private Queen City businessmen's club in downtown Cincinnati. Hunsche remembers the meeting:

> At approximately 4:15 in the afternoon, the Fund became aware for the first time of a potential problem at ESM and a potential resulting problem with a loss at Home State.
>
> At that time, Mr. Schiebel . . . advised us that he was concerned because the audit report prepared by Alexander Grant & Co., the auditors of ESM, had been withdrawn on Friday, March 1, approximately twenty-four hours after it was delivered to him. . . . We were also told that the withdrawal of the auditor's opinion caused Mr. Schiebel to engage legal counsel, whom he authorized to institute an immediate investigation of ESM.
>
> We were advised that Home State still had repurchase relationships with ESM and that they were substantially over-collateralized. We responded by requesting that the ODGF be kept fully advised of the results of the investigation Home State had undertaken in Florida.

The Home State people left Hunsche with the impression that the likelihood of Home State losses was small, because they expressed a high expectation that the bank's collateral was segregated for it at a custodian bank. Even though Home State was ODGF's largest member, Hunsche felt secure.

In the early 1980s, almost 99 percent of all savings and loan institution deposits were insured by the federal government through the Federal Savings and Loan Insurance Corporation (FSLIC). This was not true, however, for deposits at Home State and sixty-eight other thrifts in southern Ohio. Ohio was one of only five states which allowed thrifts to opt out of the FSLIC system. There were several reasons why the southern Ohio S&Ls banded together in 1955 in a cooperative deposit insurance venture.

Most importantly to the owners of the banks, the state system forced them to tie up less capital in their S&Ls. FSLIC demanded that an owner's capital be 5 percent of deposits, whereas ODGF asked for only 3 percent.

In addition, FSLIC required more detailed reporting than did ODGF, and ODGF's regulations were less stringent. For instance, FSLIC had imposed a 5.5 percent ceiling on passbook account interest; ODGF had none, and this gave its banks a competitive advantage.

Further, an ODGF member pledged 2 percent of its deposits to the fund, but was allowed to keep the 2 percent on its books as an asset. FSLIC required that a member pay an annual premium, which became an item of expense and reduced profits.

Finally, in a bold competitive move, ODGF insured deposits of whatever size. FSLIC's insurance stopped at $100,000 per depositor per institution.

The huge and essential difference between FSLIC and ODGF insurance was that, while FSLIC's resources were basically unlimited because of congressional guarantees, ODGF's were limited to 2 percent of the members' deposits. At the time of the Home State crisis, the 2 percent represented only $136 million. Congress has pledged to stand forever behind FSLIC and in 1989 must come up with roughly $100 billion to replenish FSLIC's resources after the massive savings and loan bankruptcies of recent years. Such action cements the faith of federally insured depositors that their government will cover them up to $100,000 at each institution where they leave their money; ODGF depositors had no such guarantee.

When Warner, Schiebel, and Schwab returned that afternoon to the group at Warnerton, it was decided to dispatch Hodgson to Fort Lauderdale to work with Collins, Tew, and Holtz to determine quickly what Home State's true losses were.

Hodgson arrived at ESM around noon on Sunday and met Tom Tew for the first time. Tew gave Hodgson and Collins complete freedom to research the paper trail left by Home State's collateral, which amounted to $815 million against borrowings of $670 million. They spent the entire afternoon doing this because they wanted to be thoroughly prepared for their principal task the next morning: making the proper investigative phone calls so that they could quantify Home State's position with maximum accuracy. Hodgson spoke several times during the afternoon to Marvin's wife Jody at Warnerton and to executives at Home State headquarters to report on his investigations.

Late in the day, Hodgson had a discussion with Tew which greatly disturbed Hodgson. Tew told him something that Warner had never revealed to him: Warner had had a profitable private account at ESM which had been closed only five weeks previously, on January 28.

This information presented Hodgson with a serious problem. He was representing both Warner and Home State, and now he saw a potential conflict between his two clients. Home State and its depositors, with their huge possible losses, might have a strong claim against Marvin because of his personal benefits from his ESM account. Marvin's situation was further compromised by another fact which Tew had revealed to Hodgson: son-in-law Steve Arky had had an ESM account which had also been closed the previous January.

At 8:00 P.M., Hodgson made a call to Warner in Cincinnati. Listening in at Marvin's end were Schiebel, Schwab, and another Home State lawyer. Hodgson remembers he told Warner that he had learned that Marvin had an account which was closed in January, and that Steve Arky was in the same position. And these events led Hodgson to conclude that he and Warner had a possible conflict.

Hodgson also recollects:

> The general message was that we were facing a major financial tragedy, that it would be necessary for me to resign as his counsel, that that resignation was based upon . . . A) there was some chance that Home State might have claims against Mr. Warner individually . . . if there was a conflict and 2) even if there wasn't a conflict, that this financial tragedy was likely to have very visible public perceptions and outcry and that the public would demand a thorough investigation from someone who was probably viewed as more independent than I. . . .
>
> He was unhappy and disagreed with my conclusion, thought it was unnecessary, and had a number of people on the phone who essentially sang the same tune to me.

Hodgson stuck to his guns about resigning as Marvin's lawyer. Then he said that he felt he should continue to represent Home State for at least the next few days, because they were going to be so critical for the institution. Warner agreed, and they discussed what kind of a press release Home State might issue the next day. There followed several more conference calls about the release, the last one ending at 2:00 A.M. Hodgson recalls, "We didn't reach agreement on what should be said, if anything, and I think we just decided we would wait until the events of the following day, Monday, to see really where we stood." They were hoping against hope that Home State would not be a loser in the ESM debacle.

While Hodgson was resigning as Warner's lawyer, Morris Broad was in another room at ESM surveying the probable damage to American Savings & Loan, and thinking about the wording of the statement he would issue to the media. Although his collateral of roughly $60 million was in exactly the same boat as Home State's, he was not thinking as wishfully as Warner and his crew. He believed there was a high probability that American's $60 million was lost, and he was going to state this when he put out his press release the first thing the next morning.

On Sunday, March 3, at 10:00 P.M. Tew sent telegrams to all of ESM's customers announcing that the firm was closing down. He finished his work that evening by writing the press release he would distribute at 8:00 A.M. the next day. It ended with the words, "ESM is unable to meet its financial obligations to its customers as they mature. ESM has terminated operations on the advice of its special counsel and will not open for business on Monday, March 4, 1985."

Donald Hunsche, the ODGF official who had bought Home State's optimistic appraisal of its loss exposure, thought it might be a good idea to apprise Tom Batties, the acting superintendent of Ohio's savings and loan division, of the situation. He called Batties at 11:00 P.M. on Sunday—more than twenty-four hours after his meeting with the Home State people. Batties reports, "Hunsche told me . . . that as a result of ESM's failure, they could be impaired for the entire amount of their overcollateralization, which was more than $100 million." But Batties was not alarmed, because Hunsche explained to him that he expected Home State's collateral was segregated for it at a custodian bank, and losses would be minimal.

The first thing Monday morning, Batties called his boss Kenneth Cox, director of the Ohio Department of Commerce, to tell him about his conversation with Hunsche. It was Cox's first day on the job. He had been Ohio's highway safety director and was only appointed to his Commerce position the previous Friday, March 1. He was not disturbed by Batties' news. He recalls, "From my inexperience on that first day, I did not remember being alarmed. I probably was truly not aware of the significance of it. To be honest about it, I simply acknowledged it and didn't give it much thought. I don't know that I had any conversation with anybody other than Tom (Batties)." Cox saw no reason to call his boss, Governor Richard F. Celeste.

Hodgson and Collins went to Tew's office on Monday morning and

Alan Novick, mastermind
of the ESM scam, who
died at his desk before
the fraud was discovered.

Ronnie Ewton in elegant
suit and handcuffs arriving
in court to face justice.
(Charlie Trainor/
Miami Herald)

The modest office building in Fort Lauderdale where the ESM gang
pulled off its $300 million scam.

Jose Gomez, the Alexander Grant accounting partner who covered the ESM fraud for seven years, leaving a court hearing. Gomez is currently serving a twelve-year sentence in federal prison.
(AP/Wide World Photos)

ESM cofounder George Mead leaving Fort Lauderdale federal court after he was sentenced to fourteen years in prison for his part in the ESM fraud.
(AP/Wide World Photos)

Steve Arky, the fiercely competitive lawyer who represented ESM and who introduced his father-in-law, Marvin Warner, to the ESM gang. Arky shot himself to death in July 1985 in despair over the ESM debacle and other personal troubles.
(Review Publications Inc.)

Marvin Warner in front of the
fireplace at Warnerton, his estate
and horse farm outside of
Cincinnati. This photo was taken
in early 1983, when Warner was
in the midst of a string of highly
profitable bank deals.
(Terry Drymon)

Shepard Broad, the wily real estate
and banking tycoon who smelled
a rat at ESM and caused its collapse
by demanding the return of
$108 million in collateral that his
bank had left with the ESM gang.

Bay Harbor Islands, the highly prosperous community
that Shepard Broad created in the late 1940s from a
mangrove swamp in Biscayne Bay, Florida.

A cast-iron jockey painted in Marvin Warner's red and white racing colors, standing guard in front of Warnerton Farm outside of Cincinnati. (Terry Drymon)

Ronnie Ewton's seventy-foot, $1.3 million yacht, which he named for his wife, Jerilyn. (Terry Renna/*New York Times*)

Tom Tew, the Miami lawyer who was originally hired by ESM and who became the federal trustee in ESM's bankruptcy. He won very handsome recoveries for the victims of the fraud.
(Roger Richards/*Miami Review*)

Laurie Holtz (right) and his partner, Jack Goldstrich, standing in a sea of ESM files. Laurie, the head of Holtz & Co., played a vital role in deciphering the complex fraud, helping Tom Tew recover more than $200 million for its victims. (Michael Germana/*Miami Review*)

The crowd of depositors outside Molitor Loan in the Cincinnati suburbs in the early morning of March 15, 1985. They are listening to bank officials telling them that Ohio Governor Richard Celeste has closed Molitor and sixty-seven other member banks of the Ohio Deposit Guarantee Fund (ODGF). (UPI/Bettmann Newsphotos)

Governor Richard Celeste during a press conference at the height of the Ohio banking crisis on March 19, 1985. (AP/Wide World Photos)

Lisa Neidich, Home State "Skirt Squad" member, wears a "Victims of Trust" T-shirt as she exhorts fellow depositors before boarding a bus to travel to a rally at the state capitol in Columbus on April 2, 1985. (AP/Wide World Photos)

Home State depositors during the mass organizing meeting at the Xavier University field house on March 24, 1985. Mary Lou Dysinger, a depositor from Tipp City, Ohio, holds a sign clearly stating her point of view. (AP/Wide World Photos)

Marvin Warner is an intensely interested spectator on November 17, 1986, as jury selection begins in his Cincinnati criminal trial.
(UPI/Bettmann Newsphotos)

Burt Bongard, former Home State Savings Bank president and confessed conspirator in the ESM fraud, being escorted in chains from the Ann Arbor, Michigan, federal court house after being sentenced to ten years in prison.
(AP/Wide World Photos)

David Schiebel, former Home State Savings Bank president, pictured during the Cincinnati trial where he was a codefendant with Marvin Warner and Burt Bongard. Schiebel was convicted on three securities fraud counts.

Marvin Warner leaving federal court in Fort Lauderdale on July 7, 1988, after losing a $22.7 million dollar verdict to Tom Tew. To the left behind Warner is his attorney, Andy Hall, and to the right is Marvin's son, Mark. (*Miami Herald*)

worked with Tew's staff trying to locate Home State's collateral. Their search was fruitless. ESM's records indicated that some of Home State's collateral might have been lent to other ESM customers. They called these customers and discovered that they were not borrowers and did not possess any of the securities.

Tom Tew called ESM's two custodian banks, Bradford and Security Pacific. He was dismayed to learn that the banks had liquidated $42 million and $12 million in securities, respectively, immediately upon reading his and Broad's press releases as they came across the New York Stock Exchange ticker tape machine. This represented assets held for ESM in ESM's own accounts; none of these securities were segregated for ESM customers. Bradford kept $39 million, which paid off a loan it had made to ESM, and handed over the remaining $3 million to Tew as receiver. Subsequently, it transferred to the receivership $10 million in ESM securities which it had not liquidated that day, making a total of $13 million. Security Pacific later gave Tew its full $12 million, so he recovered $25 million from the two custodian banks.

Tew had no way of knowing at that time whether Bradford's $39 million claim was valid, but he did know that the maximum amount available at the two custodians was $64 million and that none of it was segregated for specific ESM customers. He passed this information on to Hodgson and Collins.

The $25 million which was recovered from the custodians went into a pot which was later divided up among all of ESM's valid creditors. It is a paltry figure compared to the $300 million in segregated funds which the Home State directors had hoped to find at the custodians.

Hodgson remembers:

> Very early on in that day, maybe by noontime, we realized . . . that the collateral was not segregated . . . , and we concluded that in all probability Home State was going to sustain a massive loss.
>
> We informed Mr. Schiebel . . . and maybe other officials, and we had to recognize at that point that Home State had some additional disclosure obligations. . . . There were questions in our mind as to whether or not the bank would be permitted to open under Ohio law since it was clear that it was going to be insolvent.

Hodgson then placed a conference call to Home State's Board of Directors. He told them:

In my opinion, they should no longer take any instructions from Mr.
Warner. They should consider their duties were to the depositors and no
longer to the shareholders.

I thought that Mr. Warner's interests might be inconsistent with the
interest of a depositor, and I couldn't take the risk that they weren't. And
I thought the safest course of action was to advise them to make
decisions independent of Mr. Warner.

The board, which had worked so closely with Warner for years, was at
first stunned by this advice. But after Hodgson stubbornly insisted on
its correctness, they agreed to follow it.

Even though Hodgson had told them it was clear that Home State
was headed for insolvency, the directors could not bring themselves to
disclose its plight. Putting their heads in the sand, they informed
neither ODGF nor the state officials, and they did not issue a press
release.

It was business as usual on Monday at Home State's thirty-three
branches in the metropolitan Cincinnati area, Columbus, and Dayton. Only two minor defensive measures were taken. Executives called
the Federal Reserve Bank in Cleveland concerning conditions for an
emergency loan from them; and employees at Home State's headquarters were told late in the afternoon that there would be "a lot of flak"
about potential losses in the next day's newspapers. They were advised, "If you should hear anything, just tell people not to panic."

During the afternoon, Charlie Harper of the SEC decided that he
wanted Tom Tew as receiver to represent the interests of those defrauded by ESM. Hodgson spoke to Warner about this. Warner
checked with Steve Arky and told Hodgson that Steve felt Tew would
be the wrong choice and that he, Warner, agreed.

Hodgson replied that he would support Tew anyway, because he
was convinced by Harper's arguments that Tew would be the most
effective guardian of the Home State depositors in this disastrous
situation. When Hodgson and Collins accompanied Harper to federal
court where Harper asked Judge Hoeveler to appoint Tew as receiver,
the two lawyers, as representatives of Home State, backed Harper's
request.

As Monday wore on, Warner grew increasingly nervous about the
situation in Florida. In midafternoon he, Jody, and one of Home
State's lawyers boarded the Sabre jet and flew to Miami. They met
with Hodgson in the early evening. Hodgson was disturbed that

Home State had as yet made no disclosure of the day's terrible news, and he insisted that a press release be issued. There was another conference call; the four from Florida were on one end and the Home State directors were on the other.

After acceding to Hodgson's request to tone down a glowing description of Home State's assets, the directors wrote a release which fudged the issue of Home State's losses. It quoted Schiebel as follows:

> Home State had borrowed approximately $670 million from ESM, using government securities of greater value as collateral. Home State is determining the full value of the securities and the loss would be the difference between this value and the $670 million borrowed.
> We anticipate that a loss on the ESM matter is possible, but we have substantial liquidity and Home State's deposits are guaranteed by the Ohio Deposit Guarantee Fund.

Perhaps it was wishful thinking. Perhaps the directors wanted more time to plan. In any case, they did a disservice to their depositors, the public at large, and the officials of both ODGF and the state of Ohio by creating a false feeling of confidence. They could have made a clean breast of it, and said, "It is likely that we have lost $145 million and we are hopelessly broke because our net worth is just $20 million. In addition, our potential $125 million shortfall could almost wipe out ODGF, whose assets are only $136 million." Then everyone concerned could have gone immediately to work to attack the crisis. Instead, it was left to fester.

Hodgson, who was so convinced that Home State was broke that he questioned whether it should continue to accept deposits, felt that his usefulness to the bank had come to an end. He decided that he would fly to Cincinnati the next day to resign as counsel after making a final report to the directors.

Cincinnati has two major newspapers: the *Enquirer*, which publishes only in the morning, and the *Post*, which has both morning and afternoon editions.

The *Enquirer* carried a story about ESM's $300 million collapse and merely indicated that Home State was one of its customers. The *Post* used Schiebel's quote from the press release in its Tuesday afternoon edition.

The contrast between Home State's vague public stance regarding ESM losses and the more candid position taken by American can be seen in a *Miami Herald* report on Tuesday morning:

> America Savings and Loan revealed that it could lose as much as $60 million from a soured deal with ESM. "The loss will be very substantial, but we will meet our regulatory requirements," said Morris M. Broad, Chairman and Chief Executive Officer.

In response to the news that American would probably lose $60 million of its $155 million net worth, its stock plummeted 32 percent that Monday on the New York Stock Exchange.

The *Wall Street Journal* and the *New York Times* ran extensive articles on Tuesday about the ESM collapse. Each reported substantial losses for American Savings & Loan, and neither mentioned Home State.

On Tuesday morning, all the Cincinnati-area Home State branch managers were brought into corporate headquarters for a talk by Schiebel, and the Dayton and Columbus managers were hooked in via a telephone conference call. Schiebel told them that they should be prepared for a run of customer withdrawals and that arrangements were being made for emergency cash shipments from the Federal Reserve Bank branch in Cincinnati.

Dozens of nervous customers closed out their accounts, but a classic panic run did not materialize on Tuesday. Batties made a reassuring statement, and Schiebel continued to claim that he could not determine Home State's losses. He was telling the public this while Hodgson was reporting to him that, try as they might, they could find no evidence anywhere that Home State would ever see the $145 million in securities it had dropped at ESM.

Hodgson was back in Cincinnati by Tuesday evening. He reported his grim findings to Home State's board, resigned, and returned to Philadelphia the next morning. As Hodgson was leaving, Home State started to concern Ohio's governor, Richard Celeste.

Celeste, born in 1937, was one of the golden young men of American politics in the 1970s and 1980s. A Yale Rhodes scholar, he served in the Peace Corps and was then an Ohio legislator from 1970 to 1974. He was elected lieutenant governor in 1974 and directed President Carter's Peace Corps in 1979 and 1980. Running for governor in 1982, he won a landslide victory and, as the forty-five-year-old chief executive of a major state, looked forward to a prominent position in Democratic politics for decades to come.

Handsome and burly at six feet, four inches, the governor makes an imposing presence. His life-style is very different from the glittery one adopted by political ally Marvin Warner. Celeste is an informal, down-home sort of fellow who likes college basketball, folk music, and cooking Sunday pancake breakfast for his wife and six kids. He has not paid strict attention to his marital vows, however, and a 1988 presidential bid was quickly shot down by revelations of infidelities.

Celeste first became aware of the Home State situation on Tuesday afternoon, when his chief of staff, Ray Sawyer, briefed him about potential problems there. "You've got to understand how things work with the governor of Ohio," Celeste explains. Managing a $10 billion-a-year operation with hundreds of agencies, departments, divisions, and boards and nineteen thousand employees, "the governor can only respond to a blip on the radar screen." With Sawyer's briefing, the blip had arrived on Celeste's screen.

The blip started pulsating more strongly early Wednesday morning when Marvin Warner called the governor. Marvin was agitated. He had read the front-page article in that day's *Enquirer,* and he knew it spelled serious trouble. The headline read, "Cincinnati Savings & Loan Facing Loss;" the article mentioned "A loss of undetermined proportion" and contained the statements by Schiebel and Batties.

The governor remembers the call: "It was clear to me, just from the tone of his voice, that it was a matter of real concern. Warner said there was a story in the *Enquirer* and he was sure it was going to cause problems at the institution. I came into the office and asked my chief of staff and director of commerce to get on top of it."

Celeste chaired a strategy meeting at 8:30 A.M. attended by Sawyer and Director of Commerce Cox and two representatives of the industry association, the Ohio Savings and Loan League. A nervous Warner telephoned into that meeting, pleading that the state bail Home State out by making a financial commitment to guarantee its deposits.

Celeste believed that Warner was grossly overreacting and that his bailout idea was untenable politically. The governor and his advisers, unaware of Home State's true condition and the mortal danger it posed to ODGF, decided to reassure the public that the ODGF system was strong and that the state somehow would stand behind it. They issued a supportive statement, in Cox's name. Cox went on radio and TV and said:

> I want to assure depositors that their assets are protected and that there is no reason for undue concern. Their deposits are guaranteed in

full by the Ohio Deposit Guarantee Fund. In spite of potential difficulties, Home State Savings is in a sound financial condition and has a record of stability. . . .

In addition to these protections, the state of Ohio is prepared to safeguard the interests of the depositors of Home State and all depositors whose funds are guaranteed by the Ohio Deposit Guarantee Fund. . . .

The state of Ohio had no legal responsibility to stand by Home State or the private ODGF insurance system. But the state had tacitly approved of ODGF, because it had chartered the fund and all its member banks. And the public believed that the state somehow had a moral responsibility for the ODGF system. A poll taken later showed that 88 percent of the Home State customers felt that their deposits were insured by the state of Ohio, and the governor has said, "All the people thought the state was behind ODGF, that Ohio in ODGF meant Ohio. And it was my feeling that technically, even though we didn't have a responsibility in that respect, practically, we did have one."

With Cox's statement, the state of Ohio had become a leading player in the unfolding drama. But it had done so by buying into the totally unrealistic, rose-tinted view being disseminated by the Home State insiders. Sawyer felt that the statement "reflected the facts as we knew them. We had no sense of the magnitude of (the Home State problem). . . . We had enormous problems realizing the significance of it all."

Ohio's officials might have had problems realizing the significance of it all, but Home State's depositors did not.

Cincinnati is a city of solid burghers who live in substantial red-brick houses, a city of conservative Republican politics and conservative financial practices. At its core are Germanic and Anglo-Saxon populations whose roots reach deeply into the nineteenth century. They've worked hard for generations, saved their money nickel by nickel, and have strong instincts for self-preservation.

Those instincts told them that, behind all the optimistic rhetoric of Schiebel, the ODGF, and Cox, something was dreadfully wrong at Home State. In particular, they distrusted the uncertain waffling about "a loss of undetermined proportion." Faced with uncertainty, they did what they felt was prudent. They grabbed their money.

The depositors started lining up outside the Home State branches at 7:00 A.M., about the time Warner was warning Celeste about the front page of the *Enquirer*. They began pulling out their cash as soon as the doors opened, and they just kept at it. The *Enquirer* sold out early, and the lines begat lines as depositors heard about them on the radio and from neighbors. Cox's statement reassured very few.

The demand was so great that by midmorning the Federal Reserve Bank in downtown Cincinnati started dispatching Brink's armored trucks loaded with cash to the beleaguered Home State branches. Those in line watched nervously as guards, their guns drawn, carried bags of money into the vaults.

Bank managers passed out numbers to people standing in line, some of whom waited more than two hours to get at their money. Many, like Charles Little, stuffed their cash into paper bags. He got a police officer to escort him and his life savings across the street, where he deposited the money in a federally insured bank.

A fifty-six-year-old businessman cashed in a $10,000 certificate of deposit even though it meant paying a $256 penalty for early withdrawal. He was not convinced that his money was completely insured by ODGF. "I never thought in my lifetime I would see something like this. This is what's known as mixed emotions."

Cheryl Kominsky had her two preschool boys in tow as she left a branch clutching her family's $150. "My father called after he heard about it and said even though the bank was covered, it might take years to get the money repaid. One hundred and fifty dollars is one hundred and fifty dollars."

Debi Rickert and Toni Handley were more trusting than Cheryl and suffered for it. Debi, who had just moved to Cincinnati, remembers that her husband, Bill, was worried enough by the *Enquirer* article to go down to his branch. She recalls, "He talked to the manager, who assured him the bank was backed by the state of Ohio and gave him a copy of Cox's statement. We felt certain we were doing the intelligent thing by not panicking and adding to the problem. Bill even deposited his monthly paycheck into the bank."

Toni's mother had her life savings of $150,000 at Home State, and Toni's husband called to say he had read there were serious problems at the bank and she should withdraw the money. Toni went over to pick up her mother, but before they left they flipped on the TV and caught Ken Cox's news conference. Toni remembers, "Cox said there is no need to fear, this government is standing behind the banks, and if the good little citizen will sit quietly at home, the crisis will pass. And I told my Mom, 'Take your coat off. The bank might lie to us, Warner might lie to us, but by God, our government officials aren't going to lie to us.' Little did we know!"

At about 10:00 A.M., Schiebel received what he believed was "a call from heaven." It was from Oliver Waddell, chairman of the First National Bank of Cincinnati, who wanted to discuss whether a purchase of Home State by First National was in the cards.

Waddell and Warner sat down for a serious discussion at 3:00 P.M. in Waddell's office. Waddell said he felt that Home State's thirty-three branches and ninety-two thousand depositors would, under the right circumstances, fit well with First National's own branch network. With the bank's customers pulling out cash by the bucketful, Warner knew there was no time to lose. He suggested that, to quickly get down to terms, Waddell's people begin a detailed study of Home State's books the next morning. Celeste and his staff were told about Waddell's overtures and felt encouraged.

Throughout the day, Schiebel and Ohio's officialdom were determinedly upbeat. But both the *Post* and the *Enquirer* added to depositor unease by commenting on the Ewton-Warner connection at American Savings & Loan and both papers mentioned that Warner and Arky had private accounts at ESM. The *Post* reported the first sighting of Ronnie Ewton since the crisis began. Ewton's lawyer said that he was in Florida and would cooperate with the authorities.

Wednesday's tally at Home State was horrendous. The Federal Reserve had dispatched thirty-nine truckloads of cash, and by closing time $55 million had been withdrawn. The cash outflow had exceeded $100,000 per minute. Schiebel had met the massive cash demand by tapping into ODGF to the tune of $8.5 million and by selling securities in the open market and to the Federal Reserve Bank. He also started discussions with the Fed about borrowing from that institution against collateral.

In spite of all this, Cox that evening told reporters, "We don't believe we have the kind of a problem that would require emergency action," and the governor felt relaxed enough to attend an Ohio State–Michigan basketball game.

The *Wall Street Journal* and the *New York Times* continued their intense coverage of the ESM story on Wednesday. The *Journal* reported Bradford's liquidation of ESM's securities and started zeroing in on Grant's possible culpability. The *Times* highlighted the losses of municipalities such as Beaumont, Texas, Toledo, Ohio, and Pompano Beach, Florida, and reported that "the receiver and the SEC . . .

are starting to look at extensive links between the ESM group and Marvin L. Warner, a Cincinnati-based financier who controls a number of banks that dealt with ESM."

Home State depositors were already lined up in the chilly dawn of Thursday, March 7, to continue their quest for their cash. Schiebel dispatched to the branches all available midlevel managers to soothe customer fears. He ordered them to paste on their front doors the front page of that morning's *Enquirer*; the headline stated "Home State Deposits Safe, Officials Say," and the lead paragraph read "State and bank officials moved Wednesday to assure Home State Savings Bank depositors that the bank is not in danger of failing and that their money is safe."

Governor Celeste called Karen Horn, president of the Federal Reserve Bank of Cleveland, during the morning to determine how the Fed might help. Cleveland is one of the Federal Reserve's twelve senior banks and has jurisdiction over the Cincinnati operation. Horn told Celeste that there was little the Fed could do beyond lending Home State cash against valid collateral. She promised that she would expedite this process.

But she did more. Celeste, a neophyte about banking at this point, realized he needed expert help, and Horn was an experienced and able hand. She started to give him practical advice and became one of his main confidants during the crisis. Celeste says that his talk with Horn was a sobering one: "My notes indicate that there were two conclusions I had from my phone conversation. One is that there would be no easy way out of the Home State situation. And secondly, that it was going to have a profound impact on the Ohio Deposit Guarantee Fund."

The governor's sober thoughts were appropriate. All efforts Thursday to stem the run at Home State proved futile. Brink's made fifty-nine cash deliveries as customers withdrew another $45 million.

Celeste attempted to get the state's two top legislators, Democratic Speaker of the House Vern Riffe and Republican Senate President Paul Gillmor, to join him in a policy statement, but they refused because the situation looked so ominous. Celeste then issued a release which offered little encouragement. It said:

> I want to assure the depositors of Home State Savings Bank and all citizens of Ohio that our state-chartered banking system is working so far to protect the funds of depositors.

I have instructed Commerce Director Kenneth Cox to monitor the situation closely and gather information to assess what further steps should be taken. It serves no purpose to speculate on what those steps may be.

David Schiebel, who was getting three hours of sleep a night, looked totally drained as he entered the conference room at First National Thursday at 6:00 P.M. to join Oliver Waddell and twenty-five lawyers, accountants, and managers to try to negotiate Home State's sale. He had come from a meeting with Warner at which he had apprised Marvin of the full seriousness of their plight. With $100 million cash gone in two days and no end of the run in sight, Schiebel knew his position was desperate.

The group concentrated on the dreadful numbers, carefully dissecting each balance sheet item. It was Waddell's first opportunity to gauge the true extent of Home State's ESM losses. Schiebel tried to claim that they were still undetermined, but the First National people insisted on pegging them at the full $145 million.

Waddell was no fool. As the number-crunching continued into the night, he realized that there was a gaping hole at Home State at least $145 million wide, and that ODGF was going to be engulfed in it. Waddell was not going to jump into the hole unless more help was forthcoming. And the only reasonable source of such help was the state of Ohio. He decided that he could not risk the money of First National's shareholders unless he got assurances that the state would stand behind ODGF with loans. He and his accountants calculated the amount of such loans at roughly $80 million. If such a commitment were made, then First National might invest up to $50 million.

Waddell set a deadline of 8:00 A.M. Sunday for a yes or no on the deal. He felt that, to stop the run and revive depositor confidence, it was imperative that First National be in charge of the Home State branches on Monday morning.

The meeting ended at 1 A.M. after seven grueling hours with an agreement that Schiebel and Hunsche would meet with Ohio officials the next day to determine whether an $80 million state loan was in the cards.

Charlie Harper remembers working late at ESM on Thursday night when he received a call from Celeste's executive assistant: "He wanted to know about money secreted in the Bahamas or something. I said there's no indication of that. The money is gone, and that's it. Then they called me up and wanted me to tell them whether Marvin Warner was involved. I said, 'I don't know that.'" By chance a few minutes later, Charlie's boss of bosses, Chairman of the SEC John Shad, called. He—like Celeste—couldn't believe that, with all the money sloshing around ESM, Ronnie and the boys hadn't put some away in the Bahamas. Shad believed it could be as much as $100 million. But, Charlie had to tell him that they lost it all trading. Shad laughed and said, "That's tough, Charlie. It's bad news for the creditors."

The Cincinnati newspapers on Friday morning interpreted Celeste's statement of the previous day differently. The *Enquirer* headline read "Celeste Plans No Extra Help for Home State." In contrast, the *Post*'s said "Gov. Celeste Reassures Home State Customers," and its lead editorial reinforced the fantasy that all was well. Under a heading which said "Home State Deposits Safe," it concluded:

> Some clients of ESM may be badly hurt, including some cities and pension funds. But the customers of Home State Savings Bank should be reassured. Officials from the bank, state agencies and the governor's office have stated over and over that depositors are well protected.
>
> The private Ohio Deposit Guarantee Fund, which insures Home State's deposits, has a sterling reputation. And Kenneth Cox, director of the Ohio Department of Commerce, insists that the state would stand behind it in the very unlikely event that that were necessary.
>
> Nothing is more understandable than people's concern for their savings. The good news which they should take to heart is that their savings are safe.

The *Columbus Dispatch* on Friday morning reported that both Home State and the city of Toledo would be badly hit by ESM's collapse, but that Ohio State University, which had lent $2.65 million to ESM, had taken physical possession of the collateral provided by ESM and would suffer no losses.

Schiebel and Hunsche and their aides met Friday morning at the statehouse in Columbus to discuss Waddell's proposition with Batties, Cox, Sawyer, and Attorney General Tony Celebrezze. As Schiebel was describing the deal, he received a discouraging phone call from Cincinnati; the storm at Home State was continuing with hurricane force. Cash was leaving as fast as it had the previous two days. Hunsche gave him a lift when he said that ODGF would provide whatever he needed that day.

Cox immediately scheduled an afternoon meeting for the governor and the legislative leadership about the First National deal. There was little enthusiasm for Waddell's plan. Cox said later, "It appeared politically unworkable at that point in time. It was discussed with Riffe and Gillmor and their basic attitude was the same thing . . . the consensus was fairly unanimous that you couldn't come up with that type of money." Celeste's people persisted and, after much negotiation, determined that the most they might come up with for a First National buy out was $50 million. Waddell was informed of this and stated firmly that $50 million was far too little.

Celeste was delighted that the legislators had bought the idea of a $50 million contingency fund. Whether it was to be used for Home State or not, he wanted it. And he asked the leadership to begin work on a bill which would give him this financial comfort.

Although Celeste was elated by the $50 million prospect, Schiebel and Hunsche were crushed because they knew it was not enough to save Home State. At 3:30 P.M., they left the statehouse and went to the nearby offices of the Savings and Loan League. They got a mild boost when, at 4:00 P.M., they heard that Home State's loan arrangement with the Federal Reserve had been okayed. Over the next two hours, however, the news was all bad. Cash was being withdrawn at a furious pace. At day's end, Brink's had made seventy-eight shipments and more than $54 million had left Home State's coffers.

This was the last straw for Schiebel. After checking with Warner, he decided to close Home State down. He asked all key employees to meet with him at the Cincinnati headquarters at 8:00 P.M. He told them that all branches would be closed on Saturday. But then—in a burst of wishful thinking—he said they would reopen Monday because a sale to First National was imminent.

The wishful thinking persisted at 10:30 P.M., when Schiebel held a press conference and told reporters that he expected to finalize the sale of Home State to another Ohio financial institution that weekend; he would not disclose the new buyer's name. He said that Home State would be closed on Saturday, and it would be up to the new owner to decide whether to reopen on Monday. Schiebel again stated that he did not have enough information to quantify Home State's ESM losses. In an *Alice in Wonderland* twist, he placed most of the blame for the bank's run on the depositors, saying, "I believe that most of it was really inflicted by the depositors themselves. It was the panic of the individual depositors that led to the situation, the long lines and the hectic week that we've had. The depositors, if they would have taken their time and not rushed the institution in the manner they did, I think it would have been business as usual." He claimed he did not know how much cash had been withdrawn during the three-day run. The actual figure was $154.2 million, of which ODGF provided $45 million.

On Saturday morning officers of Home State, First National, and ODGF met to continue work on the bailout plan just in case the state could produce the kind of money Waddell felt he needed. Their hopes were dashed when Batties called to say that the First National plan was now moot, because he was sure that $50 million was the maximum the state would provide. Then he asked the Home State and ODGF people to fly to Cleveland to meet with a group of bank executives whom the state believed might make the deal based on a $50 million subsidy.

Schiebel and Hunsche and their men flew to Cleveland to pursue what appeared to be their last option. Cox chaired the meeting, which began at 3:00 P.M., and included representatives of five major banks from Cleveland, Toledo and Columbus. Cox wanted to know whether he was "in the ball park" with the $50 million figure. All the available numbers were presented to the bankers, and the discussion went on for nine hours. There were no takers. The last flight had left for Cincinnati, so an exhausted Schiebel, now battling the flu, had to rent a car to drive home.

Sunday morning Warner made last-ditch appeals to Ohio Senators Howard Metzenbaum and John Glenn, both of whom had received handsome campaign contributions from him. He told them that he feared a widespread panic if Home State collapsed, and asked them to try to get the Federal Reserve to step in more vigorously and save the situation. The senators said they would do all they could.

As Marvin made these calls, officials of the Federal Reserve— together with officials of the Federal Home Loan Bank Board (FHLBB), the Federal Savings and Loan Insurance Corporation (FSLIC), and the Federal Deposit Insurance Corporation (FDIC),— were meeting in Miami with Charlie Harper and Tom Tew.

The Federal Reserve is, with the exception of the presidency, the most powerful policy agency in the federal government. It is independent of the president and has ultimate responsibility for the health of our financial system, both nationally and internationally. To carry out this responsibility, it has wide powers to set interest rates, change the money supply, and affect the basic capital structure and lending power of all American banks.

The other agencies are more specialized. The FHLBB regulates savings and loans and FSLIC is its depositor insurance arm; both organizations have the same chairman. The FDIC insures commercial bank deposits; it was in Miami because some of the ODGF banks had the option of becoming commercial banks.

The entire federal banking bureaucracy had made a pilgrimage to Florida to determine if there was any money to be recovered from the ashes of ESM. Charlie Harper recalls, "The first thing they said is, 'Is there $100 million in the Bahamas?' You know, I'm starting to feel a little inadequate about not being able to locate this $100 million. And we said no, they've lost it all trading." He and Tom carefully went over the numbers for their guests and showed them that the cupboard was bare, except for a few straycrumbs. The people at the meeting were in constant touch with SEC Chairman Shad and Federal Reserve Chairman Paul Volcker up in Washington.

Volcker and the other federal banking people were trying to assess what impact a Home State and perhaps an ODGF collapse might have nationally. And even internationally. Based on this assessment, they would decide how strong a role the federal government would play in resolving Ohio's crisis.

Their consensus was that the Ohio crisis would have both national and international impact, but that the impact would be containable. The federal agencies would help with resources they already had in place, but there would be no federal bailout. This meant that FDIC and FSLIC would take under their wings any ODGF banks which met their standards, and that the Federal Reserve would open its loan window to any bank with valid collateral. But the federal government would not pour in direct aid money to save individual banks.

Underlying this decision was the thought that the federal taxpayer did not have an obligation to bail out banks which had voluntarily opted out of the federal insurance system; the ODGF thrifts went out on their own, because they did not want to shoulder the stringent financial and regulatory burdens of FSLIC. The federal people also believed that political pressure in Ohio would reach such critical levels that the governor and the legislature would be forced to come to the rescue of aggrieved depositors.

Early Sunday afternoon, with the First National deal dead and all other options closed, Schiebel threw in the towel. He got the Home

State directors to consent to a request that the state appoint a conservator to take over the operations of the bank. Celeste acceded, and he and Cox and Batties reached out with over fifty calls to their network to find an able conservator.

The winning suggestion came from Celeste's seventy-eight-year-old father, Frank, a retired housing executive who had been mayor of the Cleveland suburb of Lakewood for eight years and who had made an unsuccessful run for state attorney general in the 1960s. Frank had assiduously maintained his political and business contacts, and he recommended Arlo Smith, who had spent over forty-two years in banking and who had been the chief executive of a Cleveland savings and loan for ten years. Smith was living in retirement in Clearwater, Florida, but took the job because he was challenged by it and expected it to be relatively short-lived.

Celeste sent Batties to Florida in a state airplane to pick up Smith, and the two men discussed the crisis as they flew back to Cincinnati. They decided not to reopen on Monday and to continue efforts to find a buyer. They arrived in Cincinnati at 2:30 A.M. and drove directly to Home State headquarters where some employees were still working. As Smith walked in the door, he was greeted by a portrait of "Ambassador" Warner. He took his first action as conservator and ordered it removed. It was later replaced by a portrait of Abraham Lincoln.

With a conservator chosen, Celeste's overriding priority Sunday night was legislation. A strategy meeting was set for 6:30 P.M. at the Columbus law offices of the firm which represented Cox and the Department of Commerce—Porter, Wright, Morris & Arthur. Celeste knew that there was one man in state politics with the ability to hammer out a bill in the course of one night—Republican State Senator Richard Finan of Evendale, a Cincinnati suburb.

Finan, age fifty, had important legislative credentials; he was majority whip, chairman of the Senate Ways and Means Committee, and a member of the Finance Committee. But more than anything else, he had experience in banking and finance and credibility in that community. He had been on the board of a federally insured savings and loan since 1969 and had handled many cases for financial institutions in more than two decades as a lawyer.

A trim, wiry man with more than a passing resemblance to Johnny Carson, Finan takes a cool, practical approach to problems. He was hosting a small political meeting at his home when the governor called. Celeste summed it up by saying, "We have big trouble that could lead to even bigger trouble, and I really need your help." Finan immediately turned the meeting over to his wife and drove to Columbus.

He recollects, "Frankly . . . when I got there, I felt things were really in disarray. We had a roomful of lawyers, and I am a lawyer, but we didn't have the politicians there. The roomful of lawyers had a number of ideas and thoughts, a lot of which simply were not politically feasible."

Finan took over the meeting and started to draft a bill, sentence by sentence. Making frequent calls to other legislative leaders and to the governor, at 4:00 A.M. he finally put together a three-point proposal.

It left responsibility for Home State with ODGF, and created a "Son of ODGF" (called The Savings & Loan Assurance Corporation, or SLAC) with $50 million in borrowed state capital to back the sixty-eight ODGF banks other than Home State. The third feature gave SLAC an additional $40 million through assessments on the sixty-eight remaining ODGF members.

Since the Ohio constitution did not allow the state to lend tax funds to a private institution, SLAC's $50 million would come from $25 million in unclaimed bank accounts owned by the state and $25 million in excess lottery profits (later changed to liquor profits).

Finan believed that, by separating the fate of the sixty-eight from the Home State mess, he would improve the prospects of the non-Home State banks. Although some had financial weak spots, the sixty-eight were essentially healthy. None was remotely like the $145 million disaster area which was Home State.

On Monday Celeste and Finan were as upbeat as possible about the proposed new fund. The governor said he had strong bipartisan support for the $90 million in new protection and might have a bill to sign within forty-eight hours, and Finan told the media, "There's no way we're going to let (Home State) in the new fund until they take care of their problems. The sole reason for this new fund is to insure the assets of the approximately seventy other savings and loans in Ohio served by the current ODGF. We need prompt action to allay the concerns of other savings and loan depositors who feel they may be affected by the problems at Home State."

Unfortunately for the ODGF depositors, the statements of Celeste and Finan were the only good tidings that would come their way that day. The media also delivered to them a flood of discouraging items.

Home State remained closed, and it's ninety-two thousand depositors were separated from $525 million in deposits. Arlo Smith confirmed that the bank would not allow withdrawals or accept deposits until its thirty-three branches were sold. Senior citizens who had arranged for Social Security to deposit their checks directly to Home State could not get at their money. Most stores, including major chains such as Sears and Kroger, would not take Home State checks in payment and banks in the area wouldn't accept them for cash or deposit.

The *Wall Street Journal* highlighted Warner's personal dealings at ESM and the Warner-Ewton connection at American Savings & Loan.

The city of Toledo faced a $19 million ESM loss, and the national bond rating services demoted the city to their "credit-watch" lists. Toledo's mayor suspended its treasurer and its finance director for their roles in the debacle.

The *Columbus Dispatch* reported the failures of the Sunday meeting in Cleveland with major prospective buyers of Home State and of the First National negotiations. Arlo Smith, who had no new hot prospects, could only say, "We're moving with all haste to develop an appropriate sale."

Tom Tew announced that thus far he had only located $23 million in ESM assets, miles short of its $300 million in debt. He would search vigorously for every other dollar available, but could promise nothing.

Two Home State debenture holders filed suit against the bank on behalf of themselves and all other debenture holders. They wanted their money back and claimed that the offering circular for the debentures was false and misleading, because it said nothing about the ESM risk.

Batties and Schiebel perpetuated the unhealthy aura of uncertainty surrounding Home State by refusing to estimate its ESM losses. A guessing game started in the newspapers. The *Enquirer* estimated $130 million, the *Post* $100 million.

Home State depositors got the sickening feeling that they would never see their money again. Theodore Jones is a double amputee who uses a wheel chair. He had deposited $13,000, the bulk of his savings, in Home State, but he wasn't able to get down to his branch before the collapse and he felt sure he had been wiped out. He had difficulty accepting the reality of what had hit him. He said, "I almost fainted when it happened. They had it up there in big letters in their window—'Your Savings Guaranteed 100 Percent.' What a bunch of bunk."

Toni Handley felt angry and guilty, because she was responsible for her mother depositing her $150,000 life savings at Home State. They had originally gone to a FSLIC bank and discovered that the insurance limit was $100,000. When Toni heard that ODGF insurance was unlimited, she talked her mother into becoming a Home State customer.

Arjan Jagtiani, a senior electrical engineer, expressed deep frustration:

> Our Home State account is the overwhelming majority of our life time savings. Why save money? You might as well live high, spend, and be merry. It's just really disgusting.
>
> When I deposited the money, I asked them how safe it was. They said it was insured by ODGF. I thought that was a state organization, and that our money was as good as gold.
>
> The funniest part is, I'll be getting my masters in business administration next month. With all my degrees, I still wasn't smart enough to avoid putting all my eggs in one basket. We're going to have to pick up the pieces and start all over.

And Debi Rickert remembers, "After Bill deposited his monthly paycheck, we paid all our bills. Two days later the bank closed and for the next week our checks all came back to us stamped 'Refer to Maker' in big, bold letters. Here we were away from home and family, in a new town where we knew no one, and we had no money to even buy groceries—and now we had checks bouncing."

Almost everyone knew someone whose Home State checks had bounced, and uneasiness began to grow about the new fund. If ODGF's $136 million couldn't take care of Home State's 92,000 customers, how would $90 million protect the more than 400,000 depositors at the sixty-eight other banks? People began to realize the essential difference between private and federal insurance: ODGF and "Son of ODGF" (SLAC) had finite resources, whereas backing for the federal insurance companies, FSLIC and FDIC, was essentially unlimited. American Savings & Loan in Miami had suffered a grievous blow at ESM, but there was never a hint of a run by its depositors; it was FSLIC insured.

The significance of this was not lost on Celeste, and he began to think that the ultimate solution to the crisis might involve forcing the ODGF banks into FSLIC insurance coverage. He spoke to Paul

Volcker for the first time Monday afternoon and tried out the idea on him. Volcker gave him cautious encouragement.

Nervousness by ODGF depositors was reflected in a $6 million outflow from the sixty-eight banks on Monday.

The news on Tuesday wasn't much better. The governor announced that there were new potential buyers for Home State, but the media gave much bigger play to a statement by Batties that Home State would be closed indefinitely and that losses could top $100 million. Tuesday's ODGF deposit outflow was $13.4 million, more than double that of the previous day.

Celeste believed he could bring a sharp ending to the crisis on Wednesday, March 13. Finan and the legislative leadership had worked around the clock and would deliver to him the $90 million relief bill that afternoon.

The politicians were dealing with a delicate and volatile commodity—public confidence. There was nothing fundamentally wrong with the sixty-eight ODGF banks. The weakness of their private banking insurance system was the problem. The confidence of the Ohio depositors was fragile, because the Home State mess had shown them that the ODGF backup system was paper thin.

Celeste hoped that the relief bill would restore that confidence. He would arrange a press conference around its signing; in an upbeat statement, he would cite the legislation as proof of the state's capacity for swift action to meet and defeat catastrophe. Depositor fears would be quieted, and problems would be resolved in a calm and reasoned atmosphere.

Things didn't work out that way. Celeste's bill signing was upstaged by two other events which dominated that day's news coverage and the next day's headlines. First of all, Batties made the bombshell admission at an earlier press conference that, "I cannot make a flat-out guarantee that all depositors with funds still at Home State will get their money back." Then Marvin Warner announced his resignation as chairman of the powerful Ohio Building Authority, the post Celeste had appointed him to.

At Celeste's press conference, the first question was, "Has Warner resigned voluntarily or has he been forced out?" And the reporters rarely got off that subject. Except to ask the governor why "Son of ODGF" would provide solutions when the state couldn't assure Home State depositors that the original ODGF would take care of them.

Wednesday afternoon, depositors started crowding into the sixty-eight banks to make withdrawals. The Federal Reserve made emergency cash shipments of $23 million to seven banks, and the total outflow from the ODGF system exceeded $30 million.

Celeste called Finan and said, "It didn't work. The Warner story buried our story." He was really down. He felt that they would ride a whirlwind the next day, and he was concerned for public safety, fearing that angry people on line might get violent.

Ken Cox called a press conference for 8:00 P.M. which was meant to reassure depositors, but had the opposite affect. He said that the state was "pursuing every means conceivable to insure that Home State depositors get their money." But, like Batties earlier in the day, he would not say that the state would unconditionally insure their deposits.

A woman stood up and told Cox that she and her husband had deposited all their money in Home State as they looked for a home to buy. She protested, "They said your money is guaranteed. What am I to think now?" Cox had no adequate answer. This was featured on the eleven o'clock news, together with shots of crowds of people lining up outside the banks waiting to get at their cash in the morning.

Bill Cunningham, a popular Cincinnati radio talk-show host, is heard everywhere in southern Ohio, because his station transmits at the highest power rating allowed, fifty thousand watts. He recalls, "I had spent a week of shows telling people not to panic; the money is safe. I bought it hook, line and sinker." But on Wednesday he changed his tune. He told his listeners, "If the state is not willing to reassure Home State people, the rest of you should get on line and pull your money out of the other banks. There is going to be a disaster."

Laird Lazelle, chief executive of Charter Oak (the third largest ODGF bank), called Cunningham, accused him of being an alarmist, and volunteered to go on the show to reassure depositors. Lazelle answered questions clearly and confidently for a couple of hours, but the tactic didn't work. It only intensified the spotlight on Charter Oak, because it had the heaviest withdrawals in the system the next day.

In scenes cruelly remindful of the Great Depression, depositors waited on line all Wednesday night to pull their cash out of ODGF branches on Thursday morning. They brought kerosene heaters to warm themselves against the damp cold, and slept wrapped in blankets on lawn chairs or in sleeping bags. They ate sandwiches and drank coffee and whiskey from thermos bottles. Some sang songs. Others watched TV on portable sets or listened to transistor radios.

The lines grew all day. At closing time at 5:30 P.M., at Molitor Loan, one thousand people stood three abreast in a U-shaped line that stretched for more than one hundred yards. They vowed to stay all night to get their money on Friday morning. Scenes such as this were repeated at scores of ODGF branches throughout southern Ohio.

The Fed had made $60 million in emergency cash shipments on Thursday, exceeding by $5 million its peak daily shipment during the Home State run the week before.

In Washington, four Ohio congressmen met with Edwin Gray, chairman of both the FHLBB and FSLIC, to pressure him to expedite inspections of ODGF banks which wanted to join FSLIC. Gray, a Republican who was later accused of playing politics with the Ohio collapse, was decidedly uncooperative. Thomas Luken, a representative from Cincinnati whose son is mayor of the city, reported, "Gray was rather arrogant about it. The quote was, 'You should be in Columbus, not here.' . . . They said they didn't have enough people in the system to come in and accelerate the inspections so they offered really no relief at all, nothing." Luken and the others added their disappointing news to the truly distressing reports that Celeste had been receiving all day about the bank runs. Celeste was particularly discouraged by Gray's attitude, because he was becoming more convinced that federal insurance was an essential part of the answer to his problems.

The governor knew that it was time to make the really tough decisions. He sent out a state trooper for barbecued spare ribs and gathered his key advisers around him for what he knew would be a long night of debate and decision.

One of them was Celeste's father, Frank, who was summoned from a gin rummy game in Lake Worth, Florida. The governor said, "I like to have him around in situations like this. I like to have people I can bounce ideas off. His judgment is so sound." Also present were Sawyer, Batties, Cox, Jack Kessler (a Federal Reserve Board member and a businessman), Don Shackelford (president of a federally insured Columbus savings and loan), and Gerald Austin (manager of Celeste's 1982 campaign and his key political adviser).

The group at the statehouse threw themselves into their crucial tasks: defining and evaluating the governor's options. The telephones were in constant use as they received input from Paul Volcker, Riffe and Gillmor, Dick Finan, and a group of lawyers at Porter, Wright's Cincinnati office. And they made numerous calls to ODGF executives to get firsthand reports on the condition of their banks. Several of the weaker banks responded that they couldn't last through Friday.

Dick Finan called in at 11:00 P.M. He was distressed by the results of his own telephone survey of bank executives which confirmed Celeste's most discouraging reports, and by what he was hearing from Bill Cunningham over the radio.

Cunningham was even more vociferous than on the previous evening. He was saying, "It's time to panic. Take your cots and tents and line up. You'd better be first in line or you might not get your money."

Finan could only see matters getting worse, and he had terse advice for the governor: "Close all sixty-eight banks."

This was one of the four options which had survived the group's scrutiny by midnight. The other three were:

1. Keep the sixty-eight open without restriction and let the panic run its course;
2. Allow all banks to open but permit individuals to withdraw only 35 percent of their funds; or
3. Close only the weak banks.

The "let the panic run its course" option was the first to go. Celeste has said, "It was my firm conviction that if one more savings and loan in Ohio failed, then not only were all of the privately insured institutions in trouble, but at least potentially all of the others were in trouble too."

The "limited withdrawal" option had appeal for the governor because, "It's the politician's solution to a difficult problem—cut it down the middle. The perfect political solution. The problem was, there is no basis in statute for it."

They argued the other two options well into the morning. Around 2:30 A.M., some of the group were in need of nourishment. A search produced only a couple of quarts of milk and a box of Girl Scout cookies. They were consumed rapidly.

The third option, "closing only the weaker banks," showed at least partial faith in the system. But, it involved serious legal problems, because it discriminated against individual institutions. And some feared that partial closings would dilute the overall impact of the governor's actions. They wanted to issue a message that was simple and strong.

So most of the participants favored the fourth option, but the debate was still going on at 4:30 A.M. In the end, it was Celeste's assessment of the media affect on public confidence which sealed the decision.

One of the Porter, Wright lawyers in Cincinnati had obtained an early copy of Friday's *Enquirer*, and telephoned the governor that the headlines announced, "Savers Withdrawing S&L Funds" and "Customers Ignore Pleas, Assurances." Two-thirds of the front page was devoted to articles about the crisis, and there were two prominent photographs in color. One featured the large crowd lined up three-deep outside Molitor Loan, and the other showed only two people in front of a federally insured savings and loan. They had just deposited funds which they had withdrawn earlier from an ODGF bank.

That clinched it. At 5:00 A.M., Celeste—in shirt sleeves, unshaven, bone-tired—told the advisers slumped in chairs surrounding his desk, "Close them all."

The *Enquirer* photographs had a strong symbolic effect on him. Ken Cox has commented, "What he felt was that pretty soon the public was going to know the difference between privately funded institutions and federally funded ones and as soon as they did, they were going to act, and it would just move right on up the state. He felt he had to stop the runs, get them federally insured. He knew that he had to get them federally insured, and he couldn't do that leaving them open."

Immediately after he made his decision, Celeste called Karen Horn of the Federal Reserve and Dick Finan and asked them to join him in a press conference at Cincinnati's Lunken Airport at 7:30 A.M. They agreed, and Celeste and his advisers went to their respective homes and showered and shaved.

Two hours later, standing in front of a depression-era mural of a laborer repairing an airplane, Celeste became the first American elected official to declare a bank holiday since Franklin D. Roosevelt in 1933. He was separating five hundred thousand depositors from $4.3 billion of their assets. He said:

> In view of the severe and spreading lack of confidence, which is reflected on the front pages, not only of the Cincinnati paper this morning, but also Cleveland and other papers across the state, I have instructed the director of commerce . . . to impose a three-day bank holiday for all ODGF institutions. . . .
>
> We will set to work immediately in cooperation with our nation's central bank Federal Reserve system and with our own banking leaders

to develop an orderly plan for restructuring these institutions so that they can reopen as soon as possible.

After Horn and Finan made forceful statements of support, the governor told reporters that he hoped to obtain federal insurance coverage for the closed banks, but couldn't promise it at that time. He vowed to return to Cincinnati every day until the crisis was resolved.

Turning to the prospects for Home State depositors, he said, "It is inconceivable to me that they would lose everything, and the goal is to try to keep them as close to whole as we possibly can."Then he asked for questions.

Mike Handley, whose wife Toni was lulled by Ken Cox into leaving her mother's $150,000 life savings at Home State, had been awakened at 5:00 A.M. by a call from his boss who told him Celeste would be at Lunken at 7:30. Toni was so angry about what happened to her mother that she decided she had to be there. She said, "I thought, by God, the governor's being in my city, I'm going down to Lunken. What was very surprising is that there was not another real person there, just the media. So I found myself getting a lot of attention for asking questions." The governor's answers were so noncommittal that she left as angry as when she had arrived.

At 8:00 A.M., Christine Wright and the others who had waited all night in front of Molitor Loan heard on the radio that the governor had closed the bank. Christine's muscles felt stiff and achy; she was cold; she was exhausted. She was also very angry because her mother, Fannie Wright, had been hit by what Christine called a "double whammy." Fannie had had two banks shot out from under her; she was old enough to remember Roosevelt's bank closing and had managed to withdraw her $8,000 life savings from Home State in time. Then she turned around and put the money into Molitor, which seemed solid as a rock to her.

Christine, who had driven ninety miles from her home in Greenville, Ohio, to withdraw her mother's money, was bitter and fearful as she got back into her car. She told a reporter, "My mother has little income except a minimum Social Security check. I wasn't even aware there were two kinds of deposit insurance—state and federal. This is terrible, really terrible."

Bob Jacobson, a civil engineer, was also hit by a "double whammy."He was one of the first to pull out of Home State, and he consolidated his savings at Molitor, where he had accounts for twenty-three years. He said, "I was the thirty-sixth person in line this morning. And I'll be close to the front again, because I'll go over there Sunday night and spend the night again.

"To create a separate fund simply shows that even the governor didn't have any confidence in the banking system. I think that helped to scare the people. And now this three-day holiday simply intensifies the fear. We're at a point now where we can't trust anybody when it comes to protecting your money."

The governor spent the rest of his day Friday working on two tasks: calming the fears of people like Christine and Bob with statements that an effective action plan was in motion, and implementing that plan by starting to move the sixty-eight banks under the federal insurance umbrella.

Calming depositor fears involved a statewide political caravan. Celeste, Horn, and Finan flew from Lunken to Columbus, where they repeated their performance for the media with legislative leaders Riffe and Gillmor. These two men accompanied the group to Cleveland for an 11:45 A.M. meeting arranged by Horn; it involved her staff and executives of thirteen major Ohio banks. It lasted ninety minutes and was the first of several that weekend in which the participants grappled with the hard issues of a rescue package.

Before leaving Cleveland for Columbus, the politicians held another upbeat press conference at the Cleveland airport. During the flight, an exhausted Celeste told reporters, "I've gone from kindergarten to first grade in learning about banking. Ten days ago, I couldn't have told you the difference between federal and state-sponsored insurance funds."

While the governor was travelling around the state, Tom Batties ran a six-hour meeting at a Cincinnati hotel with 110 executives of the sixty-eight banks. Their purpose: to organize "Son of ODGF" (SLAC). After a hardball speech in which Batties implied he would subject them to bureaucratic harassment if they didn't cooperate, they voted unanimously to join the $90 million organization, which involved a $40 million commitment on their part. Celeste believed that having the SLAC monies in place would give him an important back-up resource in dealing with Gray and FSLIC.

Horn and Celeste pressed Paul Volcker for help, and found a ready ally. Volcker feared that the bank holiday could erode confidence in the entire U.S. financial system. He immediately gave Horn 150 inspectors to review the books of the sixty-eight banks to expedite federal insurance coverage, and he instructed her to cut red tape if any of the sixty-eight wished to borrow from the Fed. He called Gray at FSLIC and told him that he was concerned about Gray's frosty rejection the previous day of aid to the beleaguered ODGF institutions.

Friday evening Celeste made a short, reassuring speech on local TV, and at 11:30 P.M. he appeared on the national ABC program, "Nightline." Then he went to bed for the first time in forty-eight hours.

On Saturday morning the national media descended on Columbus, and the governor's press secretary set up a command post for them in the lieutenant governor's office, moving that official to a small cubicle down the hall.

The governor and his key aides spent most of Saturday at Horn's office in a marathon working session with Fed and FSLIC officials and banking leaders. While this was going on, an army of federal and state inspectors was crawling over the books of the sixty-eight banks. They started making flash reports to the group in Cleveland, and the dimensions of the problems concerning federal insurance started to become clear. The people in Cleveland were also in touch with Finan and his legislative cohorts in Columbus, who had begun work on a bill which would bring the sixty-eight banks under the federal insurance umbrella.

On Saturday evening, Celeste held a press conference at the Cleveland airport and then flew to Lunken to brief the Cincinnati media. He had little specific news to report.

Volcker and Gray got together on Sunday, and Horn briefed them by telephone. She reported the first round of examinations showed that thirty of the sixty-eight banks appeared to be weak, and she and Volcker convinced Gray to send one of his chief lieutenants to Cleveland to coordinate the complicated insurance application process for all of the banks.

The goal of reopening the sixty-eight on a sound footing in seventy-two hours was proving impossible. The jobs of getting a good bill out of the legislature and finishing the complex financial analyses for the feds were too large to complete over a weekend. But the media couldn't wait. While the officials struggled behind closed doors, television and the press were spreading the Ohio story all over the world, and adding fierce pressure for action.

The media zeroed in on the half million families who did not know if they would ever see $4.3 billion of their own money again. They were in shock and despair, and these feelings spilled over to the tens of thousands of people to whom they paid their bills: the landlords, the grocers, the doctors, the auto repairmen. This gave TV anchormen the opportunity to intone: "In a drama reminiscent of the Great Depression, thousands of Ohio citizens, cut off from their life savings . . . ," while on the screen the nation saw mothers crying that they couldn't buy groceries for their children, and angry depositors shouting, "We want our money back."

Celeste summoned 125 ODGF executives to a Sunday evening meeting at the statehouse to tell them that he had reluctantly decided to extend the bank holiday forty-eight hours beyond its Sunday midnight deadline. Then he flew to what had become his ritual late-evening Lunken press conference and broke the frustrating and disappointing news to the large media contingent there.

The governor's media woes were not helped by the silence of Marvin Warner, who had fast become a target of public anger and distrust. Warner had made a single statement painting himself as a victim of the debacle and then disappeared from public view. A Monday morning *Post* editorial headed "Where is Marvin Warner?" asked the following questions:

- How could you commit the faith of all your depositors and stockholders to a single man, Ronnie Ewton?
- Was it coincidence that you pulled $37 million of your own money out of ESM just before it collapsed, or did you have indications that the securities dealer was facing serious problems?
- If you did, why did you get yourself out but leave your depositors holding the bag?
- Why aren't you in the forefront of those working night and day with the other owners of Ohio thrift institutions to find a solution to this crisis and restore confidence in the system?
- Why aren't you standing next to Dick Celeste when he faces the cameras and the public?
- Marvin Warner, where are you?

On Monday, anxiety spread like a stain over the international financial markets as Celeste and the legislature continued to grapple with the crisis. The traders in London and Zurich and Tokyo didn't fully understand what was going on in Ohio, but what they did understand they didn't like. The Associated Press headline read, "Dollar Dips in London Over Ohio S&L Crisis," and the news service reported that the dollar plunged 14 percent in its worst one-day slide in fourteen years.

The American consumer was badly shaken. The influential economic research firm, Sindlinger & Co., reported:

> Ohio's banking woes gave consumer confidence its worst weekly jolt in thirty years. Nearly 17 percent of all households which had confidence in the economy before the bank closure, lost that confidence after word of the bank holiday spread between Friday and Monday. Many consumers believed the Ohio bank problems were only the tip of the iceberg and expected many more banking problems in the future.

The Ohio media dubbed March 18 "Dark Monday," and it surely seemed the bleakest of times. But the darkness was more in the perception than in the reality, because the forces of reconstruction in the federal government, the governor's office, and the legislature finally possessed the momentum and the sense of direction to resolve the crisis.

10

Reconstruction in Ohio

Celeste pleaded with Finan Tuesday morning to get him a bill that day and then made an emergency flight to Washington to cover his flanks there. He was learning fast about federal mechanisms. He said, "When things began to unravel, everybody felt that there was an emergency process by which the federal government automatically plugged in. It's clear that that doesn't happen. It's only with a great sort of to-ing and fro-ing, to put it mildly, that federal agencies come to believe this is really something they ought to be involved in." First he briefed the Ohio congressional delegation. Then he met separately with Volcker and Gray to solidify their support for a federal insurance package. Gray kept Celeste waiting an hour, but once the two men sat down together, he was conciliatory and agreed to commit all available resources to speeding FSLIC coverage for the sixty-eight banks. He extracted a price, however, getting Celeste to promise that Ohio would make good FSLIC losses incurred in accepting ODGF banks.

The legislature stayed in session seventeen hours on Tuesday, and finally passed a bill one hour past midnight, Wednesday morning. Celeste signed it at 2:47 A.M. Senate approval was delayed by a three-hour recess when Republican members left to attend a $100-a-plate fund-raiser for Paul Gillmor, who was building a war chest to run for governor against Celeste in 1986.

The bill required all sixty-eight banks to obtain federal insurance but allowed them to open for business as soon as they could prove to the state that they could meet FSLIC qualifications.

Even with expedited procedures, FSLIC approval could take several weeks. The most daunting of FSLIC standards concerned a bank's capital base. FSLIC demanded that each bank owner's capital equal 5 percent of deposits, whereas ODGF required only 3 percent. Short-term emergency help could be sought from SLAC, but over the long term, the weaker banks were faced with raising more capital or merging with stronger institutions. To help the banks, the previous

179

requirement that they contribute $40 million to SLAC was waived. Those banks which could not qualify for FSLIC within 120 days would be closed.

Other provisions of the bill allowed all depositors to withdraw up to $750 per month from their accounts, and guaranteed to compensate FSLIC for any loss. It also created a special prosecutor to pursue any criminal violators involved with the debacle.

Senate Republicans had insisted on the special prosecutor, but all commentators agree that there was a remarkable lack of political partisanship during the crisis. The politicians saw the banking catastrophe as an Ohio problem rather than a Democratic problem or a Celeste problem. Divisions were slight, and they occurred along geographic rather than party lines. That is, some northern Ohioans wanted to wash their hands of the problem, because they saw it as a southern one brought on by the south Ohioans themselves.

And there was considerable Republican restraint concerning the Celeste-Warner connection. Their relationship was political, not social, and was perceived as a marriage of convenience, with Warner providing Celeste crucial campaign funds at the right time, and Celeste appointing Warner to an important administrative post for which he was well qualified. Besides, Warner had proven to be an effective chairman of the Ohio Building Authority.

Celeste got less than three hours sleep after signing the bill, because at six o'clock he arose to go to the ABC and CBS TV stations for interviews on nationwide morning news shows.

The governor felt that he had finally brought the sixty-eight banks up onto safe ground and was looking forward to a relatively quiet day at the statehouse. But it was not to be. Home State reared its ugly head again.

Fred Kaufmann, a Home State depositor from Dayton, wanted to insure that his fellow victims would not be forgotten in the euphoria surrounding the passage of the rescue bill for the sixty-eight. He hastily organized a motorcade from Cincinnati and Dayton to Columbus to present Home State grievances to the governor, and roughly seventy-five people made the drive. Five were selected to meet with Celeste, and they delivered their message forcefully. One of the five was Toni Handley, who had heard about Kaufmann's plans on the radio.

Toni was the last person one would suspect of being a political activist. She was a conservative Republican and fit almost perfectly the profile of a prosperous Midwestern housewife. Now thirty-nine, she had left college at nineteen to marry and raise a family. She had never taken a paying job and had devoted herself to her husband, who helped run a business she had inherited, and to raising her two boys. Toni was slim, feminine, and had lustrous dark hair. From childhood, she was used to deferring to men and had rarely asserted herself. But Home State fueled her anger as nothing had before and drove her into the public arena. She found she had the will and the brains to be effective there, and her life was forever changed.

The previous night Toni had met Paula Taylor at the Cunningham radio show. She had come to spread the word about the motorcade, and Paula was there to publicize a class action suit against Home State, to which she was a plaintiff. Paula believed that a rally was needed to galvanize the Home State victims, and Toni agreed. They scheduled a planning session at Paula's home two nights later on Thursday, March 21.

On Thursday, Attorney General Tony Celebrezze appointed Lawrence A. Kane, Jr., as special prosecutor under the law passed the previous day. Kane, fifty-five, was a partner in a prominent Cincinnati law firm and a lifelong Republican whose father had served many years in the Ohio legislature. Celebrezze said, "It is important to appoint a Republican to avoid a public perception of any collusion or inside dealing."

Paula and Toni were joined for their meeting around Paula's kitchen table Thursday night by Lisa Neidich, whose mother was a friend of Paula's. Lisa, single and thirty, had just returned from a stint as a nurse in Saudi Arabia. She had planned to move to California, but was now stuck in Cincinnati because she had placed her $7,500 life savings in Home State.

Everyone agrees that Paula has extraordinary organizing skills, which she had honed as an executive of an agency serving the retarded. Aged thirty-seven, she and her husband, Harry, are parents of a nineteen year-old adopted son who is retarded and autistic.

Paula had rented the basketball field house of nearby Xavier University for 2:00 P.M. Sunday, March 24, for $325, and had bought about $200 worth of stationery and stamps. She hoped to get the full $525 back by passing the hat at the rally.

She set out a pot of coffee and went about energizing her co-workers to assure a good turnout. They enlisted Kaufmann and the Dayton contingent by phone, and they organized a leaflet blitz, recruited a telephone squad, arranged for radio appearances, and wrote a press release.

Debi Rickert was outraged because her Home State checks were bouncing right and left. When she got one back from her church with a sympathetic note, her resolve stiffened. She thought, "They're not going to do this to us. We're not going to let them. I don't know what I'm going to do about it, but I know I'm going to fight hard for what is ours." When she saw Toni's name in an *Enquirer* article about the trip to see Celeste, she called her to volunteer for work. She was chagrined that she couldn't make the meeting at Paula's, but she worked Friday and Saturday distributing leaflets in the rain all over southern Ohio, while her husband took care of their infant son.

The Governor felt that he needed a truly experienced hand to bring the sixty-eight banks into the federal insurance fold and to resolve the Home State mess; on Friday he replaced the relatively green Batties as savings and loan superintendent with a tough, politically-savvy business lawyer, fifty-two-year-old Bob McAlister. Batties remained with the agency as general counsel. McAlister, an active Democrat, quickly proved to be the man for the job. He combined sharp and tenacious negotiating skills with an articulateness and sense of humor which rapidly won over the media.·

McAlister realized that all routes to federal insurance were not direct ones, and during his first day on the job, he was able to announce that a couple of banks had achieved federal coverage indirectly. Century Savings moved under the federal umbrella because its parent was FSLIC insured, and Scioto Savings received approval of a long-pending request to become a commercial bank under FDIC protection. He also stated that he had okayed all banks for the $750 limited withdrawals, and approved eighteen of them for full service operations starting Monday the 25th.

Four thousand people showed up at the dusty old Xavier field house on Sunday afternoon. The event was decisive in making the Home State depositors a political force.

The rally began raucously as the crowd vented the outrage and frustration which had built up for three weeks. They chanted, "We want our money back," booed Celeste's name, and cheered wildly as Paula and other speakers insisted on the governor's moral obligation to get them one hundred cents on their dollars. The decibel level peaked when one speaker quoted the statement of the governor's man, Cox, saying, "The state of Ohio is prepared to safeguard the interests of the depositors of Home State and all depositors whose funds are guaranteed by the Ohio Deposit Guarantee Fund."

Just when things seemed to be getting out of hand, the organizers gave the throng a constructive outlet for their heated emotions. Lisa grabbed the microphone and directed them to tables where they signed petitions, registered their addresses and telephone numbers, and picked up form letters to mail to their legislators. All the letters came with stamped envelopes. As the crowd streamed out of the field house, the Home State Depositors Association—soon to number six thousand—was ready for action.

Paula's fundraising at the rally fell $200 short of her expenditures, but her sense of elation about the size and spirit of the crowd overwhelmed any feelings of monetary disappointment.

The day after the rally, Charlie Luken, mayor of Cincinnati, offered the Depositors Association his office as their Cincinnati base. Within twenty-four hours, Lisa and a cadre of volunteers had taken over his space and four phone lines and moved him into his secretary's office. Luken, always encouraging and affable, accepted the arrangement for the many weeks of the crisis.

Joe Rabe, a Columbus accountant with $17,000 tied up at Home State, was at Xavier because he had heard about the event on the radio. He was so fired up by the rally that during the drive home he decided to organize a depositors group in his home town. He found several willing and able people, contacted Paula and her folks, and the Home State Depositors Association now had strong bases in the three principal afflicted cities.

The day after the rally, Debi Rickert joined Paula, Toni, and Lisa as a full-fledged member of the leadership group for the Cincinnati depositors. They contrasted brightly with the all-male leadership in Dayton and Columbus, and were dubbed the "Skirt Squad" by the media.

Debi, aged twenty-five, had worked her way through night school to get her masters in human services, but her career as a drug counselor was interrupted just months before the Home State collapse when her husband was transferred from Cleveland to Cincinnati. Paula was impressed with Debi and said, "Very high energy, just bubbles over with energy, very well educated, was new to the city, a brand new mother, basically a new mom. Very attractive, all-American looking. She's very dedicated and very assertive and very direct, but she can also use her feminine wiles when she wants to."

Over one hundred people attended a follow-up meeting at a local high school on March 26, two days after the rally. They decided to mount a massive petition drive and bring the petitions via a motorcade to the Governor a week later, on April 2. Debi was appointed organizer of the motorcade, and Paula, Toni, and Lisa assumed responsibility for the petitions.

Another type of petition was being discussed in Florida on March 26 when Tom Tew presented one on behalf of ESM's creditors to a federal judge; this petition asked that ESM be placed in bankruptcy. The request was granted, and the following day Tew was appointed trustee for the creditors. Bankruptcy status for ESM gave the creditors enhanced power under federal law to pursue what was rightfully theirs.

Home State continued to be a hot potato, but during the week of March 24, there were strong signs that the crisis surrounding the sixty-eight was being defused. International currency markets calmed down, McAlister announced that three more banks had qualified for federal insurance, and Karen Horn said that her financial data indicated that depositor confidence was fully restored. A respected poll showed that 49 percent thought the governor was correct in closing the banks, and only 28 percent opposed his decision; 23 percent were uncertain. The national media drifted away from Columbus, allowing the lieutenant governor to return to his office.

On Friday March 29, Celeste had a half-hour question and answer session with a Cleveland luncheon audience and was never asked about the bank closings. Later that day, he was applauded during an Akron speech when he stressed his leadership role in the crisis; and that evening, when he invited newspaper editors to dinner, they were gentle with him as he discussed his handling of the closings and his relationship with Warner.

The Skirt Squad had reason to be satisfied when they met in Paula's kitchen Sunday night, March 31. They and their cohorts in Dayton and Columbus had collected seventy-five thousand signatures in five days, a feat which would make even a seasoned, sophisticated political organization proud. But at about nine o'clock they received news which deflated their good spirits; the legislature and a good part of the state government would be closed April 2, the day of the petition motorcade, for the funeral of a legislator who had died suddenly of a heart attack.

They weighed the possibly serious disappointment of bringing their people and their petitions to an empty governor's office against dissipating the precious energy and momentum which they had built. During their debate, they called influential politicos for advice, and Debi was asked to contact Finan. As she waited for him to come to the phone, she stepped on Paula's dog. She remembers, "Here I was trying to muster my courage to talk to this senator and the dog hauls off and bites me. 'Oh, shit,' I yelled into the phone. The dog would not take his teeth out of my foot and finally Paula disengaged him." When things settled down, Finan counseled against the motorcade; but he was on the losing side. At 2 A.M., they decided to push ahead.

Celeste can count votes, and when he got word that seventy-five thousand signatures were going to land on his desk, he decided he would work his schedule around the legislator's funeral to meet the Home State delegation.

The motorcade turnout exceeded the Skirt Squad's expectations. They were thrilled to be part of a three-hundred-car flotilla cruising with their lights on in formation up I-71 to Columbus. They met the Columbus and Dayton people at a designated parking area, and marched, one thousand strong, a mile to the statehouse.

It was fortunate that the state had beefed up its security force around the statehouse because the crowd was angry and boisterous. Seven of the leaders, including Debi, Toni, Joe Rabe, and Fred Kaufmann, were chosen to meet the governor. They pushed through a crowd of security and media people, and were ushered into a room where Celeste, McAlister, Cox, Arlo Smith and several attorneys greeted them from behind a huge, oval, mahogany table. After everyone was seated, the Home State delegation spread their petitions on the table and covered a good portion of it.

The heated mood of the Home Staters, already confrontational, was turned up a notch by the noise coming from the crowd outside. They were chanting, "Give us our money back," and "Open Home State," and even "Burn down the statehouse," and some were banging on the walls.

But the governor was ready for the people seated opposite him. He disarmed them by saying in a cool, detached voice that he had a very interested buyer who, with the aid of the state, would make Home State's depositors and debenture holders 100 percent whole. The depositors were surprised but not totally convinced. Toni Handley pressed Celeste about the strength of the purchaser's commitment, and the governor replied he expected a letter of intent momentarily. He added that he would be able to reveal the name of the buyer, an out-of-state bank, in a day or two.

Debi presented the governor with a T-shirt emblazoned with the words "Betrayal of Trust" and the group filed out to report to the crowd waiting outside. They said they were optimistic, but cautious. Most of the people driving home felt happy but were convinced that the road to their money would be long and hard.

The next day Celeste and Tew were in Washington testifying before a congressional subcommittee investigating the federal response to ESM's collapse and the Ohio banking crisis. Celeste announced that twenty-nine banks with more than 40 percent of the deposits were in full-service operation, called for greater federal regulation of the government securities market, and condemned private deposit insurance.

Tew called the ESM swindle "the most abusive corporate raping I've ever seen," and released a 166-page report to the judge handling the ESM case; it detailed the fraud and its accounting cover-up. He said he was considering suits against Warner, Arky, and Bongard as "insiders" who may have been involved in ESM's machinations. And he spotlighted Ronnie Ewton and Jose Gomez as prime players in the fraud.

Ewton and Gomez were slipping into deeper trouble that day as they were indicted, along with Nick Wallace, for forging Alan Novick's will. A Fort Lauderdale judge had thrown out the document when a handwriting expert testified that Novick's signature had been written over four times with ballpoint pens and felt markers. She said that the forgery was crude and obvious and failed every possible criteria for authenticity.

Alan, in fact, had left no will, and the document presented in court was an after-the-fact concoction; it left everything to Alan's widow, Sonya. Gomez had forged the signature and Ewton and Wallace had witnessed it in an attempt to help their friend's widow. The three fumbling perpetrators later pleaded guilty to the forgery.

On Thursday, April 4, after Celeste returned from Washington, he discovered that a legislator had leaked the news that Home State's suitor was New York's Chemical Bank. When he took a close look at Chemical's proposition, the governor realized quickly that it would take all his wiles to overcome the two big political problems which it contained.

First of all, the proposal involved lots of Ohio money; it estimated commitments of up to $100 million from the state and $90 million from ODGF and allowed Chemical to ask for more if a detailed examination of Home State's condition showed the bank to be sicker than its books indicated. Because it wanted a totally satisfied customer base, Chemical's proposition insisted on a 100 percent return plus interest to depositors and full reimbursement of $27 million to the debenture holders. For its part, Chemical would invest $46 million to gain access to the lucrative southern Ohio market.

The governor's second sticking point was that Ohio law prohibited out-of-state ownership of state banks. Repeal would involve wrangling with both the legislature and the local banking industry.

Celeste's mood was brightened on Friday, when the legislature handed him a bill increasing SLAC's capital by $10 million to $60 million, and raising the monthly withdrawal limit from $750 to $1,000 per depositor. But as he sat chewing on a Wendy's hamburger at lunchtime, he brooded about finding the political clout to deal with his problems with the Chemical proposal. And his mind kept returning to the image of those seventy-five thousand signatures spread over his big mahogany table. He had heard that the Home State Depositors Association had dozens of people in the statehouse lobbying for their cause, and he asked an aide to find some of their leaders. Within a few minutes, the aide turned up with Toni, Debi, Lisa, Fred Kaufmann, and Mark Stachler, an associate of Fred's from Dayton.

The mood Celeste set was entirely different from the one which prevailed when they had gathered around the mahogany table just seventy-two hours before. Warm, comfortable, cordial; no hint of confrontation. The governor acted like the guy next door, eating his hamburger and burping, introducing everyone to his Dad who had dropped by for a moment, taking a "wrong number" phone call and joking about it.

He told the depositors he was on their side and wished to create an advisory committee of nine of their leaders to help guide him through the difficult time ahead. The Home State people were wary, but accepted his offer. They and the governor were united by a common need, but the depositors felt that it was basically a marriage of political convenience, and their wariness never left them. The committee was set up the following week and included Toni, Lisa, Debi, Joe Rabe, Mark Stachler, and Fred Kaufmann.

Starting Monday, April 8, the depositors had at least fifty people at the statehouse every day lobbying the legislators directly, testifying before committees, and dealing with the media. Many were retirees who had lots of time available. Toni, Debi, and Lisa, who helped coordinate their efforts, became Monday to Friday residents of Columbus.

International financial markets were severely jolted April 8 by the news that government securities dealer Bevill, Bresler & Schulman was closed down by the SEC for a fraud rivaling ESM's in size. More than $240 million was missing and the modus operandi was remarkably similar to ESM's: phony bookkeeping, borrowing against customer collateral, huge speculative losses, sybaritic life-styles for the principals.

The reason for the similarities was not far to seek. Bevill, one of the main culprits, was a "Memphis bond bandit," as were several of his key employees. He, like Ewton, Mead, and Seneca, was an alumnus of Hibbard, O'Connor & Weeks, and he had employed Ewton and Mead at Bevill, Bresler in 1975. One of his principal managers worked for a time at ESM.

Bevill, Bresler's biggest casualty was an Arkansas bank that lost $40 million but survived because wealthy owners replenished its capital. The financial markets were quieted rapidly, because deposits at all but one of its seventy-five victimized banks were federally insured, and because the Federal Reserve, benefitting from its Ohio experience, immediately announced it would make emergency loans available to the fraud victims. The single bank which was not federally insured turned out to be twice bit; it was Jefferson Building and Savings, one of the ODGF sixty-eight. It suffered no loss, however, because it had firmly secured possession of its collateral.

Coming so quickly after the ESM debacle, the Bevill, Bresler fraud increased pressure on Congress to regulate the government securities industry. Such legislation was enacted in 1986, and all participants agree that the widespread suffering and dislocation caused by the ESM and Bevill, Bresler frauds were the prime catalysts in its passage.

On Monday, April 8, fifty Chemical Bank auditors arrived in Cincinnati to begin analyzing Home State's books. They promised to come up with a definitive offer within a week and plunged into a series of sixteen-hour work days. While Celeste waited on their evaluation, he was hit with a new problem. ODGF, whose total assets were earmarked for Chemical, would not cooperate.

The fund's executives wanted to hold onto its money and stay in business, because they felt they had a good chance to win multimillion-dollar lawsuits they had filed against the key players in Home State's collapse—Warner and several Home State executives, Alexander Grant, the ESM gang. They planned to distribute to the original member banks any monies recovered in the suits.

On April 12, ODGF obtained a court order prohibiting Bob McAlister from taking control of the $87 million which remained in its coffers and thus liquidating the fund. The governor said, "I am outraged. It is unbelievable to me that the very organization . . . that purported to guarantee all the deposits in the institutions, is now trying to keep that guarantee from being effective." The battle was joined in the courts and a decision was expected in early May.

Chemical's formal offer on April 16 increased its contribution from $46 million to $57 million, but to the governor's chagrin, it upped the state's subsidy from an expected $100 million to $129 million. Chemical's auditing team had found that the value of Home State's mortgage portfolio and other assets were overstated by roughly $40 million. The state's financial adviser, investment banker Kidder, Peabody & Co., did not, in Bob McAlister's words, "take great exception to the findings."

Now began an exhausting four-week round of negotiations to create an acceptable Home State bailout bill. Among the participants were the Chemical people, Finan and the legislative leaders, Celeste, McAlister, and assorted lobbying groups which included the Ohio Bankers Association and the Home State Depositors Association.

Everyone involved agrees that the Depositors Association was very effective. Sometimes they let their anger get out of hand; one day they went too far with Dick Finan, of all people, and he shouted, "God damn it, shut up. I'm on your side. Go yell at the guys who are against you." But for the most part, they modulated their pressure skillfully, organized their troops well, and worked the media like pros.

The participants in the legislative negotiations were filled with anxiety for weeks because of the court battle over ODGF's vital millions. This was removed at a dramatic hearing of the Ohio Supreme Court on Wednesday, May 8. Depositors packed the chamber. There were many more spectators than seats, and the bailiff started asking people to leave because a rule prohibited standees. But the chief justice looked up and in a booming voice said, "Mr. Bailiff, don't do that. Let the people in. They should hear this. Their money is at stake."

The crowd cheered the verdict which gave McAlister $81 million and allowed ODGF to retain $6 million to pursue its lawsuits.

Marvin Warner left Ohio the weekend of Home State's collapse and, except for a short April 4 TV interview, had been invisible to the people and the media of the state until Thursday, May 9. On that day, he held a press conference with reporters from six major Ohio newspapers—in Miami, 1,100 miles from Cincinnati. He said he had no role in causing the collapse and painted himself as a victim—of the ESM crooks, the phony Grant audit, and the unfair media.

The performance didn't wash well back home. Bill Cunningham reported a passionately negative response on his call-in show, and the *Enquirer* summed up local sentiment in an editorial:

> The Florida session with the press was a case of too little, too late. For his own reasons, Marvin Warner has methodically ducked the spotlight—precisely when he should have sought it out.
>
> If Marvin Warner is, as he insists, a victim in the Home State affair, he should have stood shoulder-to-shoulder with all the other Home State victims. If, as he maintains, he did not have his hands on the wheel, he rode very close to the driver's seat. . . . Common sense and decency say that any corporate executive, any one in a leadership position, must be accessible when trouble occurs. But, Marvin Warner shirked that responsibility.

By May 17, Finan and a determined band of legislative allies had drafted a bill which they felt stood a good chance of resolving the crisis. It dealt both with the terms of the Home State bailout and with rules governing purchases of Ohio banks by out-of-state banks. It stipulated that the state would contribute $125 million; $91 million from the sale of ten-year bonds, and $34 million from currently available state liquor profits and unclaimed bank accounts.

Repayment of the bonds would come from: collections in lawsuits against culprits in the ESM–Home State debacle, fees from out-of-state banks entering the Ohio market (Chemical's fee was set at $21 million), future state liquor profits, and future unclaimed bank accounts. In addition to its $21 million entrance fee, Chemical would invest $30 million in Home State and ODGF would contribute $81 million.

Out-of-state banks could buy Ohio banks only if they paid a fee and if they picked up at least fifty thousand accounts. Ohio banks would be given seven days to top any out-of-state purchase offer for another Ohio bank. An in-state bank had to give its consent for any takeover by an out-of-state bank.

The bill passed the Democratic House sixty-three to twenty-five at 12:45 P.M. after only twenty-five minutes of debate. Then it went to the Senate, where the Republicans had an eighteen to fifteen majority and where the vote promised to be very close.

Home State depositors, who packed the gallery, sat nervously through the roll call. Only thirty-two members were voting because one was home sick and, as they neared the end, the count was sixteen to fifteen in favor. The final vote was to be cast by Buz Lukens, a conservative Republican from a district between Cincinnati and Dayton.

Lukens, fifty-four, did not expect to live through 1985. In January, doctors had removed two pounds of cancerous tissue from his neck, and he had undergone painful and exhausting radiation and chemotherapy. His treatments caused memory lapses, and his aides stayed close to him to remind him of recent events and people's names.

Toni and Debi were with Buz before the vote and walked arm-in-arm with him to the Senate floor, begging him all the way to vote "yes." He wouldn't commit himself and told them, "Ladies, trust me, trust me. I promise you there's something working and I can't talk to you about it now." Then he voted "no" causing a sixteen to sixteen tie and the defeat of the bill.

Most of the Home State spectators rose to their feet and shouted their anger at the senators standing below. Some sat and wept. Finally they filed out and gathered on the statehouse lawn. Their leaders promised to keep fighting and then left them for a nearby bar to plot the next moves. There they decided to battle on with a massive statehouse demonstration the following week, continued pressure on key senators, and the withdrawal of funds from selected Columbus banks as a show of economic power.

But their battle was won in the quiet of Buz Lukens's home on Sunday. He hadn't told anybody, but he had voted "no" on Friday, because he preferred an Ohio solution to the crisis, and had gotten the word that Cincinnati financier Carl Lindner was readying a bid for Home State which would better Chemical's. Buz was worried about "a foreigner" taking over Home State, but he was also concerned abut the sheer size of Chemical; it was four times as big as any Ohio bank.

On Sunday morning, he received confirmation that Lindner was totally serious and Buz decided to change his vote. Lindner did not want to be identified as a bidder, and Lukens agreed to shield his name.

Carl Lindner, sixty-five in 1985, had parlayed a small Cincinnati dairy into a multibillion dollar empire which controlled corporate giants such as Penn Central, United Brands, and Great American Insurance. A privacy fanatic who never gives interviews, Lindner is a devout Baptist and paragon of Midwestern rectitude who loves to pass

out cards with sayings like "Only in America! Gee! Am I lucky!,"
"Life is hard by the yard but a cinch by the inch," "Every dog has his
day," and "The harder I work, the luckier I get." His generous
philanthropy has included Baptist causes, the Museum of Modern Art
in New York, where a gallery bears his name, and the University of
Cincinnati.

Lindner planned to bid for Home State through his Hunter Savings, the second largest FSLIC-insured thrift in the Cincinnati area.

Lukens announced his switch on Monday, May 20, and the vote was
scheduled for the following day. On Tuesday morning, five thousand
Home State depositors descended on Columbus anticipating victory.
They wore their "Victim of Trust" T-shirts and carried cowbells and
homemade signs which said things like "I'm a Home State Hostage,"
"Chemical Bank Now," and "Give Me 100 Percent or Give Me Marvin." They poured out of their buses and vans and cars, created
miniruns at three Columbus banks, and then surrounded the statehouse. Fifteen hundred of them were able to squeeze inside; of these,
five hundred packed the Senate gallery while the overflow milled
around in the central rotunda. Toni Handley remembers:

> They had called out the National Guard or the State Guard because
> they were afraid something would go wrong. Because there were thou-
> sands upon thousands of depositors. You literally could not set foot
> anywhere near the statehouse. They were lined up. They were on the
> lawn. Just shoulder to shoulder by the statehouse.
>
> A Senate aide pulled Lisa and I aside and told us that we had been so
> active they wanted to make sure we had a good seat. And they dragged
> us onto the Senate floor through a roundabout way and they stationed
> us right along the rail there, of the Senate floor. We were told people
> were never allowed within that rail, but there we were feeling like
> Queens of the May.

As the vote proceeded, the Senate ushers could not keep the spectators quiet as they booed the "no" votes and greeted each "yes" by
ringing their cowbells, cheering, and applauding wildly. When
victory came, they rushed into the rotunda to hug and kiss those who
had missed the show. Someone starting singing "God Bless America"
and the crowd joined in.

After signing the bill, Celeste came out to meet the throng. They
cheered loudly when he paid tribute to their persistence, determination, and patience.

The next day, Lindner announced his interest in Home State and on Tuesday, May 28, made a formal bid through Hunter asking for $5 million less in state aid than Chemical. That meant that his subsidy would be $201 million, $120 million from the state and $81 million from ODGF. As part of the deal, Lindner agreed to substitute for Chemical's $21 million Ohio entrance fee the same amount in additional capital for Home State. On May 30, McAlister accepted the Hunter bid. He said, "$5 million is an awful lot of money," and pointed out that Lukens's crucial vote probably would not have been obtained if an Ohio solution had not been in the offing.

Lukens credits his efforts to end the sufferings of the Home State depositors with giving him added spiritual strength to battle his cancer. He is now completely free of it and since 1986 has served Ohio's eighth district in the U.S. House of Representatives.

Lindner immediately sold twenty Home State branches to other Ohio banks—ten to AmeriTrust and ten to First National—and the grand reopening on Friday, June 14, took place under the banners of the three institutions. After fourteen weeks of hardship and anxiety, the Home State depositors had their money again. First National served them punch and cookies, AmeriTrust had coffee and danish, and the Hunter tellers wore carnations. A sense of calm and business-as-usual prevailed, and this seemed anticlimactic to many of the veterans who fought the arduous battles of the past months.

As soon as he completed the Hunter transaction, McAlister made deals to sell five banks to Chase Manhattan in New York and four to Home Savings of America in Los Angeles. As a condition, he forced the out-of-state buyers to pick up two weak thrifts in each package. He also spent SLAC money vigorously to meet FSLIC capital requirements for laggards, and by June 15 just eight ODGF banks were still on a $1,000 withdrawal basis and not open for full service. They held $227 million in deposits, or only 6 percent of the $4.3 billion in assets which had been frozen on March 15. The struggle to return the final eight to health was a slow one, and the last returned to full service on January 6, 1986.

In all, the legislature committed roughly $200 million to save the depositors of Home State and the sixty-eight. This meant that each of Ohio's eleven million citizens—man, woman, and child—was dunned $18 to make good on the bank failures.

The people of Ohio experienced pain, anxiety, financial deprivation. They were hurt, but their sufferings weren't the stuff of ultimate tragedy—Stephen Arky's sufferings were.

11

The Demons of
Stephen Arky

The demons of despair, of defeat, of self-hatred—he had fought them all his life. He had kept them at bay, but they were always there, ready to devour him.

Their chains started to come loose, for the final time, on January 21, 1985, when Bobby Schatzman, Ronnie Ewton's bankruptcy lawyer, met with Steve Arky to let him know about ESM's massive losses and imminent collapse.

Arky's reaction to Schatzman was totally out of character. Arky had always been the rough-and-tumble deal maker, the pugnacious litigator who relished combat and who would, on occasion, humiliate his opponents. When Schatzman told him Ewton estimated ESM's losses at $180 million, Steve was stunned. For several moments he could not speak. He appeared in shock, as if all the force had left his body. ESM had always had problems, but they were manageable problems, the kind that Steve could help resolve. Like the SEC investigation in 1977, the Seneca divorce case in 1980, and perhaps twenty lesser matters since then.

But a $180 million loss wasn't manageable, it was catastrophic. It would probably bring down Home State, perhaps the whole Ohio banking system; it could severely wound Marvin Warner and shake the foundations of Arky, Freed.

Betrayal—this was the word that burned into Steve Arky's mind and that robbed him of his vitality. Ronnie Ewton had betrayed him; so had Roger Bernstein.

Partnership should mean trust, and Steve felt sure that Roger, a former partner of his at Arky, Freed, had misled him into investing in an oil and gas deal by inflating the production and profit projections. Now the deal had gone sour. Some partner!

With Ronnie, it was worse. They had fought side by side in so many tough battles, had wheeled and dealed and made money together at ABI and ComBanks, were partners in the Tampa Bay Bandits. But it went beyond business. They were close friends, had been close for over fifteen years.

Steve and Ronnie were an odd couple: the chunky, 5-foot, five-inch, Jewish lawyer in his dark suits and black horn-rimmed glasses; and the slender, smooth, elegantly tailored WASP broker with the soft Tennessee accent. Ronnie was one of the few adult males that Steve felt totally comfortable with. He could confide in Ronnie. Let his hair down. Talk about his troubles—business troubles, family troubles—it didn't matter. And Ronnie had confided in him also, in bad times like the breakup with Darla, and in good times. But it was all a fake— Ronnie had used him, had played him for a sucker for all those years. Betrayed into defeat.

Betrayal and defeat. Their opposites, loyalty and victory, had been the touchstones of Steve's life. That was how he kept the demons at bay. You served others, you won for others, you never let them down. They needed you and respected you, and you felt good, and the demons were kept in their chains.

But the quest was endless; you were always driven to find others to be served. "His entertainment was business entertainment," said Alan Levan, a close friend and client. "At a party, playing tennis, jogging, swimming, sitting on a plane, he would pick up clients." His relentless drive, which some saw as conventional business ambition, was rooted in the necessity of the quest.

Some people, Steve must have felt, you could never satisfy. Whatever you gave them never seemed enough. But with Ronnie, that loyalty, that service was always enough, or so it appeared.

Now he saw that betrayers like Ronnie just glided on to the next sucker. The betrayers got off easy. Being duped by them must have brought deepest pain.

Then there was Tom Tew. Another one of those handsome WASP Southerners who glided so easily through life. Arky remembered telling a reporter that Tew's fundamental flaw was a lack of dedication, a lack of loyalty. Steve had talked about how Tew moved through four law firms and two marriages during the previous ten years. He had said, "The man can't keep his legal partners, and he can't keep his wives."

And he had added, "He wants what we have. It's simple jealousy." Steve saw Tew as one of his true rivals to be number one, king of the hill, in Miami's fiercely competitive world of corporate law. Steve seemed to have emerged from the cradle with a burning desire to be number one—at anything he did.

He was born on June 30, 1943, the son of Albert and Lillian Arky, and grew up in a Jewish neighborhood in University City, Missouri, a suburb on the edge of St. Louis. University City now has a downtown business district with shiny glass and steel office towers, but when Steve was growing up, it was a one-industry town. And that industry was prestigious Washington University.

Albert, who had come to America from Hungary as a child, worked as a counterman in a food market owned by relatives. With Lillian helping out part of the time as the manager of a laundromat, he was able to provide Steve and his younger sister Joyce with many of the comforts of lower-middle-class American life in the 1950s and 1960s. The family lived in a small, comfortable house on a tree-lined street of similar houses, and they accumulated the appliances which made life easier for so many millions in those decades. And they were able to take advantage of the excellent schools provided by University City.

Steve was a serious, directed, no-nonsense student. He told others that his main motivation was to deliver the goods to his parents, to reward them for what they had done for him. He made Albert and Lillian proud by winning a scholarship to Washington University, where he sped along—earning a bachelor of arts and a law degree in six years rather than the usual seven.

Steve drove aggressively toward the apex of the power pyramid at college. He didn't often stop "to smell the roses" and seemed to be running everything. He was elected president of his fraternity and won the Omicron Delta Kappa award for outstanding leadership in student government and social activities. The only top post which eluded him was president of the senior class; he lost out in a close election. A few years later when his sister Joyce ran for the same office and was defeated, he told her, "Thank God. It would have been awfully difficult to live with the reality of me losing and you winning."

Steve's drive for success seemed clearly to be leading him to the upper echelons of corporate America. He wanted to get there as soon as possible, and he saw law school as his launching pad for such a career. His record led him to an excellent starting job as an attorney with the SEC in 1967.

At college he met and fell in love with fellow student Marlin Blach

Warner and, over her father's objections, they were married during Steve's final year in law school. The parallels to Marvin's marriage to Jane Blach were striking. Again, the older generation was opposing an heiress's marriage to a penniless, ambitious attorney, the son of an immigrant working man.

Steve's first job with the SEC was in Washington, D.C., but he soon had himself transferred to the agency's Miami office. He wanted no part of Washington's bureaucracy and chose Miami because he wished to place himself where the action was—in a burgeoning, exciting city where business opportunity seemed everywhere at hand.

Steve quit the SEC in 1971 to join a respected, established, politically connected Miami law firm, Pettigrew & Bailey. In 1976, he and five other partners (including Pettigrew) left in a dispute over management philosophy and the division of fees and formed Arky, Freed.

Steve was far and away the biggest business getter in the new firm, in large part due to fees generated from Marvin Warner's enterprises and bank deals. But the mix of talents among the partners was excellent and by 1983, Arky, Freed had grown to forty-five lawyers plus a support staff of sixty-five.

On Steve's fortieth birthday, June 30, 1983, the *Wall Street Journal* ran an article on the partnership which focused on Steve's leadership role and featured a line drawing of him. The opening sentence read, "In a very short time the law firm of Arky, Freed . . . has risen to the top here (Miami) as an adviser to take-over minded investors in the combative world of Florida banking." The writer acknowledged that having Marvin Warner's business was a major advantage, but pointed out that Arky, Freed had attracted other major clients such as Mitsubishi, financier Victor Posner, builder Kaufman and Broad, Inc., and Juan Perez-Sandoval. He attributed the firm's success to a combination of financial sophistication and toughness, and quoted two rivals: "They're young and aggressive"—and they're "smart, prepared and extremely aggressive."

Steve was described as "really a businessman in the law business," and he told the reporter, "What really turns me on is business deals, putting deals together. Creative financing."

As the years rolled by, Steve focused more and more on deal making, and became increasingly impatient with the details of the practice of law. He was an inspired matchmaker who, instead of making the usual lawyerly arguments about why things can't be done, would sweat out ways to make deals happen. He would cajole and flatter the principals, create—when necessary—complex financial instruments such as convertible debentures, suggest ways to combine departments efficiently, and figure out how to minimize the tax effects of mergers.

His life was almost totally absorbed in his work. His wife grew accustomed to cold dinners and all-night negotiations, to postponements of vacations with their children, Todd, born in 1970, and Lisa in 1973. And Marlin remembered the Arky, Freed anniversary party when the partners made a strict rule: no shop talk. Within a half hour, Steve was gleefully describing the details of a corporate marriage he had just arranged. The partners had chuckled knowingly; there was no way they could change him.

His work was the main content of his conversation just about anywhere. If he couldn't talk about business, he became very quiet. Acquaintances who were not part of his professional world described him as "very reserved, stuffy," "always serious, the kind of guy you couldn't joke around with," and "a cold fish, totally controlled."

But those who benefitted from his total dedication saw a different Steve. One of his clients said, "I loved that little guy. He was a terrific guy. He always delivered." And another remarked, "He was always there for you as a friend. I had a lot of respect for him."

Steve almost never talked about his feelings. One of his closest friends has said, "He would talk about deals, not about emotions." When his feelings did surface, they were usually aggressive. His friend Alan Levan remembers, "Steve took a sense of delight in making the other guy look bad. If Arky, Freed beat another lawyer they rubbed his face in it, laughed about it. The loser felt not only unsuccessful, but humiliated."

In the preliminary skirmishing after the ESM collapse, Steve reacted with his customary aggressiveness and energy. He rushed to the SEC on March 15, the day Dick Celeste closed the sixty-eight banks, and volunteered for questioning. The following week he submitted to twenty hours of rigorous examination about his relationships with Ronnie Ewton and ESM.

However, when Tom Tew pulled out his big guns on April 2 in his public report to the judge handling the ESM case, Steve offered almost no resistance. The report painted Arky and Warner as ESM insiders who enriched themselves from private accounts while hundreds of thousands of innocents were being defrauded. Warner fought back vigorously, and some of Arky's partners counseled him to do likewise; but Steve declined the gambit.

The ESM mess seriously reduced the income flow of Arky, Freed. Big corporate clients were unnerved by the suggestion of scandal. They preferred their attorneys to be virtually anonymous, not in the headlines of the *Wall Street Journal*, the *Miami Herald*, and the *New York Times*. In fact, the *Herald*, an important client, sharply cut back its dealings with the firm. Referrals from other attorneys dried up, and the entrepreneurs and the CEOs, who had constantly turned to Steve Arky for counsel, stopped calling. On top of all this, Warner's empire was crumbling and there would be no more fees from the man who had been Arky, Freed's biggest source of income.

Two factions coalesced within the firm around opposite responses to the ESM debacle. They were led by the two main litigating partners—Gene Stearns and Bruce Greer. The Stearns faction wanted to adopt the old Arky, Freed tactics—the best defense is a strong offense, hit 'em and hit 'em again, attack, attack, attack.

The Greer faction argued for a strategy of retreat—let's bury this, put it behind us as soon as possible. We can't win a media war against Tew; he has too much artillery, including the prestige of the federal government, backing him.

There were mutterings in both factions about getting rid of Steve. Some partners perceived him as a liability no matter which approach was adopted.

The thought of having to leave the firm must have brought Steve almost to the point of physical illness. Nausea. Despair. The firm was his monument, living proof of his victories, his unstinting service to clients, his loyalty to partners and employees.

The problems at Arky, Freed were more than enough for one man to cope with, but Steve also faced forces outside the firm that were vectoring in on him with brutal strength. The Tampa Bay Bandits and the USFL were going under, and as a Bandits general partner, Steve's liabilities might mount into the hundreds of thousands of dollars. Another project which he had invested major time and money in, a kind of Miami Lloyds of London called the Insurance Exchange of the Americas, was tottering towards bankruptcy.

Furthermore, his expenses were going to mount as he would have to finance legal battles with creditors of these shaky enterprises, with Tom Tew, with the SEC, with litigants barely on the horizon. And he had serious monetary obligations to cover in the Bernstein oil and gas deal. Suddenly the arrows seemed to be coming at him from all directions.

In late April he sought out one of his closest friends, a fellow lawyer, and talked about his financial difficulties, emphasizing the relatively small pile of capital he had been able to accumulate during his forty-two years. He talked about how difficult it was to make real money as a lawyer. All you have to sell is your hours, and there are only so many hours in the day. And if you're going to have fancy clients, you've got to have fancy offices, and all that overhead eats you up. Steve told his friend, "After all my success and all the big cases and all the investments, my net worth is only half a million dollars. I have to do something about that." He talked about leaving the law firm and going into investment banking. After all, deal making was his forte, and it really gave him a kick.

The lawyer suggested that the two of them and a mutual friend, a broker, form an investment banking company specializing in deals—takeovers, leveraged buyouts, mergers. Steve knew and respected the broker, who had made lots of money investing astutely and boldly for clients and for himself. The three met a couple of times about organizing the new company, but they made little progress because Steve's heart wasn't in it.

During May, he fell into a funk. He virtually stopped seeing clients, and he spent endless hours reviewing the ESM files. And he would tell over and over again, to anyone who would listen, the story of his betrayal by Ronnie Ewton.

Things got worse in June; Steve's mood swung from apathy to despair and panic. On June 15, he told his partners that Arky, Freed was in desperate financial trouble. The firm was, in fact, in reasonable financial health, and Steve's partners were frightened that he was losing touch with reality. They were relieved when, on June 23, Marlin Arky called to say that Steve was at her dad's Bal Harbour condo and was taking the week off to rest and relax.

Steve was not, in fact, in Bal Harbour; he was in a bed at South Miami's Larkin General Hospital. The night before, he had tried to kill himself by taking a fearsome overdose of Restoril sleeping pills. Marlin kept the knowledge of the suicide attempt to herself, her dad, a very small circle of friends, and her psychotherapist, Evan Katz. She never told anyone at Arky, Freed.

The first thing you notice about Marlin is how straight she stands. Her posture goes beyond the strictures of the good health and hygiene books and gives her a bearing of both stateliness and strength. She is slender; she can't weigh much over one hundred pounds and stands about five feet, one inch tall. Her dark brown hair, done in 1940s pageboy style, frames an attractive face accented by the strong bone structure she inherited from her father. She listens intently to what you say, and her speech is soft yet animated. The main quality she conveys is strength—quiet strength.

A firm believer in psychotherapy, Marlin felt relieved that Steve was, for the first time, being treated by a psychiatrist, Larkin's George Metcalf. He released Steve from Larkin on Monday, July 1, put him on a regimen of antidepressant drugs, and counseled him twice a week in therapy sessions.

When Marlin left Steve at 8:30 A.M. on Monday, July 22, he was partially dressed. He had pulled on his slacks, his socks, and his T-shirt. He never finished dressing. Instead, he took a white legal pad, and in an agitated script, wrote two notes. The first was addressed "To the world at-large." It read:

> I have become severely depressed primarily because of acts of others whom I trusted totally. They returned my trust with betrayal. I will not list all the names here, because those who have failed me know who they are. I will single out Roger Bernstein and Ron Ewton.
>
> As for the ESM matter, I swear now that I did not know anything about the adverse financial conditions or even suspect that there might be problems until January 21, 1984 (sic: 1985). I am innocent of any wrong doing in that case. So are my partners and Marvin Warner.
>
> I only wish that I had the strength to keep going in order to prove my innocence and see those who perpetrated the fraud brought to justice.
>
> Thanks to those who believed in me and stayed with me through the dark days that began with the ESM disaster.
>
> Stephen W. Arky

The second was addressed to Marlin, and, indirectly, to their children Todd and Lisa:

> My depression keeps getting deeper and I cannot go on living. I have not slept for so many nights that I've lost count. My behavior while appearing to be normal for a person in depression has started becoming bizarre, and I realized that I would have to spend the rest of my life in a mental institution. That option is simply not acceptable.
>
> I love you, Todd & Lisa more than you can ever know. I have held on this long only because I couldn't bear to let you all down. It is now clear

to me that I can't hold on any longer. I can't explain it very well—except to say that I hope you will be able to forgive me someday. There is nothing that any of you could have done to help me. It's as if my mind has decided to destroy me. While I want more than anything to be with all of you, if I can only accomplish that by letting you visit me at an asylum, that is unacceptable.

Please try to understand.

All my love,

Steve

Steve put down his pen, picked up a pillow and a loaded Colt .38 revolver which he had hidden, and walked to the bathroom carrying the legal pad with the two notes still attached. He placed the pad on a counter, put the pillow on the floor, laid down on his left side with his head on the pillow, brought the gun to his right temple, and put a bullet through his brain.

The sight of Steve's car still in the garage rattled Marlin when she returned home nearly two hours later. She entered the house and called, "Steve," and there was no answer. Before she moved any further, she called Evan Katz. "I'm scared," she said. When she got to the bathroom, she looked briefly at her husband's blood-soaked body and in her shock didn't notice the gun, which had been forced under his chin by the recoil. When she called the police, she told them he had slit his wrists.

After they arrived, she asked the police to delay an announcement for twenty-four hours. Her children were at a camp in Maine, and she wanted time to fly there, tell them the terrible news herself, and take them home to Miami. The officers agreed. She called her dad, told him what had happened and what she was going to do, and set off for Maine. She and the children returned that night. The next day, Marvin called Steve's friends and partners to tell them of the tragedy.

Marlin felt that Steve's only moments of peace during his last tortured weeks occurred when he was jogging along the roads near their home. She buried him in his running shorts and track shoes. Over a thousand mourners filled every nook and cranny of Temple Beth Am for the funeral service on Wednesday, July 24. It was the largest crowd the temple had ever held at a funeral.

Steve Arky's death was the darkest chapter in the ESM saga.

12

Tom Tew—Ace Receiver

Tom Tew started work at ESM Tuesday morning March 5, 1985, in charge of the place, armed with the authority of the federal government. The last time he had been there he only possessed the authority to investigate, and it was derived from George Mead and Nick Wallace. That all changed on Monday, March 4, when Mead and Wallace released him, and Judge William Hoeveler appointed him equity receiver to safeguard the interests of those hurt by the ESM fraud. The concept of equity receiver goes back hundreds of years into British common law and gives judges broad emergency powers to protect the victims of fraud or gross mismanagement.

There was hardly space to sit down at ESM that Tuesday morning. Bodies were everywhere: Laurie Holtz's crew, Charlie Harper and his SEC investigators, three lawyers from Tom's office, FBI agents, armed guards, and the ESM employees who had elected to stay on. Tom needed the ESM employees to help him locate and make sense of the 1.5 million documents in the company files. Novick's schemes to keep ESM alive were so complex that he required complete records to make sure he did not slip up, and he never threw anything away. As one of the lawyers commented, "Novick had so many balls in the air, there was no air there."

Tom remembers that the decision to retain the ESM people was a tough one. He said, "Even though I knew one person had been pretty close to the flame, we convinced the government that on balance it was better to have them there and take the risk that some might have culpability than to throw them out and never get the job done. We took some initial heat, but it proved to be a super decision, thank God."

Tew's efforts were almost foiled by the FBI agents, who panicked the ESM employees by questioning them roughly and by making macho displays of the pistols in their ankle holsters. Tom asked Charlie

Harper to "please, for God's sake, rein these guys in," and Charlie gathered the agents in Ewton's conference room and persuaded them to ease up.

Tom faced what seemed like a thousand tasks. Some were crucial, like extracting vital information from the investigations of Holtz, the SEC, and the FBI. Others were trivial, like closing a small ESM Memphis office which Mead had set up in the mortgage brokerage business seven months before. But everything Tom did was driven by a single overriding goal: recovery for the victims of as much as possible of the missing $300 million. He had to grab every ESM asset within reach and sue everyone in sight to try to recover what was not yet within reach.

The first business of the day was to close out the $900 million in open buy and sell orders which ESM had with brokerage firms throughout the United States. Fortunately, these transactions netted a $700,000 profit to the ESM receivership, and the money was in the bank within a week.

Then, for hours, Tom fielded calls from stricken customers. Most of them were officials who had left unprotected their towns' and counties' securities at ESM and were now feeling political heat because of the losses suffered. He invited them to come to Fort Lauderdale and spent much of the next couple of weeks meeting with these people—listening to their anguished stories, researching their claims, and discussing strategies for getting their money back.

Even as he talked to them, he was putting some of these strategies to work. On March 8, he got Judge Jose Gonzalez, who inherited the case because he was federal district judge for Fort Lauderdale, to freeze the personal assets of all the ESM executives. And on March 15 he sued Alexander Grant for $315 million on behalf of the victims.

The victims were the state of Ohio's conservator, who now stood in the shoes of Home State and whose claim was $145 million, American Savings & Loan (AS&L) with a claim of $60 million, seventeen public bodies who were looking for $105 million, and miscellaneous creditors seeking $5 million. Home State and AS&L had gotten into trouble by borrowing from ESM and overcollateralizing their loans. The public bodies and the other creditors had lent money to ESM, but were sweet-talked into leaving their collateral there. In both cases, the ESM crew had used the collateral for its own purposes.

The public victims sought the following:

	Millions
Beaumont, Texas	$ 20.2
Toledo, Ohio	19.2
Clark County, Nevada	14.4
Pompano Beach, Florida	12.0
Clallam County, Washington	10.5
Memphis, Tennessee, Board of Education	8.1
Tamarac, Florida	7.1
Jefferson County, Washington	5.4
Harrisburg, Pennsylvania	3.7
Eight others	4.4
Total	$105.0

Aside from the one-day interruption in Miami on Sunday, March 10, when Tew and Harper had to meet with the federal banking hierarchy to convince them that there were no significant monies in ESM's coffers, the work went on in Fort Lauderdale seven days a week, fourteen hours a day.

Tom's discussions focused increasingly on the subject of bankruptcy for ESM. He felt uncomfortable with his powers as equity receiver because, though rooted in common law, they are not clearly defined in specific state and federal statutes. As Tom commented, "The statutory powers of the bankruptcy laws are clear; the powers of the receiver are murky. Putting ESM into bankruptcy would give me greater powers to track down and claim all its assets. I wanted to change my receivership hat for a bankruptcy trustee hat."

For a bankruptcy proceeding to be effective, there must be a consensus among the creditors concerning basic strategy. Tew held a creditors meeting on Friday, March 22, to obtain such a consensus and to give the creditors their first opportunity to examine the complex legal issues and financial data in an organized fashion. When more than one hundred people showed up and overflowed Tew's conference room, they were hurriedly shuttled to a larger room in the building.

Tew addressed the group and quickly established that he had things under control and that there was a chance for a decent recovery if they acted quickly and in concert. He was followed by Laurie Holtz who made a detailed presentation of the numbers. Tom's performance impressed Laurie who recalled, "With each lawyer thinking he was the best in the room, each thinking he had the enchilada, and the others had appetizers, each thinking what mattered was only his client, and he had the right idea of what to do, Tew did a great selling job."

The creditors were convinced by Tew's call for swift action and agreed with him that an early push for an ESM bankruptcy was in their best interests. But they had to determine whether to use Chapter 7 or Chapter 11 of the bankruptcy statute. Chapter 7 applies to a debtor who is hopelessly broke and provides for the creditors to liquidate his assets. Chapter 11 is used when there is a chance that the debtor may regain solvency; it gives him time to reorganize his affairs under the protection of the court. The creditors made the obvious choice to push for an immediate Chapter 7 filing.

They were pleased with their decisions, and they left the six-hour meeting with positive feelings about the two men who had carried the ball so well for them to that point. The creditors strongly appreciated the skill and speed with which Tew and Judge Gonzalez had worked to get at the facts, unravel the central issues, and expedite the court proceedings.

Jose Gonzalez was born poor in Tampa in 1931, the son of Spanish immigrants. In the mid-1930s, his dad went to Detroit for a couple of years to take advantage of the generous $5-dollar-a-day wage being paid by Ford Motor. The family stayed in Tampa, living off the money sent from up north.

Gonzalez had an intense and loving relationship with his father. The judge chokes up when he tells about the two ticket stubs to a 1939 baseball game at the Polo Grounds in New York which are mounted in a plastic frame in his office. Gonzalez's dad made a financial sacrifice to take him to the game to see Mel Ott, New York's feared home run hitter, in action.

The University of Florida opened broad vistas for Gonzalez, and he excelled there both as an undergraduate and in its law school. After six years in private practice, he became the state's youngest circuit judge in 1964 when he was thirty-three. His work was outstanding, and for six years running, he ranked first among thirty-six South Florida judges in a bar association poll.

This led to an appointment to the federal bench by Jimmy Carter in 1978. His reputation has grown there, and the 1988 Almanac of the Federal Judiciary notes that "he has good intellect and demeanor . . . has tremendous control of his docket . . . is well versed in evidence."

The tensions of courtroom life are broken for Gonzalez by sports and music. He favors the Florida University Gators football team, the

Boston Red Sox, and the Boston Symphony. He publishes a weekly
Gator football newsletter and his jury room is dominated by posters of
Red Sox stars Wade Boggs, Roger Clemens, and Jim Rice. He has
said, "When I die, don't send me to heaven, send me to the Berkshires,"
where he spends every summer vacation listening to the Boston
Symphony at Tanglewood.

The creditors strongly desired that Gonzalez and Tew remain with
the case when it went into bankruptcy, but given the rules of bankruptcy, such an outcome seemed very unlikely.

First of all, the rules stated that bankruptcy trustees be chosen from
a panel of lawyers, accountants, and other experts previously approved by the clerk of the bankruptcy court in Washington. Secondly,
they provided that, with few exceptions, the cases be tried in specialty
bankruptcy courts presided over by specialty bankruptcy judges.
Individual cases are assigned by blind rotation by judges at the next
highest level in the federal hierarchy, the District Court.

The problem had two parts: Tew was not a member of the bankruptcy panel and Gonzalez was not a bankruptcy judge.

Tew, who wanted the trusteeship badly, went right to work.

> I called some enforcement people in the government whom I'd been
> working with to let them know that we were going into bankruptcy and
> I would soon be off the case. That raised some concerns. I got a phone
> call back from a very high ranking government officer, whom I will not
> mention, saying, "Have your application into the U.S. bankruptcy clerk
> in Washington tomorrow by 5:00 P.M., and we'll take care of it."
>
> So we sent a runner down to the bankruptcy court to get an applica-
> tion and I quickly filled it out, signed it, and had a courier carry it to the
> office we were told to have it at in Washington.
>
> And that's how I got on the panel.

Tom then consulted with David Levine, his bright, young bankruptcy partner, about keeping Gonzalez on the case.

> David reminded me that all bankruptcy cases are filed in the district
> court and are referred by the district court down to the bankruptcy
> court. And he said, "Look. If there's an order automatically referring
> the cases, we can ask the judge to suspend it for this case. Gonzalez is
> the district judge, and if he suspends the reference, he can keep the case
> for himself."
>
> That's what we did, and it worked.

On Tuesday, March 26, Tew filed the Chapter 7 petition and on March 27 at 2:00 P.M., Judge Gonzalez appointed Tom as trustee, withdrew the reference to the bankruptcy court, and assigned the case to himself. The bankruptcy panel members who crowded the Fort Lauderdale courtroom that day in hopes of a trusteeship appointment were surprised to hear the designation of Tew, whom they had not realized had just joined their ranks.

If Tew and Gonzalez had not prevailed, the victims of the ESM fraud would almost certainly have fared worse than they did. Breaking the momentum which had been built in March 1985 and stopping to educate a new judge and a new trustee would have severely hampered the endeavor to recover assets and to bring the criminals to justice. In addition, Tew and Gonzalez, to the good fortune of the creditors, possessed skills and experience which would have been extremely difficult to duplicate in South Florida at that time. They proved to be the right men in the right place and provided an effective and continuous effort which would last into 1989.

Ewton made it clear in late March that he would cooperate fully if he could make a deal that would benefit his wife, Jerilyn, and his two-year-old son. Ronnie sat down with Tew and told him he would confess to all his crimes, work full-time with Holtz, the SEC, and the FBI to help make sense of the complex stratagems of the fraud, and go bankrupt and give the trusteeship the great bulk of what remained of his ill-gotten gains (more than $9 million was left of the $25 million which Ronnie had looted from ESM). In return, Tew let Jerilyn keep her jewelry and a Toyota.

Tom was hard-pressed to explain to the ESM creditors that two major Ewton assets were beyond his reach. He could not touch $475,000 which Ronnie had put into a prenuptial fund for Jerilyn, because Tom "could not trace any looting from ESM to those dollars." In addition, Florida's liberal Homestead Act allows a bankrupt to keep his main residence—in Ewton's case, a luxurious waterfront home in Boca Raton which Jerilyn later sold for more than $1 million.

Tew feels that the deal, which like all such negotiations had to be approved by Gonzalez, was a good one; Tom believes Ewton's cooperation shortened the investigation by months, saved the trusteeship several hundred thousand dollars in accounting, legal, and investigative expense, and quickly enabled the trusteeship to realize $8 million by selling off the assets Ronnie surrendered. They included the 5,600-acre spread in Aiken, South Carolina; farms in Greenwich, Connecticut, Lake Worth, Florida, and Boone, North Carolina; the nineteen polo ponies; the Hatteras yacht "Jerilyn," which sold for over $1 million; the $90,000 mooring which the "Jerilyn" called home; the $152,000 Aston Martin Lagonda sports coupe, and a Corvette, a Mercedes Benz, a Toyota, and a Jeep Wagoneer; half interest in the ESM office building; and various bank and brokerage accounts.

All the ESM executives, with the exception of Nick Wallace and Stanley Wolfe, a financial officer, cooperated fully with Tew, as did Jose Gomez and the trustees for the Novick estate. By September of 1985, Tew had retrieved more than $35 million for the creditors, broken down as follows:

Sources	Millions
Bradford Trust	$13.0
Security Pacific	12.0
Ronnie Ewton	8.0
Other ESM officers	1.5
Alan Novick's estate	.4
Sale of securities owned by ESM	.7
Total	$35.6

The $35 million represented what Tom could recoup quickly and relatively easily. Now he would turn to the targets which would require protracted negotiation or litigation, or both. Five of them were obvious: Alexander Grant & Company, Marvin Warner, Burt Bongard, Steve Arky, and the Arky, Freed law firm. The sixth was a surprise: American Savings & Loan (AS&L).

Tew's tactics in suing AS&L were masterful. He used a simple but brilliant concept to transform AS&L from a creditor to a debtor. He alleged that the $1 billion transaction that led to the $60 million AS&L loss was a cooperative venture, because Ronnie Ewton originated it when he was a manager of both companies. In other words, AS&L was not a creditor acting on an "arm's length" basis with ESM. Rather, it enjoyed insider status at ESM because of Ewton's dual role on the executive committee of AS&L and as chairman of the board of ESM.

Tew's arguments were so persuasive that AS&L not only dropped all claims to the $60 million, but in addition contributed $5 million to the other creditors in an out-of-court settlement. Tew had pulled off a $65 million coup which made Shepard Broad decidedly unhappy.

Tew knew that the really serious money was to be gotten from Alexander Grant & Company, and he pushed his claims against them at the same time that he was negotiating with AS&L.

In U.S. laws governing partnerships, each partner is financially

liable for the professional acts of every other member of the partnership. Thus, each of the 470 Alexander Grant partners was responsible
for the financial consequences of Jose Gomez's conduct at ESM. To
protect themselves against acts such as Jose's, they had a $500,000-
deductible, $190 million insurance policy. This meant that each of the
470 had first to pay roughly $1,000, then the insurance company
picked up the next $189.5 million, and the partners would have to
kick in again for claims exceeding $190 million. They quickly de-
cided on a strategy to limit payments to $190 million.

Tew spent the latter half of 1985 and the first six weeks of 1986
hammering out a settlement between Alexander Grant (which, because of a merger, changed its name to Grant Thornton on January 1,
1986) and the public bodies. He remembers it clearly:

> The lawyers for the public bodies knew that they could make a lot
> more money in litigating this thing forever. But they were solid people,
> sympathetic people, who I had confidence in and Grant had confidence
> in. And the public bodies were under political pressure to get money
> back quickly. I chose two of their lawyers to represent them and we
> started a series of secret negotiations to settle with Grant.
>
> The negotiations often took place in neutral cities like St. Louis,
> Missouri. We fly in, meet in a room, talk secretly, because Grant was
> very concerned about the media perception of what was happening to
> them.
>
> And so I engineered—as trustee I was the broker—got everybody in
> the room and said: What do you want? Would you give up this? Would
> you do this? That was really my role. What I thought I was functioning
> best at. I knew everybody's claim better than they knew it, many times
> over, and I knew the defenses to their claims better just because I had
> more fact-access. I wasn't a better lawyer, but I had more fact-access.
>
> Hard bargaining, marathon sessions among the creditors' lawyers,
> and the reason this went quickly was that none of these solid guys
> wanted to play the ultimate game of litigation. They all wanted to get
> the job over with.
>
> We started negotiating a package whereby, when I made my first $35
> million distribution, Grant would give the public bodies $50 million to
> settle all their claims.
>
> Home State was perceived by many creditors as a villain, or not of the
> same purity as the public bodies because of the Warner, Bongard, and
> Arky accounts and connections at ESM. So the state of Ohio, inheritor

of Home State's claims, agreed to take a lesser share of their claim in the first payment, kind of recognition that they were not as clean as the public bodies. Ohio took $10 million of the $35 million. This meant that the public bodies got $25 of my $35 million plus $50 million from Grant for a total of $75 million. This translates to seventy-two cents on the dollar—without any further litigation or expense, court time, and lawyers. And they would get more if I were successful in other suits.

Grant's $50 million payment had one proviso; they would not give the public bodies a "double dip." The case of Tew as trustee vs. Grant was still pending, and Grant got an agreement that, if they lost a judgment to Tew in that suit, it would be reduced by the share that would have gone to the public bodies. The settlement had no effect on suits which had been filed against Grant by other litigants.

Gonzalez approved Tew's accord with AS&L in the spring of 1986 and the Grant–public bodies deal in early July. The first payments to creditors went out soon after.

Gonzalez and Tew were concerned with criminal as well as civil matters in the spring of 1986. Tew and his investigators provided federal prosecutors with masses of evidence, which they used to indict nine men before Judge Gonzalez on April 2. The prosecutors charged Ewton, Mead, Wallace, Gomez, and five ESM lesser fry with sixty-five counts of conspiracy and fraud. All pleaded guilty except for the two men who would not cooperate with the investigation from the beginning, Wallace and Stanley Wolfe. The two went on trial together before Judge Gonzalez on June 6.

Wolfe's main job had been to shuffle money and collateral around among the customers, ESM, and the two custodians, Bradford and Security Pacific. He claimed that his duties were purely technical and that he had no knowledge his work abetted the fraud. His lawyer likened him to "the husband who didn't know his wife was having an extramarital affair while all the neighbors knew." The jurors believed Wolfe and acquitted him on all counts.

Nick Wallace did not fare as well. He was generally considered a lightweight who valued having a good time above all else, and his judgment was always suspect. He took a big gamble and put up a defense similar to Wolfe's. He maintained that he did not know that his work furthered the fraud and claimed that he was an unwitting tool of Novick. But these were quixotic arguments, because he had been at the center of things almost from the beginning. A HOW alumnus who had been one of Ewton's first recruits, he was a director of ESM and had served as both president and secretary.

The prosecutor presented evidence that Wallace had signed hundreds of letters, money transfers, and other documents which showed that he participated actively in the ESM crimes. There was evidence also that Novick had told Wallace in 1983 that ESM's losses totalled about $160 million, and that Mead told him about the bribes to Gomez a week before ESM collapsed. Further, Wallace had profited mightily from the fraud. From 1980 to 1985, he took $8,857,787 out of the company in salaries and loans. The jury was convinced and convicted Nick of one conspiracy and sixteen fraud counts.

In his sentencing, Judge Gonzalez sent out a clear signal that he would reward those who cooperated with the authorities. He sentenced Ewton to fifteen years, Mead to fourteen, and Gomez to twelve. In contrast, he gave Wallace thirty years. The four confessed ESM lesser fry got terms ranging from three to eight years.

One of the lesser fry was Earl Riddel. He was a bookkeeper's bookkeeper—a meticulous, precise stickler for detail. He made sure the paper trail was absolutely clear as he recorded the debits and credits to show the movement of each dollar and each security. He could do monthly accounting statements in record time and weeks later remember obscure calculations down to the penny. This was just what Novick wanted. With Riddel there, he always knew where he stood. Earl retired in 1982, but he left a system in place which his successors could use effectively and with great accuracy.

He had lived a fussy bachelor existence for forty years after being divorced in 1946. A bespectacled, bird-like figure with a large bald spot wreathed by white hair, he looked older than his sixty-six years. He suffered from ulcers and colitis and was obsessed with his diet, which included two poached eggs every day for lunch and frequent spoonfuls of Maalox.

When his lawyers advised him to plead guilty, they held out hopes that he might get a suspended sentence and never have to serve time, because his crimes were among the least serious of those charged to the ESM crew.

Gonzalez was repelled by the leniency which judges traditionally showed to white-collar crooks. He felt that such criminals were as harmful to society as the blue-collar type and should be treated the same way. He was determined that all the ESM criminals should serve time, and he sentenced Riddel to three years.

Earl told several friends that he believed his health problems would result in his death in jail, and that he couldn't face such a fate. On November 10, 1986, he received a letter telling him to report to prison on December 4. Then, in a bold hand he wrote the following note which he taped to the door of his modest, immaculate apartment:

> I have committed suicide. Please notify Jerry.
> Also call my sister, Isabel Schroeder.
> The door is unlocked.
> Earl

Then he placed his glasses, wallet, keys, and jewelry neatly on his night stand, laid down on his bed, pulled a plastic garbage bag over his head, sealed it around his neck with a drapery cord, and died when he ran out of oxygen. His was the second death, the second true tragedy of the ESM fraud. The building's exterminator found Earl the next day and called Jerry, who was the building manager. Jerry telephoned the police, and they notified Earl's sister.

Negotiations with Grant never stopped during 1986. On September 8, the firm agreed to settle out of court with AS&L for $22.5 million. Tew's winning strategy against AS&L of branding Ewton as a "double insider" at ESM and AS&L was not helpful to Grant, because its AS&L case centered on another issue. This was Grant's legal obligation as a professional accounting firm to tell the truth about ESM to any and all ESM customers, including AS&L; this responsibility was clear and unassailable and forced Grant to the negotiating table. As a result of the agreement, AS&L's $65 million loss from the ESM collapse was reduced to net damages of $42.5 million.

After Grant's agreements with the public bodies and AS&L, Tew offered to settle his remaining claims against the firm for roughly $10 million. Grant turned down the offer, because it believed it could mount a good case against Tew in court.

Tew sued for $85 million, which was all the monies taken in salaries and loans plus interest by the ESM criminals while Gomez was producing the phony audits. The principal prospective beneficiary of his efforts was the state of Ohio standing in for Home State, the last major creditor in the bankruptcy trusteeship.

Tew, as ESM trustee, hired his own firm, Finley Kumble, to press his claim, and the courtroom team was led by its chief litigator, Jose Garcia-Pedrosa.

Garcia-Pedrosa, the son of a prominent Cuban labor lawyer, arrived in Miami in 1960 as a penniless fourteen-year old refugee from Castro's Cuba. His brilliant high school record won him a scholarship to Harvard. He helped support himself there by delivering newspapers, tutoring Spanish, and swabbing toilets as a janitor, and earned both a BA and a law degree.

Garcia-Pedrosa combines an intellectualism and a zeal for public service with the pecuniary drive of a corporate lawyer. He reads Kafka and Sartre and believes in "giving something back" to the society which has been generous to him. He interrupted his lucrative corporate practice from 1982 to 1984 to work as Miami city attorney. He was then spurned in an effort to win election as state attorney, but believes that someday he will be back in the public sector. He says, "I know from an economic standpoint it doesn't make sense, but if all decent people in the world shun public service, then we leave it to undesirable people." His wife says, "He's the only man I know who thinks of creative ways to make less money."

Garcia-Pedrosa possesses two qualities which make him a great litigator: he excels at thoughtful, thorough pretrial preparation, and he has a passionate, charismatic style of argument which wins over juries.

Al Stein, Grant's lawyer, prepares his cases skillfully, but his courtroom style is bland and monotonous compared to Garcia-Pedrosa's.

The trial began before Jose Gonzalez on October 21, 1986. Stein had two main defenses. The first was that Gomez deceived his partners about the ESM work and this deception relieved them of their strict responsibility for his professional acts. Secondly he argued that ESM got what it wanted—a phony audit—and Grant, therefore, had no contractual responsibility to produce a truthful one. Stein asked, "What duty did Grant owe to ESM? What proof is there that ESM wanted audits in accordance with standard accounting principles?"

Garcia-Pedrosa attacked Stein's first defense by claiming negligence. He argued that Gomez had gotten away with his phony audits, not because he had deceived his partners, but because they were negligent in their duty to police his work.

He showed that Grant's system of "peer review" was lax to the point of breakdown. Under this system, partners were supposed to check on each other's work to insure that it was done honestly and competently. Garcia-Pedrosa got a peer review partner to admit that he only made cursory investigations of Gomez's ESM work papers from 1977 through 1982. And there was no refutation of Jose Gomez's testimony that another peer review partner said, "I don't understand this shit, so please tell me it's okay and I'll sign it."

More than forty Grant auditors put in thousands of hours working on the ESM account during the seven years that the fraud took place, and Garcia-Pedrosa pointed out that not one suspected that anything crooked was going on. This included a partner who prepared the tax returns which showed the true losses.

Garcia-Pedrosa used, to devastating effect, the testimony of the two Holtz partners who, under Laurie's direction, uncovered the fraud in about one hour on the fateful morning of Saturday, March 2, 1985.

He also elicited the following statement from Gomez: "I thought about when my own audit people would come up with questions that I wouldn't be able to answer without forcing me to lie extensively. That never happened."

Garcia-Pedrosa presented evidence that four Grant people, three of them partners, were aware that Gomez was taking money from ESM. They knew that this was at best a serious violation of the ethics of the accounting profession, and at worst illegal, but they never reprimanded Gomez or told anyone about it.

Garcia-Pedrosa countered the argument that ESM ordered a phony audit by bringing out the actual contracts between ESM and Grant. They stated that the audits must be produced in accordance with Generally Accepted Accounting Principles (GAAP) and Generally Accepted Auditing Standards (GAAS). Audits adhering to GAAP and GAAS would be, by definition, honest—not phony.

The jury found for Garcia-Pedrosa after only six hours of deliberation, and awarded Tew, as trustee, $70.9 million. This was reduced to $35.9 million in accordance with the "double dip" agreements reached before the trial began.

The state of Ohio got the lion's share, $34 million. And it was able to press for more. Under the bankruptcy laws, it was allowed to bring a separate suit against Grant and in September 1987 reached a further settlement of $46 million for a total of $80 million. When this was added to the $10 million it got from Tew's initial recovery of $35 million, its total take came to $90 million. The state kept only $75 million because, in a side deal, it gave ODGF $15 million. ODGF in turn, distributed the money to its sixty-eight non-Home State member banks.

Governor Celeste triumphantly announced on January 5, 1988, that Ohio was paying off, seven years early, the $91 million in ten-year bonds it sold to help bail out the Home State depositors. The funds came from the $75 million in recoveries and from state liquor profits and unclaimed bank deposits.

With the state of Ohio settlement, Grant's insurer had paid out $173 million, a higher amount by at least $75 million than had ever been disbursed in an accounting malpractice case. The total sum broke down as follows:

Recipients	Millions
Public bodies	$ 50.0
AS&L	22.5
State of Ohio	65.0
ODGF	15.0
Other creditors	10.5
Legal fees	10.0
Total	$173.0

The $17 million remaining from the $190 million insurance coverage was put in an escrow fund. There is an understanding that the state of Ohio and ODGF will receive monies from that fund after the insurer deducts all his expenses and makes final payments to miscellaneous creditors.

In a related suit, the state of Ohio also won a $5.5 million settlement from Arthur Andersen & Co. in April 1988. Andersen was Home State's auditor, and the state claimed that if the accounting firm's procedures were more professional, Andersen might have learned the truth about the ESM fraud early on. The state maintained that Andersen had identified the risks, but was then lax in examining the records which detailed the games Novick was playing with Home State's collateral. Coming after the Grant bribery, the settlement was another black eye for the accounting industry; Andersen is the world's largest accounting firm with annual billings exceeding $1 billion.

Tew's only loss as trustee occurred in April 1987, when Judge Gonzalez dismissed Tom's suit against Arky, Freed for $6.5 million. Tom had charged that Arky and his partners were negligent in not disclosing what Steve discovered on January 21, 1985—namely, that ESM had suffered massive losses and might be involved in fraudulent activity. Gonzalez ruled that the Arky, Freed people had no duty to tell anyone what they knew of the ESM situation, because the information was protected by attorney-client privilege, and because Steve pulled

Arky, Freed off the ESM assignment immediately on hearing the news.

The state of Ohio also sued Arky, Freed and fared better then Tew. Their case was essentially the same as Tom's, but they put considerably more emphasis on the information about ESM's financial plight which Arky, Freed obtained during the Seneca divorce case. Soon after Tew's defeat, Arky, Freed settled with the state of Ohio for more than $600,000.

Tew did win $136,000 from Arky's estate by claiming that Arky had made unfair personal profits at ESM to the detriment of the bankruptcy creditors; the state of Ohio settled with the estate for $60,000 on the same grounds.

Judge Gonzalez ruled that Tew, his attorneys, and accountants present their bills every sixty days for approval by both the creditors and the judge. The maximum allowable fee is 3 percent of dollars recovered, but this is rarely awarded. Something less than 2 percent is normal. By the end of 1987, approved billings amounted to $5.5 million, which was 1.9 percent of collections.

The creditors were happy to pay Tew's fees because he had won successes virtually unheard of in major bankruptcy cases. Most of the time, creditors are fortunate to receive twenty cents on the dollar; Tew, by the end of 1987, had recouped better than four times that amount.

He directly retrieved $76 million ($35 million in recoverable assets, $5 million from AS&L, and $36 million in his suit versus Grant), and indirectly he was responsible for recovering another $154 million from Grant's insurer. In addition, he benefitted the true creditors by $60 million by proving that AS&L was not a legitimate creditor. These three sums added together give a total of $290 million, or 92 percent of the $315 million Tew originally sought.

And he wasn't done yet. As 1987 ended, he was poised to press for more than $20 million from his final major target—Marvin Warner. But he would have to wait his turn. Ohio's special prosecutor and the U.S. attorney in Cincinnati were in line ahead of him.

13

Criminal Justice

Marvin Warner's head was throbbing, his eyes were burning, and he was dead tired, but he picked up another dreary financial document to review with his lawyers. For weeks he had been slogging through these grueling days with them, and he knew he had to keep on with it because the work they were doing together was as important as any in his entire life. He realized that who Marvin Warner was and what he had accomplished would be judged in the most nakedly public way in the criminal trial which was less than a month away.

The trial would run for fourteen weeks starting November 17, 1986, in the Hamilton County Courthouse, a massive stone monument occupying an entire square block in one of the grimier sections of downtown Cincinnati. Its long corridors are filled with people in the web of the law: a handcuffed street-pusher in a red satin windbreaker waiting to be sentenced; a chubby twenty-five-year-old housewife with a black eye entering an assault charge against her husband; a disheveled lawyer—his arms filled with files and briefs—rushing to argue a motion in probate court. That web would also ensnare Marvin, in his immaculate and expensive suits, for a long time to come.

He was there because Larry Kane, Ohio's special prosecutor had, on December 13, 1985, convinced a grand jury to indict Marvin on ninety criminal charges. Marvin would face eighty-seven of them now; three, which involved "sweetheart" loans to friends and family, were severed for a later trial because they were deemed unrelated to the other charges. David Schiebel would be Marvin's codefendant for all eighty-seven charges and Burt Bongard for eighty-two.

It seemed like the entire population of southern Ohio was caught up in the emotion of the event. Every cabdriver, every Woolworth's clerk, every executive enjoying a cigar at the Queen City Club was eager to tell you how they felt about Marvin, Burt, and David. After more than a year of waiting, the trial was the arena where Ohioans could finally come to terms with the hurt and panic they had endured, the anger they felt, and the financial hardship they had suffered.

Public passions were indeed so strong that the defense attorneys made a major issue of them. They argued that Marvin could not get a fair trial in Cincinnati because of "massive and prejudicial" publicity and asked that the proceedings be moved elsewhere in Ohio. They cited two polls which they had commissioned and which reported that sixty-four percent of potential jury members believed that Marvin had committed a crime.

But the lawyers ran into a judge who was convinced that Cincinnati could produce twelve citizens who would be fair and impartial jurors. It took three weeks of rigorous questioning by the attorneys and it was excruciatingly boring, but Judge Richard Niehaus finally swore in a jury which he felt sure would render an unbiased verdict.

The jury was basically working class. It included a woman who mixed batter at a cookie factory, a telephone lineman, a retired fireman, a salad bar attendant, and a school crossing guard. There was one Ph.D.—a physicist with General Electric; of the six male jurors, he was the only one to wear a tie.

Niehaus holds forth in Room 513—the same small, musty court-room where his father was a judge for many years. In fact, his slow-moving, mistake-prone bailiff had been inherited from his dad. Niehaus never allowed the high-profile Warner trial to interfere with his daily handling of the flotsam and jetsam of Cincinnati society. One morning he delayed Marvin's testimony to sentence a skidrow character to an alcohol abuse center and accepted a drug addict's guilty plea on a concealed weapons charge.

Sixteen men—Marvin, Burt, and David, their teams of lawyers, and the prosecuting attorneys—sat in a cramped area directly in front of the judge. It resembled an obstacle course, because jammed among the tables and chairs were two dozen filing cabinets filled with the often tedious documents presented in the case. Every time Bongard's attorney arose to address the court, seven other people had to get up and move their seats to let him through. And Schiebel's lawyer joked, "I think if there's a fire, I'll never get out of here, Judge."

In the midst of this chaotic scene, Marvin sat tautly and alertly, constantly drumming his fingers on the arms of his chair and occasionally leaning forward to scribble notes to his lawyers.

The air in Room 513 was always heavy and humid because the ventilation system was old and very tired, and the four narrow specta-tor benches were constantly crowded. The front bench was reserved for the defendants' families. The three wives were there every day, and Marvin's children—Marlin, Mark, and Alyson—were rarely absent. Jody always wore plain, dark dresses, and Bongard's and Schiebel's spouses similarly avoided any ostentatious display.

One of Marvin's fans was a local eccentric, Fifi Taft Rockefeller, whose face was caked with makeup, and who wore several layers of clothing topped by a platinum blond wig adorned with brightly colored strips of tinsel. Judge Niehaus had to eject her a couple of times when she cheered too loudly for Marvin.

The other spectators included a handful of bitter Home State depositors, lawyers and FBI men who were observers for litigants in subsequent ESM trials, a dozen journalists, and the people who prefer trials to soap operas for daytime entertainment.

Niehaus is fully in command in his courtroom. His eyes catch everything, and he comments freely on what is going on before him. A trim, blond man with a full mustache, his quick movements and bouncy step are reminders that he was a star athlete at Georgetown University in the mid-1960s.

The judge established a sense of comradeship with the jurors and frequently pitted himself and them against the attorneys whom he felt were often wordy and irritating. Before admonishing an attorney, he would look over to the jurors and say, "We aren't going to put up with this."

Politics was never far from the courtroom. Niehaus is an elected judge and would relish winning election to high state office some day. Savvy politicians say that a run for lieutenant governor in 1990 would be a logical next step in his career.

The trial was videotaped by a cameraman whose images were beamed to all the local TV stations. Before long, Judge Niehaus became a familiar and energetic presence on the nightly news.

Attorney General Celebrezze, working on the politician's belief that distance disinfects donations, helped put as much space as possible between himself and fellow Democrat Warner by naming Kane, a prominent Republican, as special prosecutor. Kane, whose father had been an Ohio state representative for twenty years, was rumored to covet a federal judgeship. His judicial future, and a large part of his reputation as a lawyer, was at stake in this highly publicized trial.

He is a small, bald, rumpled man in his late fifties who has seen almost everything that can happen in a courtroom, and who is tough and resourceful. His background is Irish Catholic and he has six children, one of whom is retarded. Most of his nonprofessional efforts are devoted to the cause of the retarded.

The role Kane assumed in court was more coach than player. He plotted strategy and left the arguments, the motions, the examination of witnesses to four young associates whom he would send into the fray like Pat Riley sending his Lakers basketball players onto the floor at the Los Angeles Forum.

The defense lawyers were very good and very expensive. Warner's lead men were Bill Jeffress and Stan Mortenson. Their Washington firm had helped Richard Nixon avoid indictment after his 1974 resignation, won acquittal for Louisiana Governor Edwin Edwards on racketeering charges, and fought a losing battle for key Reagan aide Michael Deaver in his perjury trial.

Jeffress and Mortenson are youthful and articulate and had totally mastered the evidence. They used their contrasting styles strategically, like the nice cop and his tough partner in a TV melodrama. Jeffress, short and slender, was soft-spoken, almost gentle in his handling of witnesses. Mortenson is built like a football linebacker and took a decidedly aggressive approach in his questioning.

Bill Gilliam, who led Bongard's team, is a witty and resourceful fighter who never lets up on a witness. When he had one on the run, he would snap and bark at him like an angry bull terrier. Trim and extremely fit, he is a skilled mountain climber who is proud that he has conquered Mount Kilimanjaro. He was assisted by Marvin Gersten, a prominent New York securities attorney.

Roger Makley, Schiebel's lawyer, is a large, folksy man whose self-deprecating manner masks a sharp intelligence. His fees were paid from a fund set up by Marvin Warner.

Kane, with so much at stake, had worked his way doggedly through the eight-year Home State–ESM saga, searching for a set of crimes which he believed he had a very good shot at proving. After discarding several options, he found what he felt to be clearly convictable offenses in two short episodes which together covered less than seven months. They were the time from May 31 to October 14, 1983, when Alan Novick's hedge on Home State's $700 million purchase went wildly and sadly wrong, and the period between September 25 and November 30, 1984 when Home State was selling its debentures.

During 1983, Bongard was president of Home State and Schiebel was executive vice president. Late in August 1984, Schiebel became president, succeeding Barry Winslow who had replaced Bongard in May, 1984.

Marvin Warner was never officially an officer of Home State during

1983 and 1984, but Kane held that he was a de facto officer, deeply involved in executive decisions. In fact, Kane had to prove this executive status in order to convict Warner, whom he called "the moving force and alter ego of the bank, overseeing every major (and almost every minor) decision affecting Home State."

Kane brought two sets of charges concerning the hedge transaction. The first centered on the resolution adopted April 28, 1983, by Home State's board of directors forbidding its officers from sending excess collateral to ESM. The resolution, passed due to unrelenting pressure from ODGF, defined "excess" as anything more than 105 percent on money borrowed against Treasury securities and 110 percent on money borrowed against Ginnie Mae and other federal agency securities.

The $700 million hedge transaction, with its attendant risks, was entered into in late May and soon went sour. It resulted in Home State sending to ESM between May 31 and October 14, 1983, more than $114 million in excess collateral in forty-one separate payments. Ohio law forbids executives to commit acts prohibited by a board of directors, and Kane accused Warner, Bongard, and Schiebel of violating this law 41 times, once for each collateral transfer.

The second set of hedge transition charges stated that in making the forty-one transfers, Warner, Bongard, and Schiebel committed— forty-one times—a crime called "willful misapplication of funds." Willful misapplication alleges that they put to grave and unnecessary risk the money of Home State depositors, exposing them to unwarranted financial loss in violation of a compact of trust that bank officers automatically have with their depositors. The state also had to prove that by risking the money, the accused benefitted someone other than the bank, in this case the ESM crew and indirectly the defendants themselves.

A third set of charges covered the debenture offering prospectus and accused Warner and Schiebel of deceiving buyers by lying in the document about the financial health of Home State. Kane claimed that the defendants knew that the net worth figures for the company were grossly overstated. He accused them also of omitting mention of the tremendous risk of loss to Home State resulting from its transactions with ESM.

Warner knew it would take all his wiles to beat Kane, because Kane had a strong case on the debenture charges and some compelling evidence on the misapplication of funds and board of directors charges. Marvin and his team decided on a two-pronged strategy. First, they would fight the specific charges with the best arguments they could muster, and second, they would attempt to turn the proceedings into a trial of Ronnie Ewton.

Bill Jeffress was only three minutes into his opening statement on behalf of Marvin when he told the jury, "The central question for your decision is whether he [Marvin Warner] knew the awful truth about ESM during these years. Or whether he was lied to and deceived and swindled by the man [Ronnie Ewton], who is now going to be his chief accuser." A few moments later he added, "The key to this case is . . . the lies, the deceit that was carried on by ESM and by its corrupt auditors."

Bongard's lawyer, Gilliam, who described Ewton as "a dead mackerel in the moonlight, he both shines and stinks," echoed Jeffress' refrain when he said, "There is one central question, and one only: Did Home State and by that I mean Warner, Bongard, and Schiebel, know that Ewton and Novick were engaged in a massive fraud, a scheme to swindle millions from Home State and others? If you answer that no, I submit that you will find that there has been no violation of law."

The fact was that proof of Kane's main allegations did not rise or fall on Ewton's fraud. The fraud was unrelated to lying in the debenture prospectus or violating a board resolution. And it was only indirectly involved with the misapplication charges through the benefit Ewton and ESM derived from the transfer of the collateral.

Ewton's testimony was not essential to Kane's case. It was used, with limited results, to show that a motive for the misapplication was the alleged Home State–ESM mutual support system and, with greater success, to corroborate events such as the April 13, 1983, meeting when the hedge transaction was approved, and the September 6, 1983, encounter when Warner demanded that Ewton make up his losses.

Ewton was the celebrity attraction of the trial. The surviving archvillain of ESM was making his first public appearance since the collapse, and attracted media from all over the nation. But his testimony threw off no sparks. He showed neither shame, remorse, nor any other serious emotion, and his delivery was flat and frequently off the point.

And he was not much help to Kane. He was forced to describe all his transgressions, including the forged will, and to admit that he was still plea-bargaining to minimize his jail time. Ronnie was particularly weak under cross-examination, when Mortenson involved him in enough evasions and contradictions to undermine most of his testimony about the mutual support system. Mortenson brought out that Ewton was wildly spending almost $7 million while he was allegedly telling Warner that ESM was nearly broke, "bleeding out of both ears." The questioning ended as follows:

Q: Do you recall spending $76,304.12? What was that for?
A: For a half-interest in a yacht.
Q: How about this $15,000 you spent in April 1983? What was that for?
A: It was for a polo pony.
Q: And this $14,300 later that month?
A: A Chevrolet pickup.
Q: What of this $14,000 one month later?
A: Another polo pony.
Q: And this $29,335.84 in July?
A: I bought a Corvette.
Q: What's this $32,290 for?
A: A Cadillac Eldorado.
Q: This $15,000?
A: Polo pony.
Q: Is this the third polo pony, or have I missed some?
A: You missed some.
Q: Do you recall what this $30,000 was for?
A: Down payment on an Aston Martin.
Q: Down payment?
A: Yes, paid it off at $152,000.
Q: What's this $336?
A: Hired a stretch limo.
Q: What of this $200,000?
A: Down payment on a $1.3 million yacht.
Q: Do you recall seeing on television people standing in lines, waiting to take their money out of Home State?
A: Yes, I think I did.

Kane's other main witnesses were decidedly not the type to attract intense media attention.

To prove his misapplication case, where he had to show that the depositors were exposed to unwarranted financial loss, he relied heavily on Sylvester Hentschel, two fellow regulators, and an ODGF official. They testified that they continually warned Home State executives that the bank was repeatedly risking over $125 million in depositors' money in "unsafe and unsound" unsecured loans to an obscure securities dealer.

Kane brought to the stand two of Home State's "outside" directors to give essential testimony about the charges that the directors resolution on collateral levels was disobeyed. The bank had seven directors and four of them were "insiders"—Bongard, Schiebel, and Marvin's children Mark and Alyson. The "outsiders" were Bob Braun, host of a local talk-variety TV show, and lawyers Arthur "Ace" Elliott and Nelson Schwab.

Braun and Elliott testified that the $700 million hedge transaction was never presented to them for approval and they were never informed that Warner okayed it on April 13, 1983.

They also confirmed that the board passed the April 28, 1983, resolution limiting overcollateralization to the 105 percent-110 percent guidelines, and added that they were not told about the massive collateral movements to ESM during the May-October 1983 period, or about any violations of their resolution.

Management gave them monthly reports from which they could have deduced, by doing some mathematics, that securities were moving south, but as Braun said, "We were told (by Home State officers) that we were getting within the guidelines so I had no reason to take a slide rule to the board meeting and go over this. . . . I'm not an accountant, I'm a host of television programs. Math was not one of my best subjects."

Kane used two accounting experts to testify that the debenture prospectus inflated Home State's assets by at least $25 million. These men pointed out that, on a fair market basis, Schiebel and Warner had grossly overvalued both the amount due on loans and the bank's securities holdings.

The overvaluations were enough to wipe out Home State's purported net worth. In other words, the experts concluded that prospective buyers were blatantly deceived, because Home State was really insolvent when the prospectus was issued. The experts' conclusions were buttressed by the fact that Carl Lindner needed a $201 million subsidy to make Home State whole, or $56 million more than the $145 million ESM loss.

Kane showed that the four-page prospectus made no mention of

ESM, much less the risks it posed for Home State. The only way the buyer could become aware of ESM's existence was by asking a Home State official for documents which were referred to in the prospectus as follows:

> The Company, through its predecessors, has financial and other infor-mation on file with the Securities and Exchange Commission under Commission File No. 0-3897. That information is presented in its Form 10-K for 1983, its Form 10-Q for the six months ended June 30, 1984 and Forms 8-K filed April 11, June 6 and September 5, 1984, all of which are incorporated by reference in this Offering Circular. Persons desiring further information concerning the Company may receive a copy of these documents by written or oral request without charge. . . .

If the buyer took the trouble to obtain and to read through these bulky tomes, he would find a highly technical description of the hundreds of millions of dollars in ESM–Home State transactions. He would not discover that the transactions had resulted in a $145 million unse-cured loan to ESM which exposed Home State to grave risk.

The jury was worn down by weeks of highly technical and tedious testimony by accountants, regulators, paper pushers, and securities attorneys. Almost every day a few of the jurors dozed off in the heavy air of Room 513. They expressed some of their feelings by taping to the door of the jury room a sign on which they wrote, "Judge Nie-haus's Bored Room," "Heads or Tails?," and "Are we having fun yet?"

Through it all, Marvin appeared upbeat. There was vigor in his walk and he always had cheerful comments for the reporters who clustered around him at every recess. He told them that he felt good, because he and Jody were jogging a couple of miles every day and riding their horses regularly, and the trial meant that his long-awaited vindication was near at hand.

It was hard to tell if Marvin was sincere or merely presenting a mask of confidence to hide his fears. One day, as he and Jody stepped into the elevator to go down to lunch, they stood arm in arm and smiled cheerily at the reporters as the doors closed. A moment later, due to a mechanical glitch, the doors unexpectedly slid open. The Warners looked entirely different. Jody stared straight ahead, her face a blank. Marvin, his hand gripping her arm, his jaw muscles taut, looked glumly down at his shoes. The doors closed again and they were gone.

David Schiebel, the first defendant to testify, looked like he was cast for the part of a Midwestern banker. Tall and broad-shouldered, he had a big smile, a strong handshake, and an open, friendly manner. He was "a man you could trust." He could get emotional, however, and when he did, his voice would rise and he would jab the air with his index finger for emphasis. The jury listened intently when he spoke and liked him. Its foreman later ranked David an eight on a scale of ten as a witness. In contrast, he gave Warner a five and Bongard a four.

Schiebel started his defense against the misapplication and board resolution charges by showing that he had gone on record in strong opposition to the $700 million transaction. His reason: the regulators would be very unhappy with the deal. Then he claimed that, as executive vice president, he was not responsible for policy regarding ESM; that was Bongard's job. David admitted that he had day-to-day dealings with ESM, but asserted that they were always under the direction of Burt, his boss. Bongard's lawyer never tried to challenge this testimony, and Kane's people had a difficult time with it.

Schiebel had greater problems with the counts surrounding the debenture prospectus, which was issued in 1984 after he had become Home State president. David had shown poor judgment in accepting the post following Barry Winslow's resignation. After only five months in the job, Winslow had quit because of grave misgivings about the risky way Home State's assets were being handled. In fact, Schiebel's lawyer compared assuming the presidency to becoming captain of the *Titanic* after it had hit the iceberg.

Schiebel said lamely that he "felt comfortable" with the prospectus and "found nothing in it that was irregular." He also claimed that he relied on the accounting and legal expertise of others, which was really no defense because as president the responsibility was his.

Burt Bongard, who had been wounded by Schiebel's testimony, was no Ollie North on the witness stand. The Count Basie Band used to play a tune called "Every Tub on Its Bottom." Burt's short, heavy body looked like a "tub on its bottom," his face was dour and jowly, and he sported a "five o'clock shadow" to do Richard Nixon proud. His speech was dry and monotonous and lacked conviction. In short, he probably had a negative effect on the jury.

Kane's people, attempting to establish motive for the overcollateralization, pounded away at the huge trading profits Burt had reaped at ESM. They showed that between 1980 and 1984 Bongard had made

$2.4 million at ESM, more than three times his Home State income of $700,000. They also claimed that Burt knew his ESM profits were phony. Bongard denied such knowledge, but was embarrassed by a letter he wrote on April 18, 1983. It concerned the gift of a dozen pair of expensive folding sunglasses and it read:

> Dear Ronnie and Alan,
>   Here are a dozen glasses. Split them up in a fair and equitable manner. The way we do it here is 12½, 12½ and 75. That means the guys in the trading room get nine pair, Ronnie gets three pair and Alan gets three pair.
>   However, if we use the Warner method, Ronnie gets them all.
> Very truly yours,
> Home State Savings Association
> Burton M. Bongard, President

The "12½, 12½ and 75" referred to a percentage formula Novick used to divide up trading profits among Bongard, Warner, and Home State and indicated that Burt knew more about the inner workings of ESM than he was letting on.

Bongard denied vehemently that he was aware that ESM needed the excess collateral to stay afloat, but was forced to admit that he knew he was exceeding the 105 percent-110 percent guidelines when he authorized the securities transfers. His excuse was that he had no choice. He had to meet the demands of the failed hedge or "our net worth would have been wiped out . . . it was a Catch-22." In effect, he had acknowledged guilt on the charges against him—the misapplication and board resolution counts.

Marvin Warner gave a well-orchestrated performance on the witness stand. He was not the commanding executive ordering underlings to do his bidding. He was not the man who flew into rages when crossed. He was not the hard bargainer squeezing every penny out of a supplier.

He was the courtly elder citizen with the gentle Alabama drawl. When he began, his voice quavered and he appeared overcome by emotion as he described his humble beginnings working at the Bohemian Bakery. But he grew calmer and more self-assured after he broke the tension with a joke. Describing how he was offered $150 a month for his first job as a lawyer, he said, "I wish lawyers were that cheap now."

From time to time he would ramble and when the prosecution objected, he would apologize before Niehaus had a chance to rule on the objection. He praised almost everyone in sight, including Ewton during the ComBank years, and several other prosecution witnesses.

Marvin adamantly portrayed himself as a victim of Ewton, Novick, and Gomez, not their coconspirator. He denied that he knew that his trading profits were phony, or had any knowledge before January 21, 1985, that ESM's finances were shaky. He denied also that he had been party to any mutual self-help scheme between Home State and ESM, and said he knew nothing about the "12½, 12½ and 75" profit formula described in Bongard's "sunglasses" letter, or even that Bongard had an account at ESM.

He minimized his role at Home State after his return from Switzerland:

> I would get involved in various pet projects. I guess, in a way, I was a nuisance. I was more like the owner of a sports team, tinkering a little here and there. Sometimes the fellows appreciated it, and sometimes they didn't. But they were good fellows. You have seen on the witness stand the titan quality of the people we had at Home State. Whatever I did was to protect the assets of Home State. . . . Sometimes I told Bongard what newspaper ads to run, and sometimes I complained about the dirty rugs in the branch offices. I tinkered here and there.

But the prosecutor got him to admit that he was doing more than tinkering when he approved Home State's $700 million hedge transaction on April 13, 1983. Marvin claimed that he became involved in that decision because of its size and because it was wrapped up with a companion $100 million proposal for himself.

Kane held that the April 13 decision put Marvin squarely in the saddle as a de facto manager at Home State and argued that his approval involved him in the forty-one transfers which were the basis for the misapplication and directors resolution counts. But Kane believed that his strongest case involved the last six transfers of collateral to ESM, which began on August 29, 1983, and ended on October 14.

It was on August 29, after Bongard had sent a whopping $101.9 million from Cincinnati to Fort Lauderdale, that Marvin became so concerned that he stepped in and took over. He decreed that all future transfers be approved by him and okayed a $2.5 million payment that very day. He approved five more totalling $9.7 million between August 31 and October 14, when the hedge finally turned successful and the outflows stopped.

There was ample written evidence, in the form of memos and the minutes of meetings, to tie Marvin firmly to these six transactions.

Marvin asserted that the six transfers were not misapplications, because he had approved them only to help Home State, not to benefit the ESM gang or anyone else. He had to admit that he received copies of the board resolutions, but he claimed he had never seen them because he had exercised his "senior citizen's prerogative" not to read everything he got in the mail.

Marvin reverted to his "tinkering" defense on the debenture charges. Yes, he had helped the boys out, made a few suggestions here and there, but did not delve deeply into their work because they were management "titans." As with Schiebel, relying on the expertise of others was no defense. Marvin had to admit that he had read the document and had made changes in it as it went through several drafts. Kane charged that these changes were significant and that, as a de facto manager, Marvin had a legal responsibility to review diligently all the numbers and statements in the prospectus.

A lightness, a giddiness of relief, appeared to come over Marvin as he finished his two days of testimony on February 10, during the thirteenth week of the trial. It was nearly over now—a few more witnesses, the closing arguments, the judge's charge, the jury's deliberations. In only two more weeks, he felt sure, this ordeal would be behind him.

Ronnie Ewton was pretty relaxed as he ate breakfast on February 19 with Charlie Harper of the SEC, an associate from Tew's firm, and his own lawyer. He was showing Harper how he created funny faces for his three-year-old son Brandon by arranging raisins on the surface of his oatmeal.

They were in Cincinnati for Ronnie's sentencing on nine Ohio criminal charges to which he had confessed. He was in a good mood because he expected that his Ohio term would run concurrently with the fifteen years of federal time he was slated to serve in a "country club" prison on the grounds of Eglin Air Force Base in Florida. Concurrent sentences would mean that he would get credit for Ohio time while he was in federal prison and would never spend a day in an Ohio jail.

It all depended on the sentencing judge, Fred Cartolano. Harper and Tew's man had made the trip from Miami to sing Ronnie's praises to the judge, and Larry Kane had promised to support Ewton strongly.

Judge Cartolano presided just down the hall from Room 513, where word spread quickly that Ewton was being sentenced. In spite of the fact that Kane's main deputy was in the midst of the state's closing argument, the reporters left the Warner trial en masse and rushed over to Cartolano's courtroom.

Kane told the judge that Ronnie had been extremely helpful to the state of Ohio and recommended a concurrent sentence of no more than seven years. Tew's man and Harper said that Ronnie had saved the receiver and the federal government hundreds of thousands of dollars and that his efforts had greatly expedited the restitution which Ohio had received to that time. Then Ronnie went on for ten minutes about the great remorse he felt.

Now it was Cartolano's turn. He said:

> You are not here to be sentenced on the degree of your cooperation, but for what you did. You operated with all the morality of an Oriental bazaar. You effectively picked the pocket of every citizen of the state of Ohio, causing them to lose over $200 million.
>
> You are the wealthiest man in this room. You were allowed to keep a $1.6 million house which you have converted to cash. Every time your wife strokes her fur, someone in Toledo winces. Every time she puts on her jewelry, someone in Cincinnati blinks.
>
> It would be a subversion of justice if a man who stole $200 million could serve his time at an Air Force base which is not a real prison.
>
> I have heard Mr. Kane's recommendation, but I am not party to any agreement with him. I therefore sentence you to nine years in an Ohio jail to be served before your federal sentence.
>
> Sheriff, remove the prisoner. Right now he will start serving his Ohio time.

Two burly deputies grabbed Ewton's arms, pulled them behind his back, and handcuffed him. Then they turned him around and marched him out of the courtroom. Ronnie's face had the stricken look of an animal caught in a trap.

He was taken to a cell in the small jail at the back of the courthouse, where they made him turn in his elegantly tailored suit, which had his return trip ticket to Fort Lauderdale in a pocket, and gave him a shirt and trousers in drab prison blue. He also had to hand over his Rolex watch; in its place they affixed a wristband with his prison number—49050.

George Mead, who would be sentenced by Cartolano that afternoon, became sick to his stomach when he heard about Ronnie's fate and could not face lunch. The judge, again ignoring all pleas, gave George six years for his confessed crimes and had him carted off to jail immediately.

Jose Gomez, who also pleaded guilty, fared better than Ronnie and George when he was sentenced for his Ohio crimes eight days later, on February 27. He encountered a judge who was convinced by Larry Kane's arguments for leniency and who sentenced him to eighteen months to be served concurrently with twelve years Federal time in a minimum-security prison in Tallahassee, Florida.

The Warner jury had been hard at work for a week the day Gomez was sentenced. They had finally gotten the case on Friday, February 20, when Niehaus—taking no chances—ordered them sequestered under tight security.

Marvin and the other defendants were wondering what in the world was taking them so long. Four days, five days—that seemed reasonable. But a week, or more? What the hell were they doing? Word leaked from Niehaus's clerk that each juror had chipped in a dollar for the state's lotto drawing of February 26. They had won $55 and decided to reinvest it all in the March 4 drawing the following week, a sign that they had settled in for the long haul.

Although the wait was excruciating, Marvin and his crew took an optimistic view. They reasoned that the jury must be having serious differences, and believed that gave them a better-than-even chance for a deadlock, if not an acquittal.

But they were wrong. The jury was not seriously split. They were just doing their job in a methodical, responsible manner. First they elected a foreman. Then they set up a system to handle the five hundred pounds of documents—filling thirteen file drawers—which Niehaus gave them to help make their decisions. The foreman appointed four researchers who would deal with the documents and three "finance men" who would do all the calculations as they analyzed the complex transactions which lay at the heart of the trial. The three defendants faced more than 250 counts, and the jurors argued over them and made their decisions one count at a time. The foreman kept the lengthy process on track and tallied all the votes.

The jury had little difficulty in finding Bongard guilty on all eighty-two misapplication and directors resolution counts. Regarding misapplication, they felt he was almost fatally compromised by his ESM profits, which more than tripled his Home State salary. The "12½, 12½ and 75" letter, with its implications of a cozy relationship with Novick and Ewton, was particularly damaging. One of the jurors said, "Obviously Mr. Bongard was doing it for the benefit of someone else, including himself, I'm afraid." Guilt seemed indisputable to the jury concerning the directors resolution counts; Burt was a member of the board and was involved in all decisions regarding the forty-one transfers.

Schiebel presented the jurors with no difficult problems. He had clearly proved to them that he was not in the higher echelon decision "loop" which approved the forty-one transfers, and they found him innocent on all the misapplication and directors resolution counts. It was equally clear to them that he was hip-deep in the debenture offering, and they came to a guilty verdict on three counts of lying and misrepresentation in the debenture prospectus.

They argued long and hard about Marvin. They couldn't understand him. Why would he do it? Why would a man in his mid-sixties, who had made $100 million, and whose public service career had been capped with an ambassadorship, why would such a man get involved in lying in a prospectus and breaking his trust with his depositors? Why would he get involved with Ewton, who came across to them as amoral and weak? One of the jurors compared searching for the truth about Marvin to "being in a dark room at night and knowing that a light switch is there but not being able to grab it."

After much emotional turmoil, they found Marvin innocent of misapplication. Though he bore responsibility in the collateral transfers, the jurors felt that the purpose of his actions was to benefit Home State and not to help the ESM crew or himself. They believed that his ESM trading profits did not compromise him, because they were small compared to his total net worth.

They found Marvin guilty on the board resolution counts concerning the last six collateral transfers; these were the transactions, starting August 29, 1983, which he insisted required his personal approval. The jury did not buy his excuse that he had received the board resolution, but had not bothered to read it. Nonetheless, it was a difficult decision. One of the jurors said, "I kept fighting it and fighting it. I just finally went into the bathroom and cried my eyes out."

The jurors had an easier time with Marvin's debenture prospectus counts. It seemed obvious to them that he had serious responsibilities in preparing the flawed document, and they found him guilty on three charges.

By 12:30 P.M. on Monday, March 2, the jury had made all its decisions. The court officers scrambled to find the defendants and the lawyers in nearby restaurants and they had everybody back in the courtroom by 2:00 P.M.

The court clerk began with Marvin. He droned through the first eighty-two charges and read not guilty every time, and Jody and Alyson began sobbing. Just seconds later they turned quiet when the clerk announced that Marvin was guilty on three of the debenture counts. Jeffress shook his head sadly and Warner and Mortenson stared grimly into space. The jurors looked at each other nervously. They knew their verdict had been misread, but nobody said anything because they were uncertain about what to do.

Schiebel's verdicts came down next. David had his wife, his daughter, and his sister with him, and they reacted to the bad news with stoic silence.

Finally, the clerk read the Bongard verdicts: guilty on all eighty-two charges. Burt looked stunned, as if he had been jolted by an electric cattle prod. His wife cried almost silently behind him.

The defense lawyers requested that the jury be polled. The clerk asked the first one, "Is the verdict just read your true and just verdict?" The juror hesitated, looked down the jury box at his cohorts, rose, and said, "No, it wasn't."

The courtroom went completely silent. Niehaus feared the worst. He recalled, "When the juror said 'that's not my verdict,' the whole trial passed in front of me. I thought we were going to have to start all over." Niehaus immediately called the lawyers into his chambers and then asked the first juror to join them. In about three minutes, the group returned to the courtroom. The judge announced that his clerk had become confused and misread the verdict form. He had missed the fact that Warner had been found guilty on the last six board resolution counts. As Jody and Alyson tried to comfort him, Marvin's face became a somber mask as he clenched his jaws and the skin tightened over his cheekbones.

Niehaus quickly thanked the jury and dismissed them, and after conferring with Kane, set bail at $3.5 million for Warner, $1.5 million for Bongard, and $25,000 for Schiebel. The judge gave them forty-eight hours to raise the money and set March 30 as the sentencing date.

Marvin had regained his composure when he faced the reporters who mobbed him in a corner of the courtroom. He showed a steely calm as he told them he was disappointed but not surprised:

> I guess it is not unexpected, taking into consideration the climate in Hamilton County. . . . The jury did the best it could in a case colored by the local media. . . . These people acted in good faith as citizens. But considering the complexities of this case, it would be beyond the scope of almost anyone to understand it fully. Any citizens who devote this much time to a case ought to be appreciated.
>
> And we as citizens have to follow the laws of the land. But I am innocent. . . . Naturally we will fight this thing and appeal.

Marvin left quickly. Finding $3.5 million in bail money in forty-eight hours would not be easy.

Enjoying his days of celebrity, Judge Niehaus appeared that night on the Cunningham talk show chatting with its host, answering questions, and receiving accolades from grateful listeners. He carefully avoided saying anything which would affect the defendants' appeals.

Marvin could not stop running now. He arrived with his bail just five minutes before the deadline, and then went off with Jeffress and Mortenson to deal with his appeal and to prepare for another courtroom ordeal. Just six weeks prior to the trial before Niehaus, a federal grand jury in Cincinnati had indicted Marvin and Bongard on conspiracy and fraud charges.

In mid-March, Warner, Bongard, and Schiebel entered their appeals. Kane later announced that he would delay prosecution of the "sweetheart" loan charges, separated from the Niehaus trial, until all the Niehaus appeals were settled.

Bongard couldn't meet his $1.5 million bail and he asked Marvin for help, but Marvin wouldn't oblige him. On March 26, he gave up a complicated fight to reduce his bail and entered prison.

The same day, federal Judge Charles Joiner ruled that Bongard and Warner could not receive a fair trial in Cincinnati because of the massive publicity surrounding their recent convictions and ordered their federal trial be held elsewhere. Soon after, he chose as its site Ann Arbor, a quiet college town in Michigan.

The sentencing of Warner, Bongard, and Schiebel on March 31 was a standing-room-only media event. Three local TV stations carried the proceedings live. When he entered, Marvin Warner did not look like a man waiting to be sentenced to prison. He sat down next to former Ohio Governor John Gilligan, his main character witness, and chatted amiably with him, smiling occasionally. He seemed determined to show the world that he was an innocent man caught up temporarily in adverse circumstances. In contrast, Schiebel, and Bongard, who was led in from jail with his hands cuffed behind his back, looked pale and mournful.

Bongard was excused until the next day because of an abstruse legal problem on the misapplication counts, and Schiebel and his lawyer asked for leniency, highlighting David's good works in community service.

Gilligan, Marvin's lawyers, and his family pleaded for mercy for Marvin. Warner's daughter, Marlin Arky, told the court, "My father has dedicated his life to the work ethic, to making the world a better place. Home State's collapse robbed him of his reputation, his business, and most tragic of all, it robbed Stephen Arky of his life. My husband said in his suicide note, 'As to the ESM matter . . . I am innocent of any wrong doing in that case. So are my partners and Marvin Warner.' " She and Alyson read notes from their children to the judge, and Jody told Niehaus that her husband's life had been permanently shattered and that she had "awakened at night to the sounds of his tears."

Marvin's voice cracked and he brushed tears from his eyes as he made a short statement. He emphasized his service in government and to the community and finished by saying, "My suffering is unimportant relative to the pain and suffering of the many people who were depositors. Give me the justice that you would give to any individual, and nothing less."

Next Judge Niehaus read a formal statement in which he castigated the white collar criminal.

> The well-dressed, smiling face, armed with pen and computer, can extract a greater amount of money from a greater number of citizens and be greatly more difficult to convict than armed thugs . . .
>
> These men were in positions of trust. They betrayed that trust to the detriment of . . . the depositors and debenture holders of Home State and indirectly to the detriment of the citizens of this community and this state . . .
>
> Shall we allow fiduciaries to abandon such a duty of trust and improperly benefit from the abandonment? The answer is no.

Then he sentenced Schiebel to six months in jail plus a $25,000 fine;

he did not increase his $25,000 bail and David walked out of Room 513 a free man pending his appeal.

Niehaus turned to Marvin and gave him three-and-a-half years in prison, ordered him to pay $22 million restitution to the citizens of Ohio, and increased his bail to $22 million effective that moment. Since Marvin didn't have that kind of money available, he had to go to jail. He looked defiant as he was handcuffed to a deputy sheriff and swiftly led out of the courtroom.

The next day, Niehaus sentenced Bongard to ten years in prison and ordered him to pay $114 million in restitution. The $114 million was purely symbolic, because Burt had all but exhausted his resources paying his expensive lawyers.

At the same time, Jeffress and Mortenson went to a three-judge appeals court and argued that Niehaus, in a ploy that was pure politics, was perverting the bail process to punish Marvin. The true purpose of bail, they said, was not to punish but to insure that the accused appear in court when he was scheduled to. The judges agreed and reduced bail to $5 million. Marvin came up with the money on April 2, and after three nights in jail returned to the comforts of Warnerton.

Before the Niehaus trial began, there was dissension in the Bongard camp about basic strategy. Marvin Gersten, Bongard's New York attorney, believed Kane's case against Burt was so strong that Burt should plead guilty. Gilliam took the opposite view, arguing that he could win acquittal by painting Burt as a dupe of Ewton, Novick, and Gomez. Gilliam prevailed, but after the Cincinnati conviction, Bongard accepted Gersten's counsel, and the two almost immediately began negotiating a plea with the Federal attorneys.

Bongard pleaded guilty on April 27 to one federal charge of conspiracy and three of wire fraud. He agreed to testify against Warner in the Ann Arbor trial, scheduled to begin May 5, and to cooperate with Larry Kane as well.

The federal indictment in the Ann Arbor trial charged that Bongard, Warner, and the key ESM people (Ewton, Novick, Mead, and Gomez) formed a conspiracy between 1980 and 1985 to defraud several groups—Home State's depositors and debenture holders, the state of Ohio, and ODGF. The alleged aims of the conspirators were to enrich themselves and to keep their two bankrupt companies alive via a mutual self-help scheme; ESM would send phony profits up to Home State and in return, Home State would send ESM the collateral it needed to cover its enormous losses.

Novick was dead and the other conspirators had confessed, so Marvin was now the sole defendant. He was charged with seventeen counts of wire fraud—all of which involved telephone calls or wire transfers of money—and conspiracy. The crucial count was conspiracy, because the alleged wire frauds were all committed in aid of the conspiracy. If the jury found Marvin not guilty of conspiracy, it was almost certain they would find him innocent on the wire fraud charges.

Kane had extracted testimony about such a mutual self-help arrangement from Ewton and others to strengthen his case on misapplication, but he never attempted to show that it involved a conspiracy, an illegal, organized scheme to defraud. He had stuck to more limited charges and did not believe he had the evidence to meet the challenge of establishing a conspiracy.

The federal prosecutor, Ann Marie Tracey, had decided to take on this challenge. It was a risky course, because she had no "smoking gun," no documented evidence knitting the six men together in a conspiracy scheme. Federal attorneys have been successful in proving conspiracy cases against the Mafia, corrupt politicians, and Wall Street's insider traders, because they have had concrete evidence of scheming provided by wire taps, video tapes, and compromising written materials. Tracey had none of this. What she had to rely on was the testimony of confessed conspirators Ewton and Bongard, and evidence from which the jury could infer that a conspiracy had taken place. Key evidence of this sort included the large personal trading profits Bongard and Warner made at ESM, and Warner and Ewton sending $108 million of American Savings & Loan's money to ESM when the money was crucial to ESM's survival.

Tracey would attempt to make her case in a setting which was in a world apart from Room 513 in Cincinnati. The Ann Arbor courtroom was situated in a dignified, modern building, and its large and quiet spaces were bathed in a diffused light which entered from two large skylights. The jurors sat in well-upholstered swivel chairs and each of the few spectators who attended had his own comfortable, contoured seat. There were no glaring TV spotlights. Jeffress said it's like the "Elysian Fields" compared to the "Roman circus" of Niehaus's courtroom.

Judge Joiner had made a wise decision in choosing Ann Arbor. Its citizens were so disinterested in Warner's fate that its newspaper, the *News*, did not even cover the trial. Not one of the fifty-eight potential jurors had ever heard of Marvin Warner, and it took only four hours to choose a jury as compared to three weeks in Cincinnati. As was the case in Cincinnati, the jury was basically working class.

Charles Joiner, age seventy-one, is a courtly figure, who was solicitous of the jury in a fatherly manner. He never intruded on the proceedings the way Niehaus did, but kept the trial moving briskly, nonetheless. He seemed to operate on a boredom criterion; if he felt ennui setting in, he would ask the lawyers to speed things up.

Ann Marie Tracey is a seasoned expert in white collar crime. In her late thirties, she has the perky, practical, "girl next door" demeanor of a Mary Tyler Moore. Her personality is consistently attractive and fresh, and she established a good rapport with the jury. Her dark red hair and trim figure were set off by the conservative business suits she always wore to court.

Tracey set the stage by examining Sylvester Hentschel, Ohio's senior bank examiner, and other regulators about the key ESM–Home State transactions. Then she brought on Ewton, who arrived in the courtroom handcuffed and in leg irons. Twelve weeks in jail had taken a heavy toll on Ronnie. He had lost a lot of weight and he looked haggard and spent, like the figures one often sees in the WPA photographs taken during the depression. His eyes darted around fearfully and his testimony was subdued.

Tracey took Ewton through all the major events in the Home State–ESM saga: the growing interdependence starting in 1980, the alleged revelations to Warner and Bongard that ESM had serious financial problems, the failed hedge, the "make up my losses" meeting, and the Waldorf-Astoria meeting in the spring of 1984. As Ronnie told it, the events were related, but he did not tie them firmly together with a thread of conspiracy. He did not leave the jurors with an image of criminals constantly plotting to advance illegal schemes.

Tracey knew that if she didn't bring to light the damaging facts about Ewton, Mortenson would, and she elicited from Ronnie that he was seeking to shorten his jail time in exchange for his current testimony, that he had bribed Gomez and forged Novick's will, and that he had spent millions on personal pleasures while he was purportedly convincing Warner that ESM was in serious trouble.

Mortenson did an even better job of tearing Ronnie apart than he did in Cincinnati. He had him acknowledge that he never told Marvin that Grant's ESM audits were a fraud or that Home State's and Marvin's profits were phony. He even got him to admit to a crime that hadn't been revealed in court before: Ronnie had perjured himself during Bobby Seneca's divorce trial. And following up on Tracey's inability to get Ronnie to create a consistent story of conspiracy, Mortenson asked Ewton a series of important and probing questions:

Q: When is it you conspired with Mr. Warner to disobey and disregard the law?

A: I don't know. I don't know that we did conspire to do it. I don't think that any of us intended to do it. It just happened by neglect and pride and stupidity.

Q: Did you ever come to an agreement or an understanding with Mr. Warner to provide him or Home State with fraudulently generated funds?

A: We didn't sit down and agree on it. It just happened. It just evolved.

Q: Did you ever come to an agreement with Mr. Warner that Home State would provide to ESM cash or other assets for the specific purpose of concealing massive losses?

A: Those discussions were just to continue to operate and we didn't say we need this to conceal massive losses.

This line of questioning strongly affected the jury. Ronnie impressed none of them, and one said later that, "Ewton is probably a really good liar. He is a good salesman. Lying is probably second nature to him." And another commented, "He seemed awfully smooth. I could see how Mr. Warner could be taken in." One of Tracey's big guns had been rendered ineffective.

She brought up the other one, Burt Bongard, a week later. She knew she would have to be very dexterous in handling Burt, because he operated under three handicaps. He had to be very careful not to commit another crime—perjury—by contradicting testimony he gave under oath in Cincinnati; he was a confessed conspirator seeking to reduce his jail time; and his demeanor and delivery were dull and unconvincing.

Bongard did what Ewton failed to do: he told a story of a deliberate conspiracy which allegedly started at a 1980 meeting attended by himself, Warner, Ewton, and Novick. He detailed the quid pro quo arrangement; ESM would give profits to Home State, Bongard, and Warner, and in return Bongard and Warner would send needed collateral to ESM. And he said that Warner really ran Home State, even though Marvin was neither an officer nor a director from 1977 through 1984.

Jeffress attacked this testimony skillfully. In Cincinnati, Bongard had said he did not know that Home State's profits were phony. If this were true, it severely undermined the quid pro quo story which Tracey had elicited from him the previous day. The following colloquy took place about the profits:

JEFFRESS: I believe you testified that to your knowledge there were
            no rigged trades?
BONGARD: That's correct.
JEFFRESS: But were the profits rigged, Sir?
BONGARD: Well, the profits were not rigged, but they were certainly
            good . . . trades. We didn't have any losses.

In another discussion of the trades, Jeffress engaged Bongard in an exchange about truth which brought laughter from the courtroom:

JEFFRESS: Is it not a fact that you testified in your trial in Ohio that
            you had no idea that there were any rigged trades at ESM?
BONGARD: That was true.
JEFFRESS: Was it the whole truth?
BONGARD: It was the whole truth but not the whole story.
JEFFRESS: Do you distinguish between the whole truth and the
            whole story?
BONGARD: Given a specific question, I answered very narrowly . . . I
            did tell the truth, I just didn't tell all the story.

Jeffress further attacked the quid pro quo conspiracy story by getting Burt to corroborate his Cincinnati testimony that, while he was dealing with ESM, he was duped by the Grant audits; that is, he did not know that ESM was insolvent or had suffered serious losses. This flatly contradicted testimony given by Ewton only one week earlier.

Jeffress also painted Bongard as an ingrate and a betrayer of Warner, who had been for fifteen years his father figure and mentor. He got Burt to admit that in the time between his Cincinnati conviction and his decision to confess and help the feds prosecute Warner, he had pleaded with Marvin to help him meet the $1.5 million bail imposed by Niehaus, and Warner had refused.

Fifi Taft Rockefeller, Warner's eccentric Cincinnati fan who had come to Ann Arbor in all her glitzy glory, told "Marvin, baby" that he was home free when Burt stepped down from the witness stand.

The jury wasn't impressed with Bongard's performance either. Said one, "I didn't care for Burt Bongard. He didn't seem like a believable person." "I didn't trust him," another juror commented, "I didn't like him as soon as I saw him." A third characterized Bongard and Ewton as, "the type of guys who were running a fast game, and the game caught up with them."

The two principal defense witnesses were Schiebel and Warner.

Schiebel's main role was to contradict important testimony by Bongard and Ewton. He said that Bongard was lying when he claimed that Warner really ran Home State in the 1980s. David corroborated Warner's Cincinnati testimony that after returning from Switzerland, he "tinkered" at Home State. He testified that Marvin would occasionally look at the "bottom line" but had delegated the bank's basic operations and investment policy to Bongard.

Schiebel had attended two of the meetings where Ewton claimed he told Warner that ESM was in serious financial straits. He said that Ewton was flat-out lying, that ESM's corporate health was not discussed at either occasion.

The jury was so impressed with Schiebel's performance that when he finished they rose and applauded. Judge Joiner, who was taken by surprise, quickly quieted them and admonished them never to do it again.

On the witness stand, Marvin was again the gentle senior citizen. Mortenson allowed him to ramble on about his career and how he had been duped by Ewton, the phony Grant audits, and Bongard. Marvin said that, coming so soon after the request for bail money, he "was shocked that Burt had pleaded guilty to federal charges. It was just inconceivable."

During one of his ramblings, Warner mentioned that Tracey's husband, lawyer Donald Mooney, was a member of a firm which represented Grant. Tracey objected, because months before Joiner had ruled that Mooney's role involved no conflict of interest, and the judge sustained her objection. But the jury had heard Marvin, and Tracey was furious. She was still furious when she started her cross examination, and this kept her from developing an effective line of questioning. After an hour she asked Joiner if she could stop twenty-five minutes before quitting time and finish the next morning. He granted her request, and her performance the next day was more coherent.

Marvin appeared confident as the trial neared its finish. During a recess on the day of the closing arguments, he was bantering happily with the spectators outside the courtroom. While helping a reporter adjust his tie, Marvin smiled to the people standing around him and said, "It isn't often you can get a member of the press in a situation like this." His family did not share his good spirits. Jody and his children looked drained and somber as the time for decision approached.

Joiner gave the case to the jury on the morning of Friday, June 19, almost seven weeks after the trial began. They took less than three hours to find Warner not guilty. Outside the courtroom, the jurors joined Marvin and his family in celebration. There were teary embraces and whoops of laughter, and Marvin hugged one of the women jurors and told her, "I want to thank you for giving me my life back."Another told him, "Go on now and have a good and happy life."

Whether Marvin's life was going to be good and happy was a matter of conjecture. What was certain was that it wouldn't be lived in Ohio and it would continue to be very busy. From the courthouse steps, Marvin and Jody announced that they would move to a horse farm they had bought near Ocala, Florida. Jody said, "We are happy and ready to start a new life—in Florida. After everything that has happened, it's obvious we can't make a home in Cincinnati or anywhere else in Ohio."

Marvin would be very busy, because he was beset by $4.4 billion in lawsuits and he was pushing his appeal on the Cincinnati conviction. And he had to be at his best to face his next big challenger—Tom Tew.

In the Web of the Law

The confrontation between Warner and Tew was scheduled for November 30, 1987, in a civil trial before Judge Gonzalez. Tew wanted $22.7 million from Marvin for the ESM creditors, claiming that Ewton and his boys had provided Marvin unjust and fraudulent preferential treatment in giving him those millions. Tew, as trustee for the creditors, was the plaintiff; and he totally delegated responsibility for litigating the case to Jose Garcia-Pedrosa.

Looking past Tew's case, Marvin saw a mountain of financial trouble. He was working hard to appeal the $22 million fine imposed by Niehaus, and in addition, he was beset with more than thirty lawsuits seeking more than $4 billion from him. The main cases broke down as follows:

Claimant	Amount
State of Ohio	$2.000 billion
Alexander Grant	942 million
ODGF	756 million
FDIC	179 million
Beaumont, Texas	115 million
Clark County, Nevada	115 million
Harrisburg, Pennsylvania	115 million
American Savings & Loan	97 million
Total	$4.319 billion

A realistic assessment of these suits would put them in the hundreds of millions rather than the billions, because lawyers frequently inflate their demands out of all proportion. They do this, because a judge or a jury will far more frequently reduce a claim than increase it. For example, Tew's $22.7 million claim had been whittled down by Gonzalez from an initial $182 million.

Marvin was counterattacking with eight lawsuits of his own seeking $364 million. His principal targets, from whom he was seeking a total of $357 million, were the state of Ohio ($182 million); Tom Tew ($100 million); and Alexander Grant, Arthur Anderson, and ODGF ($25 million each).

In other words, Marvin represented a miniboom to the legal industry in the late 1980s.

On March 19, 1985, only ten days after Home State's collapse, Warner started making moves whose effects were to protect his assets from the hungry litigants who would covet them. He followed a two-stage program. First, he would give away as much as possible to Jody and other family members; then he would seek the protection of the bankruptcy court for the assets which were left.

He gave Jody $1 million on March 19, 1985, and from that date to January 1, 1987, transferred roughly $50 million from himself to his wife and family. Fifteen million dollars went to Jody outright and another $18 million in securities and property were put into joint ownership with her. Mark, his son, received $3 million, and the remaining $14 million went to various Warner family trusts.

A study of Florida's Homestead Act suggests that Marvin's and Jody's move there was not animated solely by the poisoned social atmosphere they had experienced in Cincinnati. The act, which Ronnie and Jerilyn Ewton had also used to their advantage, states that a bankrupt Florida resident can retain a "homestead" with 160 acres of land; the horse farm in Ocala which the Warners moved to, and for which they paid more than $2 million, comprises 151 acres. The act also allowed Marvin to keep $3 million in life insurance policies plus his interest in nearly $12 million of the assets owned jointly with Jody. Ohio's equivalent of Florida's Homestead Act allows a bankrupt to protect only $1,000.

Marvin told the *Miami Herald* that his decision to move from Cincinnati to Ocala had nothing to do with bankruptcy planning, and everything to do with finding better breeding grounds for his horses.

On the afternoon of October 22, 1987, Tew and Garcia-Pedrosa arrived in Judge Jose Gonzalez's courtroom to make a motion in connection with the Warner trial which was less than six weeks away. Gonzalez brought them up short when he told them they couldn't do it, because that morning, in the Jacksonville, Florida federal court, Marvin had filed for bankruptcy under Chapter 11.

A Chapter 11 filing opens up a whole new ballgame for all litigation concerning the bankrupt, because it interposes a federal shield of protection between him and his creditors while he attempts to get his affairs in order.

Marvin took roughly $20 million in assets into his bankruptcy; this is what he had left for himself after transferring the $50 million to his family. He said that his main purpose in filing was to "prevent a chaotic and uncontrolled scramble" by his creditors in pursuit of the more than $4 billion they claimed he owed them. They were pressing thirty-three separate actions, and Marvin hoped that Bankruptcy Judge George Proctor would consolidate them into one omnibus lawsuit. Proctor refused to do this, arguing that there was no time in his court schedule to try such a mammoth case. On November 28, he issued an order which allowed Tew and Garcia-Pedrosa, who were first in line, to reschedule their trial for June 1988.

This was not what Marvin had expected, and on December 16, 1987, he moved to stop the proceedings and revert to his pre-bankruptcy status. He could not have known what a difficult task this was. The power to change his status now resided with Judge Proctor, who had to weigh the interests of all parties to the bankruptcy before making a decision.

In such cases the wishes of the creditors are given great weight. When they sat down with the judge, they asked him not to turn Marvin loose. Their primary reason: bankruptcy law gave them great power to investigate all of Marvin's assets and liabilities. They wanted this power mainly because they had serious questions about the legitimacy of the $50 million in gifts he had made to his family. In fact, they claimed that $45.8 million were illegitimate transfers. Proctor went along with the creditors in a ruling on February 8, 1988. Marvin was stuck to bankruptcy like a fly to flypaper.

Jeffress and Mortenson had nothing to do with the bankruptcy action, which was outside their area of expertise. In early 1988, they were busy preparing for the Tew trial and pressing Marvin's appeal on his Cincinnati conviction. The appeal was grounded in four main arguments.

Marvin couldn't get a fair trial in Cincinnati, they claimed, because of the massive adverse publicity. The lawyers cited Marvin's acquittal in less than three hours in Ann Arbor to buttress their earlier contentions on this point. Furthermore, the attorneys protested that Judge Niehaus had shown a consistent bias against Warner in his comments and rulings, and that Ohio's attorney general had no constitutional powers to appoint Kane as special prosecutor. Finally, they contended that one of the jurors, who hadn't revealed that his mother-in-law was a Home State depositor, had stated several times during the deliberations that he hated Marvin.

Jeffress and Mortenson received a setback on January 14, 1988, when a judge ruled that their motion on the biased juror was filed late and would not be accepted. When Marvin heard about it, all his old distrust of the legal profession came boiling to the surface. As he told a reporter at the time, "From my own experience with attorneys, I've concluded that some of them are better press agents for themselves than they are lawyers. Their priorities fall in the following order: Fees. Publicity. Clients. There are, of course, exceptions. Some of mine have been excellent. Still, some have been great disappointments.

They have voracious egos that must be fed constantly. I, personally, am tired of feeding those egos."

He had hired and fired lawyers for forty years. His general approach appeared to be that, if you had the money, you could always drop one and quickly find another just as good and probably hungrier; he would pull those guys off the case. On March 25, Marvin announced that he was replacing Jeffress and Mortenson with Andy Hall, a Miami attorney, to represent him against Tew.

It was a major tactical error. The Tew trial would break very little new ground. The charges were different, but by and large, the same witnesses would be telling the same old stories and the attorneys would be chewing over the same evidence.

Jeffress and Mortenson had been working on the Home State–ESM matter for more than two years, and were familiar with every nuance of the case. Andy Hall would have less than three months to come up to speed, and he was thinly staffed; at times he was forced to hire raw college students to help him read and interpret depositions. What is more, Jeffress and Mortenson had spent hundreds of hours questioning the key players and could read their every facial tic, vocal nuance, body movement. Hall would never be able to obtain this knowledge.

Andy Hall was born in Poland in 1945 to concentration camp survivors and came to America as a young boy. He both looks and acts pugnacious. He has the rugged build and flattened nose of a middleweight boxer. The dome of his head is bald, and his strong features are framed by a mustache and a short, black beard. His basic courtroom style is that of the aggressive street fighter. He was full of moral disdain for the criminals who were among Garcia-Pedrosa's main witnesses, and he attacked them at every opportunity.

The trial began on June 13, 1988. The heat and glare of the Fort Lauderdale sun were so intense that trial participants felt physically assaulted when they emerged from the air-conditioned courtroom building onto one of its several surrounding verandas.

The jury of six was chosen the first morning, and Garcia-Pedrosa began his opening arguments soon after lunch. Since this was a civil trial, he faced a lower threshold of proof than Kane and Tracey encountered in their criminal actions against Warner.

A criminal prosecutor must prove his allegations "beyond a reasonable doubt"; such proof must be so convincing that a reasonable person would not hesitate to rely upon it in his most important affairs. In a civil case, a lawyer is required to adhere to a "preponderance of the evidence" criterion. Judge Gonzalez instructed the court that "to establish a claim by a preponderance of the evidence really means to prove that the claim is more likely so than not so." There is a considerable distance from "beyond a reasonable doubt" to "more likely so than not so."

Garcia-Pedrosa sought from Warner $22.7 million, which he claimed Warner got for two illegitimate reasons: unfair preferences (which to be collectible must occur in the 12 months preceding a bankruptcy) and fraudulent transfers.

The fraudulent transfers had more serious consequences for Warner's reputation than did the unfair preferences. The preference claims said that Warner had unfairly gotten ahead of the other creditors in line and that he should put the money back in the pot and wait his turn with the others. The fraudulent transfer claims said that he took money "for the purpose of aiding the (ESM) fraud."

Garcia-Pedrosa stated that Warner received unfair preferences totaling $18.2 million at the expense of the other ESM creditors. This occurred when Marvin closed his account on January 28, 1985, and received $4.9 million, and when, in the 1983 hedge debacle, ESM made up his losses and his invested capital to the tune of $13.3 million.

To prove these unfair preferences, Garcia-Pedrosa had to show that the payments were made within twelve months of ESM's bankruptcy on March 27, 1985, and that Warner was an "insider" of the bankrupt ESM. Judge Gonzalez defined an insider as "a person who has some special advantage, knowledge, and influence."

Further, on the unfair preferences, Garcia-Pedrosa had to establish that Warner knew that ESM was in severe financial difficulty, and that the Warner transactions involved were not "repos"—a special kind of deal where the seller of a government security agrees to repurchase it within a year. A technical, legal exception puts the proceeds of a repo beyond the grasp of a bankruptcy trustee.

Garcia-Pedrosa claimed that Warner and ESM together engaged in fraudulent transfers to him totaling $4.5 million. Garcia-Pedrosa had to prove that the transfers were made by ESM with intent to hinder, delay, or defraud its creditors and that Warner took the money for the purpose of aiding the fraud. In other words, ESM gave insider Warner special illegitimate favors to the detriment of its creditors. These payments occurred more than a year prior to ESM's bankruptcy and came in three forms: phony trading profits, interest rate subsidies, and the earliest "make-up-my-losses" payments.

Garcia-Pedrosa also charged Warner with civil fraud counts of racketeering, civil theft, and unjust enrichment. Proof of these charges could have resulted in the award of damages to the plaintiff over and above the $22.7 million. During the trial, Judge Gonzalez gave Warner a big emotional lift when he threw out the civil fraud charges on the grounds of insufficient evidence.

Backing his claim that Warner was an insider with preferential knowledge, advantage, and influence, Garcia-Pedrosa pointed to the record of Marvin's transactions with ESM, and said, "Warner was able to get Ronnie Ewton and Alan Novick, and the boys at ESM, basically to do whatever he wanted. . . . Whatever Marvin Warner asked for, Marvin Warner got; he got it every time."

There were numerous incidents to prove Marvin's insider status and "economic domination of ESM," and he cited some of the most flagrant: ESM making up Marvin's personal losses on the failed hedge transaction; Ewton's agreeing to Marvin's Waldorf-Astoria demand for a $12 million interest rate subsidy for Home State; ESM absorbing Home State's $2.1 million loss in the summer of 1984; and Mead's description to Warner of ESM's horrendous financial plight three days before Warner's ESM account was closed.

Garcia-Pedrosa described others: the many times Ewton and Novick told Warner and Bongard that ESM couldn't do all the things Home State asked of it, because ESM was in terrible financial shape itself; Ewton's December 1984 disclosure to Arky that ESM might seek a bankruptcy lawyer; and the discussions among Arky, Ewton, and Warner following Shatzman's bombshell revelations to Arky on January 21, 1985.

Garcia-Pedrosa had to take the repo issue seriously, because it jeopardized $19.3 million of his $22.7 million claim. He and Hall put four experts on the stand to describe, in mind-boggling detail, what a repo is and what it is not. When they finished, it was clearly apparent that Warner's transactions were not repos. Ironically, some of Garcia-Pedrosa's most effective testimony came from one of Hall's experts.

To press his fraudulent transfer claims, Garcia-Pedrosa used Jack Goldstrich, a partner of Laurie Holtz and a precise, articulate man with an elephant's memory for figures. He testified that Warner put up zero capital and made $1.8 million from a thirty-seven-trade winning streak at ESM, and that all thirty-seven trades were fictitious. He also showed that ESM lent money to Warner at rates well below what ESM was paying, and that these subsidies amounted to $1.6 million. For a while, Warner had borrowed from ESM at 2½ percent when the prime rate, the rate banks charge their very best customers, was 9 percent.

Hall admitted that ESM gave Warner many financial favors—made up his losses, subsidized his interest rates, created substantial trading profits. However, he maintained that, from Marvin's point of view, the deals were hard bargains which he drove solely because he knew how to use influence and power. He was just being a hard-nosed businessman, not a crook, and ESM was just trying to keep their best customer happy. What is more, Hall claimed the deals were done without collusion and without knowledge of ESM's criminal intent. He reiterated that Marvin never knew his ESM profits were phony and that he was always fooled by the fake Grant audits.

As with Jeffress and Mortenson in Ann Arbor, Hall had the advantage that there was no concrete evidence—no incriminating memos or recordings—knitting Marvin and the ESM gang together in a larcenous scheme. If he could show that Marvin was the victim of the gang, he would win. In fact, in his opening statement Andy said, "The entire case rests on whether this guy was a victim or whether he was involved."

Hall figured that his best opportunity for showing that Marvin was a victim was to put "the victim" on the stand. Garcia-Pedrosa agreed, "I don't think there's any question that Marvin Warner is Marvin Warner's most important witness."

Hall faced a difficult balancing act. He had to paint Warner as the aged victim of young sharks like Ewton and Novick, but at the same time he had to show his client as a hard-bargaining businessman pushing relentlessly for his personal advantage. Finding the appropriate emphasis for these contrasting portraits was difficult. In the end, Hall opted for depicting Marvin as a gentle victim who was fatally naive about his adversaries, and he downplayed his client's aggressive business instincts.

Hall used a variation of the "I was just tinkering" defense which Marvin had deployed in his two previous trials. He was again the semiretired old man, fussing around the edges, but not getting involved in the nitty-gritty. He claimed that he didn't know what a repo was when he was purportedly trading them, and that he was unfamiliar with his cash flow, because his accountants took care of that for him. When asked about his successful thirty-seven-trade winning streak at ESM he replied, "I don't think I knew about individual transactions at all. Based on the tax meetings we had periodically during the year, I knew essentially what my income was, and those things, but it was more from an overview statement."

In answering Garcia-Pedrosa's most probing questions, he was frequently evasive, offering statements like, "I'm sorry, I don't have that information, and if I promised it to you, I apologize" . . . "Frankly, I forgot the question" . . . "I think it is a little bit difficult for me to answer these questions." All in all, it was not a convincing performance.

Garcia-Pedrosa's best counter to Warner's victim defense was evidence that Warner derived great benefit from ESM because ESM was keeping Home State alive. He contended that Warner needed Home State at all costs in the early 1980s in order to maintain his reputation as a big-stakes player in the banking game and reap millions from deals like ComBanks, ABI, Century, and American Savings & Loan. Garcia-Pedrosa told the court, "Home State wasn't just another investment for Marvin Warner. Home State was the cornerstone of his financial investments. His alter ego. The one thing we will prove to you that Mr. Warner could not permit to go under. Because if it did, he would not be able to continue to be, as he was, a national financial person. A national financial player. . . . He had to protect Home State at any expense if he wanted to continue with his financial empire and develop it any further."

Thus, the survival of Home State, according to Garcia-Pedrosa, was the motivation for Warner's participation in the whole ESM saga. To provide the essential proof that ESM was keeping Home State alive, he called Laurie Holtz, who had done an exhaustive study of the finances of both companies.

Garcia-Pedrosa received a dismaying setback when—after ten minutes of Laurie's testimony—Judge Gonzalez dismissed him from the witness stand. He ruled that Laurie couldn't testify about Home State–ESM transactions; he reasoned that since Home State was a creditor of ESM and Tew represented the creditors, Laurie's testimony was the equivalent of Tew testifying against himself.

Near the end of the trial, Hall made a legal blunder, called "opening the door," which allowed Garcia-Pedrosa to bring Laurie back. If a lawyer brings up for his client's benefit a subject which has been banned for his adversary, then he opens the door for his adversary to explore the subject. Hall introduced Home State's finances to elicit sympathy for Marvin by showing how much he lost when the bank collapsed, and immediately Garcia-Pedrosa got the judge to give permission to recall Laurie.

At last, Garcia-Pedrosa could show that continuing ESM's contribution to Home State's survival was essential motivation for Warner to play ball with the ESM gang. And the timing was excellent, because Laurie became the last major witness and his testimony would impact the jury shortly before they began their deliberations.

Holtz testified that Home State could not have stayed in business for four years, from 1981 through 1984, without the more than $36 million in phony profits provided by ESM. He told the court that these benefits enabled Home State to show a December 31, 1984, net worth of $19.7 million. Without them, the bank would have been hopelessly broke and $16.7 million in the hole.

This was the vital ammunition that Garcia-Pedrosa needed to argue that, as long as the self-help scheme could be kept going, Warner could be viewed as a beneficiary of ESM and not its victim.

Laurie testified on July 5, and the closing arguments and the charge to the jury were heard the next day.

The jury got the case on Thursday morning, July 7, and wrestled with it all day. The atmosphere in the courtroom was that of time suspended. There was an electric tension among the two sets of lawyers and Marvin and Jody, but they were powerless to release it. So they occupied themselves with trivia: talking about the baseball pennant races and the weather, doodling, working the crossword puzzles.

The reporters took a straw poll and it came out sixty to forty in Marvin's favor. The consensus was that Garcia-Pedrosa's case was too circumstantial; he had failed to put a "smoking gun" in Marvin's hands. And the reporters thought that the damnably complex, twenty-two-question verdict form, which Judge Gonzalez had created for the jurors, worked very much in Marvin's favor. Gonzalez had put it together after consulting with both sets of lawyers, but he had adopted almost all of Hall's ideas. The media contingent believed that the judge had bent over backwards to be fair to Marvin when he approved the form. Garcia-Pedrosa called it "Kafkaesque," and Tew commented, "We have to get nineteen questions answered our way before we get a penny. And they only have to get three questions answered their way to win across the board."

Although the complexity of the verdict form favored Warner, one of its questions represented a dangerous hazard for him. It was number fifteen and it read:

> . . . do you find from a preponderance of the evidence that: Marvin L. Warner actually participated in the fraudulent purpose of ESM Government Securities, Inc. or took the conveyance (of funds) for the purpose of aiding in the fraud?
> Yes ————————————————— No —————————————————

If the jury answered "Yes," Marvin would be placed in the center of the ESM fraud for the first time.

Tew was so concerned with the verdict form that it put him in a mood to compromise, to make a deal with Warner before the jury delivered its verdict.

Andy Hall also was in a mood to compromise. Like all experienced litigators, he knew how tough it was to read the minds of a jury. And he also had to be concerned about a legal doctrine called "collateral estoppel." This doctrine holds that a finding of fact by a jury in one case will be treated as fact in related subsequent cases. For example, if this jury found that Marvin was an ESM insider, then he would be considered an insider in the remaining thirty-two suits being brought by his creditors.

At about 5:00 P.M., Marvin, his son Mark, Jody, Andy Hall, and an assistant of Andy's left the courthouse for the relative privacy and the searing heat of the veranda to decide what they might accept as a settlement. Tom Tew watched the group while standing a few feet inside the building lobby and separated from them by a wall of glass. After a few moments, Hall came inside, said to Tom, "I'd like to talk to you," and marched him outside a couple of hundred feet to the end of the veranda.

They had been talking for about ten minutes when Judge Gonzalez's clerk came into the lobby to tell one of Tew's people that the jury was sending the judge a message, and the judge wanted the lawyers back in the courtroom. Tew's man told the clerk that it appeared some kind of settlement negotiation was going on, and asked for ten additional minutes. This happened three more times. And on the clerk's fourth trip, he said that the jury had reached a verdict, both they and the judge wanted to go home, and Gonzalez had a final message for Tew and Hall: "Let's fish or cut bait." It was now about 5:45 P.M. The lawyers asked for a final ten minutes.

Hall and Tew motioned for Jody to join them and they explained to her where they stood. After Hall had initiated the offer for settlement, there was a healthy give-and-take, and the two men had agreed on a figure of $6 million. She said yes, she liked the deal. Then Tew told her that before he could go ahead he had to hear a "yes" from Marvin's mouth. The three of them walked over to Marvin, who was leaning against a trash can which separated him from the building's glass wall. He pulled himself erect, flanked by Mark and Hall's assistant.

As Tew and Warner faced each other, their hands in their pockets, their weights on the balls of their feet, a janitor came up behind Marvin to bag the refuse in the trash can. He listened attentively to the short conversation. What he heard was this:

TEW: I understand we have a deal.
WARNER: Yeah.
TEW: For $6 million?
WARNER: Oh, no, for $3 million. And what's more, here's how it will be paid. I'll give you Warnerton Farm, you sell it, and keep what you realize. Later, when I recover some of my money, I'll pay down the rest.
TEW: Remember, Marvin, if this jury finds against you, it will affect your standing in all subsequent cases.
WARNER: (putting his hand to his heart): You expect me to pay with my money?

Tew had had enough. He strode back into the building followed by Hall, who was muttering, "Son of a bitch, son of a bitch." Tew later said that he would have come down to $4.8 million, but when Warner started at $3 million, he became disgusted and decided to let the jury roll the dice.

At the crucial moment, Marvin Warner had elected to haggle. It was as if he were back in Birmingham in 1947 bargaining with a subcontractor to cut the cost of window frames by $2.40 each. His earliest instincts had prevailed, blinding him to the larger, truly important issues.

Back in the courtroom, Judge Gonzalez asked the jury if they had reached a verdict. The foreman answered, "Yes," and passed the verdict form to Gonzalez who read it and gave it to his clerk to read aloud. Andy Hall sat alone at the defense lawyer's table, while Tew's team clustered quietly around their table. Behind Hall in the first spectator bench were Mark, Marvin, and Jody. Mark had his right arm around Marvin, and Marvin's right arm cradled Jody who was huddled up against his shoulder and almost trembling.

As the clerk read the answer to the third question, Hall dropped his face into his hands on the table; he didn't change that posture until the clerk finished. Mark, Marvin and Jody did not move their bodies, but tears streamed down Marvin's cheeks. Tew's team was silent.

The jury had answered all twenty-two questions in Tew's favor, awarding him the full $22.7 million.

In the end, it had come down to Marvin's lack of credibility and a superior litigating effort by Garcia-Pedrosa and his team.

The jury could not believe that a hard-nosed, savvy wheeler-dealer like Warner did not have a basic understanding of the shady dealings going on at ESM, and was not involved with them in some way. They couldn't picture him as the gentle, naive victim and they found his answers too evasive, his memory too porous. "He was like a politician," one juror said. "He'd go this way and that way and try and get out the back, but he'd never answer the question."

They were impressed by Holtz's testimony, which provided a firm Warner motive for the mutual self-help scheme and damaged the "victim" defense. And they were convinced that Marvin fell within the judge's definition of an insider by the mountain of evidence about phony profits, the making up of losses, the interest rate subsidies, and the transfers of collateral to a desperate ESM.

The lack of preparation time clearly affected Andy Hall's performance. The jurors believed that Garcia-Pedrosa knew the whole story better, understood the issues with greater clarity and was able to present them with greater conviction. Marvin should have stayed with Jeffress and Mortenson.

Tew's team left the courtroom and was immediately met in the lobby by reporters who started questioning Tom and Garcia-Pedrosa. A few minutes later, Jody, Marvin, and Mark emerged. Jody collapsed in a chair, and Mark stayed with his father. Most of the reporters deserted Tom and Garcia-Pedrosa to surround Marvin.

Warner's eyes were red, his cheeks were wet with tears, and he looked his full sixty-nine years. He told the reporters, "I feel terrible. I'm stunned. Of course, we will appeal."

Marvin was talking bravely, but he had to know he was now firmly caught in the web of the law. He wouldn't be seeing his colors ridden in the Kentucky Derby, he wouldn't be on his phone in his Sabre jet buying and selling banks and football teams, he wouldn't be sought after by senators and governors and presidential candidates. Instead, he could expect years filled with wrangling over his assets in bankruptcy court, fighting through lawsuit after lawsuit, filing endless appeals, perhaps even living behind bars.

Epilogue: Where Are They Now?

MARVIN WARNER

Marvin and his wife, Jody, live on their horse farm in Ocala, Florida, where their legal battles occupy much of their energy. They are faced with litigation on several fronts:

- *Appeals in the Niehaus criminal case.*

  Marvin won a major victory on November 15, 1989, when an Ohio Appeals Court reversed his nine criminal convictions and wiped out Judge Niehaus's $22 million fine. The decision was based on several technical, legal issues, but two stood out.

  Juror prejudice. Prior to being selected, a juror disclosed that she and her husband had $2,000 in deposits frozen at an ODGF bank for three to four weeks when Governor Celeste closed those banks. Despite the inconvenience she suffered, she asserted that she could be fair and impartial. Judge Niehaus rejected a defendant's challenge and accepted her as a juror.

  The appeals judges disagreed, saying, ". . . We find that [the juror's] subjective protestations of impartiality cannot override the objective fact that she suffered direct and immediate economic deprivation which she perceived to be attributable to the collapse of Home State." This finding undermined the entire case against Warner, negating all nine convictions.

  Computer money transfers as evidence. Warner was found guilty of six "unauthorized acts" when he disregarded a board-of-directors resolution forbidding the transfer of excess collateral from Home State to ESM. These transfers were accomplished by computers via the Federal Reserve Board's wire system.

  The law under which Warner was convicted says that unauthorized money movements must be by "assign(ment), transfer, or deliver(y) (of) a note, bond, draft or other written instrument." Prosecutor Kane asserted that a wire transfer is the functional equivalent of a draft; the judges disagreed, saying "the legislature's use of the catch-all phrase 'other written instruments' imposed upon the other instruments within the category, i.e., a 'note,' 'bond,' or 'draft,' a requirement that they be in writing."

In other words, only written transfers—not computer data— could be admitted as evidence. Since the computer evidence was thrown out, the judges ruled that Warner could not be retried on the six transfer charges. The judges allowed retrial on Marvin's three remaining securities charges.

The ruling opens a big loophole in Ohio law. Because nearly all banks and financial institutions transfer money daily by computer, a large percentage of illegal or fraudulent transfers could never be prosecuted.

There was widespread anger among the Home State depositors. Skirt Squad member Debi Rickert reflected this saying, "All of this for nothing. It's absolute and total frustration. This has shaken my belief in the whole system."

Warner issued a statement saying, "I can understand the anger of the former depositors. Their anger understandably had to be directed at someone. I was a natural target. . . .

"I was, and am, the biggest victim. I wish for no person, friend or foe, the mental torment, pressures, the diatribe, the humiliation the past five years have been to me and my family."

Assuring that litigation of the issues will continue, Larry Kane vowed to appeal the ruling to Ohio's Supreme Court. He said the reversals were "based on technical, procedural issues, not the merits of the guilt or innocence of the defendants."

- *Preparing a defense against the three "sweetheart loan" Ohio criminal charges.*

This trial will take place after the appeals on the Niehaus criminal convictions are finally settled.

- *Protecting assets against creditors in the bankruptcy filing.*

After dealing with Marvin for almost two years, bankruptcy Judge George Proctor lost patience with him on July 27, 1989. A Chapter 11 bankruptcy proceeding, which Warner was in, is deemed a success when the debtor and all his creditors reach agreement and go their separate ways. And Proctor had repeatedly urged Warner to work out a settlement with the creditors who were seeking more than $4 billion from him.

The main issue was getting back from Marvin's wife, his son, and his family trusts a fair portion of the millions which Marvin gave to them before he declared bankruptcy. Several times during

1989, Marvin, his family, and his creditors appeared ready to settle. But on each occasion, at the last minute, Marvin backed off. It was classic Warner. He would always find a clause he didn't like, a condition he wanted modified.

Finally, on July 27, Judge Proctor changed Warner's status to a Chapter 7 debtor. Under Chapter 7, reorganization efforts end and the judge appoints a trustee to liquidate the debtor's assets for the benefit of the creditors. In other words, Proctor had stripped Marvin of control of his financial affairs.

Chapter 7 apparently acted as a tonic to Warner, and in September 1989 he agreed to settle with his creditors for roughly $16 million. Proctor then allowed him to return to Chapter 11. The IRS objected to the agreement, pushing a claim against Warner for $11 million; under federal law, IRS tax claims are priority debts and the IRS must agree to any settlement.

Proctor is pushing for a final resolution that will be acceptable to all creditors and seems close to success. It appears that Warner will pay out about $23 million, $6 million to the IRS and $17 million to the other creditors. He would be left with roughly $5 million; the Ocala horse farm represents $3 million of this.

- *Seeking more than $364 million in eight lawsuits.*

Targets include the state of Ohio, Tom Tew, ODGF, and the two accounting firms, Grant Thornton and Arthur Andersen. It is expected that the suits will be dropped as part of the overall bankruptcy settlement.

SHEPARD BROAD

Shepard is finally, at age eighty, slowing down. On April 30, 1988, he arranged the $138 million sale of American Savings & Loan to Kinder-Care, Inc. Kinder-Care, a pioneer in the children's day-care business, is expanding aggressively into banking. By an ironic coincidence, Kinder-Care's original owner was Marvin Warner, who founded the company in 1969. He sold out in 1976.

Shepard busies himself with real estate and other investments and with his many philanthropies.

He never made the $26 million payment to American Savings & Loan to reimburse it for the Warner buyout. He got Marshall Cogan, a New York entrepreneur who wanted a substantial stake in American, to lead a group of investors in putting up $16 million of the $26 million in 1985. Kinder-Care, Inc., contributed the remaining $10 million with their purchase in 1988. Cogan made a substantial profit.

TOM TEW

Tom was a partner in Finley Kumble, the nation's fourth largest firm with 684 lawyers and offices in fourteen cities, when he became involved with ESM. He later became disenchanted with the firm, because he believed it had abandoned its goal of being a meritocracy and was instead favoring its business-getters and managers. When Finley Kumble, plagued by dissension and heavy debt, dissolved on January 4, 1988, Tew and two of his partners took over six of the old firm's offices employing 130 lawyers. They called their new firm Tew Jorden & Schulte (later changed to Tew Jorden Schulte & Beasley) and made its headquarters in Miami.

Tew continues to pursue the interests of the ESM creditors while serving several major corporate clients. He is active in Republican politics and is a major fund-raiser for the party.

LAURIE HOLTZ

Holtz does not like bigness, and his staff is smaller than it was when he became involved with ESM. They work in the same modest, off-the-beaten-track offices they have occupied for decades in South Miami, far from the stylish downtown operations of giants like Arthur Andersen and Grant Thornton.

Although Laurie has fewer people, his dollar volume has grown and the nature of his work has changed. Due in part to the ESM publicity, investigative fraud accounting and litigation support have grown from a small to a significant percentage of his business.

GRANT THORNTON

Alexander Grant became Grant Thornton on January 1, 1986, after a merger. With the help of its $190 million insurance policy, strong management direction, and a skillful public relations effort, it has emerged strongly from the crimes of Jose Gomez and the ESM debacle. Its business has grown and it is now the tenth largest accounting firm in America. Grant Thornton's travails have led to a tightening of oversight and quality standards throughout the accounting industry.

RONNIE EWTON

Ronnie is serving a nine-year sentence in the Chillicothe Correctional Institution in Ohio. He will probably get out in 1994, when he will begin serving a fifteen-year sentence in a federal "country club" prison at Eglin Air Force Base in Florida. His probable release date from Eglin is 2005.

Ronnie and his wife Jerilyn have become born-again Christians and Ronnie teaches Bible studies and works in the chaplain's office at Chillicothe.

Under the terms of Ronnie's plea bargain which invoked Florida's Homestead Act, Jerilyn was allowed to keep their house, which she later sold for more than a million dollars. She and their son Brandon, age six, continue to live in South Florida.

JOSE GOMEZ

In March 1987, Jose started serving a twelve-year federal term and a concurrent eighteen-month Ohio term in the minimum-security section of Tallahassee Federal Prison. He works as a computer programmer in the finance office, and he has a reasonable expectation of freedom in 1995. His wife and two teenage sons live in Miami.

BURTON BONGARD

Bongard, with the help of lawyer Marvin Gersten, plea-bargained his ten-year Ohio term down to six years to be served concurrently with a six-year federal term. He probably will be released in 1991.

He faces another criminal trial on "sweetheart" loan charges after the appeals of Warner and Schiebel in the Niehaus case are decided.

Burt sells stationery and personal items in the commissary at Ohio's Ross Correctional Institution.

His wife, a practicing attorney, lives in New York City with their three-year-old son.

DAVID SCHIEBEL

Schiebel won reversal of his three convictions on debenture security charges in the same decision that overturned Warner's convictions. The main issue, as with Warner, was the tainted juror. Schiebel is not clear yet, because Larry Kane is appealing the reversal to Ohio's Supreme Court. He faces retrial whatever the outcome of Kane's appeal, and he is still under indictment on the "sweetheart" loan charges.

He works in Cincinnati as a consultant at Mayerson Associates, a real estate developer and manager.

GEORGE MEAD

Mead is serving his six-year Ohio sentence at Pickaway Correctional facility. He could be released by 1991, when he will begin serving a fourteen-year federal sentence at a minimum-security prison. He can expect to see the light of day in about the year 2000.

BOBBY SENECA

After leaving ESM, Bobby moved to California where he has earned a sporadic living as a securities and mortgage broker and as a salesman for gold mines.

NICHOLAS WALLACE

When Judge Gonzalez sentenced Nick Wallace to thirty years in a federal prison, he stipulated that it not be the "country club" variety. Wallace is incarcerated in the maximum-security section of the federal prison in Tallahassee, Florida, and probably will not win his freedom until 2006.

RICHARD CELESTE

Celeste is entering the last lap of his stint as governor; he cannot succeed himself after two consecutive terms. He won reelection handily in 1986 and did well in the Cincinnati-Dayton-Columbus area, an indication that the voters approved of his handling of the Home State crisis. He is currently pushing education issues and is said to be angling for a college presidency when his gubernatorial term ends.

RICHARD FINAN

Finan was the first Republican to open a campaign office for the 1990 Ohio gubernatorial race. The contest for the nomination is expected to be wide open, with several strong candidates participating.

DONALD "BUZ" LUKENS

Lukens won reelection to Congress on November 8, 1988 by a 3 to 1 margin, but two days previously he committed an act which has blighted his political future. A jury has found that he had sex with a sixteen-year-old girl on November 6, 1988, and convicted him on May 26, 1989 of "contributing to the delinquency and unruliness of a minor." He has been sentenced to 30 days in jail, fined $500, and ordered to enter a therapy program for sex offenders. His difficulties have been featured in newspapers throughout the country and by Dan Rather and other national newscasters.

THE SKIRT SQUAD

Toni Handley remained in the political arena following the victory of the Home State depositors. She is one of the leaders of the Republican party in her county and is an active campaigner.

Debi Rickert toiled hard for the Republicans through 1987 but is devoting the current period of her life to being a mother. She had a second child in 1988 and has moved with her family to Illinois.

Lisa Neidich made a successful career switch from nursing to real estate after her Home State involvement and has steered clear of politics since then.

Paula Taylor threw herself into Democratic campaigns in 1986 and 1987 but found that it took too much time from her work with the retarded; she is now a political enthusiast rather than a participant.

The four women, strangers before Home State, are now close friends who feel they grew in skill and confidence through their shared experience. Paula speaks for each when she says, "If one good thing came out of Home State, it was that, in the time of the 'me generation,' we cared for each other enough to bond together for a common cause."

MARLIN ARKY

Marlin married businessman David Feldman in late 1988 and is living with him and her two teenage children in a Miami suburb.

ARKY, FREED

Arky, Freed splintered into several pieces less than a year after Steve Arky's suicide.

THE U.S. GOVERNMENT SECURITIES MARKET

The "bond daddies" are very unhappy. Their ultimate playground, the U.S. government securities market, is at long last being policed. Spurred on by Representative Dingell of Michigan, Representative (now Senator) Wirth of Colorado, and Senator D'Amato of New York, Congress in October 1986 passed a bill bringing the market under regulation. Qualified observers agree that the bill would not have been passed without the political pressure generated by the ESM–Home State debacle.

Regulatory authority is shared by the SEC and the bank regulatory agencies.

This is a major improvement over the days when the "bond daddies" robbed their customers without having to worry about the policeman on the beat. Jubilation must be curbed, however. Ivan Boesky and the other thieves in the "insider" scandals were directly under SEC jurisdiction and they were caught only after long and extremely lucrative criminal careers. The main reason: the SEC doesn't have enough policemen.

So, in spite of the 1986 bill, the best advice one can give to a player in the government securities market is: be very, very careful and make sure you know where your collateral is.

Notes

CHAPTER 1: $300 MILLION IS MISSING

Page 3.   **He was white . . . to this man.** Personal interview with Laurie Holtz.

Page 4.   **That morning, just . . . the day before.** Personal interview with Laurie Holtz.

Page 4.   **They handed me . . . transactions with it.** Personal interview with Laurie Holtz.

Page 6.   **She looked at . . . was all there.** Personal interview with Laurie Holtz.

Page 9.   **One of the . . . off the shelf.** Personal interview with Tom Tew.

Page 10. **This is unbelievable. . . . Collins were worried.** Personal interview with Laurie Holtz.

Page 10. **Tom described the . . . can't survive anyhow.** Personal interview with Tom Tew.

Page 11. **I was going . . . but they didn't.** Personal interview with Laurie Holtz.

Page 12. **Mead and Wallace . . . have to do."** Personal interview with Tom Tew.

Page 12. **More than 99 percent . . . and Stephen Arky.** Personal interview with Laurie Holtz.

Page 12. **In 1981, for . . . a cash settlement.** James Lyons, *American Lawyer*, "How Many Hats Can Steve Arky Wear?" May 1985, pages 1380-1385.

Page 13. **A Miami financial . . . of their clients."** Brian Dickerson, *Miami Herald*, "Tropic Magazine," "The Lonely Death of Stephen Arky," December 7, 1986, page 14.

Page 15. **I was going . . . pretty darn stupid.** Personal interview with Charlie Harper.

Page 15. **So I start . . . be the receiver.** Personal interview with Charlie Harper.

CHAPTER 2: THE PATRIARCH

Page 18. **Those were terrible . . . rough, rough times.** Personal interview with Shepard Broad.

Page 19. **"a place where . . . had a bellybutton."** Personal interview with Shepard Broad.

Page 20. **"no plenipotentiary put . . . to his mission."** Personal interview with Shepard Broad.

Page 20. **I went to . . . might tell you.** Personal interview with Shepard Broad.

Page 21. **"an alien with . . . means of support."** Personal interview with Shepard Broad.

Page 21. **This fellow fed . . . passed the bar.** Personal interview with Shepard Broad.

Page 23. **"My son and . . . and join us."** Personal interview with Shepard Broad.

Page 24. **"There are many . . . nobody else can."** Personal interview with Shepard Broad.

Page 24. **"The headline on . . . took the bar."** Personal interview with Shepard Broad.

Page 25. **"homelessness, in and . . . badge of shame."** Personal interview with Shepard Broad.

Page 26. **Ben-Gurion came . . . distrust and distaste.** Robert Herron, *Miami Pictorial*, "The Miami Connection," March 1973.

Page 26. **The apartment belonged . . . program so distasteful.** Robert Herron, *Miami Pictorial*, "The Miami Connection," March 1973.

Page 27. **We were skeptical . . . can to help.** Robert Herron, *Miami Pictorial*, "The Miami Connection," March 1973.

Page 27. **Jacob Dostrovsky, who . . . the master tactician.** Robert Herron, *Miami Pictorial*, "The Miami Connection," March 1973.

Page 28. **It gives me . . . through the blockade.** Robert Herron, *Miami Pictorial*, "The Miami Connection," March 1973.

Page 29. **The swamp was . . . during its investigation.** Personal interview with Shepard Broad.

Page 29. **I told Roy . . . Bank, Ben Kane.** Personal interview with Shepard Broad.

Page 30. **If you pick . . . pretty livable place.** Personal interview with Shepard Broad.

Page 31. **"The city, the . . . conflicts of interest."** Personal interview with Shepard Broad.

Page 31. **"a no-brainer industry."** Personal interview with Shepard Broad.

Page 34. **Shepard was surprised . . . father-in-law, Marvin Warner.** Personal interview with Shepard Broad.

Page 34. **He made it clear . . . run with it.** Personal interview with Shepard Broad.

Page 34. **He told the . . . and consumer lending."** *Miami Herald*, "Broad Family Releases Reins of S&L," March 23, 1984

Page 34. **First of all . . . he would choose.** Voting Trust Agreement dated as of December 8, 1982, by and between Shepard Broad, as trustee, Marvin L. Warner, as trustee.

CHAPTER 3: HE WANTED EVERYTHING

Page 37. **One of her . . . for her generation."** Personal interview with David Sokol.

Page 38. **Marvin has been . . . in him either.** Personal interview with David Sokol.

Page 38. **His college roommate . . . you are now.** Dale Keiger, "The Man Who Would Be Somebody," *Cincinnati Magazine*, September 1986, page 57.

Page 39. **The Blach family . . . from his relatives.** Personal interview with David Sokol.

Page 40. **He would say . . . $150 an hour."** Overheard by author during recess in *State of Ohio vs. Marvin Warner, et al.*

Page 40. **George has been . . . few "Yiddish words."** Personal interview with David Sokol.

Page 40.   **Marvin wanted to change . . . him and George.** Personal interview with David Sokol.

Page 43.   **Abner Johnson, who . . . and specifications completely.** Personal interview with Abner Johnson.

Page 43.   **Marvin Warner borrowed . . . side of Birmingham.** Author's notes from Marvin Warner's testimony in *State of Ohio vs. Marvin Warner, et al.*

Page 44.   **Marvin Warner was . . . financing, construction, sales.** Personal interview with Abner Johnson.

Page 44.   **If there was . . . wanted, he got.** Dale Keiger, "Rise and Fall of Marvin Warner," *Columbus Monthly*, November 1986, page 127.

Page 45.   **He hounded his . . . quite as tough.** Dale Keiger, "Rise and Fall of Marvin Warner," *Columbus Monthly*, November 1986, page 130.

Page 45.   **Back in the . . . It's not mine."** Personal interview not for attribution.

Page 46.   **Marvin and Joe . . . repay the loan."** Personal interview with Joe Kantor.

Page 46.   **We had fulfilled . . . need or not.** Personal interview with Abner Johnson.

Page 47.   **But Marvin had . . . could get started.** Polk Lafoon IV, "Warner Rolled Up His Sleeves and Plunged into Real Estate," *Cincinnati Post*, August 30, 1976.

Page 48.   **Marvin remembers the . . . and the wallboard.** Polk Lafoon IV, "Warner Rolled Up His Sleeves and Plunged into Real Estate," *Cincinnati Post*, August 30, 1976.

Page 50.   **To achieve this . . . occurred in 1958.** Personal interview with David Sokol.

Page 51.   **Jane Blach Warner . . . in other areas.** Personal interview not for attribution.

Page 51.   **Since the divorce . . . she was twenty-two.** Personal interview not for attribution.

Page 52.   **Marvin was a . . . boss was coming.** Personal interview with Dale Keiger.

Page 52.   **Marvin likes . . . of LeRoy Neiman.** "The Poor Boy Who Loves Land," *Cincinnati Enquirer*, January 17, 1971.

Page 52.   **The only jarring . . . niches, on floors.** "The Poor Boy Who Loves Land," *Cincinnati Enquirer*, January 17, 1971.

Page 53.   **A source of . . . father's thoroughbred operations.** From author's notes of Marvin Warner's testimony in *State of Ohio vs. Marvin Warner et al.*

Page 53.   **In the mid-1980s . . . thoroughbreds $30 million.** Sharon Moloney, "Warner Shaky on Horse Deal Details," *Cincinnati Post*, December 8, 1987; Sharon Moloney, "Warner Filing Says He Has $20 Million," *Cincinnati Post*, November 17, 1987; Sharon Moloney, "Marvin Warner Vague on Income," *Cincinnati Post*, November 23, 1987.

Page 53.   **By the mid . . . the national party.** Dale Keiger, "Rise and Fall of Marvin Warner," *Columbus Monthly*, November 1986, page 130.

Page 53.   **"There still should . . . a technical education."** Mary Jean Connors, "Warner's Goal: More in College," *Cincinnati Enquirer*, May 11, 1975.

Page 54.   **In January 1977 . . . friend Ronnie Ewton.** Deposition of Ronnie R. Ewton, in the United States District Court for the Southern District of Florida, Fort Lauderdale Division, *Thomas Tew, as trustee for the Estate of ESM*

Government Securities, Inc., vs. Marvin L. Warner and Burton M. Bon-gard, pages 16–18.

Page 55.   **the bank lent . . . in April 1977.** Deposition of Ronnie R. Ewton, in the United States District Court for the Southern District of Florida, Fort Lauderdale Division, *Thomas Tew, as trustee for the Estate of ESM Government Securities, Inc., vs. Marvin L. Warner and Burton M. Bon-gard*, pages 16–18.

Page 55.   **Marvin split with . . . southerner Jimmy Carter.** Personal interview not for attribution.

Page 55.   **Bob Strauss thought Marvin was crazy.** Personal interview not for attribution.

Page 56.   **He designated Burt . . . Bongard had access.** State of Ohio exhibit #275477 in *State of Ohio vs. Marvin Warner, et al*; testimony of Ronnie Ewton in United States District Court, Eastern District of Michigan, Southern Division, in *United States of America vs. Marvin L. Warner*, May 13, 1987, Volume 5, pages 132–135.

Page 57.   **And then there . . . elsewhere that night.** Personal interview with Dale Keiger.

Page 57.   **Another girlfriend was . . . after six months.** Marian Christy, *Cincinnati Post*, May 22, 1979.

Page 57.   **Susan and Marvin . . . return to Cincinnati.** Marian Christy, *Cincinnati Post*, May 22, 1979

CHAPTER 4: THE WORLD OF THE BOND DADDIES

Page 59.   **it badly depleted . . . traumatized him emotionally.** Testimony of Ronnie Ewton in the United States District Court Southern District of Florida, Fort Lauderdale Division, in *Thomas Tew, receiver for ESM vs. Jose Gomez and John Does one through one hundred d/b/a/ Alexander Grant & Company, a Partnership*, volume IB, page 50; Testimony of Ronnie Ewton in the United States District Court, Eastern District of Michigan, Southern Division, in *United States of America vs. Marvin L. Warner*, May 14, 1987, Volume 6, pages 135–136.

Page 59.   **We left Nashville . . . family back stabilized.** Ronnie Ewton testimony, Ann Arbor Federal Trial, volume 6, page 136.

Page 60.   **Darla is a . . . became his mentor.** Personal interview with Mary Ann Murphy.

Page 60.   **Your first year . . . of a high-roller.** David McClintick, "Memphis Blues, City Becomes a Center of Municipal Bonds—and Also Shady Dealing," *Wall Street Journal*, December 3, 1971.

Page 60.   **in Memphis, Tennessee . . . his name.** Peter Cary and Susan Sachs, "Founders of ESM Lived High," *Miami Herald*, March 31, 1985.

Page 61.   **For a taxpayer . . . in interest payments.** "Basic Arithmetic Tells You You Belong in Tax Free Municipal Bonds," brochure from Lebenthal & Co., Inc., June 1988.

Page 63.   **One veteran Tampa . . . above the market.** Peter Cary, "ESM Mess Is Catching Federal Eye," *Miami Herald*, April 29, 1985.

Page 65.   **Bobby Joe Fabian . . . away with murder.** James Cole, "Shadowy 'Mr. Big' Still Sought as Mysteries Swirl," *Memphis Press-Scimitar*, February 2, 1971.

Page 65.   **The head of . . . capital of the country.** Martha Brannigan, "In Fort Lauderdale, The ESM Scandal Is Unusual Only in Size," *Wall Street Journal*, April 4, 1985.

Page 66.   **Some say it's . . . built a city.** "History of Fort Lauderdale," Greater Fort Lauderdale Chamber of Commerce, 1987.

Page 66.   **The Ewtons never . . . the southeast region.** Testimony of Ronnie Ewton in the United States District Court, Eastern District of Michigan, Southern Division, in *United States of America vs. Marvin L. Warner*, May 14, 1987, Volume 6, pages 136–137.

Page 67.   **And Hibbard, O'Connor . . . to make transactions.** "NASD Board of Governors Decision in re: *District Business Conduct Committee vs. Hibbard & O'Connor Securities, Inc.*," October 23, 1975.

Page 67.   **Key operators of . . . serving prison terms.** William Power, "Bevill Ex-Aides Are Sentenced to Prison Terms," *Wall Street Journal*, September 10, 1987.

Page 67.   **Winters and Company . . . bilking numerous customers.** Fred Fogarty, "Greed: It's the Big Factor in Investment Firm's Demise," *Fort Lauderdale News/Sun-Sentinel*, September 4, 1977.

Page 68.   **at least one . . . as a result.** Peter Cary, "ESM Mess Is Catching Federal Eye," *Miami Herald*, April 29, 1985.

Page 68.   **R. J. Allen . . . years in prison.** "Ex-Broker Sentenced in POW Swindle," *Fort Lauderdale News/Sun-Sentinel*, September 2, 1977; Tom Morganthau, "Ex-POW Describes Sales as Bond Trial Begins," *Miami Herald*, October 12, 1974; Barbara Greenberg, "POW Bilkers Now Facing Criminal Trial," *Fort Lauderdale News/Sun-Sentinel*, October 21, 1974.

Page 68.   **Ewton and Seneca . . . and Mead 20 percent.** Deposition of Richard Birnbaum before the Securities and Exchange Commission in the matter of Securities Transactions at ESM Government Securities, Incorporated and Affiliates, June 7, 1985, page 26.

Page 69.   **Ronnie retained his . . . as their attorney.** Testimony of Ronnie Ewton in the United States District Court Southern District of Florida, Fort Lauderdale Division, in *Thomas Tew, receiver for ESM vs. Jose Gomez and John Does one through one hundred d/b/a/ Alexander Grant & Company, a Partnership*, volume IB, page 15.

Page 69.   **Our offices were . . . the front door.** Testimony of Ronnie Ewton in the United States District Court Southern District of Florida, Fort Lauderdale Division, in *Thomas Tew, receiver for ESM vs. Jose Gomez and John Does one through one hundred d/b/a/ Alexander Grant & Company, a Partnership*, volume IB, page 155.

Page 70.   **I went to . . . just by happenchance.** Testimony of Ronnie Ewton in the United States District Court, Eastern District of Michigan, Southern Division, in *United States of America vs. Marvin L. Warner*, May 15, 1987, Volume 7, page 43.

Page 70.   **Ronnie didn't know . . . in the United States.** "Board of Fox & Co. Approves a Merger with Alexander Grant," *Wall Street Journal*, April 12, 1985.

Page 72.   **The chief of . . . and its participants."** Daniel Hertzberg and Alan Murray,

"Treasurys on Trial, Pressure to Regulate Government Securities Rises After Ohio Crisis," *Wall Street Journal*, April 1, 1985.

Page 73.   **As Tom Tew . . . and Wall Street."** Personal interview with Tom Tew.

CHAPTER 5: ANATOMY OF A SCAM

Page 74.   **He accused . . . "Memphis Bond Bandits."** Memo from Lou Frank to Donald L. Tarleton, February 16, 1977.

Page 75.   **As a result . . . bank had suffered.** Susan Sachs, "Regulator Ignored ESM Warning Signals," *Miami Herald*, April 28, 1985.

Page 75.   **In February 1977 . . . banks and ESM.** Susan Sachs, "Regulator Ignored ESM Warning Signals," *Miami Herald*, April 28, 1985.

Page 75.   **Later, after Ronnie . . . again with ESM.** Susan Sachs, "Regulator Ignored ESM Warning Signals," *Miami Herald*, April 28, 1985.

Page 75.   **Lou Frank's boss . . . Florida's securities regulator.** Peter Cary, "ESM Mess Is Catching Federal Eye," *Miami Herald*, April 29, 1985.

Page 75.   **In an interoffice . . . and its agencies."** James Lyons, "How Many Hats Can Steve Arky Wear?" *American Lawyer*, May 1985, page 87.

Page 76.   **Steve remembered, "I . . . a new Cadillac."** James Lyons, "How Many Hats Can Steve Arky Wear?" *American Lawyer*, May 1985, page 86.

Page 76.   **They uncovered "at . . . netted only $2,500."** James Lyons, "How Many Hats Can Steve Arky Wear?" *American Lawyer*, May 1985, page 88.

Page 76.   **This was vintage . . . the best defense.** James Lyons, "How Many Hats Can Steve Arky Wear?" *American Lawyer*, May 1985, page 89.

Page 76.   **told Ewton they . . . with another investigation."** James Lyons, "How Many Hats Can Steve Arky Wear?" *American Lawyer*, May 1985, page 88.

Page 77.   **Behind it, Ewton . . . $140 million.** Report on the Condition of the ESM Companies by Thomas Tew, receiver, April 2, 1985.

Page 77.   **Their companies had . . . other key players.** Personal interview with Laurie Holtz and Jack Goldstrich.

Page 77.   **In a December . . . the balance sheet. . . .** From the actual memo, provided by the ESM Depository, document #021032.

Page 78.   **even when he . . . in South Philadelphia.** Peter Cary and Susan Sachs, "Founders of ESM Lived High," *Miami Herald*, March 31, 1985.

Page 78.   **Her name was . . . hairdressing and acting.** Peter Cary and Susan Sachs, "Founders of ESM Lived High," *Miami Herald*, March 31, 1985; personal interview with Jose Garcia-Pedrosa.

Page 78.   **They played up . . . my whole life."** Peter Cary and Susan Sachs, "Founders of ESM Lived High," *Miami Herald*, March 31, 1985.

Page 78.   **They had to . . . returned from Europe.** Deposition of Richard Birnbaum to the Securities and Exchange Commission in the matter of ESM Government Securities, Incorporated and Affiliates, June 7, 1985, pages 88–90.

Page 79.   **Steve Arky had found it.** Deposition of Ronnie R. Ewton in the United States District Court, for the Southern District of Florida, Fort Lauderdale Division, in *Thomas Tew, as trustee for the Estate of ESM, vs. Marvin L. Warner and Burton M. Bongard*, Volume I, page 17.

Page 79.   **The asking price was $3,369,750.** ESM Depository Chronology of Key Events, September 14, 1987.

Page 79.   **That's when Novick . . . of ESM customers.** Personal interview with Tom Tew; testimony of Ronnie Ewton in the United States District Court, Southern District of Florida, Fort Lauderdale Division, in *Thomas Tew, receiver for ESM, vs. Jose Gomez and John Does one through one hundred d/b/a/ Alexander Grant & Company, a partnership*, October 21, 1986, Volume IB, pages 168–171.

Page 80.   **So Alan Novick . . . on February 4.** Personal interview with Laurie Holtz.

Page 80.   **Now it was . . . couple of hours.** ESM Depository Chronology of Key Events, September 14, 1987.

Page 80.   **Marvin really liked . . . on the risk . . .** Testimony of Ronnie R. Ewton in United States District Court, Eastern District of Michigan, Southern Division, in *United States of America vs. Marvin L. Warner*, May 13, 1987, Volume 5, page 121.

Page 80.   **In addition, Marvin . . . accounts at ESM.** ESM Depository Chronology of Key Events, September 14, 1987.

Page 80.   **Marvin had already . . . on April 26.** ESM Depository Chronology of Key Events, September 14, 1987.

Page 80.   **Seneca and Novick . . . and Home State.** ESM Depository Chronology of Key Events, September 14, 1987.

Page 80.   **Marvin appeared to be . . . . roaring good time.** Deposition of Richard M. Birnbaum, before the Securities and Exchange Commission in the matter of securities transactions at ESM, June 7, 1985, page 121.

Page 80.   **The more Marvin . . . without anyone knowing.** Plaintiff's exhibit No. 205 in *Thomas Tew, as trustee for the Estate of ESM vs. Marvin L. Warner*.

Page 81.   **Their response was . . . for speculative purchases.''** Plaintiff's exhibit No. 208 in *Thomas Tew, as trustee for the Estate of ESM vs. Marvin L. Warner*.

Page 81.   **Marvin brushed aside . . . both bank chains.** ESM Depository Chronology of Key Events, September 14, 1987.

Page 81.   **Bobby Seneca went . . . in the red.''** Personal interview with Laurie Holtz; personal interview not for attribution.

Page 81.   **Bobby fell apart . . . of the year.''** Peter Cary and Susan Sachs, "Founders of ESM Lived High," *Miami Herald*, March 31, 1985; deposition of Robert Seneca before the Securities and Exchange Commission re securities transactions at ESM Government Securities, Inc. and Affiliates, March 30, 1985, page 102; personal interview not for attribution.

Page 82.   **When Ronnie asked . . . of the losses.''** Personal interview with Tom Tew.

Page 83.   **He remembers, "She . . . not aware of.** Deposition of Robert Seneca before the Securities and Exchange Commission re securities transactions at ESM Government Securities, Inc. and Affiliates, March 30, 1985, page 109.

Page 83.   **On February 1 . . . and Pete Summers.** ESM Depository Chronology of Key Events, September 14, 1987.

Page 83.   **Seneca was stripped . . . on June 21.** ESM Depository Chronology of Key Events, September 14, 1987.

Page 83.   **Bobby signed a . . . remaining ESM stock.** ESM Depository Chronology of Key Events, September 14, 1987.

Page 83.   **Jose Gomez first . . . in December 1977.** ESM Depository Chronology of Key Events, September 14, 1987.

Page 83.   **Alan Novick moved . . . the losses completely.** Deposition of Jose L. Gomez in the United States District Court for the Southern District of Florida, Fort Lauderdale Division, in re: Alexander Grant & Co., Volume I, page 90.

Page 84.   **Alan dropped more . . . speculations in 1978.** Report on the condition of the ESM Companies, by Thomas Tew, receiver, April 2, 1985.

Page 84.   **Borrowing with customer . . . taking from it.** Personal interview with Jose Garcia-Pedrosa.

Page 84.   **Alan and Ronnie . . . for energy investments.** Gary Webb and Stephen Talbot, "ESM Officers' Deals Lost $26 Million," *Cleveland Plain Dealer*, August 18, 1985.

Page 84.   **The promoters of . . . with these ventures.** Gary Webb and Stephen Talbot, "ESM Officers' Deals Lost $26 Million," *Cleveland Plain Dealer*, August 18, 1985.

Page 84.   **They invested $8,755,000 . . . the energy business.** Gary Webb and Stephen Talbot, "ESM Officers' Deals Lost $26 Million," *Cleveland Plain Dealer*, August 18, 1985.

Page 85.   **She rattled around . . . his vacuous materialism.** Personal interview with Mary Ann Murphy.

Page 85.   **Darla told him . . . you lose your ass."** Personal interview with Mary Ann Murphy.

Page 85.   **Then Darla discovered . . . moved to California.** Personal interview with Sharon Bogard.

Page 85.   **He slipped into . . . times a month.** Personal interview with Mary Ann Murphy.

Page 85.   **He fooled Jose . . . covering 1978 operations.** Deposition of Jose L. Gomez in the United States District Court for the Southern District of Florida, Fort Lauderdale Division, in re: Alexander Grant & Co., Volume I, page 98.

Page 86.   **He was $15,000 . . . debts as well.** Personal interview with Jose Gomez.

Page 86.   **Over lunch one . . . about his debt burdens.** Testimony of Jose Gomez in United States District Court, Southern District of Florida, Fort Lauderdale Division, in *Thomas Tew, receiver for ESM, vs. Jose Gomez, and John Does one through One Hundred d/b/a/ Alexander Grant and Company, a partnership*, October 28, 1986, Volume VA, page 225.

Page 86.   **Soon after Gomez . . . them do it. . . .** Martha Brannigan, "Auditor's Downfall Shows a Man Caught in Trap of His Own Making," *Wall Street Journal*, March 4, 1987.

Page 86.   **Then Novick suggested . . . had been corrupted.** Testimony of Jose Gomez in United States District Court, Southern District of Florida, Fort Lauderdale Division, in *Thomas Tew, receiver for ESM, vs. Jose Gomez, and John Does one through One Hundred d/b/a/ Alexander Grant and Company, a partnership*, October 28, 1986, Volume VA, pages 226-228.

Page 86.   **Gomez continued to . . . December 1, 1980.** ESM Depository Chronology of Key Events, September 14, 1987.

Page 87.   **Jose and Alan . . . $14,422,605.** Report on the condition of the ESM Companies, by Thomas Tew, receiver, April 2, 1985.

Page 87.   **In addition, they . . . projects in 1979.** Second report on the condition of the ESM Companies by Thomas Tew, receiver/trustee, November 4, 1985.

Page 87.   **Operating losses chart:** Compilation from Report on the condition of the ESM Companies, by Thomas Tew, receiver, April 2, 1985; Second Report on the condition of the ESM Companies by Thomas Tew, receiver/trustee, November 4, 1985; personal interview with Laurie Holtz and Jack Goldstrich.

Page 88.   **He grabbed $100 . . . he lost $93,000,000.** Personal interview with Laurie Holtz.

Page 89.   **it was in terrible financial condition.** Testimony of Laurie Holtz in United States District Court, Southern District of Florida, Fort Lauderdale Division, in *Thomas Tew, as trustee for the Estate of ESM Government Securities, vs. Marvin L. Warner and Burton M. Bongard*, July 5, 1988, Volume XII, pages 3789–3790.

Page 90.   **He was Marvin's . . . his travel plans.** Personal interview with Jose Garcia-Pedrosa.

Page 90.   **Bongard was in . . . March 21, 1980.** Testimony of Burton M. Bongard in United States District Court, Eastern District of Michigan, Southern Division, in *United States of America vs. Marvin L. Warner*, May 27, 1987, Volume 13, pages 69–75.

Page 90.   **By June 30 . . . had made $413,332.** Testimony of Burton M. Bongard in United States District Court, Eastern District of Michigan, Southern Division, in *United States of America vs. Marvin L. Warner*, May 27, 1987, Volume 13, page 68.

Page 90.   **Burt's ESM profits . . . present from Novick.** Testimony of Mary Gondek in United States District Court, Southern District of Florida, Fort Lauderdale Division, in *Thomas Tew, as trustee for the Estate of ESM Government Securities, Inc., vs. Marvin L. Warner and Burton M. Bongard*, June 20, 1988, Volume V, page 1029.

Page 90.   **The Bank, reeling . . . present of $8,851,000.** Testimony of Laurie Holtz in United States District Court, Southern District of Florida, Fort Lauderdale Division, in *Thomas Tew, as trustee for the Estate of ESM Government Securities, vs. Marvin L. Warner and Burton M. Bongard*, July 5, 1988, Volume XII, pages 3789–3790.

Page 90.   **ESM lent Home . . . ESM benefit $8,851,000.** Personal interview with Laurie Holtz.

Page 91.   **During 1980, Home . . . to $58 million.** Defendant's exhibit ("Excess collateralization and funds at risk for the period April, 1977 through February, 1985") in *Thomas Tew, as trustee for the Estate of ESM, vs. Marvin L. Warner and Burton M. Bongard.*

Page 91.   **ESM was drained . . . than $144 million.** Compilation from Report on the condition of the ESM Companies, by Thomas Tew, receiver, April 2, 1985;

Second Report on the condition of the ESM Companies by Thomas Tew, receiver/trustee, November 4, 1985.

Page 91.   **Ewton and Novick . . . in the Bahamas.** Personal interview with Sharon Bogard.

Page 91.   **When they went . . . of Alan Novick.** ESM Depository Chronology of Key Events, September 14, 1987.

Page 91.   **They got Bongard . . . from Home State.** Defendant's exhibit ("Excess collateralization and funds at risk for the period April, 1977 through February, 1985") in *Thomas Tew, as trustee for the Estate of ESM, vs. Marvin L. Warner and Burton M. Bongard.*

Page 92.   **He geared up . . . for these transactions.** Personal interview with Laurie Holtz.

Page 92.   **It's true 1981 . . . profits of $26,058,743.** Report on the condition of the ESM Companies, by Thomas Tew, receiver, April 2, 1985

Page 92.   **The memo read . . . without their knowledge.** Copy of actual memo supplied by Charlie Harper.

Page 93.   **They would have . . . combat with whips.** Personal interview with JoAnn Touri and Lisa Winbourne.

Page 93.   **He would frequently . . . grueling return trip.** Personal interview with Charlie Harper.

Page 95.   **In 1982, Novick . . . profit of $4,678,802.** Personal interview with Laurie Holtz.

Page 95.   **Alan, however, had . . . greater than ever.** Report on the condition of the ESM Companies, by Thomas Tew, receiver, April 2, 1985.

Page 95.   **Bongard cooperated by . . . totaled $125 million.** Defendant's exhibit ("Excess collateralization and funds at risk for the period April, 1977 through February, 1985") in *Thomas Tew, as trustee for the Estate of ESM, vs. Marvin L. Warner and Burton M. Bongard.*

Page 97.   **Marvin gave $38,000 . . . note for $75,000.** James F. McCarty, "Warner Cash Bailed Out Candidates," *Cincinnati Enquirer*, March 31, 1985.

Page 97.   **And got Ewton . . . and $5,000 respectively.** James Bradshaw, "ESM Officers Helped Celeste," *Columbus Dispatch*, March 14, 1985.

Page 97.   **He immediately recognized . . . and unsound practice.** Testimony of Sylvester F. Hentschel, in United States District Court, Eastern District of Michigan, Southern Division, in *United States of America vs. Marvin L. Warner*, May 11, 1987, Volume 3, page 113.

Page 98.   **Hentschel remembers The . . . by Alan Novick.** Testimony of Sylvester F. Hentschel, in United States District Court, Eastern District of Michigan, Southern Division, in *United States of America vs. Marvin L. Warner*, May 11, 1987, Volume 3, pages 115–130.

Page 98.   **He reported to . . . Home State's business.** Testimony of Sylvester F. Hentschel, in United States District Court, Eastern District of Michigan, Southern Division, in *United States of America vs. Marvin L. Warner*, May 11, 1987, Volume 3, page 132.

Page 98.   **So he was . . . out-and-out lie.** Testimony of Sylvester F. Hentschel, in United

States District Court, Eastern District of Michigan, Southern Division, in *United States of America vs. Marvin L. Warner*, May 11, 1987, Volume 3, pages 144–145.

Page 100.   **The proposal, as . . . the opposite direction.** ESM Depository Chronology of Key Events, September 14, 1987; personal interview with Laurie Holtz.

Page 100.   **In the meantime . . . the 105 percent–110 percent guidelines.** ESM Depository Chronology of Key Events, September 14, 1987.

Page 101.   **By the end . . . million in collateral.** Defendant's exhibit ("Excess collateralization and funds at risk for the period April, 1977 through February, 1985") in *Thomas Tew, as trustee for the Estate of ESM, vs. Marvin L. Warner and Burton M. Bongard.*

Page 101.   **and Warner almost $10 million.** ESM Depository Chronology of Key Events, September 14, 1987.

Page 101.   **Marvin was on . . . what was happening . . . sending down securities.** Testimony of Burton Bongard in United States District Court, Eastern District of Michigan, Southern Division, in *United States of America vs. Marvin L. Warner*, May 26, 1987, Volume 12, pages 158–163.

Page 101.   **After Bongard had . . . Marvin approved it.** ESM Depository Chronology of Key Events, September 14, 1987.

Page 101.   **Home State's paper . . . end in sight.** Personal interview with Laurie Holtz.

Page 101.   **Ewton remembers Novick . . . get you out."** Deposition of Ronnie E. Ewton, in the United States District Court for the Southern District of Florida, in *Thomas Tew, as receiver for ESM, vs. Marvin L. Warner and Burton M. Bongard*, Volume I, pages 170–172.

Page 102.   **Marvin then wrote . . . can be justified.** State of Ohio Exhibit #248A in *State of Ohio vs. Marvin L. Warner, et al.*

Page 102.   **During September and . . . totaling $8 million.** ESM Depository Chronology of Key Events, September 14, 1987.

Page 103.   **But the hedge . . . down to $70 million.** Defendant's exhibit ("Excess collateralization and funds at risk for the period April, 1977 through February, 1985") in *Thomas Tew, as trustee for the Estate of ESM, vs. Marvin L. Warner and Burton M. Bongard.*

Page 103.   **He also got . . . $3,265,157 to $919,157.** Personal interview with Laurie Holtz.

Page 103.   **On October 5 . . . present of $247,750.** ESM Depository Chronology of Key Events, September 14, 1987.

Page 104.   **He called in . . . off his back.** Karen Garloch, "Lawyer Says Home State Heads Mum," *Cincinnati Enquirer*, January 6, 1987, reporting on testimony of attorney Gary P. Kreider.

Page 104.   **Warner summoned Ewton . . . seem so much.** Deposition of Ronnie R. Ewton in the United States District Court for the Southern District of Florida, Fort Lauderdale Division, in *Thomas Tew, as trustee for the Estate of ESM, vs. Marvin L. Warner and Burton M. Bongard*, July 25, 1986, Volume V, pages 535–543.

Page 104.   **the money had . . . $300.** Personal interview with Jack Goldstrich.

Page 105.   **In early 1984 . . . cover ESM's losses.** Defendant's exhibit ("Excess collateral-
             ization and funds at risk for the period April, 1977 through February,
             1985") in *Thomas Tew, as trustee for the Estate of ESM, vs. Marvin L.
             Warner and Burton M. Bongard.*

CHAPTER 6: THE STAGS LOCK HORNS

Page 106.   **He counseled with . . . for Mr. Warner.** Personal interview with Shepard
             Broad.

Page 107.   **Cooper remembers, "Warner . . . jobs they had.** Testimony of William
             Cooper in United States District Court, Eastern District of Michigan,
             Southern Division, in *United States of America vs. Marvin L. Warner,*
             Volume 15, pages 169–170.

Page 107.   **He told Cooper . . . with Ronnie Ewton."** Personal interviews with William
             Cooper and Shepard Broad.

Page 107.   **He didn't mention . . . had accounts there.** Personal interview with Shepard
             Broad.

Page 107.   **Marvin told his . . . had. Ever. Period."** Personal interviews with William
             Cooper and Shepard Broad.

Page 108.   **The telephone was . . . his right ear.** "The Poor Boy Who Loves Land,"
             Cincinnati Enquirer, January 17, 1971.

Page 108.   **On May 6 . . . call from ESM.** Personal interview with Laurie Holtz.

Page 108.   **A government bond . . . remarkably similar fraud.** Michael Quint, "State
             Units Face Loss In Lion Capital's Filing," *New York Times,* May 8, 1984.

Page 108.   **Ewton and Novick . . . need $100 million."** Personal interview with Laurie
             Holtz and Jack Goldstrich.

Page 108.   **After the formal . . . million, that day.** Personal interview with Shepard
             Broad.

Page 109.   **Ronnie Ewton told . . . crisis behind it.** Personal interviews with William
             Cooper and Shepard Broad.

Page 110.   **Cooper and Mahoney . . . Marvin in 1983.** Personal interview with Shepard
             Broad.

Page 110.   **In 1985, he . . . as a fugitive.** Personal interview with James Catlin.

Page 110.   **Ewton's response was . . . this deal quickly."** Personal interview with
             Shepard Broad.

Page 110.   **Marvin told him . . . review the contracts.** Deposition of Edward P. Mahoney
             before the Securities and Exchange Commission, re securities transactions
             at ESM, May 2, 1985, pages 112–118.

Page 111.   **Cooper remembers, "When . . . the Freedom transaction.** Deposition of
             William Cooper before the Securities and Exchange Commission re ESM
             Government Securities, May 7, 1985, page 272.

Page 111.   **At about the . . . the Vernon contract.** Deposition of Edward P. Mahoney
             before the Securities and Exchange Commission, re securities transactions
             at ESM, May 2, 1985, pages 179–181.

Page 111.   **When Shepard came . . . issue of power.** Personal interview with Shepard Broad.

Page 112.   **And, to top . . . price was wrong.** Personal interview with Shepard Broad.

Page 112.   **Shepard was also . . . on June 7.** Personal interview with Shepard Broad.

Page 112.   **Shepard explains, I . . . fuzzy to me.** Personal interview with Shepard Broad.

Page 113.   **When Shepard called . . . offered no opposition.** Personal interview with Shepard Broad.

Page 113.   **Home State was . . . June 30, 1984.** Personal interview with Laurie Holtz.

Page 113.   **So Home State . . . Treasury note position.** Personal interview with Laurie Holtz.

Page 113.   **Marvin turned from . . . and the Broads.** Personal interview with William Cooper and Shepard Broad.

Page 115.   **In a May . . . whatever means possible.** Testimony of Barry Winslow in United States District Court, Eastern District of Michigan, Southern Division, in *United States of America vs. Marvin L. Warner*, May 21, 1987, Volume 10, pages 109–113.

Page 115.   **Winslow called Cooper . . . May 18 memo.** Deposition of William Cooper before the Securities and Exchange Commission re ESM Government Securities, May 7, 1985, pages 126–130.

Page 116.   **he took Mahoney . . . not be his.** Deposition of Edward P. Mahoney before the Securities and Exchange Commission, re securities transactions at ESM, May 2, 1985, pages 185–189.

Page 117.   **Cooper remembers what . . . Board meeting together.** Personal interview with William Cooper.

Page 117.   **Arky tried to . . . turned it down.** Personal interview with William Cooper and Shepard Broad.

Page 119.   **Shepard started the . . . represented to us."** Personal interview with Shepard Broad.

Page 119.   **Marvin chimed in . . . were so strong.** Personal interview with Shepard Broad.

Page 119.   **He finally said . . . back to American.** Personal interview with Shepard Broad.

CHAPTER 7: MASTERFUL MANEUVERS

Page 121.   **Ed Mahoney explains . . . had been hired.** Deposition of Edward P. Mahoney, before the Securities and Exchange Commission re securities transactions at ESM, May 2, 1985, pages 245–246.

Page 123.   **Marvin charged his . . . tag of $8,095.61.** Warner National Corporation Flight Billing Forms.

Page 123.   **When the examiners . . . to roughly $300,000.** *Federal Home Loan Bank Board Memorandum*, from Patricia G. Morgan, Examiner, to Lamar Heath, district director, October 10, 1984.

Page 123.   **Trish Morgan was . . . to the company.** Federal Home Loan Bank Board
            letter, from Park T. Zimmerman, supervising agent, to Mr. Gerald A.
            Lewis, comptroller, State of Florida, March 14, 1984.

Page 124.   **Ewton and Novick . . . and his crew.** Deposition of Ronnie R. Ewton, in the
            United States District Court, for the Southern District of Florida, Fort
            Lauderdale Division, in *Thomas Tew, as trustee for the Estate of ESM
            Government Securities, vs. Marvin L. Warner and Burton M. Bongard,*
            July 23, 1986, Volume I, pages 162–173; testimony of Ronnie R. Ewton in
            United States District Court, Eastern District of Michigan, Southern
            Division, in *United States of America vs. Marvin L. Warner,* May 14, 1987,
            Volume 6, pages 80–87.

Page 125.   **They read: Dear . . . in the third.** Letter and agreement proper from Marvin
            L. Warner to Shepard Broad, dated October 26, 1984.

Page 126.   **Marvin, with his . . . let that happen.** Personal interview with Shepard
            Broad.

Page 127.   **He told Carl . . . of his life.** Personal interview with Shepard Broad.

Page 127.   **I wouldn't give . . . or Warner management.** Personal interview with
            Shepard Broad.

Page 128.   **Kamp felt like . . . the danger list.** Testimony of Carl Kamp in hearings
            before the Subcommittee on Oversight and Investigations of the Commit-
            tee on Energy and Commerce, House of Representatives, December 16,
            1985, pages 525–539.

Page 130.   **A few days . . . sweeter for him.** Testimony of Ronnie R. Ewton in the United
            States District Court for the Southern District of Florida, Fort Lauderdale
            Division, in *Thomas Tew, as trustee for the estate of ESM, vs. Marvin L.
            Warner and Burton M. Bongard,* July 29, 1986, Volume IV, pages 614–615.

Page 130.   **"Alan was a . . . couldn't run it."** Personal interview with Charlie Harper.

Page 130.   **He had to . . . and personal suggestions.** Testimony of Ronnie R. Ewton in
            the United States District Court for the Southern District of Florida, Fort
            Lauderdale Division, in *Thomas Tew, as trustee for the estate of ESM, vs.
            Marvin L. Warner and Burton M. Bongard,* June 15, 1988, Volume III,
            pages 455–457.

Page 131.   **"Pursuant to the . . . the 'Selling Shareholder.'"** Minutes of a special
            meeting of the board of directors of American Savings & Loan Associa-
            tion of Florida held at the administrative offices of the association, 17801
            N.W. 2nd Avenue, Miami, Florida, on December 21, 1984 at 10:00 A.M.

Page 131.   **"Kindly advise directors . . . make their selection."** Minutes of a special
            meeting of the board of directors of American Savings & Loan Associa-
            tion of Florida held at the administrative offices of the association, 17801
            N.W. 2nd Avenue, Miami, Florida, on December 21, 1984 at 10:00 A.M.

Page 131.   **"While I wish . . . telephone yesterday morning."** Minutes of a special
            meeting of the board of directors of American Savings & Loan Associa-
            tion of Florida held at the administrative offices of the association, 17801
            N.W. 2nd Avenue, Miami, Florida, on December 21, 1984 at 10:00 A.M.

Page 132.   **On December 21st . . . by the Notice.** Letter from Marvin L. Warner to
            Shepard Broad, December 31, 1984.

CHAPTER 8: THE FIRST DOMINO FALLS

Page 134.   **Gomez spent more . . . Novick's obfuscating techniques.** Deposition of
Ronnie R. Ewton in the United States District Court for the Southern
District of Florida, Fort Lauderdale Division, in *Thomas Tew, as trustee
for the Estate of ESM, vs. Marvin L. Warner and Burton M. Bongard*, July
29, 1986, Volume VII, pages 642-646, 655, 671-675; personal interview
with Tom Tew; deposition of Robert A. Schatzman before the Securities
and Exchange Commission in the matter of trading in the securities of
ESM, May 21, 1986, pages 36-37.

Page 134.   **It involved obtaining . . . on ESM's survival.** Deposition of Ronnie R. Ewton
in the United States District Court for the Southern District of Florida,
Fort Lauderdale Division, in *Thomas Tew, as trustee for the Estate of ESM,
vs. Marvin L. Warner and Burton M. Bongard*, July 29, 1986, Volume VII,
pages 642-646, 655, 671-675; personal interview with Tom Tew; testimony
of George Mead in United States District Court, Eastern District of
Michigan, Southern Division, in *United States of America vs. Marvin L.
Warner*, May 22, 1987, Volume 11, page 84.

Page 134.   **When Ewton returned . . . to him soon.** Deposition of Ronnie R. Ewton in
the United States District Court for the Southern District of Florida, Fort
Lauderdale Division, in *Thomas Tew, as trustee for the Estate of ESM, vs.
Marvin L. Warner and Burton M. Bongard*, July 29, 1986 Volume VII,
pages 651-652.

Page 135.   **On Monday the . . . from Arky Freed.** Deposition of Ronnie R. Ewton in the
United States District Court for the Southern District of Florida, Fort
Lauderdale Division, in *Thomas Tew, as trustee for the Estate of ESM, vs.
Marvin L. Warner and Burton M. Bongard*, July 29, 1986, Volume VII,
page 653.

Page 135.   **On December 18 . . . for his wife.** Report by Donald Gropman on Testimony
of Ronnie R. Ewton in *State of Ohio vs. Marvin L. Warner, et al.*, January
16, 1987.

Page 136.   **he suggested that . . . seek criminal counsel.** Deposition of Ronnie R. Ewton
in the United States District Court for the Southern District of Florida,
Fort Lauderdale Division, in *Thomas Tew, as trustee for the Estate of ESM,
vs. Marvin L. Warner and Burton M. Bongard*, July 29, 1986, Volume VII,
page 657.

Page 136.   **The depths and . . . frightening to me.** Deposition of Ronnie R. Ewton in
the United States District Court for the Southern District of Florida, Fort
Lauderdale Division, in *Thomas Tew, as trustee for the Estate of ESM, vs.
Marvin L. Warner and Burton M. Bongard*, July 29, 1986, Volume VII,
page 658.

Page 136.   **Steve was speechless. . . .and he agreed.** Deposition of Robert A. Schatzman
before the Securities and Exchange Commission in the matter of trading
in the securities of ESM, May 21, 1986, page 195.

Page 137.   **Arky was truly . . . to call Marvin.** Personal interview with Tom Tew.

Page 137.   **He immediately telephoned . . . consumed five hours.** Personal interview
with Tom Tew.

Page 137.   **Marvin and Steve . . . resigned as counsel.** Testimony of Marvin L. Warner in United States District Court, Eastern District of Michigan, Southern Division, in *United States of America vs. Marvin L. Warner*, June 16, 1987, Volume 24, page 179.

Page 137.   **Ewton says that . . ."ESM had problems."** Testimony of Ronnie R. Ewton in United States District Court, Eastern District of Michigan, Southern Division, in *United States of America vs. Marvin L. Warner*, May 14, 1987, pages 95–96.

Page 137.   **Warner Ron, I've . . . the best I can.** Deposition of Ronnie R. Ewton in the United States District Court for the Southern District of Florida, Fort Lauderdale Division in *Thomas Tew, as trustee for the Estate of ESM, vs. Marvin L. Warner and Burton M. Bongard*, July 29. 1986, Volume VII, pages 663–664.

Page 137.   **Marvin recalls, "It . . . was greatly disturbed."** Testimony of Marvin L. Warner in United States District Court, Eastern District of Michigan, Southern Division, in *United States of America vs. Marvin L. Warner*, June 16, 1987, Volume 24, page 182.

Page 138.   **Schiebel recalls, He . . . replied, 'Not really.'"** Testimony of David Schiebel in United States District Court, Eastern District of Michigan, Southern Division, in *United States of America vs. Marvin L. Warner*, June 9, 1987, Volume 19, page 127.

Page 138.   **Ronnie's version is . . . solve the problems.** Testimony of Ronnie R. Ewton in United States District Court, Eastern District of Michigan, Southern Division, in *United States of America vs. Marvin L. Warner*, May 14, 1987, pages 100–101.

Page 138.   **Marvin says that . . . kept stonewalling him.** Testimony of Marvin L. Warner in United States District Court, Eastern District of Michigan, Southern Division, in *United States of America vs. Marvin L. Warner*, June 16, 1987, Volume 24, pages 180–181.

Page 139.   **He also told . . . out Warner's account.** Testimony of Ronnie R. Ewton in United States District Court, Eastern District of Michigan, Southern Division, in *United States of America vs. Marvin L. Warner*, May 14, 1987, page 103.

Page 139.   **Jose still hadn't . . . at $256 million.** Testimony of George Mead in United States District Court, Eastern District of Michigan, Southern Division, in *United States of America vs. Marvin L. Warner*, May 22, 1987, Volume 11, page 68.

Page 139.   **He asked George . . . could be hurt."** Testimony of George Mead in United States District Court, Eastern District of Michigan, Southern Division, in *United States of America vs. Marvin L. Warner*, May 22, 1987, Volume 11, pages 155–156.

Page 139.   **According to George . . . pick it up.** Testimony of George Mead in United States District Court, Eastern District of Michigan, Southern Division, in *United States of America vs. Marvin L. Warner*, May 22, 1987, Volume 11, page 73.

Page 139.   **they cleared up . . . $300,000 was profit.** ESM Depository Chronology of Key

Events, September 14, 1987; personal interview with Laurie Holtz.

Page 140.   **When Hodgson arrived . . . generate a panic.** Personal interview with Clark Hodgson.

Page 141.   **In the days . . . be turning hostile.** Personal interview with Tom Tew.

Page 142.   **He was bleeding . . . handle this alone.** Personal interview with Tom Tew.

Page 142.   **Cagney suggested that . . . a criminal lawyer.** Personal interview with William Cagney.

Page 143.   **I concluded that . . . a lawsuit.** Testimony of Jose Gomez in United States District Court, Southern District of Florida, Fort Lauderdale Division, in *Thomas Tew, receiver for ESM, vs. Jose Gomez, and John Does one through one hundred d/b/a/ Alexander Grant and Company, a partnership*, October 28, 1986, pages 234–235.

Page 143.   **He was tense . . . unwind these transactions.** Personal interview with Clark Hodgson.

Page 144.   **His voice trembled . . . is Tom Tew."** Personal interview with William Cagney.

Page 144.   **This has been . . . all our records.** Personal interview with Tom Tew.

Page 144.   **The next morning . . . subsequent legal struggles.** Personal interview with Tom Tew.

CHAPTER 9: DEVASTATION IN OHIO

Page 146.   **Seven men had . . . base in Philadelphia.** Personal interview with Clark Hodgson.

Page 146.   **Collins called early . . . charges at once.** Personal interview with Clark Hodgson.

Page 147.   **Hodgson felt that . . . Guarantee Fund (ODGF).** Personal interview with Clark Hodgson.

Page 147.   **At approximately 4:15 . . . delivered to him.** Statement of Donald Hunsche before a Subcommittee of the Committee on Government Operations, House of Representatives, April 3, 1985, page 56.

Page 147.   **We were also . . . investigation of ESM.** Randy Ludlow and Mike Kelly, "The Brink of Collapse," *Cincinnati Post*, June 1, 1985.

Page 147.   **We were advised . . . undertaken in Florida.** Statement of Donald Hunsche before a Subcommittee of the Committee on Government Operations, House of Representatives, April 3, 1985, pages 56–57.

Page 149.   **At 8:00 P.M., Hodgson . . . where we stood.** Deposition of Clark Hodgson in United States District Court, Southern District of Florida, May 18, 1988, pages 51–55.

Page 150.   **He believed there . . . the next morning.** Personal interview with Clark Hodgson.

Page 150.   **He called Batties . . . would be minimal.** Randy Ludlow and Mike Kelly, "The Brink of Collapse," *Cincinnati Post*, June 1, 1985.

Page 150.   **He recalls, "From . . . than Tom (Batties)."** Randy Ludlow and Mike Kelly, "The Brink of Collapse," *Cincinnati Post*, June 1, 1985.

Page 151.   **He was dismayed . . . two custodian banks.** Personal interview with Tom Tew.

Page 151.   **Hodgson remembers: . . . very . . . of Mr. Warner.** Deposition of C. Clark Hodgson, Jr., in United States District Court, Southern District of Florida, May 18, 1988, pages 55–61.

Page 152.   **Only two minor . . . not to panic."** Randy Ludlow and Mike Kelly, "The Brink of Collapse," *Cincinnati Post*, June 1, 1985.

Page 152.   **Warner checked with . . . this disastrous situation.** Testimony of C. Clark Hodgson, Jr., in United States District Court Southern District of Florida, Fort Lauderdale Division, in *Thomas Tew, as trustee for the Estate of ESM Government Securities, vs. Marvin L. Warner and Burton M. Bongard*, June 23, 1988, Volume VIII, pages 2063–2066.

Page 152.   **Hodgson was disturbed . . . day's terrible news.** Deposition of C. Clark Hodgson, Jr., in United States District Court, Southern District of Florida, in *Thomas Tew, as trustee for the Estate of ESM, vs. Marvin L. Warner and Burton M. Bongard*, May 19, 1988, page 56.

Page 153.   **After acceding to . . . wrote a release.** Deposition of C. Clark Hodgson, Jr., in United States District Court Southern District of Florida, Fort Lauderdale Division, in *Thomas Tew, as trustee for the Estate of ESM Government Securities, vs. Marvin L. Warner and Burton M. Bongard*, June 21, 1988, Volume VI, page 1499.

Page 153.   **Hodgson, who was . . . to accept deposits.** Deposition of C. Clark Hodgson, Jr., in United States District Court Southern District of Florida, Fort Lauderdale Division, in *Thomas Tew, as trustee for the Estate of ESM Government Securities, vs. Marvin L. Warner and Burton M. Bongard*, June 21, 1988, Volume VI, page 1495.

Page 155.   **He has not . . . revelations of infidelities.** Alex S. Jones, "Ohio Paper Stirs Storm on Governor's Sex Life," *New York Times*, June 5, 1987.

Page 155.   **"You've got to . . . the radar screen."** Arienne Bosworth, Herb Cook, Jr., Max S. Brown, "Should Celeste Have Closed the S&L's?" *Columbus Monthly*, May 1985.

Page 155.   **The blip started . . . spelled serious trouble.** Randy Ludlow and Mike Kelly, "The Brink of Collapse," *Cincinnati Post*, June 1, 1985.

Page 155.   **The governor remembers . . . top of it."** Randy Ludlow and Mike Kelly, "The Brink of Collapse," *Cincinnati Post*, June 1, 1985.

Page 155.   **A nervous Warner . . . guarantee its deposits.** Randy Ludlow and Mike Kelly, "The Brink of Collapse," *Cincinnati Post*, June 1, 1985.

Page 155.   **Celeste believed that . . . was untenable politically.** Arienne Bosworth, Herb Cook, Jr., Max S. Brown, "Should Celeste Have Closed the S&L's?" *Columbus Monthly*, May 1985.

Page 156.   **A poll taken . . . State of Ohio.** Steve Kemme, "Poll Offers Saver Profile at Home State," *Cincinnati Enquirer*, April 24, 1985.

Page 156.   **All the people . . . did have one.** Personal interview with Richard Celeste.

Page 156.   **Sawyer felt that . . . of it all.** Randy Ludlow and Mike Kelly, "The Brink of Collapse," *Cincinnati Post*, June 1, 1985.

Page 157.   **Many, like Charles . . . Federally insured bank.** Karen Garloch, "Withdrawals Continue at Home State," *Cincinnati Enquirer*, March 8, 1985.

Page 157.   **A fifty-six-year old . . . as mixed emotions."** "Home State Depositors Line Up for Funds," *Cincinnati Enquirer*, March 7, 1985.

Page 157.   **Cheryl Kominsky had . . . and fifty dollars."** "Home State Depositors Line Up for Funds," *Cincinnati Enquirer*, March 7, 1985.

Page 157.   **He talked to . . . into the bank.** Personal interview with Debi Rickert.

Page 157.   **"Cox said there . . . did we know!"** Personal interview with Toni Handley.

Page 158.   **At about 10:00 A.M. . . . in the cards.** Randy Ludlow and Mike Kelly, "The Brink of Collapse," *Cincinnati Post*, June 1, 1985.

Page 158.   **Wednesday's tally at . . . $100,000 per minute.** Randy Ludlow and Mike Kelly, "The Brink of Collapse," *Cincinnati Post*, June 1, 1985.

Page 158.   **Cox that evening . . . require emergency action."** John Byczkowski, "Home State Deposits Safe, Officials Say," *Cincinnati Enquirer*, March 7, 1985.

Page 159.   **My notes indicate . . . Deposit Guarantee Fund.** Personal interview with Richard Celeste.

Page 159.   **Brink's made fifty-nine . . . another $45 million.** Randy Ludlow and Mike Kelly, "Collapse Forced Action," *Cincinnati Post*, June 3, 1985.

Page 159.   **Celeste attempted to . . . looked so ominous.** Randy Ludlow and Mike Kelly, "Collapse Forced Action," *Cincinnati Post*, June 3, 1985.

Page 160.   **He had come . . . of their plight.** Randy Ludow and Mike Kelly, "Collapse Forced Action," *Cincinnati Post*, June 3, 1985.

Page 160.   **The first National . . . full $145 million.** Randy Ludlow and Mike Kelly, "Collapse Forced Action," *Cincinnati Post*, June 3, 1985.

Page 160.   **Waddell set a . . . in the cards.** Randy Ludlow and Mike Kelly, "Collapse Forced Action," *Cincinnati Post*, June 3, 1985.

Page 160.   **"He wanted to . . . don't know that.'"** Personal interview with Charlie Harper.

Page 161.   **He—like Celeste . . . for the creditors."** Personal interview with Charlie Harper.

Page 162.   **It appeared politically . . . far too little.** Randy Ludlow and Mike Kelly, "Collapse Forced Action," *Cincinnati Post*, June 3, 1985.

Page 162.   **At day's end . . . Home State's coffers.** Randy Ludlow and Mike Kelly, "The Brink of Collapse," *Cincinnati Post*, June 1, 1985.

Page 162.   **"He told them . . . National was imminent.** Randy Ludlow and Mike Kelly, "Collapse Forced Action," *Cincinnati Post*, June 3, 1985.

Page 162.   **I believe that . . . business as usual.** John Byczkowski, "Home State Negotiating for Sale," *Cincinnati Enquirer*, March 9, 1985.

Page 163.   **The actual figure . . . provided $45 million.** Randy Ludlow and Mike Kelly, "The Brink of Collapse," *Cincinnati Post*, June 1, 1985.

Page 164.   **The first thing . . . it all trading.** Personal interview with Charlie Harper.

Page 164.   **Early Sunday afternoon . . . of the bank.** Randy Ludlow and Mike Kelly, "Collapse Forced Action," *Cincinnati Post*, June 3, 1985.

Page 165.   **As Smith walked . . . of Abraham Lincoln.** Randy Ludlow and Mike Kelly, "Collapse Forced Action," *Cincinnati Post*, June 3, 1985.

Page 166.   **"Frankly, when I . . . not politically feasible."** Randy Ludlow and Mike Kelly, "Collapse Forced Action," *Cincinnati Post*, June 3, 1985.

Page 166. **"There's no way . . . at Home State."** Keith White, Jackie Jadrnak, "State Plans New Bank Insurance Fund," *Cincinnati Enquirer*, March 12, 1985.

Page 167. **Theodore Jones is . . . bunch of bunk."** "The Ohio Thrift Panic," *Newsweek*, April 1, 1985.

Page 168. **Toni Handley felt . . . Home State customer.** Personal interview with Toni Handley.

Page 168. **Arjan Jagtiani, a . . . start all over.** Steve Berry, "Dream Crumbles Along with S&L," *Columbus Dispatch*, March 21, 1985.

Page 168. **And Debi Rickert . . . had checks bouncing."** Personal interview with Debi Rickert.

Page 169. **Nervousness by ODGF . . . banks on Monday.** James Breiner, "How Home State Fell," *Columbus Dispatch*, June 2, 1985.

Page 169. **Tuesday's ODGF deposit . . . the previous day.** James Breiner, "How Home State Fell," *Columbus Dispatch*, June 2, 1985.

Page 170. **The Federal Reserve . . . exceeding $30 million.** Randy Ludlow and Mike Kelly, "Thrift Crisis Spread," *Cincinnati Post*, June 4, 1985.

Page 170. **Celeste called Finan . . . buried our story."** Personal interview with Richard Finan.

Page 170. **"I had spent . . . be a disaster."** "Closing of Ohio S&L's After Run on Deposits Is One for the Books," *Wall Street Journal*, March 18, 1985.

Page 170. **It only intensified . . . the next day.** "Closing of Ohio S&L's After Run on Deposits Is One for the Books," *Wall Street Journal*, March 18, 1985.

Page 171. **The Fed had . . . the week before.** James Breiner, "How Home State Fell," *Columbus Dispatch*, June 2, 1985.

Page 171. **who was later . . . the Ohio collapse.** Arienne Bosworth, Herb Cook, Jr., Max S. Brown, "Should Celeste Have Closed the S&L's?" *Columbus Monthly*, May 1985.

Page 171. **"Gray was rather . . . at all, nothing."** Randy Ludlow and Mike Kelly, "Thrift Crisis Spread," *Cincinnati Post*, June 4, 1985.

Page 171. **"I like to . . . is so sound."** Kevin Close, "All-Night Session Precedes Ohio's S&L Shutdown," *Cincinnati Enquirer*, March 16, 1985.

Page 172. **Several of the . . . all sixty-eight banks."** Personal interview with Richard Celeste.

Page 172. **Celeste has said . . . in trouble too."** Personal interview with Richard Celeste.

Page 172. **"It's the politician's . . . statute for it."** Personal interview with Richard Celeste.

Page 173. **One of the . . . Ignore Pleas, Assurances."** Personal interview with Robert Trafford.

Page 173. **That clinched it. . . ." Close them all."** Randy Ludlow and Mike Kelly, "Thrift Crisis Spread," *Cincinnati Post*, June 4, 1985.

Page 173. **Ken Cox has . . . leaving them open.** Randy Ludlow and Mike Kelly, "Thrift Crisis Spread," *Cincinnati Post*, June 4, 1985.

Page 173.   **In view of . . . soon as possible.** Edited transcript of governor's press conference, *Cincinnati Enquirer*, March 16, 1985.

Page 174.   **he said, "It . . . we possibly can."** Edited transcript of governor's press conference, *Cincinnati Enquirer*, March 16, 1985.

Page 174.   **"I thought, by . . . she had arrived.** Personal interview with Toni Handley.

Page 174.   **At 8:00 A.M. . . . terrible, really terrible."** "Closing of Ohio S & L's After Run on Deposits Is One for the Books," *Wall Street Journal*, March 18, 1985.

Page 175.   **Bob Jacobson, a . . . protecting your money.** Allen Howard, "Worried Depositor Wins One, Loses One," *Cincinnati Enquirer*, March 17, 1985.

Page 175.   **During the flight . . . State-sponsored insurance funds."** "Closing of Ohio S&L's After Run on Deposits Is One for the Books," *Wall Street Journal*, March 18, 1985.

Page 175.   **After a hardball . . . on their part.** Randy Ludlow and Mike Kelly, "Thrift Crisis Spread," *Cincinnati Post*, June 4, 1985.

Page 177.   **Warner had made . . . where are you?** "Where Is Marvin Warner?," *Cincinnati Post*, March 19, 1985.

Page 178.   **Sindlinger & Co. . . . in the future.** "Consumers Shaken by Bank Problems," *Cincinnati Enquirer*, Wednesday, March 20, 1985.

CHAPTER 10: RECONSTRUCTION IN OHIO

Page 179.   **When things began . . . to be involved in.** Personal interview with Richard Celeste.

Page 179.   **He extracted a price . . . accepting ODGF banks.** "Ohio Moves to Aid S&Ls," *Fort Lauderdale News/Sun Sentinel*, March 19, 1985.

Page 179.   **The bill required . . . with the debacle.** "Ohio Lawmakers Put Politics Aside to Resolve Dispute," *Cincinnati Post*, March 20, 1985.

Page 180.   **The politicians saw . . . rather than party lines.** "Ohio Lawmakers Put Politics Aside to Resolve Dispute," *Cincinnati Post*, March 20, 1985.

Page 181.   **Celebrezze said . . . or inside dealing."** "Republican Likely to Lead Probe," *Columbus Dispatch*, March 22, 1985.

Page 182.   **They're not going . . . for what is ours.** Personal interview with Debi Rickert.

Page 182.   **The State of Ohio . . . Deposit Guarantee Fund.** Personal interview with Paula Taylor.

Page 183.   **"Very high energy . . . when she wants to."** Personal interview with Paula Taylor.

Page 184.   **A respected poll . . . 23 percent were uncertain.** "Celeste's Handling of Crisis Draws Support in Poll," *Columbus Dispatch*, March 29, 1985.

Page 184.   **Later that day . . . relationship with Warner.** "S&L Issue a Quiet One," *Columbus Dispatch*, March 30, 1985.

Page 185.   **"Here I was . . . Paula disengaged him."** Personal interview with Debi Rickert.

Page 186.   **"the most abusive . . . I've ever seen."** Personal interview with Tom Tew.

Page 186.   **He said he . . . in the fraud.** Personal interview with Tom Tew.

Page 186.   **She said that . . . criteria for authenticity.** "ESM Official's Will Is Fake, Judge Rules," *Miami Herald*, March 21, 1985.

Page 188.   **Bevill, one of the . . . of his key employees.** "Brokerage Closes Down, Assets Frozen," *Miami Herald*, April 9, 1985.

Page 189.   **"I am outraged . . . from being effective."** "Home State Sale Hits Roadblock," *Columbus Dispatch*, April 13, 1985

Page 189.   **"take great exception to the findings."** "Home State Sale Hits Roadblock," *Columbus Dispatch*, April 13, 1985.

Page 189.   **"God damn it . . . are against you."** Personal interview with Richard Finan.

Page 189.   **"Mr. Bailiff . . . is at stake."** "ODGF Loses Court Battle," *Columbus Dispatch*, May 8, 1985.

Page 189.   **Marvin Warner left . . . Thursday, May 9.** "Marvin Warner—The Florida Session with the Press Was a Case of Too Little, Too Late," Editorial, *Cincinnati Enquirer*, May 10, 1985.

Page 190.   **The performance didn't . . . on his call-in show.** Personal interview with Bill Cunningham.

Page 190.   **The *Enquirer* summed . . . shirked that responsibility.** "Marvin Warner—The Florida Session with the Press Was a Case of Too Little, Too Late," editorial, *Cincinnati Enquirer*, May 10, 1985.

Page 190.   **It stipulated that . . . out-of-state bank.** "House OKs Home State Bailout Bill," *Columbus Dispatch*, May 17, 1985.

Page 191.   **"Ladies, trust me . . . about it now."** Personal interview with Paula Taylor.

Page 191.   **He hadn't told . . . shield his name.** "Home State Deal Has Enough Votes," *Columbus Dispatch*, May 20, 1985.

Page 191.   **A privacy fanatic . . . luckier I get."** "Home State Buyer Contrast to Warner," *Columbus Dispatch*, May 30, 1985.

Page 192.   **Toni Handley remembers . . . Queens of the May.** Personal interview with Toni Handley.

CHAPTER 11: THE DEMONS OF STEPHEN ARKY

Page 194.   **on January 21, 1985, when . . . imminent collapse.** Deposition by Stephen Arky before the Securities and Exchange Commission, April 25, 1985, Volume III, pages 292–293.

Page 194.   **When Schatzman told . . . left his body.** Brian Dickerson, "The Lonely Death of Stephen Arky," *Miami Herald*, *Tropic Magazine*, December 7, 1986.

Page 194.   **Steve felt sure that . . . and profit projections.** Personal interview with Tom Tew.

Page 195.   **Ronnie was one . . . totally comfortable with.** Brian Dickerson, "The Lonely Death of Stephen Arky," *Miami Herald*, *Tropic Magazine*, December 7, 1986.

Page 195.   **"His entertainment was . . . pick up clients."** Brian Dickerson, "The Lonely

Death of Stephen Arky," *Miami Herald, Tropic Magazine*, December 7, 1986.

Page 195.   **"Arky remembered telling . . . It's simple jealousy."** Brian Dickerson, "The Lonely Death of Stephen Arky," *Miami Herald, Tropic Magazine*, December 7, 1986.

Page 196.   **A few years later . . . and you winning."** Personal interview with Joyce Arky Lewin.

Page 198.   **And Marlin remembered . . . he had just arranged.** Brian Dickerson, "The Lonely Death of Stephen Arky," *Miami Herald, Tropic Magazine*, December 7, 1986.

Page 198.   **His friend Alan . . . unsuccessful, but humiliated."** Brian Dickerson, "The Lonely Death of Stephen Arky," *Miami Herald, Tropic Magazine*, December 7, 1986.

Page 199.   **Two factions coalesced . . . approach was adopted.** Brian Dickerson, "The Lonely Death of Stephen Arky," *Miami Herald, Tropic Magazine*, December 7, 1986.

Page 200.   **After all my . . . heart wasn't in it.** Personal interview with confidential source.

Page 200.   **On June 15 . . . desperate financial trouble.** Brian Dickerson, "The Lonely Death of Stephen Arky," *Miami Herald, Tropic Magazine*, December 7, 1986.

Page 200.   **The night before . . . Restoril sleeping pills.**   Death scene investigation report, Metro-Dade Police Department, Dade County, Florida.

Page 202.   **When Marlin left Steve . . . slit his wrists.** Death scene investigation report, Metro-Dade Police Department, Dade County, Florida.

CHAPTER 12: TOM TEW—ACE RECEIVER

Page 203.   **Even though I . . . to ease up.** Personal interview with Tom Tew.

Page 205.   **The statutory powers . . . Chapter 7 filing.** Personal interview with Tom Tew.

Page 207.   **He has said . . . to the Berkshires."** Personal interview with Jose Gonzalez.

Page 207.   **I called some . . . and it worked.** Personal interview with Tom Tew.

Page 208.   **Ewton made it . . . looted from ESM).** Personal interview with Tom Tew.

Page 209.   **He alleged that . . . board of ESM.** Personal interview with Tom Tew.

Page 210.   **He remembers it . . . in other suits.** Personal interview with Tom Tew.

Page 211.   **Wolfe's main job . . . abetted a fraud."** David Satterfield, "ESM Aid Denies Knowing of Fraud," *Miami Herald*, June 27, 1986.

Page 211.   **His lawyer likened . . . the neighbors knew."** John G. Edwards, "Jury Considers Fate of ESM Officers," *Fort Lauderdale News/Sun-Sentinel*, July 2, 1986.

Page 211.   **He was generally . . . was always suspect.** Personal interviews with Mark Raymond, Lisa Winbourne, JoAnn Touri, and Mary Ann Murphy.

Page 211.   **He maintained that . . . tool of Novick.** David Satterfield, "ESM Court Strategy Tries to Lay Blame on Key Exec Who Died," *Miami Herald*, June 30, 1986.

Page 211. **A HOW alumnus . . . president and secretary.** Peter Cary, "ESM Mess Is Catching Federal Eye," *Miami Herald*, April 29, 1985.

Page 212. **Wallace had signed . . . the ESM crimes.** Peter Cary, "ESM Mess Is Catching Federal Eye," *Miami Herald*, April 29, 1985.

Page 212. **Novick had told . . . about $160 million.** David Satterfield, "Ewton: Wallace Knew of Huge Losses," *Miami Herald*, June 18, 1986.

Page 212. **Mead told him . . . bribes to Gomez.** John G. Edwards, "Ex-ESM President Denies Associate's Charge," *Fort Lauderdale News/Sun-Sentinel*, July 1, 1986.

Page 212. **Wallace had profited . . . salaries and loans.** "Report on the Condition of the ESM Companies," by Thomas Tew, receiver, April 2, 1985.

Page 213. **Earl told several . . . such a fate.** Personal interview With Jack Goldstrich.

Page 213. **I have committed . . . out of oxygen.** Offense Report #86-187086, Police Department, Fort Lauderdale, Florida, November 11, 1986.

Page 213. **The building's exterminator . . . notified Earl's sister.** Offense Report #86-187086, Police Department, Fort Lauderdale, Florida, November 11, 1986.

Page 214. **He reads Kafka . . . generous to him.** David Satterfield, "He's a Rich, Highly Successful Lawyer, There's Just One Thing He Wants," *Miami Herald*, August 1, 1988.

Page 214. **He says, "I . . . make less money."** David Satterfield, "He's a Rich, Highly Successful Lawyer, There's Just One Thing He Wants," *Miami Herald*, August 1, 1988.

CHAPTER 13: CRIMINAL JUSTICE

Page 218. **Marvin Warner's head . . . his entire life.** Personal interview with Stan Mortenson.

Page 219. **They cited two . . . committed a crime.** *Joint Motion of All Defendants For a Pretrial Change of Venue Hearing and a Change of Venue*, filed May 28, 1986, in the case of *State of Ohio vs. Marvin L. Warner, et al.*, in the Court of Common Pleas, Criminal Division, Hamilton County, Ohio.

Page 221. **four young associates.** Mark A. Vender Laan; Lawrence R. Elleman; Carl J. Stich; Kenneth S. Resnick; with assistance from M. Gabrielle Hils and Paul R. Mattingly: State of Ohio's Trial Brief, filed December 8, 1986, in *State of Ohio vs. Marvin L. Warner, et al.*

Page 221. **His fees were . . . by Marvin Warner.** Sharon Moloney, "Former Friends Now Enemies in Court," *Cincinnati Post*, May 26, 1987.

Page 226. **One day, as . . . they were gone.** Personal report by researcher Gropman.

Page 227. **Its foreman later . . . Bongard a four.** Personal interview with Herman Cooper.

Page 230. **There was ample . . . these six transactions.** For example, State's Exhibit #33481, Interoffice memorandum to the file from David J. Schiebel of the minutes of the meeting with Marvin L. Warner on August 29, 1983.

Page 230. **Ronnie Ewton was . . . of his oatmeal.** Personal interview with Charlie Harper.

Page 232. **First they elected . . . all the votes.** Personal interview with Herman Cooper.

Page 233.   **One of the . . . himself, I'm afraid."** Mary Yost, "Doubts Linger About Warner, Juror Says," *Columbus Dispatch*, March 3, 1987.

Page 233.   **One of the . . . to grab it."** Mary Yost, "Doubts Linger About Warner, Juror Says," *Columbus Dispatch*, March 3, 1987.

Page 233.   **One of the . . . my eyes out."** Mary Yost, "Doubts Linger About Warner, Juror Says," *Columbus Dispatch*, March 3, 1987.

Page 234.   **Niehaus feared the . . . start all over."** Transcript of Bill Cunningham Show on Radio WLW, March 2, 1987.

Page 235.   **I guess it . . . the local media.** Howard Wilkinson, "Reactions: Calm, Shock, Indignation," *Cincinnati Enquirer*, March 3, 1987.

Page 235.   **These people acted . . . I am innocent.** Sharon Moloney, "Calm Warner Praises Jury But Insists He's Innocent," *Cincinnati Post*, March 3, 1987.

Page 235.   **Naturally we will . . . thing and appeal.** Mary Yost, "Warner, 2 Others Await Sentencing," *Columbus Dispatch*, March 3, 1987.

Page 235.   **Bongard couldn't meet . . . wouldn't oblige him.** Howard Wilkinson, "Bongard: Warner Part of Conspiracy," *Cincinnati Enquirer*, May 29, 1987.

Page 237.   **Before the Niehaus . . . the Federal attorneys.** Personal interview with Marvin Gersten.

Page 238.   **Jeffress said it's . . . of Niehaus's courtroom.** Sharon Moloney, "Warner's Anonymity Makes Jury Selection Easy," *Cincinnati Post*, May 6, 1987.

Page 240.   **and one said . . . be taken in."** Sharon Moloney, "Jurors Couldn't Believe Warner Would Want More," *Cincinnati Post*, June 20, 1987.

Page 242.   **The jury wasn't . . . up with them.** Sharon Moloney, "Jurors Couldn't Believe Warner Would Want More," *Cincinnati Post*, June 20, 1987; Howard Wilkinson, "The Decision: Jurors Saw Warner as a Victim," *Cincinnati Enquirer*, June 20, 1987; Howard Wilkinson, "Boxes of Evidence Untouched by Jury," *Cincinnati Enquirer*, June 21, 1987.

Page 242.   **Tracey was furious. . . .her cross examination.** Personal report from researcher Moloney.

Page 242.   **and this kept . . . was more coherent.** Transcript of *United States of America vs. Marvin L. Warner*, United States District Court, Eastern District of Michigan, Southern Division, Volume 24, Tuesday, June 16, 1987, page 255 and Volume 25, Wednesday, June 17, 1987, pages 6–22.

Page 243.   **While helping a . . . situation like this."** Eyewitness account by author.

Page 243.   **There were teary . . . my life back."** Sharon Moloney, "Warner Cleared of All Federal Charges," *Cincinnati Post*, June 20, 1987.

Page 243.   **Another told him . . . and happy life."** Sharon Moloney, "Jurors Couldn't Believe Warner Would Want More," *Cincinnati Post*, June 20, 1987.

Page 243.   **Jody said, "We . . . else in Ohio."** Howard Wilkinson, "Couple Seeks a New Start," *Cincinnati Enquirer*, June 20, 1987.

CHAPTER 14: IN THE WEB OF THE LAW

Page 244.   **he was beset . . . $4.319 billion.** Voluntary Petition in re Marvin Leon

Warner, Executed on October 20, 1987, United States Bankruptcy Court for the Middle District of Florida.

Page 244.   **Marvin was counterattacking . . . $25 million each).** Sharon Moloney, "Warner Filing Says He Has $20 Million," *Cincinnati Post*, November 17, 1987.

Page 245.   **He gave Jody . . . Warner family trusts.** Sharon Moloney, "Warner Gave Millions to Wife After S & L Fell," *Cincinnati Post*, June 17, 1988.

Page 245.   **states that a . . . for his horses.** Rosalind Resnick, "Bankruptcy Laws Favor the Wealthy; Florida Provision Lets Rich Keep Homes," *Miami Herald*, April 24, 1988.

Page 245.   **Marvin took roughly . . . to his family.** Sharon Moloney, "Warner Gave Millions to Wife After S & L Fell," *Cincinnati Post*, June 17, 1988.

Page 246.   **He said that . . . he owed them.** Sharon Moloney, "Warner Tries to Halt Bankruptcy Bid," *Cincinnati Post*, December 17, 1987.

Page 246.   **They were pressing . . . such a mammoth case."** Howard Wilkinson, "Warner wants to Drop Bankruptcy Proceeding," *Cincinnati Enquirer*, December 17, 1987.

Page 246.   **In fact, they . . . were illegitimate transfers.** Sharon Moloney, "Creditors Allege Warner Hid $45.8 Million," *Cincinnati Post*, April 24, 1988.

Page 247.   **From my own . . . feeding those egos."** Bill Adams, "A Case for Marvin Warner," *View*, February 1988, page 38.

Page 247.   **On March 25 . . . him against Tew.** Sharon Moloney, "Attorneys Part Ways with Warner," *Cincinnati Post*, March 25, 1988.

Page 247.   **at times he . . . and interpret depositions.** Personal interview with legal aide.

Page 250.   **Hall figured that . . . most important witness."** Personal report by researcher Gropman.

Page 252.   **The reporters took . . . in Marvin's favor.** Personal report by researcher Gropman.

Page 253.   **Tew commented, "We . . . across the board."** Lane Kelley, "Warner Owes ESM $22 Million, Jury Says," *Fort Lauderdale News/Sun-Sentinel*, July 8, 1988.

Page 253.   **At about 5:00 P.M. . . . roll the dice.** Personal report by researcher Gropman.

Page 255.   **In the end . . . with greater conviction.** Personal interviews with Leonard Mead, Naomi Ruth "Penny" Meola, Ruth Brown, and Yolanda D. Hankerson.

Page 255.   **He told the . . . we will appeal."** Martha Brannigan, "Fighting on in Court, Marvin Warner Strives to Salvage His Fortune," *Wall Street Journal*, August 3, 1988.

EPILOGUE: WHERE ARE THEY NOW?

Page 258.   **After dealing with . . . settlement among them.** Glenn Ruffenach, "Liquidation Order Imposed on Estate of E.S.M. Figure," *Wall Street Journal*, July 31, 1989; Sharon Moloney, "Judge Orders Warner Assets to be Sold Off," *Cincinnati Post*, July 29, 1989; personal interview with Lawrence Kellogg.

Page 259.   **By an ironic . . . company in 1969.** Personal interview with Laurie Holtz.

Page 259.   **He got Marshall . . . on his investment.** David Satterfield, "Bank Board Orders Broad to Put $9.86 Million in American S & L," *Miami Herald*, February 3, 1987; David Satterfield, "American S & L Shareholder Boosting Stake," *Miami Herald*, March 12, 1987; David Satterfield, "Friedman Takes Over American Savings," *Miami Herald*, April 30, 1988; personal interview with Edward P. Mahoney.

Page 260.   **When Finley Kumble . . . headquarters in Miami.** Rosalind Resnick, "Lawyers Spin Off New Firm," *Miami Herald*, December 25, 1987.

Page 260.   **Ronnie and his . . . office at Chillicothe.** Personal interview with Mary Ann Murphy.

Page 261.   **He works as . . . the finance office.** Personal interview with Jose Gomez.

Page 261.   **Burt sells stationery . . . Ross Correctional Institution.** Sharon Moloney, "'Nightmare' Imprisons Bongard," *Cincinnati Post*, November 27, 1987.

Page 261.   **After leaving ESM . . . for gold mines.** Deposition of Robert Charles Seneca before the Securities and Exchange Commission into securities transactions at ESM, March 30, 1985, pages 12–16.

Page 262.   **A jury found . . . of a minor.** "Ohio Congressman Is Convicted in Sex Case, but Aide Says He'll Run for Re-election," *New York Times*, May 27, 1989; Howard Wilkinson, "Judge Hands Lukens 30 Days in Jail, Fine," *Cincinnati Enquirer*, July 1, 1989.

Sources

The material for this book came from five main sources: interviews, publications, legal documents, legislative documents, and other documents.

Interviews

More than one hundred persons were interviewed by our research team. Fourteen of them asked that their names not be mentioned, and we have honored their wishes.

Of the principal players in our drama, only Marvin and Jody Warner and Ronnie Ewton refused requests to be interviewed. We engaged in informal conversations with Marvin, Jody, and Mark Warner that yielded no information of significance. We have had access to legal depositions by Marvin Warner and Ronnie Ewton and to all trial testimony by the Warners and Ewton.

Those interviewed include the following: Eddie Bapst, former executive secretary, Ohio State Racing Commission; Fran Bermanzohn, senior vice president and general counsel, Public Securities Association; Richard Birnbaum, June Seneca's lawyer, 1979–1980; Sharon Bogard, formerly Ronnie Ewton's secretary at ESM; Burton Bongard, formerly Home State CEO, confessed participant in ESM fraud; Shepard Broad, retired chairman of the board, American Savings & Loan; Cher Brooks, senior staff, U.S. House of Representatives; E. T. Brown, Birmingham, Alabama, political consultant; Ruth Brown, juror, Fort Lauderdale trial of Thomas Tew, as trustee for the Estate of ESM Government Securities, vs. Marvin L. Warner and Burton M. Bongard (*Tew vs. Warner*); William Cagney, lawyer for ESM, George Mead, and Nick Wallace in 1985; Ott Cefkin, media relations specialist, Fort Lauderdale Police Department; Richard Celeste, governor of Ohio during Home State crisis; Marti Cochran, chief counsel and staff director, Subcommittee on Securities of the U.S. Senate Banking Committee; Tessie Cohen, friend of Warner family, knew Marvin as a child; Herman Cooper, jury foreman, *State of Ohio vs. Marvin L. Warner, et al.* (Cincinnati trial); William Cooper, chief operating officer, American Savings & Loan, 1984–1985; Bill Cunningham, Cincinnati radio talk show host (WLW) and lawyer; Mike Curtin, Ohio state legislature reporter, *Columbus Dispatch*; Jeff Davis, administrative aide to Ohio Senator Richard Finan; Brian Dickerson, reporter who wrote long feature on Arky suicide, *Miami Herald*; Richard Finan, Republican member of Ohio State Senate; Mike Flanigan, senior staff, U.S. House of Representatives; Marvin Gersten, lawyer for Burton Bongard; Jack Goldstrich, partner, Holtz & Company; Jose Gomez, participated in ESM fraud while partner in Alexander Grant & Company; Jose A. Gonzalez, federal judge who presided over ESM bankruptcy and key ESM civil and criminal trials; B. Z. Goodwin, attorney/consultant, Holtz & Company; Rabbi Milton Grafman, clergyman who married Marvin and Jane Blach Warner; Toni Handley, member of Home State "Skirt Squad"; Yolanda D. Hankerson, alternate juror, *Tew vs. Warner*; Charles Harper, chief, Miami SEC office; Connie Harris, superintendent, Ohio Division of Savings and Loans; Dr. James Henry, formerly track physician, Beulah Park Race Track, Grove City, Ohio; Clark Hodgson, formerly lawyer for Home State and Marvin Warner and Warner Director on American Savings & Loan board; Laurie Holtz, partner, Holtz & Company; Donald Hunsche, executive vice president, Ohio Deposit Guarantee Fund (ODGF); Paul Jacobson, partner, Goldman, Sachs & Company; Abner Johnson, Birmingham, Alabama, FHA officer when Warner-Kanter companies worked with agency in late 1940s; Lawrence Kane, state of Ohio special prosecutor in cases stemming from collapse of Home State; Joe Kanter, Marvin Warner's partner in real estate and construction enterprises, 1948-1957; Bob Keefe, executive director of Democratic National Committee, 1973-1975, currently political consultant; Dale Keiger, freelance journalist who wrote magazine articles about Marvin Warner; Lawrence Kellogg, partner, Tew Jorden Schulte & Beasley; Randy Kroner, senior staff, Holtz & Company; Laird Lazelle, CEO of Charter Oak Savings (ODGF bank); David Levine, partner, Tew Jorden Schulte & Beasley; Immaculata "Betty" Rohner Loughlin, formerly Alan Novick's secretary; Donald "Buz" Lukens, formerly Republican member of Ohio State Senate, now member of the U.S. House of Representatives; Edward P. Mahoney, holder of several top executive positions at American Savings & Loan since 1978; Leonard Mead, jury foreman, *Tew vs. Warner*; Naomi Ruth "Penny" Meola, juror, *Tew vs. Warner*; Sharon Moloney, reporter, *Cincinnati Post*; R. Stan Mortenson, lawyer for Marvin Warner; Mary Ann Murphy, wife of Tim Murphy, confessed participant in ESM fraud; Anthony Nales, town manager, Bay Harbor Islands; Arthur Nascarella, retired New York City detective; John W. Osborn, partner specializing in securities law, Cadwalader, Wickersham & Taft law firm; Jim Otte, broadcaster, Columbus radio station WOSU; Fay Paskowitz, Birmingham, Alabama, friend of Warner family; Jose Garcia-Pedrosa, partner, Tew Jorden Schulte & Beasley; Richard Pettigrew, leading Miami corporate lawyer; James Pohlman, partner, Porter, Wright, Morris & Arthur, law firm which represented state of Ohio in Home State/ODGF matters; Joe Rabe, organizer of Home State Depositors Association in Columbus; Irene Raymond, Marvin Warner's cousin in Birmingham, Alabama; Mark Raymond, senior associate, Tew Jorden Schulte & Beasley; Paige Reefe, associate, Washington law firm Cutler & Stanfield; Debi Rickert, member of Home State "Skirt Squad"; James Russell, financial editor, *Miami Herald*; Thomas A. Russo, partner specializing in securities law, Cadwalader, Wickersham & Taft law firm; Harold Satz, Missouri judge who provided background on Jewish life in St. Louis area; Raymond Sawyer, formerly chief of staff for Governor Celeste of Ohio, now in private practice of law; Robert Sax, partner, Holtz & Company; David Schiebel, president of Home State when it collapsed, convicted on securities counts in *Ohio vs. Warner, et al.*; Ellen Seidman, special assistant to the undersecretary, U.S. Department of the Treasury; Mary Ann Sharkey, political journalist, *Cleveland Plain Dealer*; Jerry Sklar, formerly president, Birmingham Stallions football team; David Sokol, roommate of Marvin Warner at University of Alabama; Tom Suddes, political journalist, *Cleveland Plain Dealer*; Paula Taylor, member of Home State "Skirt Squad"; Cotton Tew, private investigator, Tom Tew's father; Tom Tew, partner, Tew Jorden Schulte & Beasley; JoAnn Touri, formerly bookkeeper at ESM, then comanager of the ESM Depository; Robert Trafford, partner, Porter, Wright, Morris & Arthur, law firm which represented state of Ohio in Home State/ODGF matters; Nancy Van Sant, SEC Attorney, Atlanta office; Lisa Winbourne, formerly a computer operator at ESM, then comanager of the ESM Depository; Claudia Winkler, formerly editorial page editor, *Cincinnati Post*; Michael Wollensky, formerly SEC regional administrator, Atlanta office; Jack Wingate, executive vice president, Heritage Savings (ODGF bank); John Wrinkle, Birmingham, Alabama, political consultant; Mary Yost, political journalist, *Columbus Dispatch*; and Sydney Ziff, friend of Marvin Warner's family when Marvin was a child.

Publications

Relevant materials from the July 30, 1920, *Montreal Star* to the present day have been culled from the following publications: *Aiken County*; *Aiken Lifestyles*; *American Lawyer*; *Bailout: An Insider's Account of Bank Failures and Rescues* (book by Irvine H. Sprague); *Barron's*; *Boston Globe*; *Bulletin of the U.S. Treasury*; *Business Week*; *Cincinnati Enquirer*; *Cincinnati Magazine*; *Cincinnati Post*; *Cincinnati: The Queen City* (book by Daniel Hurley); *Cleveland Plain Dealer*; *Columbus Dispatch*; *Columbus Monthly*; *Congressional Quarterly*; *Debt Management*; *Dog World*; *Economic Review-Federal Reserve Bank of Atlanta*; *Fannie Mae Guide to Debt Securities*, October 4, 1988; *Federal Reserve Bank-Annual Statistical Digest*; *Federal Reserve Bank of Cleveland-1985 Annual Report*; *Federal Reserve Bulletin*; *Florida Trend*; *Forbes*; *Fort Lauderdale News/Sun Sentinel*; *Fortune*; *Freddie Mac Annual Report* 1987; *Great American Bond Market* (book by Sidney Homer); *History and Origins of the Public Securities Association* 1912–1986; *Housing America—An Overview of Fannie Mae's Past, Present, and Future*, *Institutional Investor*; 1987 *International Finance Yearbook*; *Investor's Daily*; *Journal of Accountancy*; *Kennel Review*; *Los Angeles Times*; *Manhattan, Inc.*; *Mason, Ohio Pulse-Journal*; *Memphis Commercial Appeal*; *Memphis Commercial and Financial Chronicle*; *Memphis Press-Scimitar*; *Miami Herald*; *Miami News*; *Miami Pictorial*; *Miami Review*; *Montreal Star*; *National Journal*; *National Law Journal*; *National Thrift News*; *Newark Star-Ledger*; *Newsweek*; *New York*; *New York Post*; *New York Times*; *Ocala Star-Banner*; *Ocala View*; *Ohio Business*; *Public Securities Association 1987*; *Annual Report*; *Securities Regulation & Law Report*; *Sport*; *Sports Illustrated*; *St. Petersburg Times*; *Time*; U.S. government fiscal year budget for 1988; *U.S. Mortgage Securities for International Investors* (pamphlet by Andrew S. Carron of the First Boston Corporation, dated September, 1987); *U.S. News and World Report*; *Wall Street Journal*; *Washington Post*; *Who's Who in America*; *Who's Who in Memphis Business*; and *World Almanac*.

Legal Documents

At least one member of our research team was present each day at the three Warner trials: *State of Ohio vs. Marvin L. Warner et al.*, in Cincinnati; *United States of America vs. Marvin L. Warner*, in Ann Arbor; and *Thomas Tew, as trustee for the Estate of ESM Government Securities, vs. Marvin L. Warner and Burton M. Bongard*, in Fort Lauderdale. We have full transcripts of the Ann Arbor and Fort Lauderdale trials and a partial transcript of the proceedings in Cincinnati. We also have a full transcript of the proceedings in *Thomas Tew, receiver for ESM, vs. Jose Gomez, and John Does one through one hundred* d/b/a Alexander Grant & Company, a Partnership (Tew vs. Grant in Fort Lauderdale).

We possess and have studied depositions given by the following: Stephen Arky, Richard Birnbaum, Burton Bongard, Shepard Broad, William Cooper, Ronnie Ewton, Jose Gomez, Bruce Greer, Gilbert Haddad, Clark Hodgson, Gary Kreider, Robert Luther, Edward P. Mahoney, Robert Schatzman, Robert Seneca, Eugene Stearns, Charles Streicher, Marvin L. Warner, and Barry N. Winslow.

Other important legal documents used in our research included notes and files from June Seneca's lawyer (Richard Birnbaum), indictments, trial briefs, bankruptcy petitions, and verdict forms.

Legislative Documents

We studied acts of Congress and the Ohio State Legislature, hearings and reports of Congress and the legislatures of Ohio and New York, and reports of the U.S. General Accounting Office.

Other Documents

We found several hundred other documents useful. Many had become part of the public record because they were used as evidence in trials which we covered.

The variety of the materials was great; among them were Marvin Warner's desk calendars from 1983 and 1984, minutes of Home State and American Savings & Loan directors' meetings, the hand-written diary of a Skirt Squad member, police reports on the suicides of Stephen Arky and Earl Riddell, Warner's handwritten "make-up-my-losses" memo, and fifty-four volumes (1907–1960) of the city of Birmingham, Alabama, annual directory of residents' occupations and addresses.

Index

AIMEE coal operation, ESM scam
      involving, 84-87
Alexander Grant & Company. *See also*
      Gomez, Jose
   certification of ESM statements by, 8
   change of, name to Grant Thornton,
      210
   civil suits against, 209-11, 213-16
   hiring of, as audit firm for ESM, 70
   Jose Gomez as supervisor of ESM
      account at, 8
   out-of-court settlement of, 213
   responsibility of, for Gomez's actions,
      213, 214, 215
   structure of, 85-86
   system of peer review at, 214-15
   use of, by Ronnie Ewton as
      accountant, 69-70
   withdrawal of, from 1984 audit of
      ESM, 4, 146-47
Allen, Mel, 37
Allen, R. J., & Company, case, 68
American Bancshares, Inc. (ABI)
   change of name to Great American, 56
   interest of ESM in, 75
   purchase of controlling shares in, by
      Ewton and Seaton, 75
   Warner's purchase of Culverhouse's
      shares in, 56
American Savings and Loan (AS&L)
   "buy-sell" provision in contract
      between Broad and Warner, 35
   chartering of, 32
   financial position of, prior to buyout
      offer, 121
   impact of ESM fraud on, 10-11, 150
   investment by Marvin Warner in,
      34-35
   losses of, 10-11, 153-54
   management of, by Shepard, 31-35,
      107-8

rejection of Home State contract by, 123
rejection of Perez-Sandoval contract
      by, 123
and use of back-to-back arbitrage, 109
need for additional investors, 34
Ronnie Ewton as head of executive
      board for, 35
success factors needed for, 31-32
Tew's tactics in suing, 209
troubles following deregulation, 32-34
Warner as CEO of, 106
AmeriTrust, purchase of 10 Home State
      branches by, 193
Anderson, Arthur, & Co., loss of suit by
      Ohio, 216
Arky, Albert, 196
Arky, Freed, Stearns, Watson, Greer and
      Weaver, 12, 13
   faction fights in, 199
   financial status of, 200
   Gonzalez dismissal of Tew's suit
      against, 216-17
   growth of, 197
   impact of ESM on income flow of, 199
   lack of bankruptcy department at, 135
   litigation against, 216-17
   present status of, 263
   Tew's suit against, 209
Arky, Joyce, 196
Arky, Lillian, 196
Arky, Lisa, 198
Arky, Marlin Blach Warner, 42
   marriage of, 51, 196-97
   present status of, 263
   relationship with mother after divorce,
      51
   at sentencing of father, 236
   and suicide/suicide attempt of Steve,
      200-2
Arky, Stephen, 1, 12, 13
   and ABI deal, 79

advising of, concerning ESM problems, 136
attempt to stall by, in dealing with ESM crisis, 138
attempt to undue buyout by Shepard, 132–33
as attorney for ESM, 54, 69
betrayal of, by Roger Bernstein, 194, 201
betrayal of, by Ron Ewton, 194, 201
building of shield around ESM by, 77
closing of ESM account by, 149
contacting of Broad by, concerning investment in, American, 34
demons of, 194–202
designation of, as chief lieutenant by Warner, 56
early life of, 196
financial problems of, following ESM crisis, 200
focus of, on deal making, 197–98
and formation of Arky, Freed, 197
friendship of, with Ewton, 75–76
handling of SEC investigation of ESM, 76–77, 91–92
as investment advisor to Warner, 54–55, 106, 197–98
knowledge of, of problems at ESM, 130
marriage of, to Marlin Blach Warner, 51, 196–97
meeting with Bobby Schatzman, 194
mood swings of, following ESM crisis, 200
in National Guard, 75
opposition of, to Tew as receiver, 152
painting of, by Tew as ESM insider, 198
preparation of buyout proposal for Shepard, 125–26
relationship with Tew, 195
resignation of, as ESM counsel, 136–37
role of, in purchase of Freedom Savings & Loan, 110, 111
as SEC staff lawyer, 75, 197
shock of, concerning ESM losses, 137
suicide/suicide attempt of, 200–2
Tew's suit against, 209
treatment of, by psychiatrist, 201
Arky, Todd, 198
Austin, Gerald, 171

Back-to-back arbitrage, 109, 113
Bailey, Pierre, 29
Bank holiday
declaration of, in Ohio, 173–74

extension of, 177
Banking Deregulation Act (1980), 32
Batties, Tom, 171
appraisal of, by Donald Hunsche as to Home State status, 150
replacement of, with Bob McAlister, 182
role of, in handling of Home State crisis, 150, 154
Bay Harbor Islands, Broad's investment in, 29–31
Ben-Gurion, David, 25–27
Bernstein, Roger, betrayal of Steve Arky by, 194, 201
Berra, Yogi, 37
Bevill, Bresler & Schulman
Ronnie Ewton at, 68
scandal at, 67
SEC shutdown of, 188
Birmingham Stallions, management of, 108
Blach, Mervin, 39–40
Blach's department store, 39
Bobrowicz, Szmuel. See Broad, Shepard
Bobrowicz, Usher, 19
Boggs, Wade, 207
Bogus, Melvin, 60–61
Boiler rooms, origin of, 62
Bond daddies
coining of, as term, 65
operations of, 60–62
promises of, 63–64
scams used by, 64
and the U.S. government securities market, 68
and use of leverage, 70
Bongard, Burt, 12, 13
criminal prosecution of, 219
criminal trial of, 228
decision to resign, 102–3
defense strategy at trial of, 237
designation of, as Home State president, 56
financial problems of, 90
guilty plea to federal charges against, 237
guilty verdict of, 232–33, 234
involvement of, in ESM scam, 90
opening of account at ESM by, 90
present status of, 261
as president/CEO of Unity Bank and Trust, 89–90
pressure from, to insure Home State profits, 95
and sale of ComBanks, 96

sentencing of, 235-36, 237
testimony of, at Warren's federal trial,
    240-41, 242
testimony of, at own trial, 227-28
Tew's suit against, 209
Bradford, as ESM custodian bank, 151
Braun, Bob, 225
Bricker, Senator, 42
Briggs, Schaedle and Co., 73
Broad, Ann, birth of, 23
Broad, Daniel, 22
Broad, Morris, 14
  birth of, 23
  decision of Warner to buy out, 120
  lack of drive by, 34
  and management of American Savings,
      106, 107-8
  role of, in purchase of Freedom
      Savings, 110, 117
  survey by, on impact of ESM fraud on
      American, 150
Broad, "Pop" Daniel, 19, 20, 22, 24
Broad, Ruth Kugel
  European vacation of, 115
  marriage of, 22-23
  move to Miami, 24
Broad, Shepard, 14
  arrival of, in Canada, 18, 21-22
  attempt by Warner and Arky to undue
      buyout offer, 132-33
  attempt to raise buyout money, 127-28
  as attorney in Brooklyn, 23-24
  birth of daughter, Ann, 23
  birth of son, Morris, 23
  buyout of Warner by, 131-32, 134
  as candidate for political office, 23
  change of partnership to Broad and
      Cassel, 31
  deal between Kamp and, concerning
      buyout, 130-31
  decision of Warner to buy out, 120
  decision to purchase American, 131
  decision to fight buyout offer, 126-27
  early life of, 18-21
  expense account of, 123
  friendship with Roy Calamia, 24
  investment of, in Bay Harbor Islands,
      29-31
  involvement of, in Palestine cause, 26-29
  Jewish contributions of, 28
  and the Kelley Drye report on ESM
      transaction, 113, 115, 118-19, 120,
      122
  and management of American Savings
      & Loan, 31-35, 106, 107-8

marriage of, to Ruth Kugel, 22-23
meeting with Ben-Gurion over
    Palestine, 26-28
meeting with Henry Montor over
    Palestine, 25, 26
move to Miami, 24
organization of Miami Beach chapter
    Zionist Organization of America,
    25
partnership with Ed Fleming, 24-25
present status of, 259
as prudent man, 32
and purchase of Freedom Savings &
    Loan, 111-20
relationship with John J. Flannery, 23
request for return of Treasury notes,
    142
return from Europe, 118
role of, in real estate financing for
    American, 109
and state charter for American Savings
    & Loan, 31
travel of, to U.S., 19-21
treatment of risk by, 122
during World War II, 25
Broad and Cassel, formation of, 31

Cagney, William (Bill)
  acceptance of retainer fee, 144
  as counsel for ESM, 14
  decision not to represent ESM, 3
  introduction of Tew to Mead, 3
  meeting with Mead over need for
      criminal lawyer, 142
  recommendation of Tew, 144
  telling of ESM fraud, 10-11
Calamia, Roy, 24, 29
Capehart, Senator, 42
Carter, Jimmy, 32, 55, 73
  appointment of Gonzalez to federal
      bench by, 206
Cartolano, Fred, 230-31
Cassel, Alvin, partnership with Broad,
    31
Celebrezze, Tony, 161
  appointment of Lawrence Kane as
      special prosecutor, 181
  as attorney General, 220
Celeste, Frank, 165, 171
Celeste, Richard F. (Gov.), 1
  and approval of Home State-Home
      State Financial merger, 124
  connection with Warner, 180
  political campaign of, 97
  present status of, 262

handling of Home State crisis by, 150,
154–55, 159–60, 161, 162, 168–78,
179–80, 182, 184–87, 192–93, 198,
216
Century Banks
merger of, with Sunbanks, 95
Warner's investment in, 95–96
Century Savings, FSLIC coverage of, 182
Charter Oak Bank, 170
Chase Manhattan, sale of Home State
branches to, 193
Citibank, 72
Clemens, Roger, 207
Clough, Susan, 57
Cogan, Marshall, 258–59
Collins, Don, 11, 14, 16
arrival of, in Fort Lauderdale, 142–43
concerns of, over 1984 ESM financial
report, 3, 4
decision to investigate Grant audit, 5
and the impact of ESM troubles on
Home State, 146
as lawyer for Home State, 3
ComBanks
control of, by Warner, 56
financial management of, under
Ronnie Ewton, 58
sale of, 96
Warner's purchase of controlling
interest in, 54
Cooper, Alice, 84
Cooper, Bill, 114
as chief operating officer at American
Savings, 106–7
and purchase of Freedom Savings, 111,
116–17, 120
role of, in FHLBB investigation of
American, 122
Cox, Kenneth, 173
as director of Ohio Department of
Commerce, 150
press conferences of, 157–58, 170,
182–83
role of, in handling of Home State
crisis, 155
Culverhouse, Hugh, Jr.
and investigation of Ewton and
Seneca, 81
purchase of Warner's controlling
interests in Tampa Bay Bucs, 56
role of, in ESM scam, 80–81
as SEC lawyer, 81
Culverhouse, Hugh, Sr., 54
Cunningham, Bill, on crisis at Home
State, 170, 172, 181, 190

D'Amato, Senator, 262
"Dark Monday," 178
Deaver, Michael, 221
Delta Securities, Ronnie Ewton at,
60–61, 65
Depository Institutions and Monetary
Control Act (1980), 32
DiMaggio, Joe, 37
Dingell, Senator, 262
Dory, Jacob (Jacob Dostrovsky), 27–28
Dostrovsky, Jacob (Jacob Dory), 27–28

Edwards, Edwin, 221
Elliott, Arthur "Ace," 225
ESM Financial Group, Inc., transfer of
losses to, via financial
statement footnote, 77, 82
ESM Government Securities, Inc. (ESM)
appetite for collateral, 104
Arky as counsel to, 54, 69
banning of National Bank from doing
business with, 75
building of shield around, by Arky, 77
custodian banks of, 151
decision of Pete Summers to leave, 92
and decision on filing for bankruptcy,
81–82
excess collateral of Home State at, 105
financial plight of, in Dec. 1984, 134
financing of, by Home State, 108–9
Gomez bailout plan of, 134, 135
hiring of Alan Novick as office
manager, 69
hiring of Alexander Grant, CPAs as
audit firm, 70
Home State Savings Bank of
Cincinnati as customer of, 3
impact of Lion collapse on, 108, 109
interest of, in ABI, 75
interest of, in secondary dealers, 73
launching of, 68–69
location of, 6
need of, for excess collateral, 90–91
negotiating of parting settlement with
Summers, 93
1980 Christmas party in Bahamas, 91
as only active company, 77
organization of, 54
pattern in handling of bank
transactions, 74
problems caused by buyout of Warner
by Shepard, 134–45
role of Alan Novick in running, 7–8,
69, 88
SEC investigation of, 75–77, 91–92

shift of losses of, to ESM affiliate,
    83–84
and support trial of Bobby Seneca,
    87–88
$300 million loss of, 104
Unity Bank and Trust of Chicago as
    big customer, 89
and use of customer firms by, 79–80
and use of leverage, 70
ESM scam
    American Savings and Loan as loser
        in, 10–11, 150
    and ABI deal, 79–80
    and AIMEE coal operation, 84–87
    anatomy of, 74–105
    Home State as loser in, 10, 153
    and Marion County,Tennessee, mine, 84
    planning of, 77–78
    role of Gomez in coverup of, 89
    role of Novick in, 77–78, 79, 80, 85
    with S-J Minerals, 84
Essex House, construction of, 46–47
Ewton, Darla
    ambitions of, 60
    breakup with Ronnie, 195
    concern of, over Ronnie's values and
        lifestyle, 85
    divorce of Ronnie by, 85
    lack of knowledge of, concerning
        scam, 85
    life of, in Fort Lauderdale, 66
    marriage of, 59–60
    move of, to Little Rock, 60
    physical description of, 59–60
    remarriage of, 85
    as Ronnie's mentor, 60
Ewton, Jerilyn Moroney, 208
    marriage of, 94–95
    present status of, 260–261
    protection of assets by, 245
Ewton, Ronnie Restine, 1
    betrayal of Steve Arky by, 194–95, 201
    at Bevill, Bresler & Schulman, 67
    birth of, 59
    as bond daddy, 65, 74–75
    breakup with Darla, 195
    concerns of, over ESM problems, 134
    criminal charges against, 211
    Darla as mentor of, 60
    family of, 59
    financial worth of, 66
    and hiring of Alexander Grant, CPA
        by, 69–70
    hiring of, by Hibbard, O'Connor &
        Weeks, Inc. (HOW), 65

and death of Alan Novick, 130
and decision on filing for bankruptcy,
    81–82, 134–35
defense strategy of Warren to turn
    proceedings into trial of, 223–24
at Delta Securities, 60–61, 65
desire of, to make deal, 208–9
divorce of, by Darla, 85
end of career at Hibbard, O'Connor &
    Weeks, Inc., 67
estimates of, concerning ESM losses,
    194
FHLBB concern of conflict of interest
    of, 122–23
and financial management of
    ComBanks and Great American,
    58
following sentencing of, 231–32
friendship of, with Arky, 75–76
as head of executive board for
    American Savings & Loan, 35
impact of divorce on, 85
indictment in forgery of Alan Novick
    will, 186
as insurance salesman, 59
interest of, in U.S. government
    securities market, 68
involvement of, in bond market, 60–73
at Kidder, Peabody & Co., 67
lack of ambition in, 59
and launching of ESM, 68–69
loan to, by Home State, 55
marriage of, to Darla, 59–60
marriage of, to Jerilyn Moroney, 94–95
meeting with Schatzman, 135
as member of boards of Great
    American and ComBanks, 56
move to Ft. Lauderdale, 65–66
move to Little Rock, 60
physical description of, 60
need of, for criminal lawyer, 136, 138
office of, 7
present status of, 260–261
problems of, following death of Alan
    Novick, 130–31
protection of assets by, 245
purchase of American Bankshares, Inc.
    (ABI) by, 54–55, 75
resignation of, as outside man with
    ESM, 7, 138, 139
role of, at Home State, 107
role of, in ESM scam, 79
and sale of ComBanks, 96
sentencing of, 212, 230–32
spending sprees of, 135

testimony of, at Warner's trial, 223,
239–40, 242
treatment of ESM customers by, 74
tax problems of, 69
use of WATS lines by, 65
at Winters and Company, 67
Ewton, Stephanie, 66, 85

Fabian, Bobby Joe, conviction of murder
of George Lenox, 65
Federal Home Loan Bank Board
(FHLBB)
examination of American's books by,
121–22
investigation of Unity Bank and Trust
by, 91
Federal Housing Administration (FHA)
Section 603 housing under, 49
Section 608 housing under, 40, 42–49
Federal Reserve, 163–64
Federal Savings and Loan Insurance
Corporation (FSLIC)
difference between ODGF insurance
and, 148
standards of, concerning bank's capital
base, 179–80
Federal Securities Act (1975), 68
Feldman, David, 262
Finan, Richard, 165, 171, 172, 173–74,
179, 189
present status of, 262
Finley Kumble Wagner Heine Underberg
Manley Myerson & Casey, 4, 12
role of, in ESM litigation, 213
First National Bank of Cincinnati
interest of, in purchase of Home State,
158
negotiations of sale of Home State, 160
purchase of 10 Home State branches
by, 193
First U.S. Corporation, formation of, 62
Flannery, John J., as client of Shepard
Broad, 23
Fleming, Ed, partnership of, with
Shepard Broad, 24–25
Fleming and Broad, formation of, 24–25
Florida Fruit Lands Company, 66
Forest Park, construction of, 49, 50
Fort Payne, Ala., set up of prehab
facility at, 46–47
Foxton Securities, assignment of Bobby
Seneca to, 83
Frank, Lou, as investigator for U.S.
Controller of the Currency, 74–75,
77

Freedom Savings & Loan of Tampa
Broad's ownership of stock in, 34–35
deal to purchase control of, 110–20
and purchase of ComBanks, 96

Garcia-Pedrosa, Jose
as chief litigator, 213–15
at Warren's civil trial, 247–56
and Warren's petition for bankruptcy,
245
Gersten, Marvin, as member of
Bongard's defense team, 221, 237
Gilliam, Bill, as member of Bongard's
defense team, 221, 223
Gilligan, John, 53, 236
Gillmor, Paul, 159, 171, 179
Glenn, Sen. John, 56, 163
GLL Farms, and murder of George
Lenox, 64
Goldman, Sachs, 72, 73
Goldstrich, Jack, 250
Goldwater, Barry, Jr., 57
Goldwater, Barry III, 57
Gomez, Jose, 1. *See also* Alexander Grant
& Company
corruption of, 86
debts of, 86
decision of, to pull audit and tell
partners of coverup, 143–44
estimates of ESM losses by, 139
first involvement of, with ESM, 83
fooling of, in audit, 85
friendship of, with Alan Novick, 86
indictment in forgery of Alan Novick
will, 186
involvement of, in AIMEE scheme,
86–87
knowledge of ESM audit, 140
lifestyle of, 86
making of partner in Alexander
Grant, 85–86
missing of ESM shift of losses by, 84
as partner in Alexander Grant, 86
offer to, to replace Novick, 130
present status of, 261
questioning of, concerning audit
problems, 143
request of 24th copy of audit from
Schiebel, 144
role of, in ESM scam coverup, 89
role of, in falsification of audit, 92
sentencing of, by Gonzalez, 212, 232
as supervisor of ESM account at
Alexander Grant, 9
Tew and Holtz on bribery of, 146–47

Gonzalez, Jose, 206–7
approval of Tew's accord with AS&L by, 211
cooperation of, with Tew, 209
desire to keep on ESM case, 207–8
freezing of ESM executive assets by, 204
as judge at civil trial of Warren, 248–49, 251, 253–55
as trial judge, 214–17
and Warren's petition for bankruptcy, 245
Grant Thornton
change of Alexander Grant & Company's name to, 210
present status of, 259
Gray, Edwin, 171, 176, 179
Great American
change of American Bancshares to, 56
financial management of, under Ronnie Ewton, 58
sale of, 96
Greer, Bruce, as partner in Arky, Freed, 138, 199
Greer, Evelyn, 138
Greutli gas property, 84

Haddad, Gil, 136
Ewton's request to, for bankruptcy lawyer, 134–35
Mead's request to, for criminal lawyer name, 142
Hall, Andy, as attorney for Warren, 247, 252–55
Handley, Bill, impact of Home State crisis on, 157
Handley, Mike, impact of Home State crisis on, 174–75
Handley, Toni
impact of Home State crisis on, 157, 168, 174–75
present status of, 262
and the skirt squad, 180–81, 182, 183–84, 185, 187–88, 191, 192
Harper, Charles, 14–17
as chief of South Florida SEC office, 66
decision to close ESM down and name Tell as receiver, 14–17, 152, 203–5
on Fort Lauderdale as white collar fraud capital, 66
and National Bank of South Florida case, 75
and possibility of funds secreted in Bahamas, 160–61
and replacement of Novick, 130

and sentencing of Ronnie Ewton, 230–31
Heatter, Gabriel, 41
Hemingway, Margaux, 84
Hentschel, Sylvester, 225, 239
discovery of Home State scam by, 98–99
as senior field examiner of Ohio Savings and Loan Association, 97–99
Hibbard, O'Connor & Weeks, Inc. (HOW)
decision of Weeks to leave, 67
decision to close Ft. Lauderdale office by, 67
founding of, 65
hiring of Ronnie Ewton by, 65–66
move of headquarters to New York City, 66
trouble of, with NASD, 67
Hodgson, Clark, 14, 16
as attorney for Home State, 149–50
decision of Warren to seek legal advice from, 140
and the impact of ESM troubles on Home State, 146
legal adviser of, to Warren, 141
resignation of, as Marvin's lawyer, 149–50
Hoeveler, William
appointment of Tew as receiver, 16–17, 152–53, 203
as judge in ESM fraud case, 16–17
Hogan, Jay, representation of Ewton by, 138
Holtz, Laurie, 1, 3–9, 11, 14, 16
on bribery of Gomez, 146–47
confirmation of loss by staff of, 8–9
desire of Tew to meet with, 144–45
discovery of $300 million loss by, 8
first meeting with Tew, 3–4
and Grant audit, 5–7
investigations of, 77
knowledge of Gomez, 9
present status of, 259
role of, in investigation of ESM, 203, 205–6
structure of firm of, 86
testimony of, in Warren civil trial, 251–52, 255
Home Savings of America (Los Angeles), sale of Home State, branches to, 193
Home State Savings Bank of Cincinnati
attempt to learn true losses of, 148
debenture issue at, 123–24

decision of close down, 162
designation of Burt Bongard as
    president of, 56
and disclosure issue, 141
excess collateral of, as ESM, 105
financial problems of, 58, 113–14, 89,
    118
financing of ESM Government
    Securities, Inc., 108–9
growth of excess collateral at ESM, 91
and guidelines on excess collateral, 99
impact of crisis, on depositors, 156–57
interest of First National Bank of
    Cincinnati in
purchase of, 158
involvement of, in ESM scam, 97–105
as largest customer of ESM
    Government Securities, Inc, 3
Lindner sale of branches of, 193
loaning of funds to Seneca and Ewton
    by, 55
losses of, 10, 148, 153
merger of, with Home State Financial,
    118, 123–24
negotiations on sale to First National,
    160
opening of trading accounts at ESM
    by, 80
profits made by, under Alan Novick, 98
purchase of, by Warner, 51
SEC investigation of, 117–18
unsecured lending to ESM, 124
withdrawals from, 169–73
Home State Depositors Association, 189
Home State Financial, Inc. (HSFI)
    need of, for money, 95
    merger of, with Home State, 118,
        123–24
Homestead Act (Florida), 245
Horn, Karen, role of, in handling of
    Home State crisis, 159, 173–76, 184
Huddleston, Larry, concern of, over
    Home State collateral, 124–25
Hunsche, Donald
    appraisal of Batties as to Home State,
        150
    and impact of ESM fraud on Home
        State, 147
Hunter Savings, interest of, in
    purchasing Home State, 192–93

Insurance Exchange of the Americas, 199
Israel, Mel, 37

Jackson, Sen. Scoop, 55

Jacobson, Bob, impact of crisis on,
    174–75
Jagtiani, Arjan, impact of losses on, 168
Jeffress, Bill
    firing of, by Warren, 247
    as member of Warner's defense team,
        221, 223, 234, 237, 241, 246
Johnson, Abner, handling of 608 FHA
    projects by, 43, 44, 46–47
Johnson, Lyndon, 53
Joiner, Charles, and moving of trial to
    Ann Arbor, 235, 238–39
Jones, Theodore, 167
Josephs, Mike, representation of Ewton
    by, 136

Kamp, Carl
    FHLBB authority of, over American,
        125
    and Shepard's attempt to buyout
        Warner, 127–28, 131
Kane, Lawrence A., Jr., 218
    and sentencing of Ronnie Ewton, 231
    as special prosecutor, 181, 220–22
    trial strategy of, 225–28
Kanter, Joe
    in army, 43
    and building of Stratford Manor, 48–49
    completion of Forest Park, 50
    and construction of Essex House,
        46–47
    decision to break up Warner-Kanter
        Company, 49–50
    as FHA builder, 44
    and formation of Warner-Kanter
        Company, 44
    interest of, in post World War II
        housing market, 43–44
    marriage of, 50
    move to Miami, 50
    movie-making involvement of, 50
    partnership of, with Marvin Warner,
        44
    physical description of, 45–46
    and set up of prefab facility at Fort
        Payne, Ala., 47
    as winner in Alabama state oratorical
        contests, 36–37, 43
Katz, Evan, 200, 202
Kaufman and Broad, Inc., 197
Kaufmann, Fred, 180, 181, 187
Kelley Drye & Warren, review of Freedom
    transaction by, 113, 115, 118–19, 120,
    122
Kessler, Jack, 171

Kevil (Ky.) Bank, sale of, 63–64
Kidder, Peabody & Co., 67
  Ronnie Ewton at, 68
Kominsky, Cheryl, impact of Home State
  crisis on, 157

Lanston, Aubrey G., & Co., 73
Lazelle, Laird, 170
Lenox, George
  ambition of, 62
  attraction of, to use of WATS lines,
    62–63
  birth of, 62
  capacity of, for work, 62
  and formation of First U.S.
    Corporation by, 62
  murder of, 64–65
Levan, Alan, 195, 198
Levine, David, consultation with Tew on
  keeping Gomez on case, 207–8
Lewis, Gerald
  Florida's securities regular, 75
  lack of action by, 75
Lindner, Carl, 191–93, 225
Lion Capital Group, collapse of, 108,
  109, 113
Lippman, Walter, 41
Little, Charles, impact of Home State
  crisis on, 157
Luken, Thomas, 171
Luken Charlie, 183
Lukens, Donald "Buz," 191, 193
  present status of, 262

Mahoney, Ed
  as deputy CEO at American Savings &
    Loan, 107
  and FHLBB examination of
    American's books, 121–22
  and purchase of control of Freedom
    Savings & Loan, 110, 116–17
Makley, Roger, as Schiebel's lawyer, 221
Mantle, Mickey, 37
Marion County, Tennessee, mine, ESM
  scam involving, 84
McAlister, Bob
  handling of Home State bank crisis by,
    189
  replacement of Batties by, 182
McGovern, George, 55
McNamara, Bob, 50
Mead, George, 1, 10, 11, 12, 16, 203
  concerns of, over withdrawal of Grant
    from audit, 5
  criminal charges against, 211

and death of Alan Novick, 129–30
hiring of Tew as special legal advisor,
  3
involvement of, in ESM, 88
and launching of ESM, 68–69
meeting with Cagney over need for
  criminal lawyer, 142
meeting with Warner, 139
present status of, 261
as replacement for Ewton, 138–39
role of, in audit investigation, 6
sentencing of, 212, 232
Merrill Lynch, 72
Metcalf, George, 201
Metzenbaum, Howard, 56, 163
Molitor Loan, impact of crisis on, 171,
  173, 174–75
Montor, Henry
  as director of United Jewish Appeal, 25
  and meetings with Ben-Gurion, 25–26
Mooney, Donald, 242
Morgan, Trish, and FHLBB
  examination, 121–23, 125, 127
Mortenson, Stan
  firing of, by Warren, 247
  as member of Warner's defense team,
    221, 234, 237, 239, 242, 246
Moscowitz, Grover, 22
Mundt, Senator, 42
Murphy, Tim, involvement of, in ESM,
  88

National Association of Security Dealers
  (NASD), and problems of HOW,
  Inc., 67
National Bank of South Florida
  banning of, from doing business with
    ESM, 75
  routine inspection of books of, 74
Neidich, Lisa
  present status of, 262
  and the skirt squad, 181, 184, 187
New York Chemical Bank, interest of, in
  purchasing Home State, 186–91
New York Stock Exchange (NYSE), daily
  volume of, 70
New York Yankees, purchase of, by
  Steinbrenner and friends, 54
Niehaus, Richard, 219, 220, 234, 236
Neiman, LeRoy, 52
Nixon, Richard, 221
Novick, Alan
  appearance of, 69
  blaming of problems of ESM on
    Seneca, 82

burial of, 130
business sense of, 82
concern of, over closeness with Home
    State, 94
death of, 128–30
family of, 93
forgery of will of, 186
friendship of, with Jose Gomez, 86
as inside man with ESM, 7–8
office of, 7
as office supervisor at ESM, 69
relationships with Warner, 124–25
role of, in turning Home State into
    black, 90
role of, in ESM scam, 77–78, 79, 80, 85
role of, in running ESM, 7–8, 69, 88
tensions of, 93
thoroughbred and dog diversions of,
    93–94
and use of leverage, 88–89
Novick, Sonya, 186

Ohio
    as recipient of money in ESM
        litigation, 215–17
    responsibility of, in Home State crisis,
        156
Ohio Bankers Association, 189
Ohio Building Authority, 97
Ohio Deposit Guarantee Fund (ODGF),
    99–101
    difference between FSLIC insurance
        and, 148
Ohio Savings and Loan League, 155
Ott, Mel, 206

Perez-Sandoval, Juan, 197
    as Freedom shareholder, 110, 112
Pettigrew & Bailey, Arky as member of,
    197
Phenix City, Ala., building of shopping
    center in, 51
Phipps, Ogden, 53
Pinsk Relief Society, 20
Posner, Victor, 197
Presley, Elvis, 84
Proctor, George, 246

Rabe, Joe, 183, 187
Rafiel, Hymie, 23
Rafiel, Leo, 23
Randman, Philip, 37, 38
Reconstruction efforts in Ohio, 179–93
Rice, Jim, 207
Rickert, Bill, impact of losses on, 168

Rickert, Debi
    impact of Home State crisis on, 157,
        168
    present status of, 262
    and the skirt squad, 182, 183, 184, 185,
        187, 191
Riddel, Earl
    involvement of, in ESM, 88
    sentencing of, by Gonzalez, 212–13
Riffe, Vern, 159, 171
Riley, Pat, 221
Rockefeller, Fifi Taft, 220, 241–42
Roosevelt, Franklin D., 40–41

Saipan Gardens, construction of, 43–44
Saunders, Tom, involvement of, in ESM,
    88
Sawyer, Ray, 171
    role of, in handling of Home State
        crisis, 155
Scanning the orbits scam, 64
Schatzman, Bobby
    concern of, over criminal aspects of
        ESM solution, 135–36
    as Ewton's bankruptcy lawyer, 194
    meeting with Ewton, 135
    as recommended bankruptcy lawyer,
        135
Schiebel, David, 11, 218
    concerns of, over 1984 ESM audit, 3, 4,
        5
    criminal prosecution of, 218, 219
    decision to have Warren tell about
        ESM problems, 141
    decision to investigate Grant audit, 5
    as executive vice president of Home
        State, 104
    guilty verdict of, 233, 234
    and the impact of ESM troubles on
        Home State, 146–49
    meeting with Holtz and Tew, 3
    and negotiating sale of Home State to
        First National, 160
    present status of, 260
    as president of Home State Savings
        Bank of Cincinnati, 3
    pressure on, concerning Home State
        collateral, 124
    request for ESM audit, 141–42
    return to Cincinnati, 5
    role of, in handling of Home State
        crisis, 154
    sentencing of, 235–37
    testimony of, at Warner's federal trial,
        242

testimony of, at own trial, 227

Schwab, Nelson, 225
and the impact of ESM troubles on
Home State, 146–49

Scioto Savings., FSLIC coverage of, 182

Security and Exchange Commission
(SEC)
interest in National Bank of South
Florida case, 75–76
investigation of Home State, 117–18

Security Pacific, as ESM custodian bank,
151

Seneca, Bob
assignment of, to run Foxton
Securities, 83
blaming of problems of ESM on, 82
as bond daddy, 74–75
burnout of, 81
and divorce of June, 82–83
force out of, 83
and launching of ESM, 68–69
loan to, by Home State, 55
love of, for bond business, 78
marriage of June by, 78–79
as partner of ESM, 78
present status of, 261–262
purchase of controlling shares in ABI
by, 75
representation of, in divorce action, 83
role of, in ESM scam, 79
romance of, with June Bellas, 78
as "S" in ESM, 54
separation of, from June, 81
signing of "Quiet Statement" by, 83
use of cocaine by, 78, 81

Seneca, June Bellas
divorce of, 82–83
marriage of, to Bobby, 78–79
problems caused by, in ESM office, 83
romance of Bobby with, 78
suing of Bobby for support payments,
87–88

Shackelford, Don, 171

Shad, John, as chairman of SEC, 161

Simon, Norton, 50

Singer, Allen, as Freedom shareholder, 110

S-J Minerals, ESM scam involving, 84

Skirt Squad
formation of, 180–82
fundraising by, 183
present status of, 262–263
role of, in coordinating legislative
lobby, 187–88
role of, in resolution of bank crisis,
180–91

successes of, 184–85

Smith, Arlo, appointment of, as
conservator, 165, 167

Sokol, Dave
as college roommate, 38–39
on Marvin, 45

Sonneborn, Rudolf G., 26–27

Sonneborn Institute, 26–27

Sparkman, John, 45, 47–48, 53, 56

Stachler, Mark, 187

Stark, Adolf, 21

Stearns, Gene
handling of support suit for Bobby
Seneca, 87–88
as partner in Arky, Freed, 199
representation of Bobby Seneca by, in
divorce action, 83

Stein, Al, as attorney for Alexander
Grant, 214

Steinbrenner, George, friendship with
Marvin Warner, 54

Stratford Manor, construction of, 48

Strauss, Robert, 55

Streicher, Charlie, involvement of, in
ESM, 88, 92–93

Stuffed pig scam, 64

Summers, Pete
decision to leave ESM, 92
negotiating of parting settlement with
ESM, 93
ownership interest of, in ESM, 83

Sunbanks, merger of, with Century
Banks, 95

Tampa Bay Bandits, 97, 195, 199

Tampa Bay Buccaneers
investment of, by Warner, 54
sale of controlling interests in, by
Warner, 56

Taylor, Harry, 181

Taylor, Paula
present status of, 262
and the skirt squad, 181–82, 183, 184

Tew, Tom, 1
acceptance of retainer fee, 144
as ESM receiver, 14–17, 152–53, 203–17
bankruptcy petition for ESM, 184
on bribery of Gomez, 146–47
confirmation of $300 million loss to, 9
confirmation of ESM fraud to, by
Holtz, 9
confrontation between Warren and,
244–56
consultation with David Levine on
keeping Gomez on, case, 207–8

as counsel for ESM, 14
desire to meet with Holtz, 144–45
Gonzalez dismissal of suit against
    Arky, Freed, 216–17
hiring of, by ESM, 3
and informing of government
    authorities concerning, ESM
    fraud, 14
introduction to George Mead, 3
investigation into ESM custodian
    banks, 151
legal specialities of, 3–4
location of ESM losses by, 167
meeting with Don Collins, 11
meeting with Laurie Holtz, 3–4
need to be released as ESM attorney, 16
painting of Arky and Warner as ESM
    insider by, 198
present status of, 259
relationship of, with Arky, 195
and shutdown of ESM, 150
Toledo, Ohio, ESM loss of, 167
Tracey, Ann Marie, 238, 239
Triple Chick, Warner's interest in, 52
Twisting scam, 64

U.S. government securities market, 263
daily volume of, 70
dominance of, by U.S. Treasury, 71
size of, 70–71
Unity Bank and Trust of Chicago
as big customer of ESM, 89
investigation into books of, 91
issuance of cease and desist order
    involving ESM, 91

Vernon, Harold, as Freedom shareholder,
    110
Veteran's Emergency Housing Act (1946)
passage of, 41–42
Section 603 of, 49
Section 608 of, 42–43
Volcker, Paul, 168–69, 171, 175–76, 179

Waddell, Oliver, on purchase of First
    National Bank of Cincinnati, 158
Wallace, Nick, 1, 10, 11, 12, 16, 203
criminal charges against, 211–12
hiring of Tew as special legal advisor,
    3
indictment in forgery of Alan Novick
    will, 186
involvement of, in ESM, 88
lack of cooperation of, with Tew, 209

ownership interest of, in ESM, 83
present status of, 260
role of, in audit investigation, 6
Warner, Alyson, 234
birth of, 50
relationship with mother after divorce,
    51
Warner, George, 40, 42
Warner, Jane Blach, 42
divorce of Marvin by, 51
marriage to Marvin, 39–40, 197
Warner, Jody Piehowicz, 226, 234, 243,
    253–54, 255
marriage of, 118–19
present status of, 257–58
romance with Marvin, 97
Warner, Mark, 253
birth of, 50
involvement of, in father's business, 51
relationship with father after divorce,
    51
relationship with mother after divorce,
    51
Warner, Marvin Leon, 12, 13–14
and ABI deal, 79
acceptance of Hunter bid in
    purchasing Home State, 193
ambitions of, 50–51
appeal of, on Cincinnati conviction,
    246–47
appointment of, as ambassador to
    Switzerland, 56–57
art collecting interests of, 52
attempt of, to portray innocence of,
    189–90
attempt to buy out Broads, 121
attempt to get more information on
    ESM problems, 138
attempt to help Ewton with ESM
    problems, 138–39
attempt to undue buyout by Shepard,
    132–33
bachelor lifestyle of, 51–52
bankruptcy petition of, 245–46
birth of, 36
and birth of Mark and Alyson, 50
and building of Essex House, 45–46
and building of Forest Park, 49, 50
and building of Phenix City (Ala.)
    shopping center, 51
and building of Stratford Manor, 48–49
as businessmen, 45
as candidate to put up money to save
    ESM, 134
as CEO of American Savings & Loan, 106

civil lawsuits against, 244
civil trial of, 247–56
closing of ESM account by, 139, 149
and college roommate, Dave Sokol,
    38–39
composure of, at trial, 226
concern of, over conspiracy
    involvement, 139
confrontation between Tew and,
    244–56
connections with Celeste, 180
criminal case against, 218, 219, 222,
    223
decision of, to become Section 608
    builder, 42–43
decision of, to blame Alexander Grant
    for audit problems, 140
decision of, to buy out Broads, 120
decision of, to close ESM account, 137
decision of, to move from Cincinnati
    to Ocala, 245
decision of, to seek legal advice from
    Clark Hodgson, 140
decision of, to split up Warner-Kanter,
    49–50
decision of, to tell Schiebel of ESM
    problems, 138
divorce from Jane, 51
divorce from Susan Goldwater, 57
as de facto officer of Home State,
    220–21
desire to energize American Savings &
    Loan, 106
early life of, 36
expense account of, 123
family of, 37–38
formation of partnership with Joe
    Kanter, 44
formation of Warner-Kanter Company,
    44–45
friendship with George Steinbrenner,
    54
first knowledge of, concerning ESM
    losses, 137
guilty verdict of, 232–35
horse breeding interests of, 52–53
interest of, in Jewish causes, 50
interest of, in post World War II
    housing market, 40–42
and the impact of ESM troubles on
    Home State, 146–50
investment of, in American Savings &
    Loan, 34–35
investment of, in Century Banks,
    95–96

involvement of, in management of
    Home State, 95
jetset lifestyle of, 108
key to success of, 123–24
not guilty verdict at federal trial, 243
legal counterattack of, 244–45
and management of Birmingham
    Stallions, 108
management skills of, 34
marriage of, to Jane Blach, 39–40, 197
marriage of, to Jody Piehowicz, 118–19
meeting with Mead, 139
as member of board of regents for
    Ohio State University, system,
    53–54
and merger of ABI with ComBanks, 80
net worth of, in 1980s, 53
opening of trading accounts at ESM
    by, 80
opposition of, to Tew as receiver, 152
painting of, by Tew as ESM insider,
    198
physical description of, 45–46
political interests of, 44–45, 47–48,
    55–56
posting of bail for appeal, 235
preparation of buyout proposal for
    Shepard, 125–26
present status of, 257–59
pressure from, to insure Home State
    profits, 95
pressure on, concerning Home State
    collateral, 124
and problems with Home State, 89
profitable account of, at ESM, 149
profit received following buyout of, 133
protection of assets by, 245
and purchase of controlling interest in
    ComBanks, 54
and purchase of Home State, 51
and purchase of New York Yankees, 54
and purchase of Stallions franchise, 97
and purchase of Tampa Bay Bandits,
    97
and purchase of Tampa Bay
    Buccaneers, 54
relationship of, with Arky, 106
relationship with father, 38
relationship with Mark and Alyson
    after divorce, 51
relationship with mother, 38
representation of, by Steve Arky, 197–98
resignation from position at DNC, 56
resignation of, from board of regents,
    56

resignation of, as chairman of Ohio
    Building Authority, 169
return of, from Switzerland, 89
romance with Jody Piehowicz, 97
romance and marriage to Susan
    Goldwater, 57–58
romance with Susan Clough, 57
sale of ComBanks by, 96
sale of Great American by, 96
sentencing of, 235–36, 237
and set up of prefab facility at Fort
    Payne, Ala., 46–47
as target of public anger and distrust,
    177
testimony of, at trial, 228–30, 242
Tew's suit against, 209
use of political system by, 53
verdict in civil case, 254–56
as winner in Alabama state oratorical
    contests, 36–37, 43
work of, for uncle, George Warner, 40
during World War II, 40
Warner, Rose, 37–38, 42
Warner, Samuel, 37–38
Warner, Susan Goldwater, marriage and
    divorce of, 57–58
Warner-Kanter Company
    breakup of, 49–50

and construction of Essex House,
    46–47
expansion of, into Midwest, 47–49
formation of, 44
and set up of prefab facility at Fort
    Payne, Ala., 46–47
Warnerton, interest of Marvin in, 51–52
WATS lines, use of, in bond scams,
    62–63, 65
Weeks, decision of, to leave HOW, Inc.,
    67
Whitty, Joe, 23
Winslow, Barry, 114–15, 221
    resignation of, 124, 227
Winters and Company
    Ronnie Ewton at, 68
    scandal at, 67–68
Wirth, Senator, 262
Wolfe, Stanley
    criminal charges against, 211
    lack of cooperation of, with Tew, 209
Wright, Christine, impact of Home State
    Bank crisis on, 174
Wright, Fannie, impact of Home State
    Bank crisis on, 174–75

Zionist Organization of America, role of
    Shepard Broad in organizing Miami
    chapter, 25